A Medieval Punishment Cemetery at Weyhill Road, Andover, Hampshire

A Medieval Punishment Cemetery at Weyhill Road, Andover, Hampshire

by

K.E. Walker, Sharon Clough and Jeremy Clutterbuck

with contributions from

Philip Armitage, Kayt Hawkins, Sarah Cobain, Frances Healy, Mandy Jay,
Katie Marsden, Rebecca Phillips and Andrew Reynolds

Illustrations by Daniel Bashford

Cotswold Archaeology Monograph No. 11
Cirencester 2020

Cotswold Archaeology Monograph No. 11

Published by Cotswold Archaeology
Building 11, Kemble Enterprise Park, Cirencester, Gloucestershire GL7 6BQ

ISBN 978-0-9934545-6-1

British Library Cataloguing in Publication Data
A catalogue record of this book is available from the British Library

Front cover: Illustration by Mark Gridley
Back cover: The cemetery under excavation; Silver penny of Aethelred II, Obverse Diademed bust right; the cemetery under excavation showing disturbance from modern services

Cover design by Aleksandra Osinska
Produced by Past Historic, Kings Stanley, Gloucestershire
Printed by Henry Ling Ltd, Dorchester

CONTENTS

List of Figures

List of Tables

Acknowledgements

The fieldwork was commissioned and the post-excavation analysis and publication were financed by Aldi Stores Ltd. The support of Mr Lee McCandless and his colleagues at Aldi Stores Ltd throughout the project has been very much appreciated. Thanks are also due to Mr Alan Williams, from Planning Potential Ltd.

Jeremy Clutterbuck led Cotswold Archaeology's Andover field team on site, and Richard Greatorex managed the fieldwork. The post-excavation was managed by Karen Walker. Daniel Bashford produced the illustrations.

Like fieldwork, post-excavation is very much a group effort and, with apologies for not naming everyone who helped during the course of this project, we would particularly like to thank the following people: David Hopkins, in his role as County Archaeologist, Hampshire, Ross Turle and Sam Butcher of the Hampshire Cultural Trust for their assistance with access to archives, David Rymill of the Hampshire Record Office, Winchester, and Suzanne Foster of Winchester College. David Bird, Pippa Bradley, Greg Chuter and Paul McCulloch all provided information on comparative sites. Frances Healy, Richard Massey and Alyxandra Mattison generously commented on earlier versions of the text which was also kindly read by Richard Greatorex, David Hopkins and Andrew Reynolds. The volume was copy-edited by Rachel Tyson.

We would also like to take this opportunity, to thank for their assistance, the many volunteers who helped in various ways, and who generously give their time to Cotswold Archaeology.

Karen Walker thanks the late David Farwell for his thoughtful and generous assistance with this project, and for very much more.

The scope of this project grew as the results of the post-excavation analysis emerged, taking some of us into new periods and areas of study. To try and set the site in its context we have used and referred to a huge body of work by scholars much more familiar with the sources, and any mistakes in interpretation are entirely our own.

Summary

Cotswold Archaeology began an archaeological watching brief for Aldi Stores Ltd, at the brownfield site of a new supermarket at Weyhill Road, Andover, Hampshire, in April 2016. It soon became apparent that human remains were present within the south-west corner of the site and an excavation was carried out that was completed in September that year.

The excavation recorded the remnants of sparse and truncated Iron Age and Roman features, but the principal interest of the site was the discovery of a cemetery containing the articulated human remains of 124 individuals and a probable 39 further individuals identified through examination of the disarticulated bone. Estimation of sex was possible for 100 individuals, of whom, three were identified as female and the rest were male, or probable/possible male with an age distribution with peak incidence in the young adult (18–25) category. Burials included individuals who had been interred in a prone position, some who had been decapitated and others with their hands behind their backs. There were also multiple burials. These are all traits indicative of a judicial punishment cemetery.

Very little artefactual evidence was recovered from the site and finds from graves comprise two examples of articulated parts of a sheep, two worked bone objects probably from graves, and several metal items. With the exception of a single silver coin, (dateable to AD 979–85), the other metal objects are of iron, and they include a number of buckles. Isotope analysis showed that the majority of the individuals were probably local.

Twenty radiocarbon dates were obtained and the calibrated date-range extends from the 8th to the 14th centuries cal AD. Chronological modelling of the results suggests that the calibrated age-range for the earliest individual spans more than 200 years so that the young man in question could have died at any time between the 8th and the mid 10th century cal AD. However, even with a conservative interpretation of the radiocarbon dates, we can confidently place the duration of use of the cemetery from at least the 10th to the 13th centuries and the evidence for both pre and post-Conquest burials is compelling.

Preface

The post-excavation phase of this project had a limited number of aims: to refine our understanding of the date and nature of late prehistoric and Roman activity before the establishment of the cemetery, to confirm the chronology of the cemetery, to discover where the cemetery population came from and to learn what the remains could tell us about the nature of political, social and cultural change at a local rural level. To a large extent these aims have been fulfilled, and this book addresses these themes in its various chapters.

As the post-excavation progressed, our understanding of the site and its significance changed and so did the focus of the work. The final two chapters address in particular the last, and in our view most difficult, of the aims. The principal authors are not historians, still less legal historians; however, we recognise both the central place and importance of the law in medieval life, and the undeniable value of preserved documentary records to help interpret contemporary archaeological remains. We have examined the limited local preserved records and drawn on standard translations and interpretations of British legal documents as well as more recent secondary sources to provide a framework, that while it cannot be absolute, seems to provide a credible explanation for the cemetery. We cannot know exactly who the people within it were but we can make reasoned guesses as to why they might have been there.

The absolute dating of the cemetery challenges some of the previously held expectations about some aspects of burial during the medieval period and adds to our understanding of the practical outcomes of continuity and change in a period of much political, legal and social upheaval. Simple calibrated date-ranges extend from the 8th to the 14th centuries cal AD. Chronological modelling of the results suggests that the earliest date obtained falls on a particularly flat stretch of the radiocarbon calibration curve, and has a calibrated age-range of more than 200 years, so that the young man in question could have died at any time between the 8th and the mid 10th century cal AD. Even with a conservative interpretation of the radiocarbon dates we can confidently place the duration of use of the cemetery from at least the 10th to the 13th centuries. Despite the disadvantages of the radiocarbon calibration curve for this period, and the resulting widely calibrated date-ranges, the evidence for both pre and post-Conquest burials is compelling. The generous support of our client has allowed us to take the work this far. We also make some suggestions for future work in a research environment.

Chapter 1
Introduction and Background

Between April and September, 2016, Cotswold Archaeology carried out an archaeological watching brief and excavation for Aldi Stores Ltd, at the site of a new supermarket at 278, Weyhill Road, Andover, Hampshire. The site, centred on National Grid Reference 434115 145870, comprised a roughly rectangular parcel of land of 0.47ha, a brownfield plot previously occupied by a car showroom and garage. Planning permission for the demolition of the existing buildings and construction of a food store, with associated access, parking and landscaping, was granted by Test Valley Borough Council, in September, 2015. The store was located within the northern part of the site, with access and parking to the south. The work was undertaken at the request of David Hopkins, County Archaeologist at Hampshire County Council.

It became apparent with the commencement of ground works, that human remains were present within the south-west corner of the site. Ground works ceased until an appropriate strategy for archaeological mitigation was in place. It was agreed that a watching brief would continue on the northern half of the site, but that the southern half would be stripped under archaeological supervision, in order to record sensitive archaeological remains. By the end of the excavation, some 91 graves had been excavated, which were found to contain a minimum number of 124 individuals and a considerable volume of disarticulated bone. The burials had been accompanied by very few grave goods. One such item was a Late Saxon coin, which prompted an initial interpretation of the cemetery as being entirely of later Saxon date. The nature of some burials (with prone burial postures, and often in intercutting graves), the condition of some bodies (some with tied hands and possibly decapitated), and the overwhelmingly male character of the burial population, provided an initial interpretation of this burial group as a Saxon execution cemetery. Aldi Stores Ltd generously funded a programme of post-excavation and scientific analysis, during which the interpretation of the cemetery has been

developed to that presented in this volume. Although the nature of the site and the construction programme required that the find was not reported publicly until after completion of the excavation, there has been a high level of local interest, and preliminary interim reports have been made available (Cotswold Archaeology 2017; Clutterbuck 2018a and b).

The archive

The archive has been deposited with the Hampshire Cultural Trust, in Winchester, under Accession number A2016.39.

The site

The site (Fig. 1.1) is located within the western margins of modern Andover, within an industrial park, with residential and industrial premises situated to the west, north and east. It is bounded to the south by the Weyhill Road, which provides access from the town to routes to the south and west, opposite its junction with Monxton Road at Hundred Acre Corner (Figs 1.2 and 1.3). Weyhill is located approximately 20 miles (32km) north-west of the city of Winchester and north-east of Salisbury, 30 miles (64km) north of the city of Southampton and 17 miles (27km) south-west of Newbury.

The land lies at an elevation of approximately 90m above Ordnance Datum (AOD), on a ridge of between the valleys of the River Anton to the north and the Pillhill Brook to the south (Fig. 1.4). The River Anton, which is a tributary of the River Test, rises just to the north of the town of Andover, and flows through its centre. The underlying geology of the site comprises Cretaceous sedimentary chalk of the Newhaven Chalk Formation, with no recorded superficial deposits (British Geological Survey 2015).

Local place-name evidence is instructive and discussed in Chapter 7 and in Andrew Reynolds' concluding

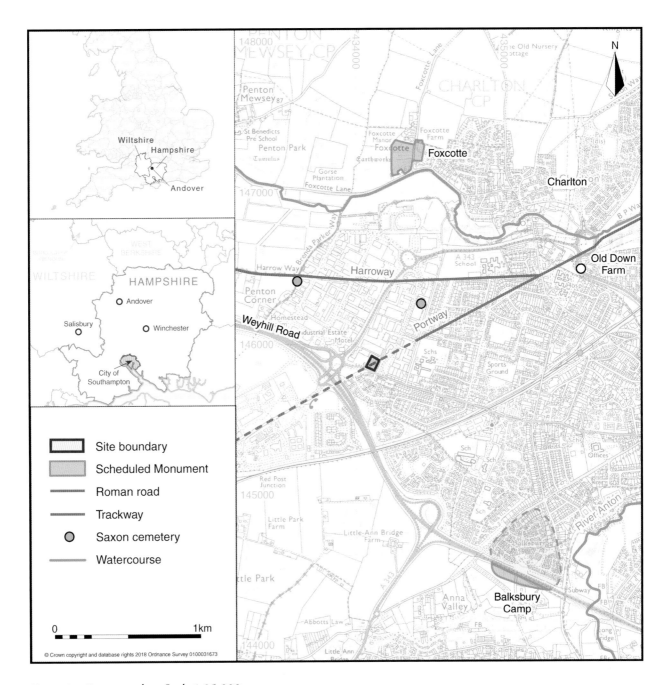

Fig. 1.1   Location plan. Scale 1:25,000

remarks. Documented previous land-use for the site includes arable cultivation and a subsequent sequence of modern buildings (Fig. 1.5). Previous site levelling operations, of unknown extent, have also disturbed archaeological levels. The natural chalk was revealed at varying depths below ground level (BGL); at *c.* 0.9m at the northern end of site, and up to 0.24m BGL at the southern end. The chalk was covered by a mid-brown, clayey silt subsoil, which also varied in depth (0.7m BGL and up to 0.16m BGL respectively). In places within the east and centre of the site, subsoils had been completely truncated by modern development. Topsoil survived in a few locations at the periphery of the northern end of

the site, to a depth of *c.* 0.2m. Heavy disturbance of features had occurred where building foundations, gas, electrical and other services had been inserted (Fig. 1.6).

Archaeological background

Earlier prehistoric evidence from the site was limited to a single flake of worked flint, probably of local origin. It is not closely dateable, and displays little edge damage. Palaeolithic and Mesolithic activity in and around Andover is largely represented by findspots of worked flints, often found in association with the River Anton, located over 1km north of the site.

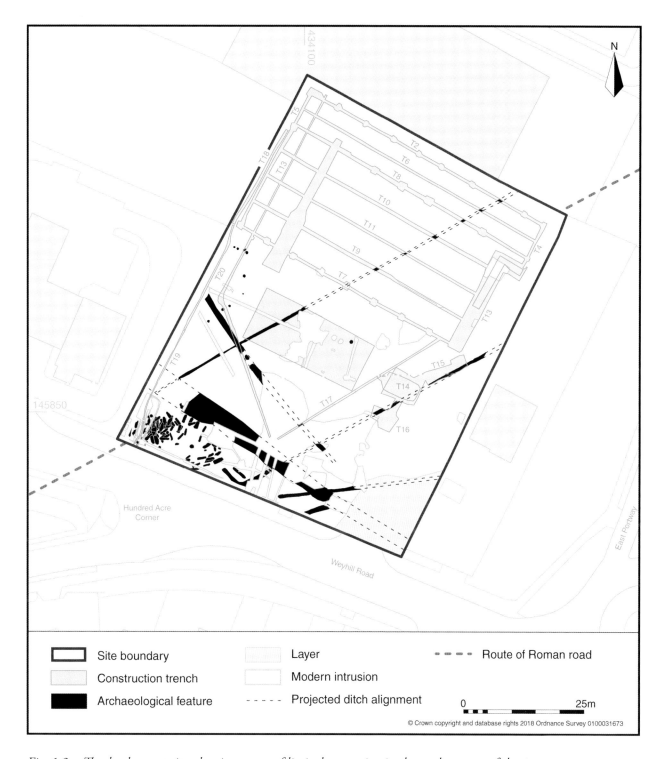

Fig. 1.2   The development site, showing extent of limited excavation in the southern part of the site

While recorded Palaeolithic material is limited to a few stray finds of hand-axes, there is more evidence that Mesolithic people visited and used the landscape. For example, over 400 pieces of worked flint of Mesolithic date were found within aeolian silt deposits at Goch Way near Charlton, and such an assemblage suggests an occupation site, possibly a riverside camp (Wright 2004). Some 752 pieces of worked flint, ranging in date

from the Mesolithic to Early Bronze Age, were found at Foxcotte 1.5km to the north of the site (Russel 1985).

Neolithic pottery and worked flint, and other worked stone artefacts, including a polished axe, a mace-head and an adze, have been found on excavated occupation and funerary sites around the town. Features dated to the Neolithic period were found at Old Down Farm (Fig. 1.1; Davies 1981), and Balksbury Camp, located

Fig. 1.3   Hundred Acre Corner

to the south-west of Andover, and 1.6km to the south-west of the present site (Fig. 1.1; Wainwright 1969, 34–6). Some 19 pieces of Neolithic Grooved Ware pottery were also found in a pit at Goch Way, near Charlton (Wright 2004). This indicates that people were using the landscape in the Neolithic period, and settling in the area. There is also evidence for Early and Late Bronze Age occupation in the surrounding area, for example at Balksbury Camp (Fig. 1.1; Wainwright and Davies 1995; Ellis and Rawlings 2001). Closer to the site, Bronze Age activity is largely represented by the round barrow cemeteries investigated at the Portway Industrial Estate, 550m to the north-east of the site, and 330m to the north-west (Cook and Dacre 1985).

There is a wealth of cropmark and excavated evidence for prehistoric settlement and agriculture in the general area (see Fig. 8.2). The valley of the River Anton was densely populated in later prehistoric periods. A prehistoric trackway, known as the Harroway, ran to the north of Andover, passing from east to west, to Weyhill and beyond, approximately 550m to the north of the site.

South of the Harroway, a large Iron Age enclosure was excavated at Vigo Road in the 1970s and early 1980s (Stoodley 2013, 42–6). Among a number of hillforts in the wider landscape, locally there was occupation at the hillfort of Balksbury Camp throughout the Iron Age (Wainwright and Davies 1995; Ellis and Rawlings 2001). An Early Iron Age hillfort was also created on Bury Hill (Cunliffe and Poole 2000), and succeeded by

a massive defended enclosure in the Late Iron Age.

In the immediate vicinity of the present site, Iron Age settlements have been investigated at Portway Industrial Estate, approximately 540m to the north-west (Stoodley 2013), and Iron Age pottery has been widely found within the local area (Hopkins, pers. comm.). A large, enclosed Iron Age settlement was investigated at Old Down Farm (Fig. 1.1; Davies 1981).

There is also extensive archaeological evidence from the Roman period (Fig. 1.7). On the eastern side of Andover, the north-eastern quadrant of a 2nd to 4th-century roadside settlement at East Anton has been investigated. Remains included 12 flint-built later Roman grain dryers or malting kilns, with four more suspected from geophysical survey results. The scale of this agri-industrial complex for the processing of grain is impressive (AC Archaeology 2011, 17). Two coffined inhumation burials were also recorded (*ibid.*, 14). Excavations had also been undertaken in the north-western quadrant, by the former Department of the Environment Central Excavation Unit. A number of authors (e.g. Rivet and Smith 1979, 389; Smith 1987, 263; Spaul 1999) agree that East Anton may be the *Leucomagus* or *Leucomago* mentioned in the Ravenna Cosmography. This is a list of place-names of the known Roman world, compiled by an anonymous 7th-century monk. Fitzpatrick-Matthews (2013, 20) states that Richmond and Crawford (1949, 37) successfully predicted the existence of this settlement, using the Cosmography. East Anton is located at the

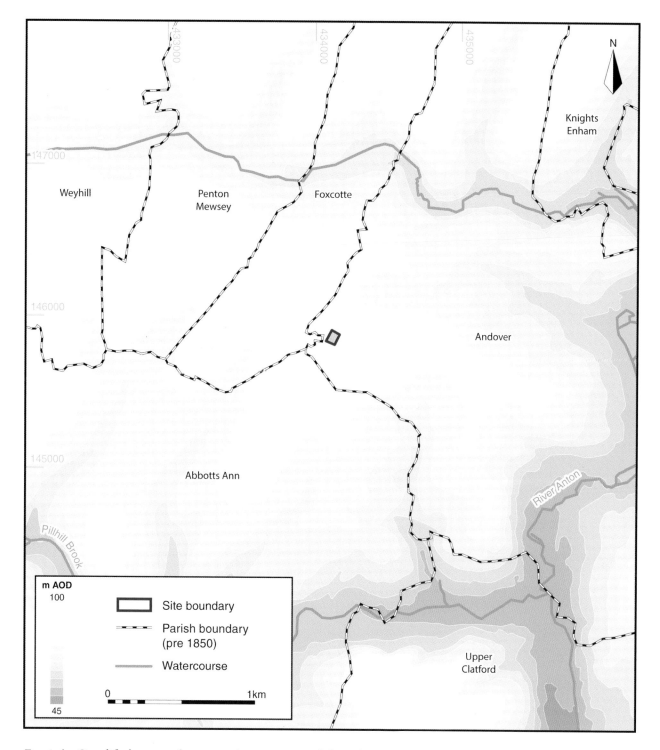

Fig. 1.4   Simplified topography map and pre-1850 parish boundaries

intersection of the road from Winchester to Mildenhall with that from Silchester to Old Sarum, known as the Portway (Margary 1973, 4b). This settlement might also have been expected to have grown up at a convenient crossing-point of the River Anton, but evidence for this remains unproven.

Within *c.* 5km of the site there is evidence of a number of Roman buildings - mostly villas or aisled farmhouses recorded by 19th and 20th-century antiquarians. These include examples at Fyfield, Appleshaw, Penton Grafton, Penton Mewsey, Thruxton and Abbotts Ann (Pastscape monument numbers 223640, 228060, 228030, 228041, 223606 and 228300, Historic England 2018) and Grateley. A number of these buildings were associated with hypocaust heating systems, bath-houses, and tessellated pavements, and attest to the general

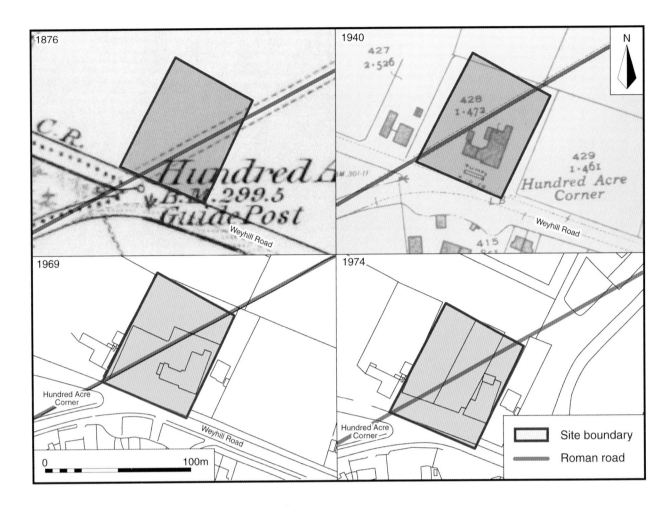

Fig. 1.5   Development of the site (1876 to 1974)

Fig. 1.6   Photograph showing disturbance by modern services with SKs1355–59 and 1362

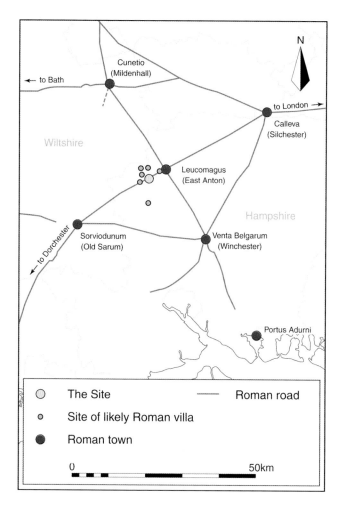

Fig. 1.7   The site in its Roman context

prosperity of the surrounding area. Such villas would have been the centres of farming estates which used the local road system to transport produce to developing market centres such as East Anton, and from there to *civitas* capitals at Winchester and Silchester.

Pre-existing roads and trackways appear to have been significant for both the development of Andover and the cemetery itself. Williams (2006, 185) has pointed out that it is often difficult to reconstruct the patterns and status of roads, tracks and paths in the early medieval landscape. However earlier routeways, including prehistoric trackways and Roman roads, often continued in use in this period, and certainly did so in this case. The site produced evidence for the Roman Portway, in the form of roadside ditches (B and C). The ditches had partly survived the effects of long-term cultivation, but direct evidence for the *agger* within the site had been lost. Comparison of this evidence with better-preserved sections of the same road presents a compelling argument that the cemetery did indeed straddle the line of the Roman road.

In the 17th century, Camden described the Portway as traversing the Forest of Chute (Lawes Long 1836,

5). Henry Lawes Long (1836, 24) debated the routes of local Roman roads, in print, and cites an antiquarian, Mr Leman, who described a road near St Mary Bourne, between Finkley Farm and Wyke, as 'a fine boundary ditch, having its vallum toward the Wykes and its ditch westerly towards Andover', which he called the Portway. Thomas Codrington, writing at the beginning of the 20th century, described the Portway as 'formerly visible on the south of East Anton, but there are now few traces of it for two and a half miles across arable land, until the Andover and Weyhill road is reached' (1919, 247). He also says that, at a location half a mile west of St Mary Bourne, the paving of the road was removed in 1879, for a length of a quarter of a mile, 'on account of its interference with farming operations'. It was found at four to eight inches below the surface, and 'was about eight yards wide' (*ibid.*). Margary (1973, 97–8) cites a description of an excavated section of the road ('Port Way', no. 4b) by Wright (1936), who in 1936 examined the Portway by trenching at Newton Tony, to the west of the Amesbury Branch Railway, where the *agger* was very clear:

> The road was found in excellent preservation, and it appeared that in the construction the surface soil had been cleared away, layer of chalk rubble laid down and cambered to give thickness seven inches at the centre. Upon this was a layer of large flints, hand-laid, three to four inches thick, bedded in soil and with a thin sprinkling of chalk flush with the top of the flints, to make the surface even. This was topped with a layer of local gravel, six inches-thick at the centre and well cambered, showing ruts. There were well-cut, V-shaped small ditches on each side, 32 ft out from the south curb and 34, and ¼ ft from the north curb, making a total width for the road zone of 84.5 ft to the ditch centres (Margary 1973, 97–8).

The ditches had a loosely packed chalk rubble primary fill *c.* six inches deep and a secondary fill of about five inches of flinty soil (Wright 1936, 515). Wright noted that, at Newton Tony, the un-metalled verge between the ditches was not rutted, although it was used as a sheep-drove until 1905 (*ibid.*, 516).

River and coastal traffic was an important aspect of trade and communication, but inland trade routes for carting goods were also established from at least the Roman period onwards. By the middle of the 14th century, a highly developed national road system was centred on London (Crittall 1959b). One important inland route developed from Southampton, north to Andover, Newbury, Oxford and Leicester (Duxbury, 2011, 26). 'Southampton, with its sheltered port near the mouth of the River Itchen, and close to the head of Southampton Water, grew rapidly. This growth, particularly during the 12th century, also reflected the geopolitical fact that England's trade, as part of the Norman and Angevin Empires, was more firmly established across the Channel' (Edwards 1987, 447). By contrast, Winchester, a valuable and populous place at the time of the Conquest, had declined in wealth by the mid 14th century, partly because of political and administrative changes, and partly because the River Itchen was becoming less navigable because of obstacles in the form of mills (*ibid.*). Andover gained an economic advantage from its position on road networks, particularly for local and regional trade in commodities such as wool, cloth and wine. Its location would also have brought a regular influx of travellers passing through the town, bringing with them opportunities, news and potential trouble. At least parts of the prehistoric east–west Harroway track were used as a long-distance pilgrim route in the medieval period. The road from Andover to Weyhill is not depicted on the Kitchin map of 1751, but is present on Harrison's 1788 map, so was probably a late 18th-century development. It seems probable, however, that some sort of earlier track to Weyhill would have existed in this vicinity, particularly given the significance of the Weyhill Fair. According to the cartographers, such a track might have joined a track or road from Monxton to Andover which pre-dated the Weyhill Road.

Further information is available from works undertaken within the Andover 'in hundred' and nearby manors. This includes a concentration of occupation evidence around the settlement of Charlton, to the north of the Harroway (Fig. 1.1). This prehistoric trackway continued to be used during the medieval period as a pilgrim route. Excavated evidence includes occupation remains from Charlton itself (Dacre and Warmington 1977), in addition to Goch Way, with three sunken-featured buildings (Wright 2004); Charlton Link Road and Armstrong Rise (Stoodley 2013, 73); Gymnasium and Car Park (Hampshire Archaeology 1997); and six sunken-featured buildings at Old Down Farm (Davies 1980). These excavations have variously produced Late Roman and Early Saxon pottery (Stoodley 2013, 73), pottery of 5th to 7th-century date (Wright 2004; Hampshire Archaeology 1997), and 6th-century pottery (Davies 1980). At Foxcotte, the archaeological evidence for occupation in this period consisted of a post-built structure and associated finds, including quernstones, a glass bead, a silver coin and quantities of pottery (Russel 1985, 159–72). As Russel points out (1985, 218), Foxcotte is one of a number of manorial holdings within Andover parish, and two other nearby holdings, Charlton and Kings Enham, to have possible place-name evidence which supports the probability of king's bequests and service provision within a royal manor. Two Saxon cemetery sites have been excavated in the immediate vicinity of the Weyhill Road cemetery, and these are discussed in Chapter 8.

Evidence for a small enclosed settlement, of probable 12th to 13th-century date, has been found near East Anton (NGR SU 376 479). Structural remains suggest that it was a farm, with a planned group of three timber buildings, of slot and posthole construction, with pottery suggesting a relatively short-lived sequence, dating from the later 10th century to the 12th century (AC Archaeology 2011, 11). One of the timber buildings was larger than the others, and its aisled form suggested a barn, or possibly a hall. Such halls may reasonably be expected on larger farms of a certain status during the period spanning the Norman Conquest (*ibid.*, 12).

There has been little excavated evidence for Saxon occupation within the centre of Andover itself. Archaeological evidence from the town is restricted to sherds of 6th/7th-century and 'Late' Saxon pottery, the distribution of which has suggested that the settlement would have been located to the north and west of the church (Campling 1989, 12). Hopkins (2004, 7–12) summarised what is known of Andover's medieval development, elements of which can be found in the historic core of the town, including High Street (recorded from 1298), Newbury Street and West Street (1379). Long, narrow medieval burgage plots were still reflected in the land units of the Tithe map and Apportionment of 1850. Excavations in the 1980s suggested intensive occupation on the northern side of Chantry Street. Two areas of suburbs developed, one to the north-east of the church, and another to the south of the town centre (Fig. 7.2).

Andover church

An Andover church of St Mary is mentioned in the Domesday Survey (see below), and it is possible that the Norman church was built on the same, prominent site, overlooking the River Anton. As Hadley and Dyer (2017, 9) point out, many churches were constructed in stone during the 11th century, to replace earlier timber churches, a process that had begun in the decades leading up to the Conquest, and which continued to *c.* 1100. Some smaller Anglo-Saxon churches 'through the architectural transition opened up by the Conquest', may have been integrated into larger-scale Norman churches (Coppen 2015, 9–10). Coppen suggests that this Saxon church originally served as a 'mother church' for its hundred, or as a monastery or a minster, as was the case for many cruciform churches built by the Normans. Hase (1975, 311–13) suggests that Andover may have been a mother church, which in earlier times controlled Penton Mewsey. He also speculates that Amport may have been an equivalent presence in the western half of the 'out hundred', with control of a number of parishes, including Thruxton and Quarley. The evidence is circumstantial, but if correct would suggest a significant boundary between areas of religious administration close to our site.

The church of St Mary, with a hide of land and all

its tithes, was bestowed on the Benedictine abbey of St Florent, Saumur, by William the Conqueror, and in 1087 the abbey established a fraternity of monks at Andover and established a priory. An assessment of English and Welsh parish churches for taxation purposes was carried out, on the orders of Pope Nicholas IV, in 1291–2. At that time, a small church at the settlement of Hatch Warren, near Basingstoke, was valued at £4 6s 8d. Several of the local churches had a higher, but not wildly dissimilar, value: St Michael at Weyhill (a cell of St Grestain Abbey, Normandy), was valued at £7 6s 8d, Holy Trinity, Penton Mewsey (patron Thomas le Rych) at £6 13s 4d, and St Michael and All Angels, Knights Enham (patron, John de Handle, knight) at £8 0s 0d. By contrast, the alien priory church of St Mary, was valued at £80 0s 0d (Denton *et al.* 2014).

The priory was seized by Edward I in 1294, and became the property of Winchester College by purchase from the last prior, in the year of 1413 (Kirby 1896, 283). Coppen suggests that, in the first half of the 19th century, the old priory buildings to the north of the Norman church were removed in order to extend the churchyard for new burial space (2015, 10). The churchyard lay to the south of the church as depicted in several illustrations, and Coppen (*ibid.*, 6) suggests that the soil level to the south of the church was higher due to the many interments within what he describes as a small area. The chancel, tower and north and south transepts of were demolished in late 1840/early 1841, in preparation for the building of the present church, above and on new ground, to the east of the old. The old church nave was demolished, and the new church tower and west-end flight of steps up from the road were finished by May, 1846. Little now remains of the Norman church, although the floor of the crypt of the present church nave comprises the original chalk floor of the tower, south transept chancel and chancel chapel. Some old memorial stones and wall monuments have been reset, and the Norman West doorway was preserved and rebuilt in Upper High Street (*ibid.*, 10–21).

Hospitals

Another important medieval building, no longer extant, which may have had burial grounds attached, was a hospital of St John the Baptist, which received a royal charter in 1247, and was closed by Henry VIII in 1536. Tanner (1744, 168) said that the hospital had a master, and both brothers and sisters. Bennett (1931), states that the duty of the brothers and sisters was to offer hospitality to travellers and to pray for the souls of those buried in the unconsecrated ground adjacent. The site of the Andover hospital is usually thought to have been at the bottom of New Street, on the east side. The hospital was granted a licence, in 1250, for a cemetery and chapel on a piece of royal land which lay opposite the hospital (Page 1911a, 356). A seal believed to be

from this hospital depicts St John the Baptist, holding in his left hand a representation of the Agnus Dei (Caley *et al.* 1846, 761). The St Mary Magdalene leper hospital of Andover was founded before the mid 13th century, and was dissolved in 1547. There are documentary examples elsewhere, of leper hospitals burying executed criminals. This includes a hospital at Lincoln, where at some time before 1335, the responsibility for burying people whose names were inscribed in the 'book of the fraternity of St John the Baptist', and who had been hanged on the Lincoln gallows, was transferred to the leper hospital (Pugh 1981, 567).

In pre-Reformation times, religious houses, such as the Order of St John, the Knights Hospitallers, habitually took an interest in ensuring the proper burial of executed felons in their own and other cemeteries (Pugh 1981; Gilchrist and Sloane 2005, 73). An example of this interest may be found at Ilchester, Somerset, where, in 1276, on the arrival of the Hospitallers' men at the gallows to claim the bodies of thieves recently hanged, the local tithingmen had left them strewn on the ground (Pugh 1981, 566). Another example is of probable 15th-century date, in Salisbury, where a prisoner who was being taken to execution escaped his guards in a *frary* cart (a cart for the dead) 'ensigned with a banner'; he claimed sanctuary and subsequently escaped to a church. This tale may also refer to the Hospitallers themselves (*ibid.*, 569), in that Hospitallers' carts may have been considered part of consecrated premises and therefore capable of providing temporary sanctuary.

Historical background

Hampshire represents one of the earliest and most historically stable shires in England. During the early 6th century, the West Saxon kingdom, based in Hampshire and Wiltshire was formed by Cerdic (r. 519–34), who took the title of king in AD 520. During the 7th century, Hampshire was 'a hotly-contested region, and one under increasing pressure from neighbouring kingdoms' (Stoodley 2006, 76, citing Yorke 1989). Although struggles continued, with both the Britons to the west and the Mercians to the east, by the time of King Ine (r. 688–726), a core area, representing the later kingdom of Wessex had become identifiable. King Egbert of the West Saxons (Ecgberht: r. 802–39), having defeated Mercians, Britons and Vikings, formed around Wessex a powerful kingdom that eventually achieved the political unification of England.

Later documentary evidence includes law codes – primarily regarding monetary compensation – which date back to at least the beginning of the 7th century (Aethelberht, r. *c.* 589–616) (Mattison 2016, 11). King Ine (r. 688 to 726) laid down the first laws of Wessex, although many more followed. By the time the earliest burials were made in the Weyhill Road cemetery at, it is probable that Hampshire had been an integral part of the kingdom of the West Saxons, more recently, Wessex, for almost 400 years. The 7th to the 9th centuries witnessed major changes, including a revival of trade networks, the development of a large-scale silver coinage, and the formation of *wics* (trading centres). Throughout the 9th and earlier 10th centuries, a series of Viking/Danish invasions dominate recorded history. These were some of the most turbulent times in English history (Reynolds 2009b, 78), and regionally there were military campaigns and battles such as those at Reading, Ashdown, Basing and Wilton in 871 alone. It is unlikely that local people would not have known of, or been unaffected by, such events even if they had not been called to serve in a *fyrd* (local militia) by their local *ealdorman*, shire-reeve or thane. Inland settlements of economic, religious and/or political importance, like Winchester, were re-fortified as *burhs* (*ibid.*). By the middle of the 10th century, the legacy of Alfred of Wessex (r. 871–99) and the later wars and treaties under Edward the Elder (r. 899–924) and his son Athelstan (r. Mercia and Wessex 924–39 and England 927–39), had stabilised Wessex and united much of the rest of the country.

From the 7th century, justice was administered through monthly public meetings, often in rural locations (Reynolds 2009a, 18–21; Russel 2016, 105). The Hundred as an administrative unit appears in historical texts by the 10th century; the Hundred Shire and Borough courts may have been well established by the time the first reference to the Hundred as a unit of organisation appeared in law (III Edmund) (Trousdale 2013, 289; cf Stenton 1971, 298ff). An anonymous document, the *Hundred Ordinance* (Wormald 1999, 378–9, cited in Russel 2016, 105), which may have been written between the reigns of King Edmund (r. 939–46) and King Edgar of Wessex (The Peaceful, r. 957–75), laid down the rules for local courts (Trousdale 2013, 290). We have no definite way of knowing whether the cemetery was located at, or near to, a site for the monthly meetings for the hundred of Andover. This subject will be discussed below, in Chapter 7.

This period also witnessed the gradual Christianisation of Anglo-Saxon England, and the building of ecclesiastical buildings with adjacent burial grounds (churchyards). These followed the 7th-century activities of Christian missionaries, and the slow adoption of a 'new' religion and new practices. By the middle of the 8th century, burials were being made in churchyards (Cherryson 2008; Buckberry 2008; Riisøy 2015, 52). There were a number of established minsters by this date, and very probably a significant church in Andover itself. Separate execution cemeteries emerged alongside this trend, from the 7th century onwards. These continued to be used throughout the later Anglo-Saxon period, and sometimes as late as the 12th century (Buckberry 2014, 131). Rules in England which prevented the burial of certain persons in the parish churchyard were

based, as in Norway, not only on Christian teaching, but 'were also very much rooted in a heathen secular way of thinking about the punishment of criminals' (Riisøy 2015, 50). A long-established body of Anglo-Saxon law codes, from Athelstan (r. 924–39) onwards, specified the death penalty. Exclusion from consecrated ground is explicitly coupled with the death penalty during the reign of Aethelred (r. 978–1016) (Thompson 2002, 175ff).

The later 10th and the first half of the 11th century certainly represent a significant period of cultural change in England. Scandinavian influence reached its apogee under Cnut (r. 1016–35), and in Europe, the ruling families of Normandy traced their origins to the group of Viking migrants who had settled at the mouth of the Seine in the 10th century (Hadley and Dyer 2017, 6). Before 1066, England was closely connected to the Continent, and after the Conquest, when Norman rule was imposed under William I (r. 1066–87), such links became more direct, and influenced all levels of society in England.

The Normans consolidated their hold over the country, and strengthened its ties with Europe, and notably with France. At higher levels, the French-speaking aristocracy came from Normandy and other parts of north-western France, although some native-born Englishmen were retained. Land changed hands as the new king rewarded his followers. Queen Edith (widow of Edward the Confessor) was apparently confirmed in her lands (Williams 1995, 10), but by 1086, Penton Grafton, with Weyhill, had been given to the abbey of Grestain (Sainte-Marie and Saint-Pierre), founded in Normandy by the mother of William I. At other levels of society, more new settlers from northern France came to live and trade in towns like Southampton (Hadley and Dyer 2017, 8). It has been argued that the aftermath of the Conquest 'reflected the ruthlessness and violence which had characterised the "feudal mutation" on the Continent, and in many parts of England the Conquest was not a matter of a distant battle and an unknown new king, but was marked by the seizure of land, forced marriage for women with land and demands for money (Williams 1995)' (Hadley and Dyer 2017, 5).

The return to stability under the rule of England's great Angevin dynasty (the Plantagenets, 1154–1216), saw England as generally prosperous and fully engaged with the Continent. The civil wars of 1215–17 (the First Barons' War) and 1263–7 (the Second Barons' War) were quickly supressed. In a charter of about 1175 by Henry II, the men of Andover were given (for a payment) 'a gild merchant, with freedom from toll, passage and custom' (Page 1911a).

Despite episodic wars with France, stability for most returned under Edward I (1272–1307). The dating evidence from the cemetery suggests that its use ended around the end of the 13th century, or at least declined (although the latest simple calibrated date was of the

14th century, and possibly as late as 1389). In the later Middle Ages, most craftsmen formed associations or guilds, but the cloth industry was in advance of the others; the weavers and fullers of important centres such as Winchester gained permission to set up guilds which then exercised a monopoly for cloth-working within a certain radius, in return for an annual rent (Poole 1951, 85). Wool and cloth production were of great importance to Andover, and between 1271–4 it had 15 licensed merchants (compared to Winchester (40), Southampton (19), Portsmouth (1) and Basingstoke (2)). It is notable that, by 1270, prominent Andover merchants such as Alexander le Riche and Nicholas Adele de la Pole were forming business partnerships with other merchants, and buying wool across large areas of southern England (Lloyd 1977, 51–3). In 1273, five Andover wool merchants were granted licences to export 124 sacks of wool (Parsons 1945, 178).

Taxation returns for 1334 show that, by the standards of Hampshire, Andover was a relatively wealthy town. Although Winchester and Southampton were valued at more than twice the rate for Andover, the town was rated above both Portsmouth and Basingstoke, and had more than five times the value of Stockbridge at that time (Letters 2005a). This was, however, by no means a time of peace and prosperity for all. Eleanor of Provence (mother of Edward I) demanded the removal of Jews from the lands that she held in dower, which included Andover, and this was granted by Edward, in 1275. Jews were removed from Andover, as demonstrated by one Jacob Cok, who brought a charge of felony against Guy de Tanton, who had forcibly removed him from Andover on Eleanor's orders (Mundill 2003, 57–8). The court records for Hampshire and Wiltshire discussed below show high levels of poverty, with many plaintiffs described as having 'no chattels' and large numbers of crimes of burglary and theft reported.

During the 14th century, after the Weyhill Road cemetery had probably gone out of use, considerable local disruption and distress resulted from crop failures, civil and foreign wars, the Black Death (1348–9, 1361–2 and 1368–9) and rebellion (1381).

Grant (2009, 183) suggested that in 1603, Andover had a population of 1,308; by 1676, this had increased to 2,175 (up 66%), and by 1811 to 3,367 (a 55% increase between 1676 and 1811). There appears to have been only limited settlement growth beyond the probable medieval core of the town (*ibid.*, 186; fig. 3), although Grant notes that some of this growth may have been accommodated by hamlets within the rural environs of Andover. In broad terms, the majority of this expansion was of late 18th-century and/or early 19th-century date, piecemeal in nature, and located on the periphery of the town, along existing routes (*ibid.*, 197).

By the 19th century, Andover borough and parish boasted a fairly substantial population (3,304 in 1841 and 4,748 in 1821), and an annual rental value in 1815 of £8,975. Weyhill, by contrast, had a population of only 408 in 1821, while its annual rental value was not recorded (House of Commons 1831, 231, 237). The Tithe map of Andover cum Foxcotte (1849) shows the site as plot 694, 'The Hundred Acre', an arable field owned by Sir John Walter Pollen, Baronet, and occupied by John Wolfe and Brothers. A direction post is depicted at the corner of the Weyhill road and the southerly route of the old Roman road from Silchester to Old Sarum. The Pollens of Andover had risen to prominence in the neighbourhood of Penton Mewsey, towards the end of the 17th century (Page 1911b). The Pollens' estate, comprising the manor of Fyfield, with land in Fyfield, Thruxton, Kimpton and Andover, has always been known as the Redenham Estate, and their house as Redenham House (Page 1911h). No less than three Sir John Pollens had served as Members of Parliament for Andover: Sir John Walter Pollen (1784–1863) was the Second Baronet Pollen of Redenham, and like his father was apparently a Hampshire magistrate assiduous in performing his duties (*Gent. Mag.* (1814), ii. 294; (1863), i. 791–2, cited in Salmon and Spencer 2009). He was Colonel of the South Hants Militia (1827–53), and served as MP for Andover between 1820–30 and 1835–41 (*ibid.*).

Introduction to the cemetery

Radiocarbon dating has for many years formed the basis of chronological analysis in archaeological reports. However, where archaeological dates have been found to overlap with the historical record, the limitations of any single radiocarbon date in matching precise year-by-year, recorded history becomes apparent. In the case of the cemetery at Weyhill Road, we are fortunate to have a body of 20 radiocarbon dates which span a critically important period for the formation of the English State. The radiocarbon-dating programme has demonstrated a period of use, in simple calibrated dates from the 8th to the 14th centuries, that most probably covers a period from the 10th century to around the end of the 13th century. It highlights a particular aspect of society during a period of great change in England, and displays a degree of continuity, neither expected nor previously demonstrated by excavation results with absolute dating.

The site was a burial ground of a very specific type: a field used for the disposal of the bodies of persons excluded from churchyard burial, who are presumed to have been executed criminals. It is not known whether other types of outcasts who could be denied access to a Christian burial such as arsonists, heretics and excommunicants, were also buried there. With that proviso, this cemetery demonstrates the continuity of both burial practice and locale from the later Anglo-Saxon period, through the Norman Conquest, and well into the medieval period for a punishment cemetery.

The use of the cemetery in the post-Conquest era, and into the 12th and 13th centuries, suggests that local societal custom and authority was relatively uninterrupted. Invasions, civil wars and local rebellions occurred during this time, but Hampshire appears to have remained relatively calm. For instance, the 'Anarchy Period' in England and Normandy (1135–54) is widely seen as having led to a breakdown in law and order (see, for example, the *Anglo-Saxon Chronicle* for 1137), and distress throughout England. Certainly, Andover suffered a large fire in 1141, during the civil war, when Queen Matilda (also known as Maud or Matilda of Boulogne, d. 1152) was besieging Matilda, also known as Maud the Empress, in Winchester (Page 1911a). Some local reaction would have occurred but no major changes are reflected in the cemetery itself.

Chapter 2
Excavation Results

Site chronology

Excavated features, and a limited number of dateable artefacts, indicate activity on the site from the later prehistoric period onwards. The bulk of this evidence relates to the Late Saxon and early medieval periods. Archaeological features can be divided into the following distinguishable phases of activity:

Period	Features allocated
Pre-cemetery	
Late Iron Age (100 BC–AD 43)	Ditches, postholes
Roman (AD 43–410)	Road ditches
Cemetery	
AD 850–1066	?Holloway Pre-Conquest burials - probably 10th century
AD 1066–1154	Burials allocated to the 11th–12th century Gallows post-pits
AD 1154–*c*. 1300	Burials allocated to the Angevin period - probably 13th century ?Gibbet post-pit
Post-cemetery	
Post-medieval to modern (AD 1540–present)	Disturbance

Pre-cemetery features

Late Iron Age

The earliest phase of archaeological activity on site was of the Late Iron Age (LIA) period (Fig. 2.1). Ditch A (Figs 2.2 and 2.3) was aligned north-west/south-east, and followed a slight contour. It displayed a distinct,

steep-sided profile, with a flat base, and was on average 0.98m wide and 0.54m deep. The remnants of four undated, but possibly associated, ditches (E, F, G and H) were found in the south of the site. Ditch A was dated to the LIA on the basis of a single fragment of pottery, and its relationship to Ditch B. Ditch B was a probable roadside gully of the 1st century AD, which had been cut across the line of Ditch A.

Ditches E and H were located some 15m further down-slope, and were on roughly the same alignment as Ditch A. Ditch E had a shallow U-shaped profile, with an average width of 0.47m and depth of 0.08m. It may represent the remnants of a more substantial ditch, as both ends were shallow and amorphous and so may not represent the original terminals of this feature. Ditch H ran parallel to Ditch E, approximately 2m apart. It had moderately steep sides and a flat base, and was 0.71m wide and 0.24m deep.

Ditches F and G were located to the east of E and H, and ran across the slope. They appeared to be roughly parallel, and about 3.5m apart. Ditch F measured on average 0.48m in width and 0.14m in depth, and displayed a shallow, U-shaped profile. Its extent was not determined, as it was truncated by modern services at its western end, and continued below a modern deposit of construction material at its eastern end. It was cut by the holloway comprising Ditch D. Ditch G had moderately steep sides and a flat base, and was 0.8m wide and 0.35m deep.

A group of eight postholes (1016, 1018, 1020, 1022, 1024, 1026, 1028 and 1035) were arranged in a roughly curvilinear configuration, towards the western edge of the site, to the north of, and adjacent to, Ditch A. A single, very small sherd of late prehistoric flint-tempered pottery, believed to be of LIA date, was retrieved from posthole 1028, but due to its condition may be residual. None of these postholes provided any other dating evidence, and they were not consistent in either diameter or depth, ranging from 0.2m to 0.53m and 0.08m to 0.17m respectively.

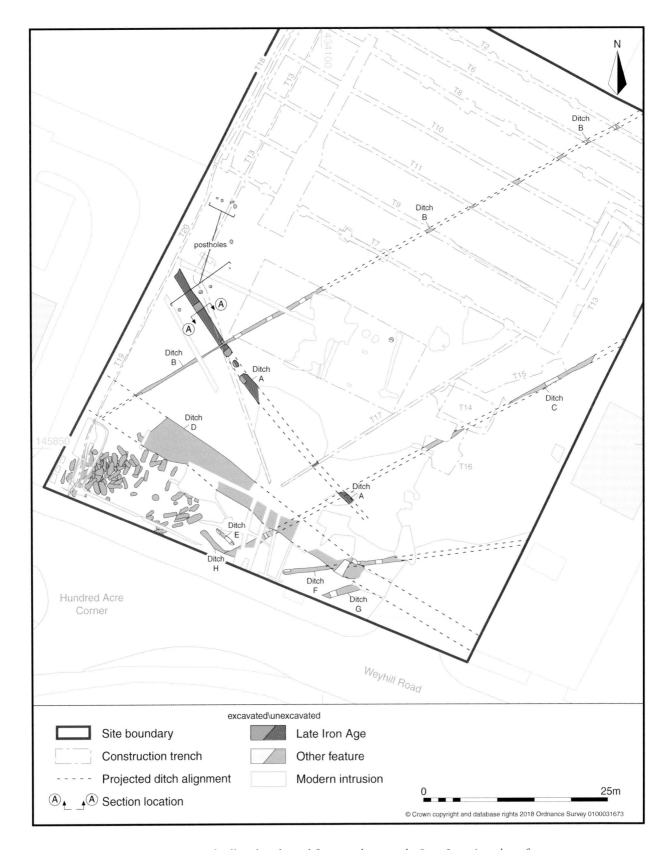

Fig. 2.1   The development site with all archaeological features showing the Late Iron Age phase features

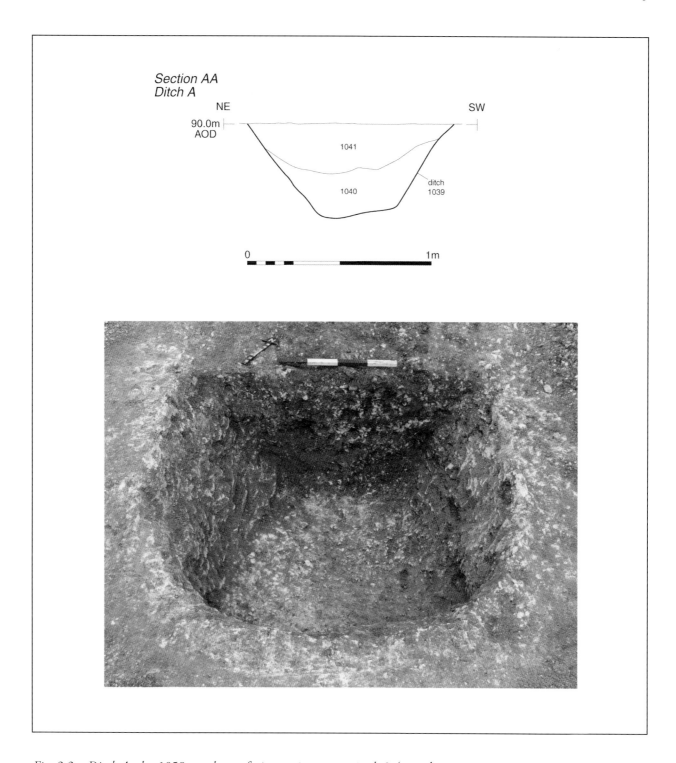

Fig. 2.2   Ditch A, slot 1059, south-east facing section at terminal. 0.4m scale

Three residual sherds of likely LIA date were recovered from the later cemetery area: a flint-tempered sherd from the fill of grave 1390; a reduced-fired, sandy body sherd, from grave 1117; and a sherd of a sand- and grog-tempered everted rim jar was found in the fill of grave 1135 (Hawkins, Chapter 4). A single worked flint, a flake, was recorded from pit 1171 (fill 1172).

This small group of badly preserved residual finds and features are insufficient to offer a coherent narrative of Late Iron Age activity on the site. However, this evidence does suggest some form of low-level agricultural activity, encompassing potential land boundaries, enclosures, trackways and other structures in the immediate area.

Roman

Before works commenced, the site was thought to have straddled the presumed route of the former Silchester to Old Sarum Roman road (the Portway). However,

*Fig. 2.3   View north-east across Ditch A.
1m scale*

during excavation, no evidence of a metalled road surface was revealed, although two parallel ditches (B and C) crossed the site from the south-west to northeast, on the predicted alignment based on better-preserved sections of the road. Ditch B (Figs 2.4–2.6) contained a single fragment of 1st-century pottery (a single rimsherd, from a necked, cordoned jar (fill 1012, ditch 1011)), and had an average surviving width of 0.45m and depth of 0.16m. Ditch B cut through Late Iron Age Ditch A and Ditch B was itself cut by a later holloway (Ditch D). It is probable that Ditch C was similarly cut by holloway D, but this relationship was partly obscured by modern services. Ditch C had an average width of 0.62m and depth of 0.24m.

Flanking Ditches B and C were 25m apart, which is very close to the recorded measurements for the Portway mentioned above in Chapter 1, i.e. 84.5 feet. If the central *agger* was of similar width (27 feet), it would have covered a section about 5m wide running diagonally across the area of the later cemetery (Fig. 2.4). The line of the road would have been known during the intervening Saxon period, even if this section of the route had fallen into disuse by that time. It would probably have featured as a known boundary, or possibly

as an open quarry for gravel and cobble. There was no doubt an increasing demand for wall rubble and hard-standing materials as Andover and Weyhill progressed through the Saxon and medieval periods. This area could, therefore, have been both well-used and also of marginal agricultural value in the succeeding periods.

The cemetery

Introduction

The main focus of activity within the site comprised the digging of a substantial number of inhumation graves (Fig. 2.7), which were concentrated within the south-western corner. Figure 1.3 shows part of this concentration, prior to excavation. The cemetery measured 21m in minimum east–west extent, and 14m in north–south extent. It seems likely that, prior to the impact of modern developments, the graves continued beyond the southern, and possibly western, boundaries of the site. Considerable disturbance of the graves occurred during the 1960s and 70s, when the industrial estate was developed. Many graves had been reduced during the late 20th century, both by the insertion of service trenches, and by the general reduction and

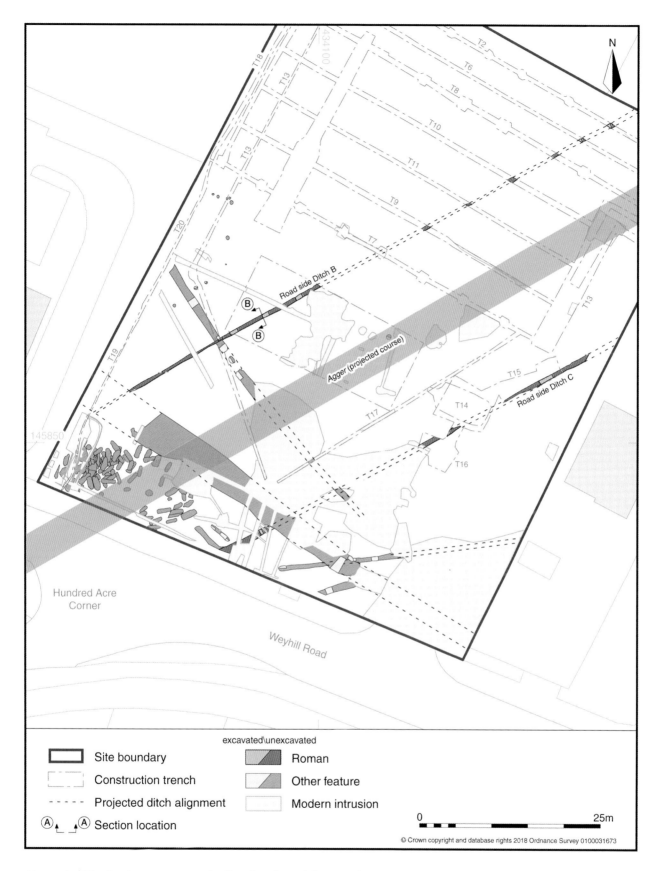

Site boundary

Construction trench

Projected ditch alignment

(A)◄ ►(A) Section location

excavated\unexcavated

Roman

Other feature

Modern intrusion

0   25m

© Crown copyright and database rights 2018 Ordnance Survey 0100031673

Fig. 2.4   The development site with all archaeological features showing the Roman features

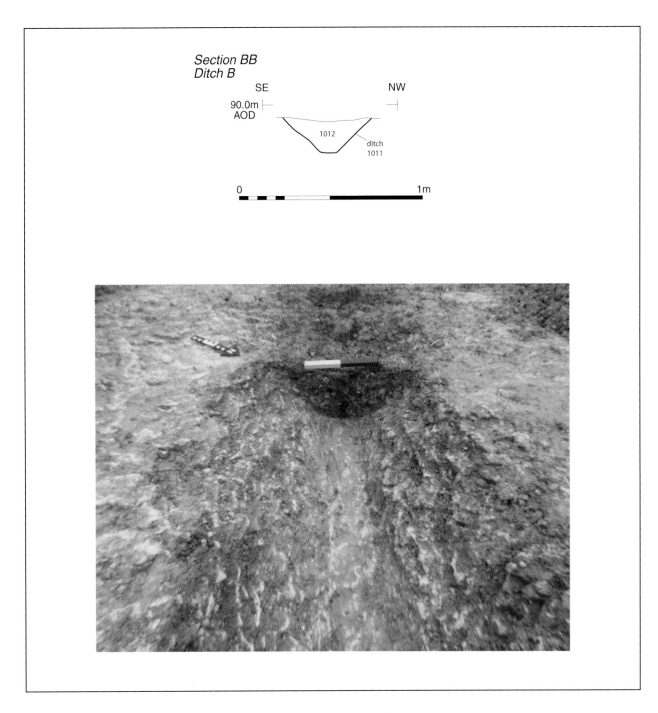

Fig. 2.5   North-east facing section through Ditch B (1011). 0.2m scale

levelling of the area. It was also apparent that, although some grave outlines were complete and evenly spaced, with an evident degree of alignment, many, as well as being recently disturbed, had been inserted into a compressed space, without concern for earlier graves. In total, some 91 possible grave cuts were identified, and subsequently excavated, during the watching brief and limited excavation.

For a local community, the concept of an inhumation cemetery implies the definition of both place and the specific rites to be undertaken within that location.

It often follows that the owners and/or organisers of that space will allocate carefully considered positions within it. This in turn results in a layout comprising relatively orderly rows of graves, with some variations in dimension, content and plan reflecting the status of the individuals concerned and the common wishes of their surviving contemporaries. From the outset, it was apparent that this cemetery demonstrated some conflicting traits. There were traces of orderly patterns and common alignments, especially in the north and east of the cemetery. However, most of the graves

Fig. 2.6 View north-east across Ditch B. 2m scale

at Weyhill Road were crammed into a very limited area. The use of a compressed area for burials is often interpreted as reflecting some local disaster, natural or otherwise, requiring the speedy disposal of a large number of corpses. This frequently results in the need for a large common grave, containing numerous bodies, which was not apparent here. Neither has the span of radiocarbon dates obtained (Healy, Chapter 5) supported that hypothesis.

The graves

The grave plan (Fig. 2.7) shows that individual burials exhibit a variety of orientations. While it is simpler to use the alignment of the grave outline to indicate orientation, and also more realistic, in that the grave aligns the body and not vice versa; the levels of disturbance and overall reduction of the graves have caused problems with this approach. Accordingly, the orientation of bodies was measured by reference to the skeleton, where enough survived *in situ* to allow this. The alignment of the body was given a compass bearing, and the results were divided into eight groups. Ninety-six individuals were assigned an orientation (Fig. 2.8). Of these, *c.* 77% were aligned with their heads to the

south, south-west or west. The head to the south-west category was noted most often, at *c.* 30%. Only *c.* 19% were recorded with head to the west, the expected alignment from a cemetery dated within the Christian period. It therefore follows that the orientations must owe more to other influences. Possible changes of burial alignment over time, and the influence of pre-existing and contemporary features, are covered in detail in Chapter 8.

The most intact graves measured *c.* 2m in length and 0.5m in width, with double graves being about 0.9m wide. (See Figs 2.9 and 2.10, graves 1055 and 1173). They displayed approximately parallel sides, with occasional suggestions of narrowing towards the foot end. Many showed irregularities in shape, probably the result of their reduction to their surviving base level. Almost 17% of graves were only 0.10m deep, or less, at the time of excavation. Sixty per cent of the group were between 0.1m and 0.3m deep, with only one example, grave 1249, recorded as more than 0.6m deep. Figure 2.11 shows one of the few examples of reasonable surviving depth, in this case grave 1111, of *c.* 0.35m depth. Many of the fills were described as light to mid-greyish brown in colour with clay/silt components.

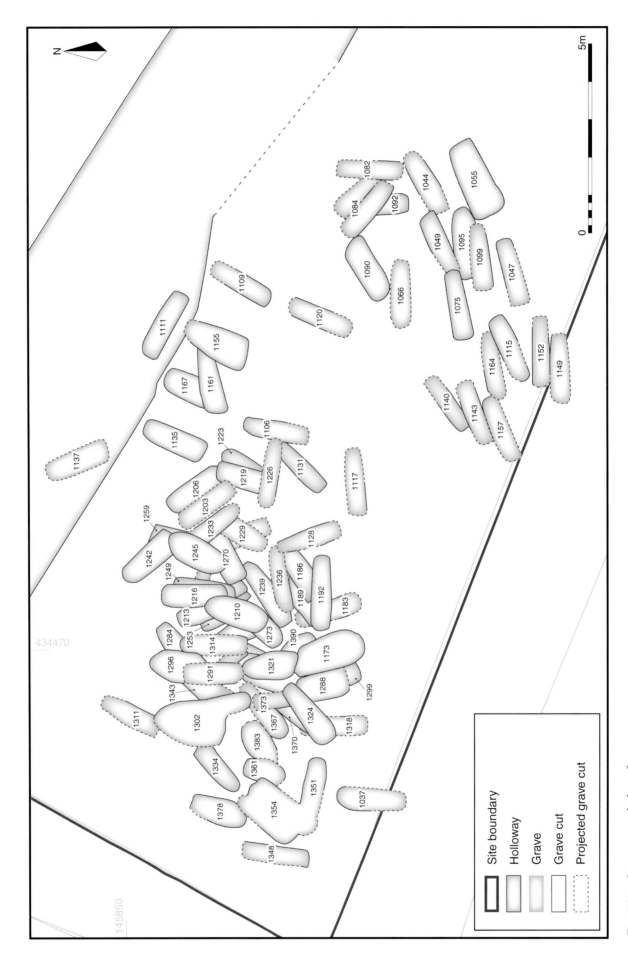

Fig. 2.7 Reconstructed plan of graves

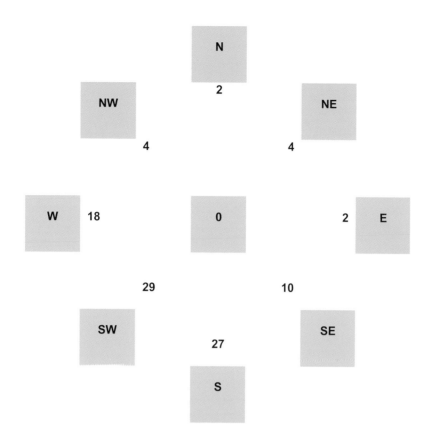

Fig. 2.8 *Diagram showing spread of skeleton alignments (head end) where discernible*

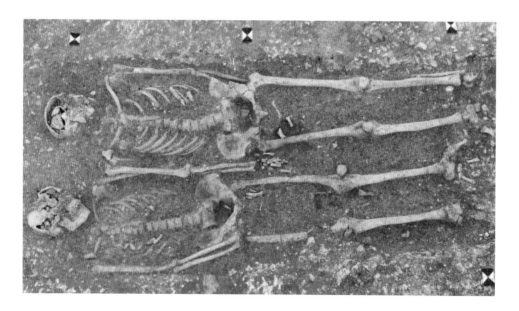

Fig. 2.9 *Double grave 1055 with SKs1056 and 1057*

There was no evidence of coffins or coffin fittings, with only single nails found in graves 1131 and 1378 and 1236. Some graves (e.g. Fig. 2.12, grave 1135), while of reasonable depth, did not appear to have been large enough to accommodate the body.

No 'empty graves' were encountered, and indeed, a substantial volume of disturbed bone was recovered from grave fills, presumably the result of ongoing disturbance to earlier graves during the lifespan of the cemetery. Therefore, it is possible that some graves may already have been completely obliterated during this process. As grave outlines were followed down and excavated, it was

Fig. 2.10 Double grave 1173 with SKs1174 and 1175

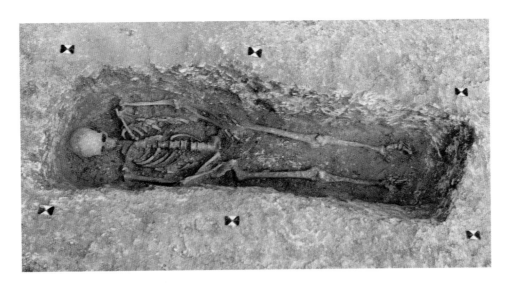

Fig. 2.11 Grave 1111 with SK1112

Fig. 2.12 Grave 1135 with SK1160

found that two (1364 and 1332, see below) represented the remains of pits containing substantial amounts of disarticulated bone, and these are not considered as graves.

A number of grave outlines were found to be the resting place of more than one individual. On seven occasions, two skeletons were found within what appeared to be a single grave; five pairs roughly side by side, and two placed one above the other. Eleven other grave features were found to contain the remains of parts of more than one articulated skeleton. Some apparently represented the remnants of former occupants, and others were too limited in extent to determine whether the grave outline represented a single event or traces of more.

A layer of soil in the south-west corner of the site (the western half being allocated the number 1015 and the eastern half 1004), also contained disarticulated human bones. It comprised both mixed deposits of subsoil and recently made ground, and probably resulted from late 20th-century levelling operations. It clearly contained material from disturbed graves, but the exact location, extent and fate of said graves remains unknown. Context 1004 encompassed an area of disturbed graves between grave 1183 and grave 1095, where there were fewer surviving burials. It is possible, therefore, that the pattern of burials as recovered has been materially altered, but as this is unprovable we have to consider the overall distribution as presented at the time of excavation.

In spite of these disturbances, both ancient and modern, the articulated or at least partly articulated remains of at least 124 individuals were identified. Even more promising was the fact that 44 of the 124 individuals were represented by 75%, or more, of recovered skeletal material. A thorough examination of the human remains (see Clough, Chapter 3), indicated that the overwhelming majority of the burials were of adult males, a significant proportion of which displayed skeletal or positional evidence of possible execution processes. The significance of this subset of the population, and how they met their end, is shown in Table 2.1 below, and considered further in Chapters 7 and 8. The nature of the interments provides a strong indication of the specific purpose of the cemetery. There is osteological and circumstantial evidence from the human remains and the nature of their burials for forcible execution as the cause of death.

Table 2.1 Evidence suggestive of execution

Evidence suggestive of execution	Examples
Hands tied behind back	27
Decapitation: either cut-marks to cervical vertebrae or cranium (sharp-force trauma)	Minimum of 10
or skull position in grave, or both	Maximum of 23–25
Hands cut off	1
Possible fracture of CV2	2

Finds from the cemetery

Very little artefactual evidence was recovered from the site generally. Small amounts of ceramic building material, glass and other clearly intrusive modern objects were occasionally noted in upper layers, and are not discussed. Finds from graves were restricted to two examples of articulated parts of a sheep (graves 1037 and 1183), two worked bone items (graves 1120 and 1341), and several metal objects (Marsden, Chapter 4). With the exception of a single silver coin (grave 1219, dateable to AD 979–85), the other 11 metal objects are of iron, and include a number of buckles which have a broad date-range. Four of the buckles are provisionally only dateable to Anglo-Saxon to early medieval (graves 1149 and 1299), or to a late 6th to 14th-century date (graves 1167 and 1189), i.e. they potentially span the known date-range of the cemetery. Two iron nails and one probable nail were also recovered from fills of graves (graves 1131, 1378 and 1236), but again these items cannot be closely dated, and may represent accidental incorporations. A single cattle tooth was recovered from a grave (grave 1242), but also seems unlikely to have been a 'grave good'. See Armitage (Chapter 4) for further descriptions of the faunal remains.

Structural elements associated with the cemetery

Post-pits

Five probable post-pits, (1125, 1171, 1265, 1276, 1280), were recorded within the area of the cemetery (Figs 2.13–2.14). These pits were approximately circular or slightly oval in shape, with reasonably well-defined, near-vertical edges. Their overall dimensions were roughly similar, and the differences in depth may be explained by differential levels of truncation across the site. The most obvious post-pit was 1280, which clearly displayed a post-pipe and packing in section.

In plan, it can be seen that four of the post-pits may have represented two pairs of substantial posts (1171 and 1265, 1276 and 1280), each pair some 3m apart, and located within the most densely used area of the cemetery. It is also possible that the post-pits represent the remains of a larger, more elaborate, fan-shaped structure, but this seems less supportable from surviving evidence. The fifth post-pit, 1125, which was 0.85m in diameter with a surviving depth of 0.25m, was an isolated feature, within an apparently open area of the site.

The northernmost pair, 1276 and 1280, was aligned roughly east–west, and could be associated with the cemetery on the basis of stratigraphic relationships (see Fig. 2.15).

These confirmed that post-pit 1276 was later than SK1240, radiocarbon-dated to the 10th century, and earlier than SK1254 which was radiocarbon-dated to the 11th to 12th centuries. Post-pit 1276 measured 0.53m in diameter, with a surviving depth of 0.44m, and 1280 was 0.65m in diameter, with a surviving depth of 0.58m.

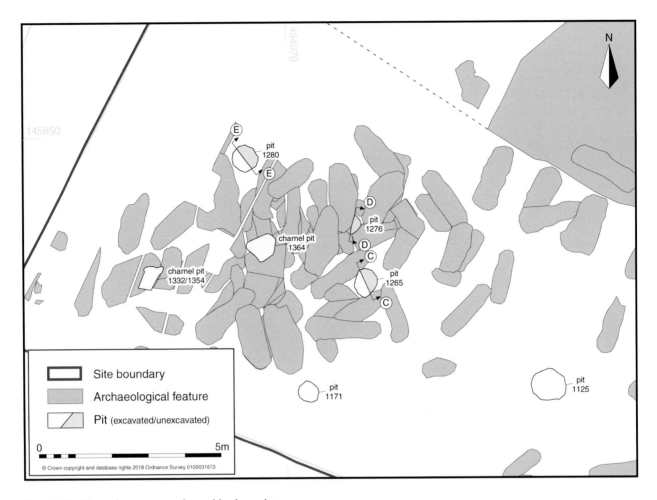

Fig. 2.13 Plan of post-pits and possible charnel pits

The central pair, 1171 and 1265, was aligned roughly north–south and was dated by a single pottery sherd. The single, hard, sand- and flint-tempered pottery sherd, with an oxidised surface, was recovered from the single fill (1172) of post-pit 1171, and is typical of the 11th to 13th centuries (Hawkins, Chapter 4). Post-pit 1171 measured 0.52m in diameter with a surviving depth of 0.13m, and 1265 measured 0.65m in diameter, with a surviving depth of 0.27m.

Other features associated with the cemetery

Feature 1364, interpreted as a charnel pit, was irregular in plan, with a flat base, and measured 1.27m at its widest extent and 0.50m in depth (Fig. 2.13). This feature cut graves 1341, 1367 and 1390, and was itself cut by grave 1321 (see Fig. 2.16).

The fill (1366, described as a mid-brown clayey silt with moderate chalk component) contained bones from a minimum of five different adults, and one child. A 12th-century iron swivel fitting (hook) was recovered from pit 1364.

Feature 1332, initially recorded as a grave, appears to have been another small charnel pit. This very shallow, irregular feature (fill 1333, described as a mid-greyish brown clayey silt) contained only cranial remains, but

from four individuals (SKs1327, 1328, 1328b and 1329).

Feature D, interpreted as a holloway, was a consistently wide and shallow linear feature, with a flat base measuring 4.8m at its widest extent and 0.13m in depth (Fig. 2.1). Holloway D cut the Early Roman gully B. This feature may be contemporary with the use of the cemetery, as it ran to the north of the main cemetery area, and could represent an access route. However, due to the similarity of the subsoil, 1002, to the fill of holloway D (described as a mid to dark brown silt with a humic content), and the disturbance caused by modern services and foundations at its western end, the exact edge of the holloway was not clear. The presence of at least one grave (1111), and possibly two (1137), which had been either dug into or cut by the holloway, may reflect a slight parallel shift of holloway D over time, or could indicate that the true southern edge of holloway D was further to the north.

The people

The human remains are fully discussed by Clough (Chapter 3). The results can be summarised as follows. The identified total of 124 individuals is a minimum

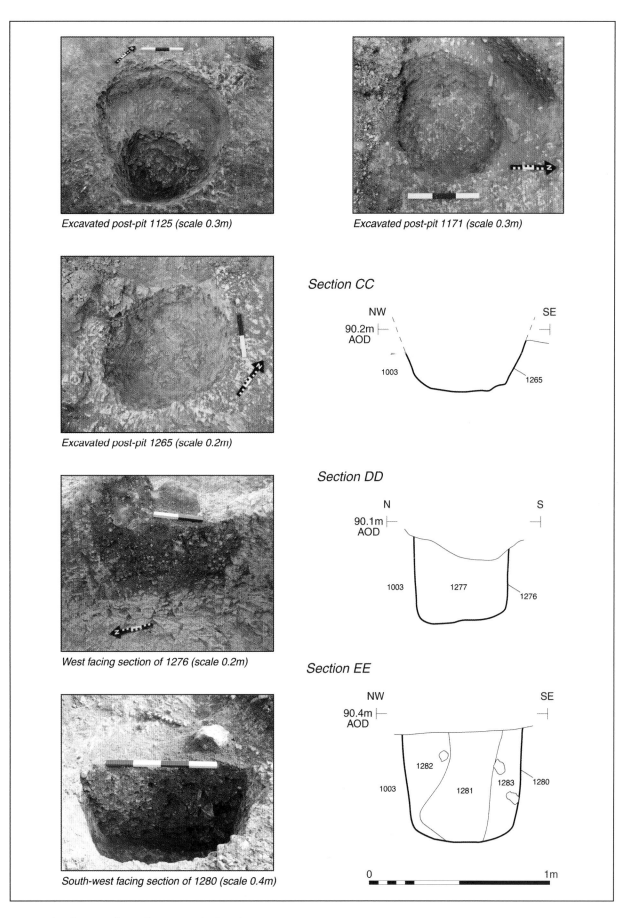

Excavated post-pit 1125 (scale 0.3m)

Excavated post-pit 1171 (scale 0.3m)

Section CC

NW

90.2m
AOD

SE

1003   1265

Excavated post-pit 1265 (scale 0.2m)

Section DD

N

90.1m
AOD

S

1003   1277   1276

West facing section of 1276 (scale 0.2m)

Section EE

NW

90.4m
AOD

SE

1282   1280

1003   1281   1283

0   1m

South-west facing section of 1280 (scale 0.4m)

Fig. 2.14 Photographs and sections of selected post-pits

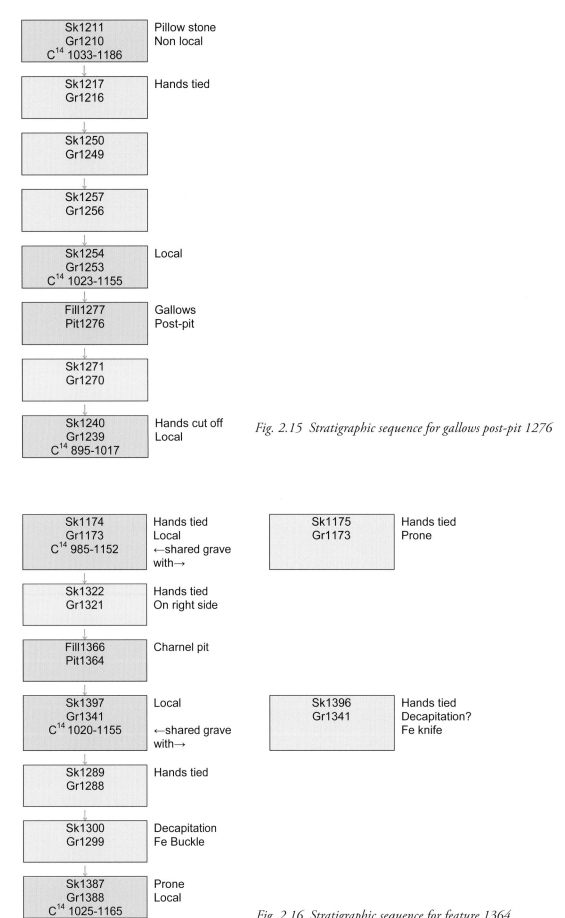

Sk1211
Gr1210
C^{14} 1033-1186
— Pillow stone / Non local

Sk1217
Gr1216
— Hands tied

Sk1250
Gr1249

Sk1257
Gr1256

Sk1254
Gr1253
C^{14} 1023-1155
— Local

Fill1277
Pit1276
— Gallows / Post-pit

Sk1271
Gr1270

Sk1240
Gr1239
C^{14} 895-1017
— Hands cut off / Local

Fig. 2.15 Stratigraphic sequence for gallows post-pit 1276

Sk1174
Gr1173
C^{14} 985-1152
— Hands tied / Local / ←shared grave with→

Sk1175
Gr1173
— Hands tied / Prone

Sk1322
Gr1321
— Hands tied / On right side

Fill1366
Pit1364
— Charnel pit

Sk1397
Gr1341
C^{14} 1020-1155
— Local / ←shared grave with→

Sk1396
Gr1341
— Hands tied / Decapitation? / Fe knife

Sk1289
Gr1288
— Hands tied

Sk1300
Gr1299
— Decapitation / Fe Buckle

Sk1387
Gr1388
C^{14} 1025-1165
— Prone / Local

Fig. 2.16 Stratigraphic sequence for feature 1364

number. Examination of the disarticulated bone has identified another 39 potential additional individuals. Amongst this material were non-adult bones, some of which could relate to the older child category, or '6–12 years' range. These could represent further parts from an already identified non-adult, but some may indicate another child, whose grave has been completely lost.

Estimation of sex was possible for 100 individuals. Of these, three were identified as female (two articulated skeletons and one cranium) and the rest were male, or probable/possible male. The age distribution has peak incidence in the young adult (18–25) category. Documentary evidence suggests that the presence of two older children in the 6–12 years range would not necessarily rule out the predominant, or even exclusive, use of the cemetery for executed criminals.

The statures for the cemetery population, estimated from long bones, fit average values and ranges for this time-period. Physical examination and reconstruction of crania, to observe varying cranial shapes and facial features, did not identify any dissimilar individuals. They appear, metrically and non-metrically, to comprise a homogenous group. There was little evidence for age-related disease, although there was some congenital disease, together with a limited amount of metabolic bone disease and some (though still low) evidence for trauma.

Twenty samples from human bone or teeth were submitted for stable isotope analysis, to determine whether the burial population was local, and to gain some indication of their diet. Animal bone from the site was very limited, but a sample (GU-44454) from a single sheep deposited in grave 1037 was also sampled for comparative purposes. The results are presented below (Jay, Chapter 6). In summary, the majority of the samples appear to come from a local population. Two individuals are consistent with a Scandinavian origin and another has strontium data which are not consistent with the site, and may well be an immigrant, while a fourth individual has a nitrogen value which is an outlier in the context of the group, and an oxygen isotope ratio which is suggestive of mobility, at least within Britain.

Cemetery chronology

The disadvantage of dealing with a mass of intercutting graves had one distinct advantage for the post-excavation assessment. In a cemetery with a well-spaced, orderly layout, there would be few, if any, obvious sequential relationships between graves. In this case, a stratigraphic matrix could be constructed for a reasonable proportion of the graves in the western half of the cemetery. The longest stratigraphic sequence is presented in Figure 2.17, with radiocarbon-dated SK1240 (assigned to the 10th century) at the base of the sequence and SK1211 (assigned to the 11th to 12th century) at the top. It contains evidence for locals, non-locals and both definite and implied punishments.

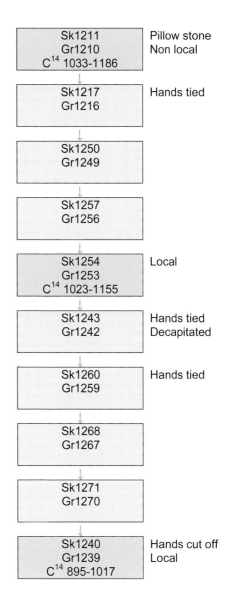

Fig. 2.17 The longest stratigraphic sequence

In plan view, it was also noted that the lack of a predominant head-to-west alignment allowed the outlying, less-disturbed groups to the north and east to be considered by reference to more local, group alignments. In order to test a number of possible hypotheses regarding the development and internal organisation of the cemetery, 20 samples of human bone were selected, largely on the basis of spatial and stratigraphic grounds, and the bone was submitted for radiocarbon dating. While dates were obtained from all samples, a number of these fall on one of three recognised plateaux in the radiocarbon calibration curve, relating to the 9th, 10th, and 11th to 12th centuries cal AD. This makes the calibrated age-ranges of the samples wider than they would otherwise be, and emphasises, even exaggerates, any breaks in burial. A simplified table of radiocarbon results is presented here (Table 2.2). These full results of the Bayesian analysis are discussed by Healy (Chapter 5).

Radiocarbon dating by Sarah Cobain

Radiocarbon dating was undertaken in order to confirm the date of skeletons 1056, 1108, 1225, 1112, 1207, 1240, 1274, 1387, 1379, 1254, 1397, 1297, 1211, 1292, 1174, 1286, 1228, 1074, 1209, and 1138. The samples were analysed during August 2017 and March 2018 at Scottish Universities Environmental Research Centre (SUERC), Rankine Avenue, Scottish Enterprise Technology Park, East Kilbride, Glasgow, G75 0QF, Scotland.

The uncalibrated dates are conventional radiocarbon ages. The radiocarbon ages were calibrated using the University of Oxford Radiocarbon Accelerator Unit calibration programme OxCal v4.3.2 (2017) (Bronk Ramsey 2009) using the IntCal13 curve (Reimer *et al.* 2013).

Table 2.2 Radiocarbon-dating results with Oxcal calibration data by Sarah Cobain

Feature	Lab no.	Material	$\delta^{13}C$	$\delta^{15}N$	C/N ratio	Radiocarbon age	Calibrated radiocarbon age 95.4% probability	Calibrated radiocarbon age 68.2% probability
SK1056 Grave 1055	SUERC-74061	Human bone: Right femur	-20.0‰	9.1‰	3.0	691 ± 30 yr BP	1265–1312 cal AD (69.8%) 1359–1388 cal AD (25.6%)	1275–1299 cal AD (55.6%) 1370–1380 cal AD (12.6%)
SK1074 Grave 1075	SUERC-78126	Human bone: Left fibula: proximal fragment	-19.6‰	10.2‰	3.2	757 ± 29 yr BP	1220–1285 cal AD (95.4%)	1249–1280 cal AD (68.2%)
SK1108 Grave 1109	SUERC-74062	Human bone: Right femur	-19.9‰	10.3‰	3.1	1116 ± 30 yr BP	895–930 cal AD (34.8%) 939–972 cal AD (33.4%)	778–789 cal AD (1.3%) 831–837 cal AD (0.5%) 868–999 cal AD (93.0%) 1004–1012 cal AD (0.7%)
SK1112 Grave 1111	SUERC-74064	Human bone: Right femur	-20.0‰	8.4‰	3.0	1181 ± 30 yr BP	729–736 cal AD (0.9%) 768–901 cal AD (87.7%) 921–951 cal AD (6.8%)	778–793 cal AD (11.5%) 801–846 cal AD (32.2%) 853–886 cal AD (24.6%)
SK1138 Grave 1137	SUERC-78128	Human bone: Femur fragments	-20.0‰	9.4‰	3.2	1003 ± 29 yr BP	981–1050 cal AD (76.1%) 1083–1126 cal AD (15.3%) 1136–1151 cal AD (4.0%)	991–1040 cal AD (65.4%) 1110–1115 cal AD (2.8%)
SK1174 Grave 1173	SUERC-74082	Human bone: Left femur	-19.7‰	8.3‰	3.0	998 ± 30 yr BP	985–1052 cal AD (67.9%) 1081–1152 cal AD (27.5%)	993–1041 cal AD (61.5%) 1108–1117 cal AD (6.7%)
SK1207 Grave 1206	SUERC-74065	Human bone: Right femur	-19.8‰	8.0‰	3.0	961 ± 30 yr BP	1020–1155 cal AD (95.4%)	1024–1049 cal AD (23.4%) 1085–1142 cal AD (34.3%) 1137–1150 cal AD (10.5%)
SK1209 Grave 1152	SUERC-78127	Human bone: Left humerus: distal shaft	-19.5‰	9.7‰	3.2	681 ± 29 yr BP	1270–1315 cal AD (61.7%) 1356–1389 cal AD (33.7%)	1279–1300 cal AD (48.2%) 1369–1381 cal AD (20.0%)
SK1211 Grave 1210	SUERC-74077	Human bone: Left femur	-20.1‰	9.2‰	3.2	913 ± 27 yr BP	1033–1186 cal AD (95.4%)	1045–1095 cal AD (40.6%) 1120–1142 cal AD (16.6%) 1147–1161 cal AD (11.0%)
SK1225 Grave 1223	SUERC-74063	Human bone: Right radius	-19.4‰	10.3‰	2.9	1093 ± 30 yr BP	891–1015 cal AD (95.4%)	899–924 cal AD (25.2%) 945–988 cal AD (43.0%)

Feature	Lab no.	Material	$\delta^{13}C$	$\delta^{15}N$	C/N ratio	Radiocarbon age	Calibrated radiocarbon age 95.4% probability	Calibrated radiocarbon age 68.2% probability
SK1228 Grave 1226	SUERC-78122	Human bone: Left clavicle: medial body	-19.8‰	12.3‰	3.2	798 ± 29 yr BP	1187–1276 cal AD (95.4%)	1221–1261 cal AD (68.2%)
SK1240 Grave 1239	SUERC-74066	Human bone: Right femur	-19.7‰	8.2‰	2.9	1081 ± 27 yr BP	895–929 cal AD (27.1%) / 939–1017 cal AD (68.3%)	900–922 cal AD (20.4%) / 950–995 cal AD (47.8%)
SK1254 Grave 1253	SUERC-74074	Human bone: Left femur	-19.8‰	8.4‰	3.0	952 ± 30 yr BP	1023–1155 cal AD (95.4%)	1028–1050 cal AD (18.7%) / 1083–1126 cal AD (37.1%) / 1136–1151 cal AD (12.4%)
SK1274 Grave 1273	SUERC-74071	Human bone: Right humerus	-19.6‰	10.3‰	2.9	1110 ± 30 yr BP	879–1013 cal AD (95.4%)	895–928 cal AD (32.7%) / 940–976 cal AD (35.5%)
SK1286 Grave 1285	SUERC-78121	Human bone: Left scapula: mid lateral border	-20.0‰	9.9‰	3.3	936 ± 29 yr BP	1027–1160 cal AD (95.4%)	1039–1052 cal AD (10.8%) / 1081–1152 cal AD (57.4%)
SK1292 Grave 1291	SUERC-74081	Human bone: Left femur	-19.7‰	9.0‰	3.1	907 ± 27 yr BP	1036–1191 cal AD (93.8%) / 1198–1205 cal AD (1.6%)	1045–1095 cal AD (39.5%) / 1120–1142 cal AD (15.3%) / 1147–1165 cal AD (13.4%)
SK1297 Grave 1296	SUERC-74076	Human bone: Right tibia	-19.5‰	8.5‰	3.1	918 ± 30 yr BP	1030–1185 cal AD (95.4%)	1045–1098 cal AD (41.4%) / 1120–1159 cal AD (26.8%)
SK1379 Grave 1378	SUERC-74073	Human bone: Right femur	-19.9‰	8.4‰	3.1	924 ± 30 yr BP	1026–1170 cal AD (94.2%) / 1175–1183 cal AD (1.2%)	1045–1099 cal AD (42.4%) / 1120–1155 cal AD (25.8%)
SK1387 Grave 1388	SUERC-74072	Human bone: Left femur	-20.2‰	8.0‰	3.0	931 ± 30 yr BP	1025–1165 cal AD (95.4%)	1040–1058 cal AD (12.7%) / 1075–1154 cal AD (55.5%)
SK1397 Grave 1341	SUERC-74075	Human bone: Right femur	-19.7‰	9.3‰	3.2	962 ± 30 yr BP	1020–1155 cal AD (95.4%)	1023–1049 cal AD (23.8%) / 1085–1124 cal AD (34.0%) / 1137–1150 cal AD (10.4%)

The results of the radiocarbon-dating samples, the stratigraphic sequence and the alignment groups were correlated to produce a proposed sequence of burial events. Three distinct phases have been identified. Ten individuals have been assigned to the earliest phase which spanned the 10th century. Thirty-five have been included in the second phase, which is roughly dated to the 11th and 12th centuries, and fifteen individuals were assigned to the final phase, which is of 13th-century date. A number of other individuals could be seen to post-date the earlier group, or pre-date the later group, but could not otherwise be closely assigned to phase. The significance and validity of this tripartite division will be discussed further in Chapter 8.

10th century

The radiocarbon results suggest that five skeletons could be included in the 10th-century group (Fig. 2.18: SKs1108, 1112, 1225, 1240 and 1274). The grave of SK1112 lay at the north-eastern extent of the burial ground, perhaps within the bounds of, and parallel to, holloway D. The exact relationship between the holloway and the grave was not obvious, but is assumed to have been roughly contemporary. Two of these skeletons were located south of, and perpendicular to, SK1112 and holloway D: SKs1108 and 1225. The other two, SKs1240 and 1274, were located within the main cluster of burials. Two further burials, SKs1160 and 1168, have been included in this group, on the grounds of their proximity to burial 1112 and general alignment. Skeletons 1184, 1190 and 1394 all appear to be at the base of the stratigraphic sequence, and could represent more examples of disturbed earlier burials within the main 11th to 12th-century burial area.

11th to 12th centuries

Eleven of the burials, from graves predominantly located in the main cluster, produced probable or definite 11th to 12th-century dates (Fig. 2.19). These comprised:

SKs1138, 1174, 1207, 1211, 1254, 1286, 1292, 1297, 1379, 1387 and 1397. Two of these burials were in shared graves, adding SKs1175 and 1396. Stratigraphic relationships linking radiocarbon-dated burials in the main group place twelve more individuals within the sequence dated to the 11th to 12th centuries (Fig. 2.20) with a further ten of probable late 10th to early 12th-century date (Fig. 2.21).

13th century

Four skeletons (SKs1056, 1074, 1209 and 1228) produced radiocarbon dates which could be ascribed to the 13th century. Since three of the dated examples occur in the eastern group, from which no other dates have been retrieved, eleven further burials (SKs1043, 1046, 1057, 1089, 1097, 1098, 1101, 1114, 1148, 1162 and 1237) have been assigned to this period. The group is, therefore, defined by limited radiocarbon dating, a shared alignment, generally west to south-west, and the presence of four shared graves (Fig. 2.22).

Post-medieval and modern

It is known from 20th-century OS maps that the site continued to be in use as agricultural land until 1940 (see Figs 1.5 and 8.2). This phase of the site was evidenced by plough scars crossing the chalk in different places, but also cutting across graves, where post-medieval pottery and ceramic building material was found redeposited in the tops of grave fills.

Subsequent development of the site as a garage, prior to the current development, also left deep chalk-cut foundations and waste pits, which truncated the eastern edge of the Saxon cemetery and holloway D. In places to the east of the site, and in the centre, the subsoil had been completely truncated by modern development. An area of graves measuring 66m² was disturbed between graves 1183 and 1095, and approximately 23m³ of material was removed, potentially accounting for this apparent gap in the cemetery.

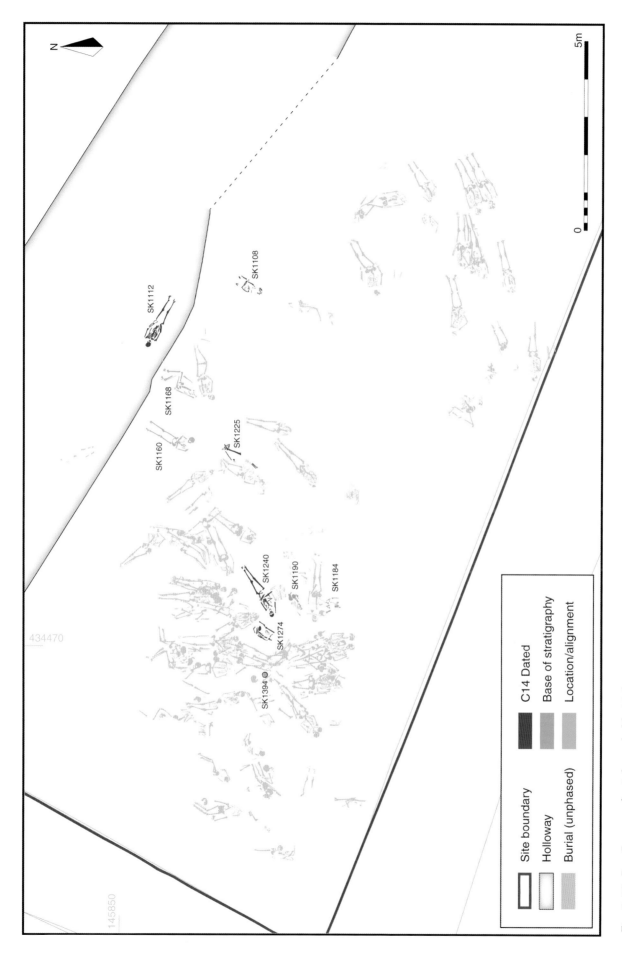

Fig. 2.18 Pre-Conquest burials, probably 10th century

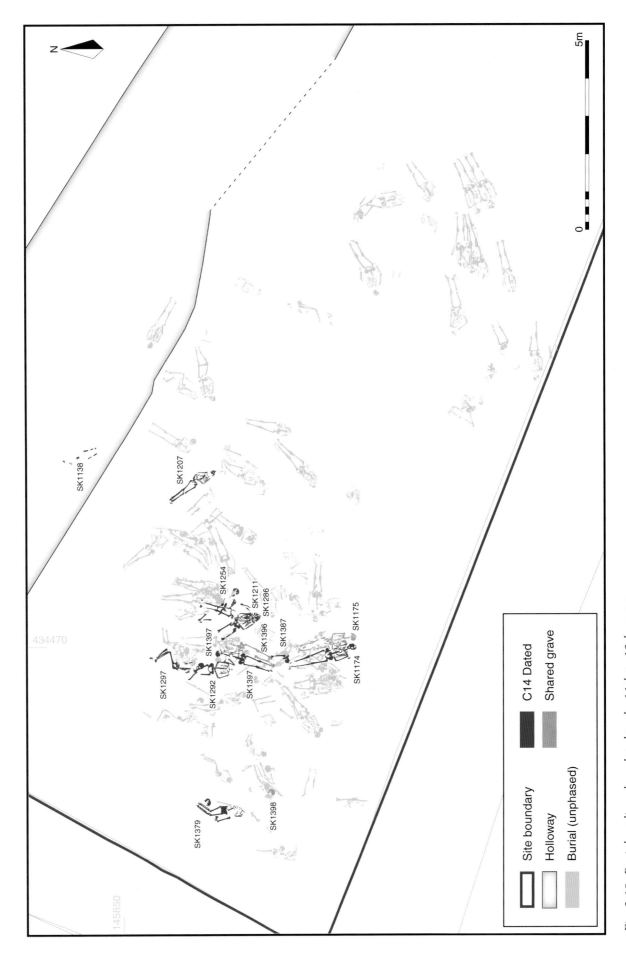

Fig. 2.19 Burials radiocarbon-dated to the 11th to 12th century

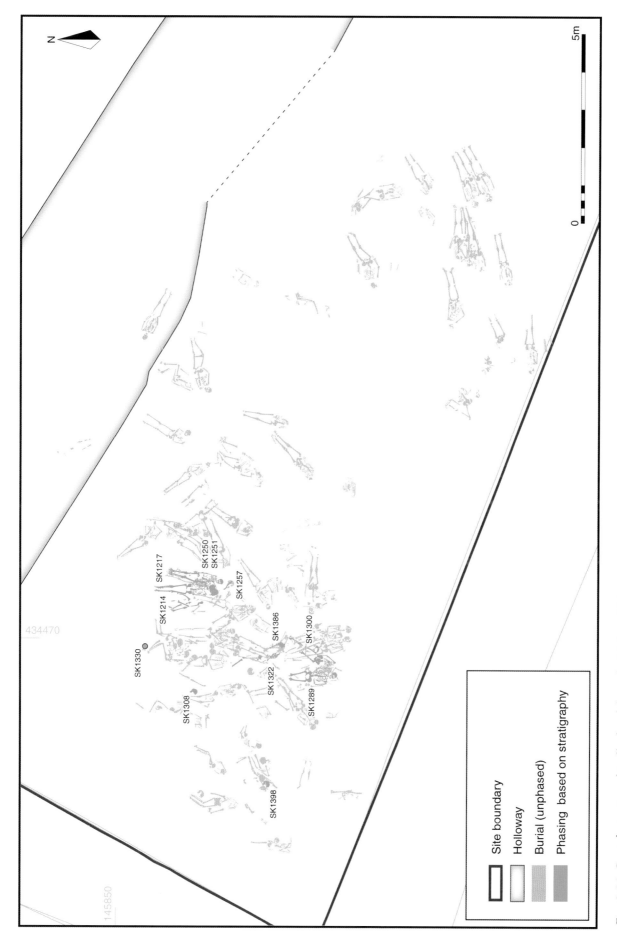

Fig. 2.20 Burials stratigraphically dated from the 11th to 12th century

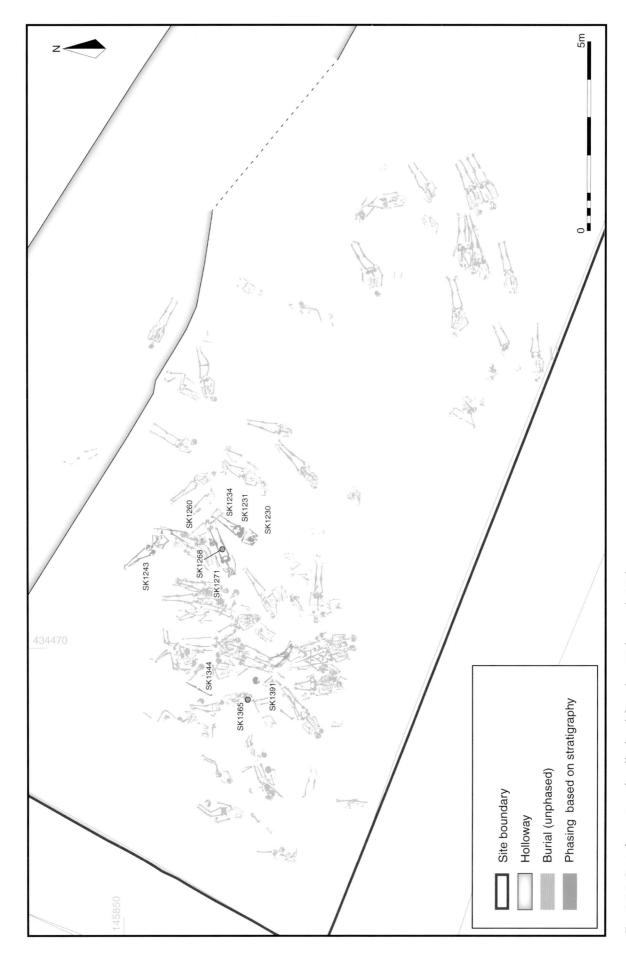

Fig. 2.21 Burials stratigraphically dated from late 10th to early 12th century

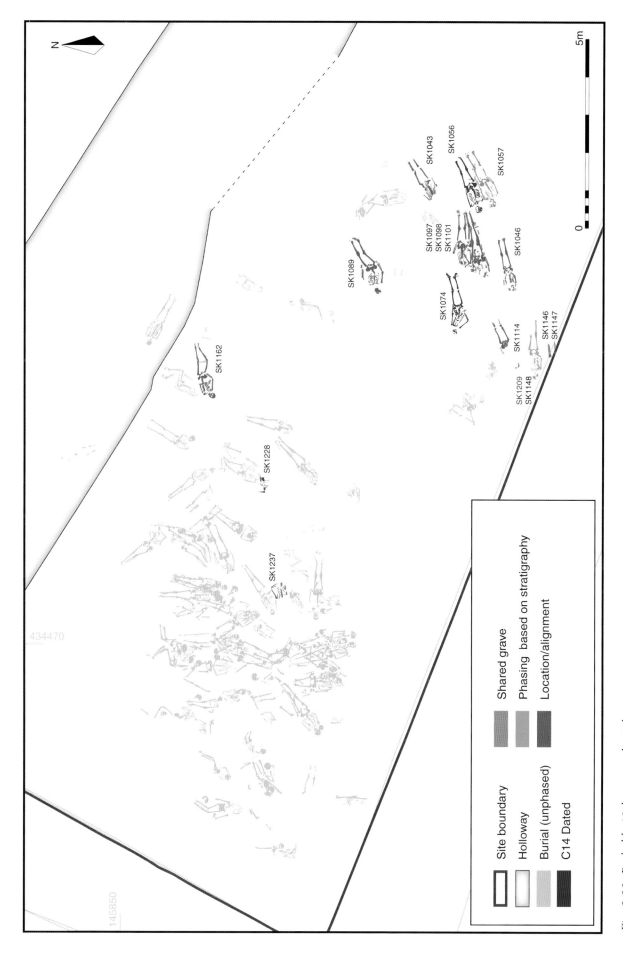

Fig. 2.22 Probable 13th-century burials

Catalogue of inhumation burials
by Jeremy Clutterbuck and Sharon Clough

The burials catalogue is organised in skeleton (SK) number order and the skeleton number is followed by the grave (Gr) number. The shallow and often disturbed nature of many of the grave cuts means that they have not been shown in the illustrations below. Projected grave outlines where it was possible to record them can be found on Fig. 2.7. Illustrations additional to those presented within the catalogue are listed in the catalogue entries. Preservation of a few individuals was too poor to merit illustration and these are cited as 'Not illust'.

For each entry, the age (estimated age-range based on the skeletal indicators present, each skeleton has also been allocated a category for analytical purposes, the category is detailed after the range and represents the best fit), and sex, are given if determinable. The orientation, where given, is that of the head end of the skeleton. The posture is given if enough of the skeleton survived to determine this. The % is an estimate of the completeness based on the presence of bones compared to a whole skeleton. The bones described are roughly those present.

The summary description of the human skeletal remains is by S. Clough. Pathology is detailed elsewhere (Clough, Chapter 3, Tables 3.1–3.23). Very few artefacts or faunal remains were found within the graves. Where present these are noted, with a position, if determined, and the material and object type. If the find is considered to have been a deliberate deposition, i.e. a 'grave good', this is stated. Further information on the artefacts and faunal remains are presented elsewhere (Chapter 4).

Radiocarbon dates are cited here calibrated at 95.4% probability (OxCal v4.3.2 (2017) (Bronk Ramsey 2009) using the IntCal13 curve (Reimer *et al.* 2013)) and as radiocarbon age BP. Further information including a complete list of the radiocarbon results can be found in Chapter 2. Bayesian analysis of the radiocarbon data by F. Healy can be found in Chapter 5.

If it has been possible to suggest a specific period for the burial (see Chapter 2), then this is given. Isotope sample numbers are presented and further data is presented by M. Jay in Chapter 6.

Abbreviations

Century	C.
cervical vertebra	CV
fragment(s)	frag./frags
illustrated	illust.
lumbar vertebra	LV
metacarpal	MC
metatarsal	MT
Registered Artefact	RA
thoracic vertebra	TV

SK1036 [Gr.1037]
Age: 14–20 years, Adolescent   Sex: Male?
Orientation: South
Posture: Supine
Human remains: 25–50%. Cranium, mandible, CV1–3, left distal humerus, left radius and ulna, left femur, patella, tibia and fibula. Left hand, talus and calcaneus
Objects in grave: Animal bone. ASK1042. Part of female sheep, 30–42 months, no butchery marks. Lying over left leg. Grave good
Isotope sample no: GU-44454 (sheep innominate bone)

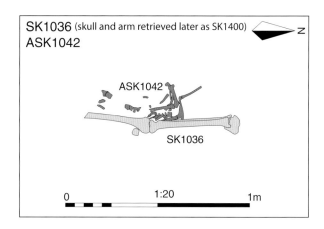

SK1043 [Gr.1044]
Age: Adult, Adult   Sex: Male
Orientation: South-west
Posture: Supine. Extended. Left arm bent at elbow over pelvis
Human remains: 50–75%. Lower thoracic and lumbar vertebrae, frags of 1st sacral vertebra, left and right ilium, frags of rib, frags of right metacarpals, frags of left and right scapula, left humerus shaft, right humerus distal. Left and right femur, right ulna and radius shaft. Left and right tibia and fibula shafts
Assigned period: 13th C. by association

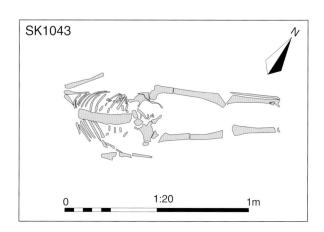

SK1046 [Gr.1047]
Age: 15–16 years, Adolescent Sex: Male??
Orientation: West
Posture: Supine. Extended. Hands in front of pelvis
Human remains: 75+%. Mandible and right maxilla. Most of the vertebrae (1 CV and 2 TV absent) and sacrum. Nearly all os coxae, ribs, manubrium and sternum. Left and right hands nearly complete. Left humerus mid shaft, right mid and distal, radii and ulnae parts absent. Left and right scapula frags, clavicles nearly complete. Left and right femori, tibiae and fibulae. Left and right talus, calcaneus, some tarsals
Assigned period: 13th C. by association

SK1050 [Gr.1049]
Age: Over 30 years, Prime Adult Sex: Male
Orientation: North-east
Posture: Prone. Skull on right side with lower right arm bent behind back centrally
Human remains: 25–50%. Frontal bone frags, right petrous, left zygomatic and maxilla. Left mandible. Top cervical and arches of TV. Shafts of humerii, clavicles, ulna and right radius. Scapula glenoid frags
Evidence for execution: Hands tied?

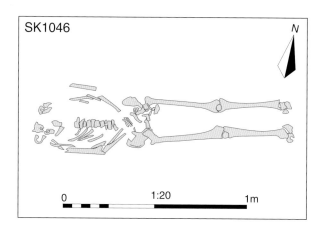

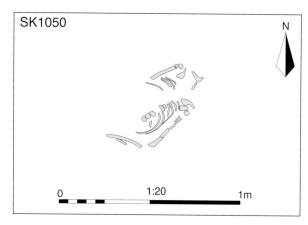

SK1056 [Gr.1055]
Age: 17–22 years, Young Adult Sex: Male
Fig. 2.9
Orientation: South-west
Posture: Supine. Extended. Arms to sides with left arm under SK1057 right arm
Human remains: 75+%. Fragmented cranium, maxilla and mandible. All vertebrae, sacrum and os coxae. Ribs, manubrium and sternum. All long bones mostly complete, except fibulae. Both patellae. Left and right hands mostly complete, though left mixed with SK1057 as overlapping in grave. Feet mostly present up to MTs where the heads are not present
Radiocarbon date: SUERC-74061 1265–1388 cal AD
691 ± 30 yr BP
Assigned period: 13th C.
Isotope sample no: GU-44439/GU-44455 (local)

SK1057 [Gr.1055]
Age: 16–21 years, Young Adult Sex: Male
Fig. 2.9
Orientation: South-west
Posture: Supine. Extended. Skull on left side. Arms by sides crossed with SK1056
Human remains: 75+%. Most of posterior cranium and mandible. Spine, sacrum, os coxae, ribs and parts of manubrium and sternum. Left and right humerii, radii, ulnae, clavicles, femori, tibiae, fibulae, patellae. Most of superior part of scapulae. Right hand MCs and phalanges, left mixed with SK1056. Right foot tarsal and MTs, left foot frag. of calcaneus only
Assigned period: 13th C. by association

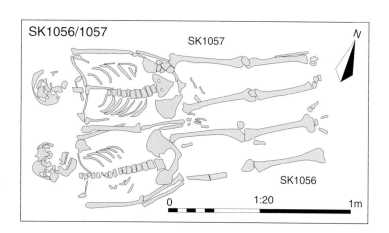

SK1065 [Gr.1066]
Age: Adult, Adult   Sex: Indeterminate
Not illust.
Orientation: West
Posture: Supine
Human remains 0–25 (5)%. Only left and right distal fibulae

SK1074 [Gr.1075]
Age: 19–24 years, Young Adult   Sex: Male
Orientation: West
Posture: Supine. Extended. Left arm by side, right arm flexed towards body at elbow, wide, as if around something.
Human remains: 75+%. Occipital and posterior parietals, partial right mandible. Hyoid arms. All vertebrae, sacrum. Most of left os coxa and right ilium. Most ribs. All long bones and scapula. No patella. Hands and feet very well represented
Radiocarbon date: SUERC-78126   1220–1285 cal AD
757 ± 29 yr BP
Assigned period: 13th C.
Isotope sample no: GU-46926 (local)

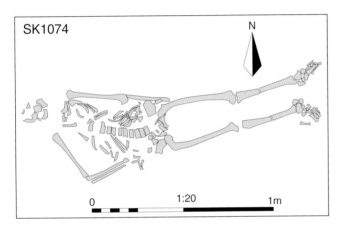

SK1081 [Gr.1082]
Age: Adult, Adult   Sex: Indeterminate
Not illust.
Orientation: South
Posture: Supine
Human remains: 0–25 (1)%. Frags of ribs and left humerus and clavicle frags

SK1086 [Gr.1092]
Age: 16–18 years, Adolescent   Sex: Male
Orientation: South
Posture: Supine. Extended. Arms by sides
Human remains: 50–75%. Mid TV–LV5. Sacrum, left and right ilia. Some ribs. Left and right humeri, clavicles, ulnae, radii, femori. Left patella. Very proximal tibiae and frag. left fibula. Left and right scapula frags. Right MC shafts and phalanges

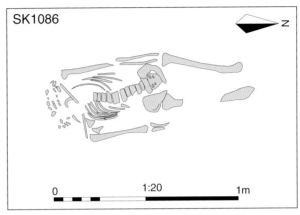

SK1087 [Gr.1084]
Age: 20–29 years, Young Adult   Sex: Male
Orientation: North-west
Posture: Prone. Flexed. Arms behind back
Human remains: 25–50%. Lower 4 lumbar vertebrae, sacral vertebrae 1–2. Left and right ilia. Right humerus. Left and right radii and ulnae. Left and right femora, patellae, fibulae shaft. Right tibia except distal, left tibia shaft frag. only. Left and right mostly represented. Left talus
Evidence for execution: Hands tied?

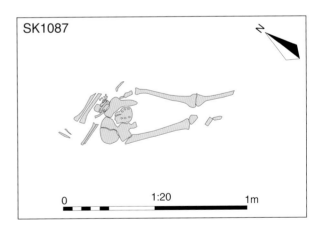

SK1088 [Gr.1084]

Age: Adult, Adult   Sex: Male??

Not illust.

Orientation: North-west

Posture: Supine. Extended

Human remains: 0–25%. Frag. of proximal right femur and ilium frag. only

SK1089 [Gr.1090]

Age: 20–25 years, Young Adult   Sex: Male

Orientation: South-west

Posture: Supine. Flexed. Arms by sides

Human remains: 75+%. Occipital, vertebrae CV3–LV5. Sacrum, ribs, sternum, Left and right pelvis. All long bones (except mid and proximal humerus), frags of scapulae and both patellae. Majority of hands and feet

Assigned period: 13th C. by association

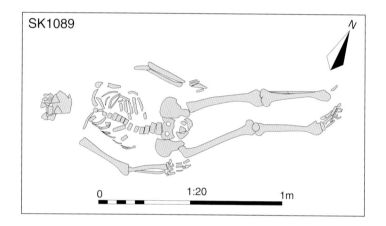

SK1097 [Gr.1095]

Age: 30–35 years, Prime Adult   Sex: Male

Orientation: West

Posture: Supine. Extended. Skull on right side. Arms by sides, hands over pelvis

Human remains: 75+%. Mandible and lower facial areas – maxilla and zygomatics. All vertebrae and sacrum. Both pelves and all ribs, sternum and manubrium. Nearly all long bones except proximal left humerus and proximal fibula. Both patellae. Nearly all hands and feet bones. Right scapula most, left inferior angle only

Assigned period: 13th C. by association

SK1098 [Gr.1095]

Age: 16–21 years, Adolescent   Sex: Male

Orientation: West

Posture: Supine. Extended. Skull on left side. Arms by sides hands over pelvis

Human remains: 75+%. Most long bones, except proximal right humerus and ulna. Right hand less than left, most feet. All spine except LV5, sacral vertebra 1 only. Ilia, but minus pubis. Left and right ribs represented, partial sternum and manubrium. Left mandible and partial right. Left cranial frags and occipital. Low fragmentation except skull

Assigned period: 13th C. by association

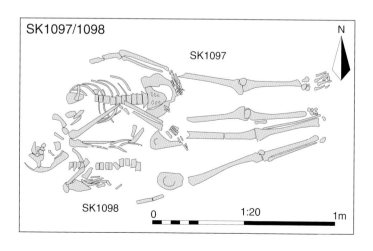

SK1101 [Gr.1099]
Age: 30–39 years, Mature Adult   Sex: Male
Orientation: West
Posture: Supine. Extended. Arms by sides
Human remains: 50–75%. Lower TV, LV and sacrum. Left and
    right pelves. Rib frags. All long bones except left humerus
    and clavicles and left scapula. Most of hands and feet. Both
    patella
Assigned period: 13th C. by association

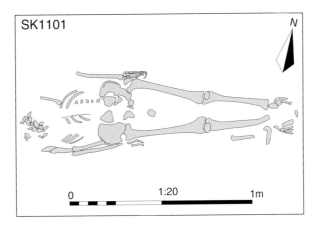

SK1105 [Gr.1106]
Age: 40–44 years, Mature Adult   Sex: Female
Orientation: South
Posture: Supine. Extended. Hands in towards pelvic area
Human remains: 50–75%. Left and right legs, bilateral calcanei
    and tali, right proximal radius and ulna, lower spine, upper
    sacrum, frags of pelvis and lower ribs

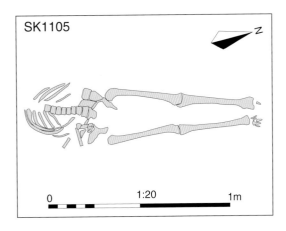

SK1108 [Gr.1109]
Age: Less than 25 years, Young Adult   Sex: Male
Orientation: South-west
Posture: Supine. Extended. Upper half only. Right arm straight,
    left bent at elbow 90 degrees across body, hand on other arm
Human remains: 25–50%. Left and right arms (partial). Frags
    left metacarpals and phalanges. Frags right pelvis. Frags
    thoracic vertebrae. Frags ribs. Frags cranium
Radiocarbon date: SUERC-74062   895–972 cal AD
    1116 ± 30 yr BP
Assigned period: 10th C.
Isotope sample no: GU-44440/GU-44456 (local)

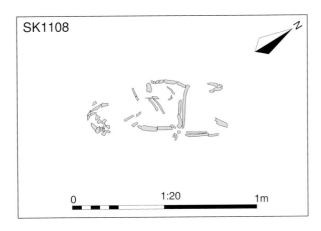

SK1112 [Gr.1111]
Age: 16–21 years, Young Adult   Sex: Male
Fig. 2.11
Orientation: North-west
Posture: Supine. Extended. Arms by sides hands on thighs
Human remains: 75+%. Skull - upper cranium, maxilla and
    mandible, spine, sacrum, both os coxa, ribs, manubrium,
    frags sternum. All long bones, scapulae and clavicles. Most
    of hands and feet
Radiocarbon date: SUERC-74064   729–951 cal AD
    1181 ± 30 yr BP
Assigned period: 10th C.
Isotope sample no: GU-44442/GU-44457 (local)

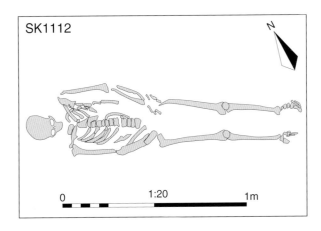

SK1114 [Gr.1115]
Age: 25–30 years, Prime Adult   Sex: Male
Orientation: South-west
Posture: Supine. Extended
Human remains: 25–50%. Posterior cranium, axis, atlas. Sacrum,
    left pelvis. Left and right femori and proximal tibia, fibulae
    shaft. Left radius and ulna. Left carpals
Assigned period: 13th C. by association

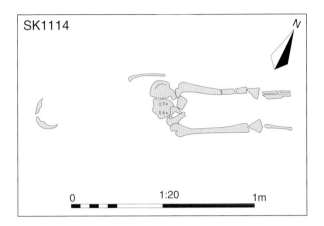

SK1118 [Gr.1117]
Age: Probably 35–44 years, Mature Adult   Sex: Male
Orientation: West
Posture: Supine. Extended. Right arm flexed to middle, hands
    together
Human remains: 25–50%. Right arm and both hands. Frags of
    spine, cranium and ribs, sacrum, hyoid.
Objects in grave: Position not recorded. Iron buckle. RA2. Not
    illust. 1 sherd LIA pottery

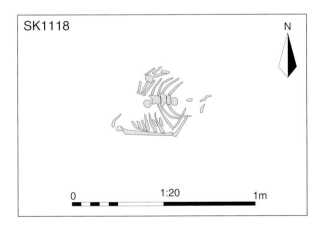

SK1122 [Gr.1120]
Age: Adult, Adult   Sex: Male??
Orientation: South
Posture: Right side. Flexed. Right side legs and hand only
Human remains: 0–25%. ?Right femur frags. Right tibia and
    fibula. Left distal tibia and fibula shaft. Right foot, left part
    foot. Left radius and frag. of ulna. Left hand
Objects in grave: Position not recorded. Worked bone. Socketed
    handle, probably from a knife. (Cat. no. 2). Mid 10th C.
    parallel

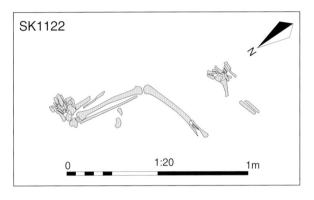

SK1123 [Gr.1120]
Age: Adult, Adult   Sex: Indeterminate
Not illust.
Orientation: Not known
Posture: Articulated fingers
Human remains: 0–25%. Phalanges, left calcaneus

SK1124 [Gr.1120]
Age: Adult, Adult   Sex: Indeterminate
Not illust.
Orientation: Not known
Posture: Articulated foot
Human remains: 0–25%. Right foot bones

SK1129 [Gr.1128]
Age: Adult, Adult   Sex: Indeterminate
Orientation: Not known
Posture: Supine. Extended? Mostly axial skeleton
Human remains: 0–25%. Thoracic spine arches, right ilium frags.
    Right rib frags. Left and right hand. Radial shaft, scapula
    blade frag.
Objects in grave: Bones from two different mice - not grave goods
Assigned period: 10th C. or later

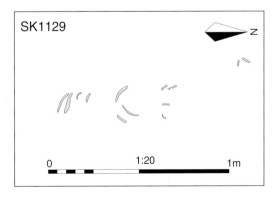

SK1132 [Gr.1131]
Age: 18–30 years, Prime Adult   Sex: Male
Orientation: South
Posture: Supine. Extended. Arms behind back
Human remains: 75+%. Part mandible and occipital. Lumbar, some thoracic and cervical. Sacrum, left pelvis and partial right. Sternum and ribs. Left arm and right clavicle. Left and right femori. Left and right lower legs and feet. Left and right hands
Evidence for execution: Hands tied?
Objects in grave: Position not recorded. Iron nail. RA3. Not illust.

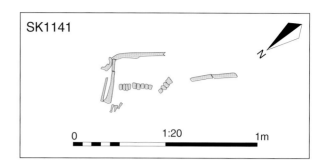

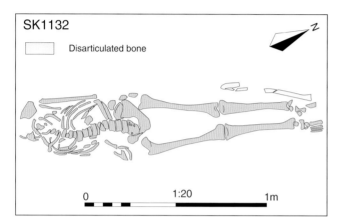

SK1134 [Gr.1131]
Age: Adult, Adult   Sex: Indeterminate
Not illust.
Orientation: Not known
Posture: Disarticulated in grave
Human remains: 0–25%. Left humerus shaft and distal. Right tibia frags, distal fibula. 2nd cuneiform and foot distal phalanx

SK1138 [Gr.1137]
Age: 18–25 – teeth only, Young Adult   Sex: Male?
Not illust.
Orientation: North-west
Posture: Not known
Human remains: 0–25%. Frag. of mandible and lumbar vertebral bodies. Left femoral head and right shaft and distal frag.
Radiocarbon date: SUERC-78128   981–1151 cal AD 1003 ± 29 yr BP
Assigned period: 11th to 12th C.
Isotope sample no: GU-46928 (local)

SK1141 [Gr.1140]
Age: 26–35 years, Prime Adult   Sex: Male?
Orientation: South-west
Posture: Prone. Right torso and arm only. Large amount of disarticulated at head end. Arm bent at elbow probably behind back
Human remains: 0–25%. Right humerus (without head), radius and ulna. Right hand phalanges. Thoracic vertebrae, and 2 lumbar. Sternum and right ribs. Frag. right pelvis
Evidence for execution: Hands tied?

SK1144 [Gr.1143]
Age: early 20s years, Young Adult   Sex: Male
Orientation: East
Posture: Supine. Extended. Cranium found between femora, but may or may not be associated with the post-cranial. Also further cranium frags, but separate individual (recorded as disarticulated)
Human remains: 25–50%. Front cranium, 3x CV, lower thoracic and lumbar. Sacrum and both pelves. Lower ribs. Left and right hands. Right leg. Left femoral head, radius and ulna
Evidence for execution: Hands tied? Decapitation? from skull position

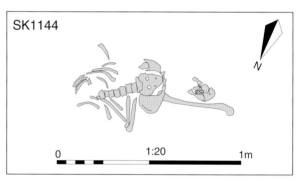

SK1146 [Gr.1149]
Age: 21–57 years, Prime Adult   Sex: Male?
Fig. 3.10
Orientation: West
Posture: Prone. Rest beyond baulk
Human remains: 25–50%. Right half pelvis. Left and right femur. Right tibia and fibula. Left tibia frags and distal fibula. Right foot, some left. Right hand, some left
Assigned period: 13th C. by association

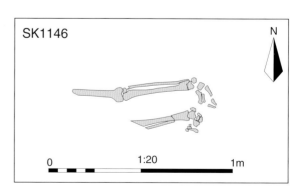

SK1147 [Gr.1149]
Age: Adult, Adult   Sex: Indeterminate
Not illust.
Orientation: West
Posture: Supine. Heavily fragmented. Rest beyond baulk
Human remains: 0–25%. Frag. sacrum, frag. left pelvis. Right hand partial. Right mid and distal humerus. Right proximal ulna shaft. Right femoral head and shaft frags. Left foot frags
Objects in grave: Iron buckle. Cat. no. 1. RA4
Assigned period: 13th C. by association

SK1147a [Gr.1149]
Age: 7–12 years, Older Child   Sex: Indeterminate
Not illust.
Orientation: Not known
Posture: Not known
Human remains: 25–50%. Right radius and ulna, left radius. Left and right hands (partial). Left and right pelves (3 parts). Left and right femori (proximal 2/3s). Lumbar vertebrae

SK1148 [Gr.1152]
Age: 18–25 years, Young Adult   Sex: Male
Orientation: West
Posture: Supine. Extended. Left side truncated. Right hand in towards pelvis
Human remains: 75+%. Left parietal and some temporal, partial left mandible. Most of frontal bone, occipital and maxilla. Spine, sacrum, Left and right pelvis, ribs. Right arms, leg, ankle and partial MTs. Left femur and patella. Both hands
Assigned period: 13th C. by association

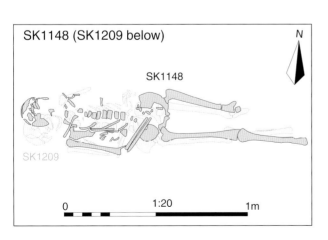

SK1154 [Gr.1155]
Age: Adult, Adult   Sex: Indeterminate
Not illust.
Orientation: South-west
Posture: Not known
Human remains: 0–25%. Left and right femur shaft. Right humerus and scapula frag. Left scapula and clavicle frag. Left distal ulna shaft. Left tibia and fibula frags. Thoracic spine arches. Left and right acetabulum. Left ribs

SK1158 [Gr.1157]
Age: 18–25 years, Young Adult   Sex: Indeterminate
Not illust.
Orientation: Not known
Posture: Articulated left foot
Human remains: 0–25%. Left distal tibia, fibula shaft frag. Left foot

SK1160 [Gr.1135]
Age: 26–35 years, Prime Adult   Sex: Male
Fig. 2.12
Orientation: South-west
Posture: Supine. Skull detached to right side of neck. Hands together over pelvis
Human remains: 75+%. Cranium, spine, sacrum, left pelvis, ribs and sternum. All long bones and hands and feet
Evidence for execution: Hands tied? Decapitation from skull position
Objects in grave: 1 sherd LIA/RB pottery. Iron object
Assigned period: 10th C. by association

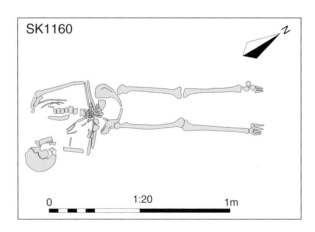

SK1162 [Gr.1161]
Age: 40+ years, Mature Adult   Sex: Male
Fig. 8.3
Orientation: West
Posture: Supine. Slightly flexed with skull tilted to one side. Right arm bent slightly and left hand over body. Space for object? Hand looks to be resting on something
Human remains: 75+%. Most of the skeleton present. Some distal areas absent such as MTs, Phalanges, facial bones
Assigned period: 13th C. by association

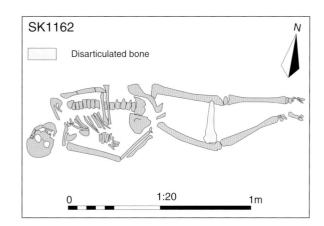

SK1165 [Gr.1164]
Age: 40–55 years, Mature Adult   Sex: Male
Orientation: West
Posture: Supine. Extended? Only pelvis area with lower lumbar
    vertebrae. Right arm across pelvis, left arm above stomach area
Human remains: 25–50%. Lower thoracic and lumbar spine.
    Partial sacrum. Right ilium and frags of the left ilium. Left
    ribs. Left zygomatic. Left hand, humeral head and scapula
    frags. Left distal radius and ulna, right femoral head and
    upper 1/3 shaft. Right radius and ulna (not head). Right 1st
    MT distal and cuneiform

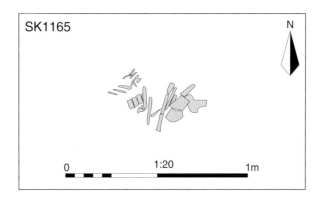

SK1168 [Gr.1167]
Age: 45+ years, Older Adult   Sex: Male
Fig. 8.3
Orientation: South-west
Posture: Supine. Legs flexed up bent to right. Arms by sides
Human remains: 75+%. Most areas represented
Objects in grave: Iron buckle. Cat. no. 5. RA5
Assigned period: 10th C. by association

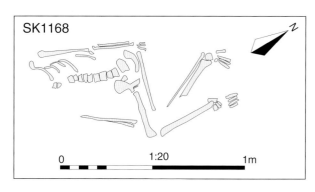

SK1174 [Gr.1173]
Age: 22–27 years, Young Adult   Sex: Male
Figs 2.10; 3.12; 8.11
Orientation: South
Posture: Supine. Extended. Hands behind back
Human remains: 75+%. Most areas represented, except skull of
    which only posterior and maxilla and mandible survive
Evidence for execution: Hands tied behind back?
Radiocarbon date: SUERC-74082   985–1152 cal AD
    998 ± 30 yr BP
Assigned period: 11th to 12th C.
Isotope sample no: GU-44453/GU-44465 (local)

SK1175 [Gr.1173]
Age: 30s years, Prime Adult   Sex: Male
Figs 2.10; 8.11
Orientation: South
Posture: Prone. Extended. Hands behind back
Human remains: 75+%. Most skeleton represented, except facial
    area
Evidence for execution: Hands tied behind back?
Assigned period: 11th to 12th C. by association

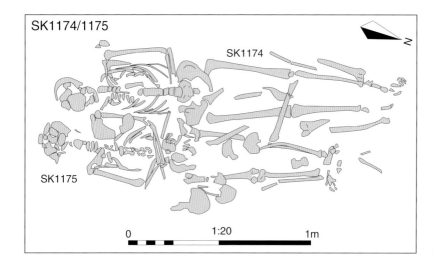

SK1184 [Gr.1183]

Age: 45+ years, Older Adult   Sex: Male

Orientation: South

Posture: Prone. Only partial torso with arms and hands drawn up together at front

Human remains: 0–25%. Lower spine, partial sacrum, frags of left and right pelvis. Some ribs. Right arms and left (part of) ulna. Right hand

Objects in grave: Animal bone. ASK1202. Skull, female sheep, 2–3 years. Placed on top of torso. Grave good

Assigned period: 10th C. by association

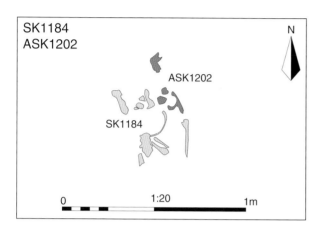

SK1187 [Gr.1186]

Age: 21–46 years, Prime Adult   Sex: Male

Orientation: North-east

Posture: Left side. Flexed/crouched, both arms to front

Human remains: 25–50%. Frag. of cranial base. Some thoracic spine. Sternum and manubrium. Left public symphyses. Left humerus, radius and ulna. Right partial clavicle, distal radius and ulna. Right distal femur. Left femur and fibula shaft. Right foot – tarsals and some MTs. Both hands

Assigned period: 10th C. or later

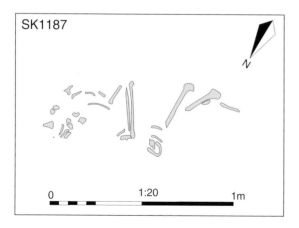

SK1190 [Gr.1189]

Age: 16–20 years, Adolescent   Sex: Male

Orientation: South-west

Posture: Supine. Extended. Hands behind the back. Skull found in grave 1192 (SK1193) to side of skeleton. Likely but not conclusively from this skeleton. Included for recording

Human remains: 50–75%. Right radius and ulna. Left upper 1/3 femur. Left distal half of radius and ulna. Left medial half clavicle and frags of scapula. Both hands. Sacrum, left pelvis. Lower thoracic and lumbar spine. Lower ribs. Fragmented cranium, right mandible and maxilla

Evidence for execution: Hands tied behind back?

Objects in grave: Iron buckle. Cat. no. 6. RA7

Assigned period: 10th C. by association

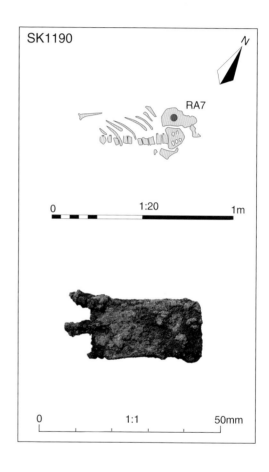

SK1193 [Gr.1192]
Age: 30–35 years, Prime Adult   Sex: Male
Fig. 3.8
Orientation: West
Posture: Supine. Extended. Hands behind back. Head slightly to
   left with disarticulated long bone across neck
Human remains: 75+%. Most of skeleton represented except
   right foot
Evidence for execution: Hands tied behind back
Assigned period: 10th C. or later

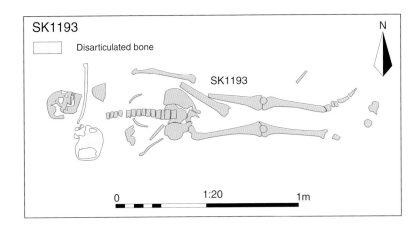

SK1204 [Gr.1203]
Age: Adult, Adult   Sex: Male
Orientation: South-east
Posture: Supine. Extended. Hands behind back
Human remains: 25–50%. Right femur, radius and ulna, frags of
   tibia and fibula. Left leg femoral and tibial frags, distal radius.
   Right pelvic frags and frag. of left
Evidence for execution: Hands behind back

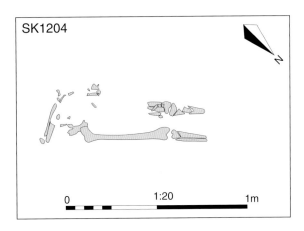

SK1207 [Gr.1206]
Age: 15–17 years, Adolescent   Sex: Male?
Orientation: South-east
Posture: Supine. Extended. Hands tied behind back
Human remains: 75+%. Mandible and partial maxilla, fragmented
   cranium. Some cervical and lumbar spine, thoracic arches.
   Some ribs. Right pelvis, left pelvis frags. Sacrum. Long bones
   represented, but none complete. Right MC2, left MC5. Left
   and right talus, calcaneus and navicular
Evidence for execution: Hands tied behind back
Radiocarbon date: SUERC-74065   1020–1155 cal AD
   961 ± 30 yr BP
Assigned period: 11th to 12th C.
Isotope sample no: GU-44443/GU-44458 (local)

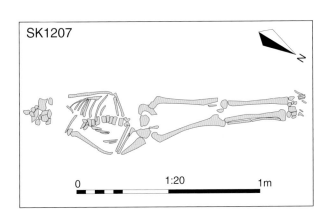

SK1209 [Gr.1152]
Age: 14–19 years, Adolescent Sex: Male
Orientation: West
Posture: Supine. Extended. Arms crossed right across body
Human remains: 75+%. Cranium - but not frontal, mandible and
    maxilla. Spine, sacrum, pelves, ribs, sternum, manubrium.
    Right arm, right leg. Left humerus proximal half, left distal
    radius and ulna, clavicle. Left femur, left proximal tibia. Left
    and right patellae. Left and right hands
Radiocarbon date: SUERC-78127   1270–1389 cal AD
    681 ± 29 yr BP
Assigned period: 13th C.
Isotope sample no: GU-46927 (local but note that $\delta^{13}C$ towards
    the higher end of the range (-19.5‰))

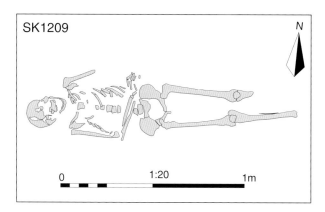

SK1211 [Gr.1210]
Age: 30–34 years, Prime Adult   Sex: Male
Figs 8.6; 8.10
Orientation: South
Posture: Supine. Extended. Left arm bent over chest, hands absent
Human remains: 75+%. Posterior cranium, maxilla and
    mandible. Cervical and thoracic spine, 1st sacral vertebra.
    Frags of pelves and ribs. Most of lower limbs and upper left.
    Right arm radius absent. Most of feet. Left hand 1 carpal and
    phalanx only
Objects in grave: Large stone on right side of skull; smaller stone
    on other side of skull
Radiocarbon date: SUERC-74077   1033–1186 cal AD
    913 ± 27 yr BP
Assigned period: 11th to 12th C.
Isotope sample no: GU-44451/GU-44464 (not local)

SK1214 [Gr.1213]
Age: 25–39 years, Mature Adult   Sex: Male
Fig. 8.10
Orientation: East
Posture: Supine. Extended. Skull below shoulder prone. Right
    side and torso mostly truncated
Human remains: 25–50%. Left and right tibia and fibula. Left
    femur. Left humerus and both clavicles. Right radius shaft
    and ulna. Both feet. Some left hand. Left ilium. 1 TV. Cranial
    bones, left zygomatic and partial maxilla
Assigned period: 11th to 12th C. by association

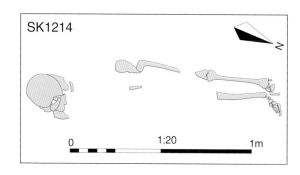

SK1217 [Gr.1216]
Age: 25–30 years, Prime Adult   Sex: Male
Fig. 8.10
Orientation: South
Posture: Supine. Extended, hands behind back
Human remains: 75+%. Nearly complete skeleton, some small
    areas damaged and some hand and foot phalanges absent
Evidence for execution: Hands tied behind back?
Assigned period: 11th to 12th C. by association

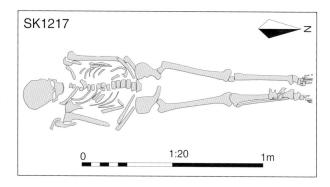

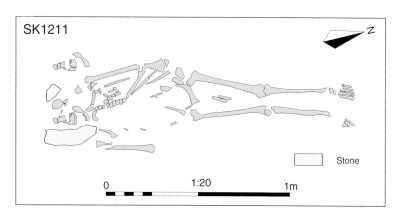

SK1220 [Gr.1219]
Age: 17–24 years, Young Adult   Sex: Male
Orientation: South-west
Posture: Prone. Lower legs slightly leaning up the side of grave.
    Hands behind back
Human remains: 75+%. Facial area of skull. Most of spine,
    sacrum and pelves. Ribs and sternum. All long bones, hands
    and partial feet
Evidence for execution: Hands tied behind back?
Objects in grave: Near left hand. RA 8 Silver Penny of Aethelred
    II (AD 978–1016). Dateable to AD 979–85. Grave good.
Assigned period: 11th to 12th C. or later

SK1228 [Gr.1226]
Age: 16–19 years, Adolescent Sex: Indeterminate
Orientation: West
Posture: Prone. Axial skeleton only
Human remains: 0–25%. Vertebra (not CV1–2). Mandible not
    alveolar. Frag. sacrum. Ribs and frag. sternum. Left and right
    mid clavicles
Radiocarbon date: SUERC-78122   1187–1276 cal AD
    798 ± 29 yr BP
Assigned period: 13th C.
Isotope sample no: GU-46925/ GU-48377 (not local)

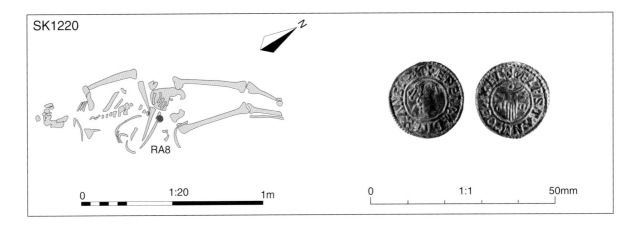

SK1225 [Gr.1223]
Age: Adult, Adult   Sex: Male??
Orientation: South-west
Posture: Supine. Extended
Human remains: 0–25%. Right tibia, fibula and foot. Left fibula
    and foot. Right hand and left 5th MC. Upper thoracic body
Radiocarbon date: SUERC-74063   891–1015 cal AD
    1093 ± 30 yr BP
Assigned period: 10th C.
Isotope sample no: GU-44441 (not local)

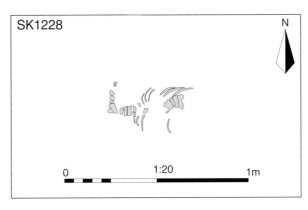

SK1230 [Gr.1229]
Age: 40–45 years, Mature Adult   Sex: Male
Fig. 3.17
Orientation: South-west
Posture: Supine. Extended. Left arm bent across. Skull placed
    behind back.
Human remains: 75+%. Most skeleton present except right
    radius and ulna and CV5–7. Foot phalanges also not present
Evidence for execution: Decapitation
Objects in grave: Inside pelvis. Iron buckle. Cat. no. 3. RA10
Assigned period: 10th to 12th C. by association

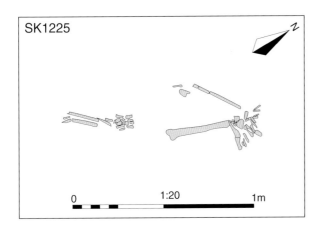

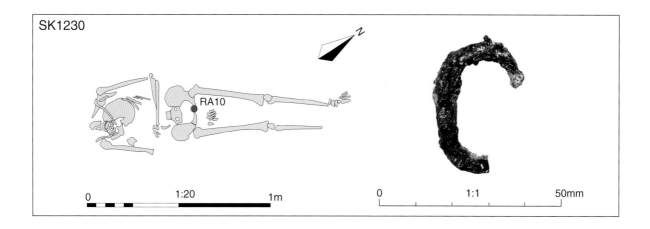

SK1231 [Gr.1229]
Age: 40–44 years, Mature Adult   Sex: Male
Orientation: South
Posture: Supine
Human remains: 0–25%. Right femoral head, right MC3 and phalanges. Left and right partial pelves. Sacrum. Lower lumbar vertebrae
Assigned period: 10th to 12th C. by association

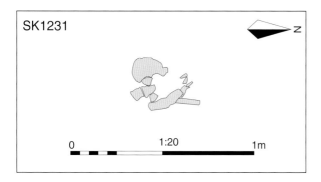

SK1234 [Gr.1233]
Age: 45+ years, Older Adult   Sex: Male
Orientation: South-east
Posture: Supine. Extended. Hands behind back
Human remains: 50–75%. Left and right femori. Right radius, ulna and humerus, clavicle. Left distal radius and ulna, mid clavicle. Left and right partial hands. Left and right pelves and sacral vertebra 1. Thoracic and lumbar vertebrae. Ribs
Evidence for execution: Hands tied behind back?
Assigned period: 10th to 12th C. by association

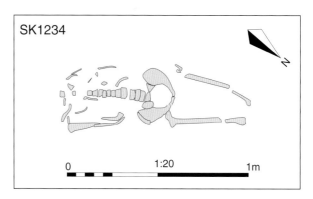

SK1237 [Gr.1236]
Age: 24–29 years, Young Adult   Sex: Male?
Orientation: West
Posture: Supine. Extended. Arms behind back.
Human remains: 25–50%. Spine, ribs, left iliac crest frags, mandible. Left distal radius and ulna, clavicle and scapula frags. Right radius, ulna, clavicle, scapula, humerus. Both hands
Evidence for execution: Arms tied behind back?
Objects in grave: Iron nail. RA9. Not illust.
Assigned period: 13th C. by association

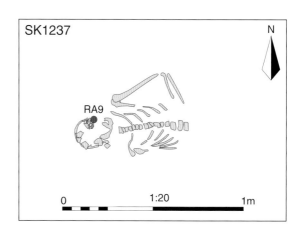

SK1240 [Gr.1239]
Age: 35–45 years, Mature Adult   Sex: Male
Fig. 3.19
Orientation: South-west
Posture: Supine. Extended. Left arm bent at elbow across body, right arm bent at elbow across chest. Hands placed under pelvis
Human remains: 75+%. Most of skeletal elements present. Distal right humerus and proximal ulna absent
Evidence for execution: Mutilation. Hands had been cut off
Radiocarbon date: SUERC-74066   895–1017 cal AD   1081 ± 27 yr BP
Assigned period: 10th C.
Isotope sample no: GU-44444/GU-44459 (local)

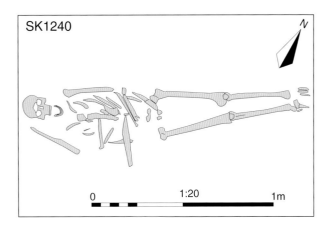

SK1243 [Gr.1242]
Age: 26–30 years, Prime Adult   Sex: Male
Orientation: South-east
Posture: Supine. Extended. Arms behind back with hands together on the left side. Head slightly elevated to rest of body
Human remains: 75+%. Most of skeleton represented
Evidence for execution: Hands tied. Damage to CV4, which may be post-mortem, but cannot completely rule out decapitation? (Not counted in the possible total)
Objects in grave: Single cattle tooth lower left third molar
Assigned period: 10th to 12th C. by association

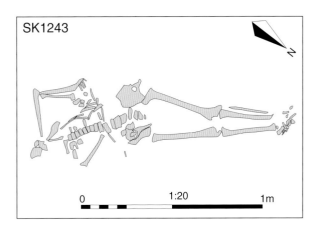

SK1246 [Gr.1245]
Age: 16–20 years, Adolescent   Sex: Male?
Orientation: North-east
Posture: Prone. Hands/arms at front
Human remains: 75+%. Lower thoracic spine and upper sacrum. Left and right pelves present. Some ribs. Left humerus (not head), radius and ulna. Right humerus, radius and ulna, clavicle and scapula frag. Left and right legs. Right foot (not phalanges), left talus. Left and right hands (few carpals)
Assigned period: 11th to 12th C. or later

SK1247 [Gr.1245]
Age: 14–18 years, Adolescent   Sex: Male??
Orientation: North-east
Posture: Prone. Upper torso on left side and head on left
Human remains: 75+%. Thoracic and lumbar vertebrae, CV1 and 2. Sacral vertebrae 1–2. Fragmented cranium, mandible and right maxilla. Left and right pelves, ribs. Left humerus (no head), right shaft and head frag. Right scapula frags. Right shaft of radius and ulna. Left and right femori. Left tibia, right fragmented Left fibula. Right talus. Right MCs and phalanges. Left MC1
Assigned period: 11th to 12th C. or later

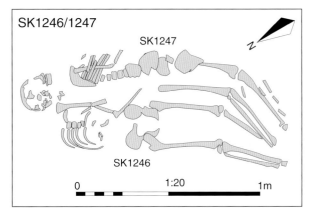

SK1250 [Gr.1249]
Age: 45+ years, Older Adult   Sex: Male
Figs 8.10; 3.13
Orientation: South
Posture: Supine. Extended
Human remains: 75+%. Most long bones, hands and feet. Cranium, ribs, sternum. Left pelvis, some frags of right. Distal sacrum. Partial vertebrae
Assigned period: 11th to 12th C. by association

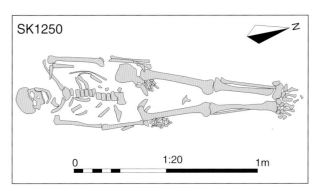

SK1251 [Gr.1249]
Age: 21–44 years, Mature Adult   Sex: Male
Fig. 8.10
Orientation: Not known
Posture: Scattered around grave
Human remains: 25–50%. Cranium. Left and right pelves. Lumbar vertebra. Right femur, right humerus
Assigned period: 11th to 12th C. by association

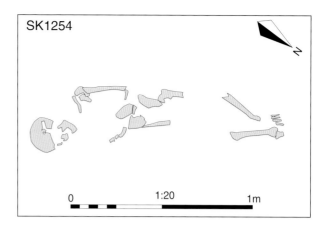

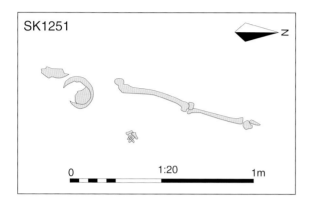

SK1254 [Gr.1253]
Age: 45+ years, Older Adult   Sex: Male
Fig. 8.10
Orientation: South-east
Posture: Supine. Knees bent up. Skull on right side
Human remains: 25–50%. Left humerus upper third absent. Left scapula and clavicle. Left proximal femur. Right scapula frags. Left MC5. Left and right fibula shafts. Bilateral talus and frags calcaneus. Left MTs shafts. Posterior cranium, mandible. Cervical vertebrae. Left and right pelves
Radiocarbon date: SUERC-74074   1023–1155 cal AD 952 ± 30 yr BP
Assigned period: 11th to 12th C.
Isotope sample no: GU-44448/GU-44461 (local)

SK1257 [Gr.1256]
Age: Adult, Adult   Sex: Male?
Not illust.
Orientation: South-east
Posture: Supine
Human remains: 0–25%. Shoulders, left humerus and back of skull
Assigned period: 11th to 12th C. by association

SK1260 [Gr.1259]
Age: 40–59 years, Older Adult   Sex: Male
Orientation: South
Posture: Prone. Head on right side. Hands probably behind back.
Human remains: 50–75%. Left leg. Right femur. Left and right foot. Bilateral clavicle. Right humerus and radius shaft. Right hand. Cranium, mandible and maxilla. Fragmented vertebrae. Sacral bodies. Right pelvis. Ribs
Evidence for execution: Hands tied behind back?
Assigned period: 10th to 12th C. by association

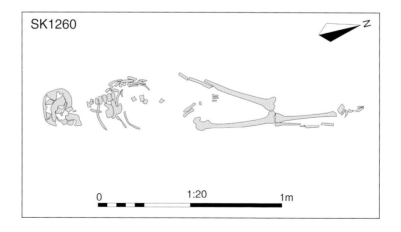

SK1268 [Gr.1267]
Age: Adult, Adult   Sex: Indeterminate
Not illust.
Orientation: Not known
Posture: Articulated foot
Human remains: 0–25%. Left tarsals and 5th MT, right calcaneus and distal fibula
Assigned period: 10th to 12th C. by association

SK1271 [Gr.1270]
Age: 17–18 years, Adolescent Sex: Male
Orientation: West
Posture: Supine. Extended. Arms by sides
Human remains: 75+%. Spine from lower cervical–lumbar. Sacral vertebrae 1–2. Left and right pelvis. Sternum. Left and right legs and feet. Right arm. Left and right hands
Assigned period: 10th to 12th C. by association

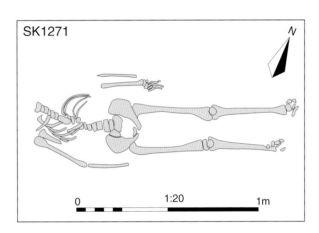

SK1274 [Gr.1273]
Age: 35–45 years, Mature Adult   Sex: Male
Orientation: South-west
Posture: Supine. Right arm straight, left across body. Skull possibly between lower legs, where mandible and frag. of maxilla found.
Human remains: 50–70%. Mandible. Spine lower CV–LV. Left and right pelvis and sacrum. Ribs, sternum, manubrium. Left and right hands. Bilateral radius and ulna. Right clavicle and bilateral scapula frags. Distal left humerus. Right tibia and distal left and right fibula. Right calcaneus and talus
Evidence for execution: Decapitation
Radiocarbon date: SUERC-74071   879–1013 cal AD
     1110 ± 30 yr BP
Assigned period: 10th C.
Isotope sample no: GU-44445 /GU-44460 and GU-48378 (not local)

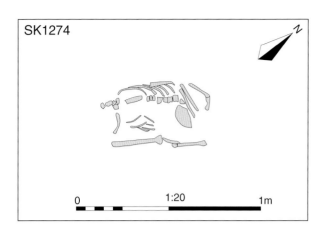

SK1286 [Gr.1285]
Age: 25–35 years, Prime Adult   Sex: Male
Fig. 8.10
Orientation: South-east
Posture: Prone. Hands behind back
Human remains: 50–70%. Left femur, radius and ulna. Left and right clavicle and scapula. Left and right metacarpals. Left and right pelvis. Sacrum, frags sternum and manubrium, ribs. Vertebrae (except LV5). Skull
Evidence for execution: Hands tied behind back?
Radiocarbon date: SUERC-78121   1027–1160 cal AD
     936 ± 29 yr BP
Assigned period: 11th to 12th C.
Isotope sample no: GU-46924 (local)

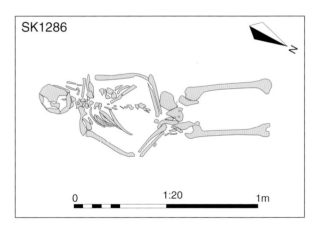

SK1289 [Gr.1288]

Age: 45–60 years, Older Adult   Sex: Male

Fig. 8.11

Orientation: South

Posture: Supine. Extended. Covered in large amount of disarticulated bone. Arms behind back. Lower legs truncated

Human remains: 75+%. Nearly all present except lower legs and feet

Evidence for execution: Arms tied behind back?

Assigned period: 11th to 12th C. by association

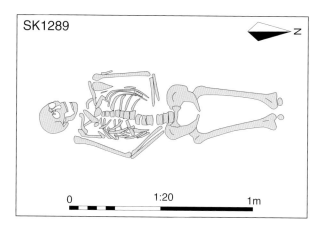

SK1292 [Gr.1291]

Age: 25–29 years, Young Adult   Sex: Male

Fig. 8.12

Orientation: South

Posture: Supine. Extended.

Human remains: 50–75%. Spine bodies (arches broken). Left temporal. Sacrum partial. Both pelves. Some upper ribs. Left and right arms. Left and right hands. Right femur, left femur (not distal)

Evidence for execution: Hands tied?

Radiocarbon date: SUERC-74081   1036–1205 cal AD
907 ± 27 yr BP

Assigned period: 11th to 12th C.

Isotope sample no: GU-44452 (local)

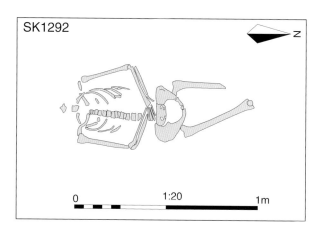

SK1294 [Gr.1284]

Age: 35–45 years, Mature Adult   Sex: Male

Fig. 3.14

Orientation: South-west

Posture: Supine. Legs bent at knees upwards

Human remains: 75+%. Axial skeleton, spine without CV1–5. Right arm, left humerus and clavicle, scapula only. Left and right legs. Bilateral talus, left calcaneus. Right MC and left MC5

Evidence for execution: Skull from CV5 upwards absent, probably intentionally. Grave looks too short

Assigned period: 11th to 12th C. or earlier, by association

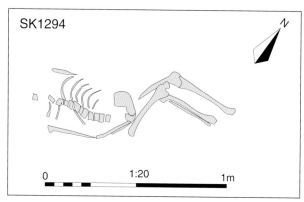

SK1297 [Gr.1296]

Age: 22–34 years (25–30 likely), Prime Adult   Sex: Male

Orientation: South

Posture: Supine. Legs bent together over to the right. Left hand up on left shoulder

Human remains: 75+%. Skull, spine, sacrum, pelves, ribs, sternum and manubrium. Left arms and leg. Right leg, clavicle and scapula. Both feet, left hand and some right. See SK1330

Evidence for execution: Possible decapitation

Radiocarbon date: SUERC-74076   1030–1185 cal AD
918 ± 30 yr BP

Assigned period: 11th to 12th C.

Isotope sample no: GU-44450/GU-44463 and GU-48379 (not local)

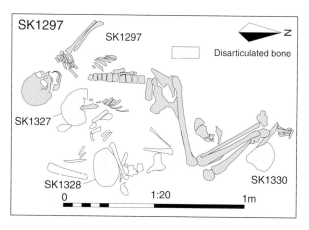

SK1300 [Gr.1299]

Age: 30–35 years, Prime Adult   Sex: Male

Fig. 8.11

Orientation: South-west

Posture: Supine. Extended. Skull was adjacent to right pelvis with CV1–4. Right arm flexed gently over top leg/hip, hands probably close as phalanges mixed. Left arm bones found near legs (disturbed?). Iron stain on the left lateral iliac blade

Human remains: 75+%. Right frontal parts of cranium. Spine – lower thoracic and lumbar, CV1–6. Sacrum. Left and right pelvis. Ribs, sternum and manubrium. Right arm and leg and foot. Left femur and upper ulna. Right hand

Evidence for execution: Decapitation

Objects in grave: Under pelvis. Iron buckle. Cat. no. 2. RA17

Assigned period: 11th to 12th C. by association

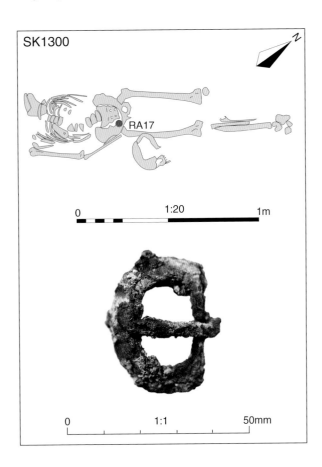

SK1303 [Gr.1302]

Age: Adult, Adult   Sex: Male?

Orientation: South

Posture: Supine

Human remains: 25–50%. Thoracic vertebrae. Skull and CVs absent. Sternum, ribs, right humerus, proximal radius and ulna. Left and right clavicle and scapula. Left shaft humerus. Some left and right carpal and metacarpal and phalanges

Evidence for execution: Disarticulated material in the area where skull should be, so maybe decapitation

Assigned period: 11th to 12th C. or later, by association

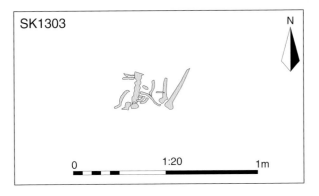

SK1306 [Gr.1305]

Age: Adult, Adult   Sex: Indeterminate

Not illust.

Orientation: Not known

Posture: Prone? Right arm articulated

Human remains: 0–25%. Right distal humerus, proximal radius and ulna. Right metacarpals. Left tibia and fibula shaft. Left ischium. Ribs and one thoracic vertebra

Assigned period: 11th to 12th C. or earlier, by association

SK1308 [Gr.1302]

Age: 30–35 years, Prime Adult   Sex: Male

Orientation: Not known

Posture: Cranium found by SK1312 right knee. Mandible found further down

Human remains: 0–25%. Cranium, maxilla and mandible

Evidence for execution: Decapitation?

Assigned period: In grave 1302 which is of 11th to 12th C. date

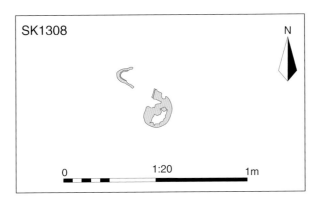

SK1309 [Gr.1302]
Age: 45+ years, Older Adult   Sex: Male
Orientation: South
Posture: Supine. Arms bent at elbows crossed at top of body.
    Right leg bent at knee to accommodate a skull (SK1310).
    Feet possibly together, though hard to say due to truncation.
    SKs1309 and 1310 are assumed to be same individual
    (decapitated) due to the leg position
Human remains: 50–75%. Skull, thoracic and lumbar spine
    CV1–2 with skull. Right side sacrum, right ilium, ribs,
    sternum. Right femur shaft. Right radius and ulna. Left
    clavicle, radius and ulna. Right tibia and fibula shaft. Left
    hand, carpals right. Right foot, left partial talus
Evidence for execution: Decapitation?
Assigned period: 11th to 12th C. or later, by association

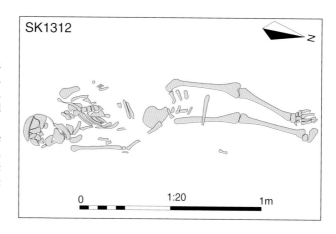

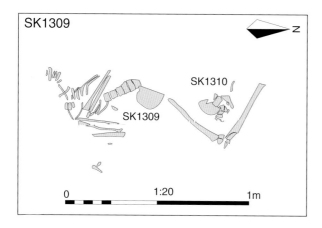

SK1312 [Gr.1302]
Age: 18–20 years, Young Adult   Sex: Male
Orientation: South
Posture: Supine. Extended. Hands over pelvis. Skull very frag-
    mented, but was in position turned to right side
Human remains: 75+%. Skull, spine (not lower lumbar), frag.
    of sacrum. Right pelvis, left ischium and pubis only. Left
    ribs and sternum. Legs and feet. Right arm, left proximal
    humerus and distal radius and ulna, shaft clavicle. Right
    hand and partial left
Assigned period: 11th to 12th C. or later, by association

SK1315 [Gr.1278]
Age: Adult, Adult   Sex: Indeterminate
Not illust.
Orientation: South
Posture: Left articulated arm only, in twisted position.
Human remains: 0–25%. Left humerus, radius and ulna, hand
Objects in grave: Iron buckle. Found on outside of arm. Cat. no.
    4. RA12

SK1315a [Gr.1278]
Age: 40–44 years, Mature Adult   Sex: Male
Not illust.
Orientation: Not known
Posture: Prone. Adjacent to SK1315 and originally thought to
    be the same
Human remains: 0–25%. Left pelvis, ribs and lower spine, lumbar

SK1316 [Gr.1314]
Age: 18–25 years, Young Adult   Sex: Male
Fig. 8.12
Orientation: South
Posture: Supine. Extended. Arms bent at elbow behind back,
    hands together
Human remains: 75+%. Most of skeleton present except right
    hand
Evidence for execution: hands tied?
Assigned period: 11th to 12th C. or later, by association

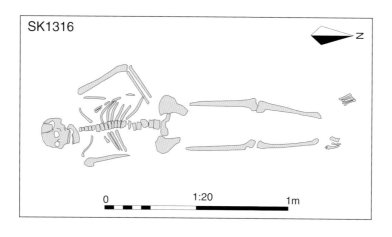

SK1319 [Gr.1318]
Age: Adult, Adult   Sex: Indeterminate
Orientation: South
Posture: Not known
Human remains: 0–25%. Frags lower thoracic and lumbar. Frags of ribs. Right clavicle and left mid clavicle
Assigned period: 11th to 12th C. or earlier by association

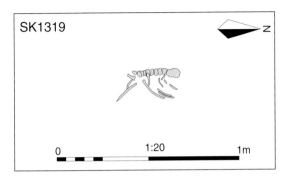

SK1322 [Gr.1321]
Age: 26–35 years, Prime Adult   Sex: Male
Figs 8.4; 8.12
Orientation: South-east
Posture: Right side. Hands behind back
Human remains: 75+%. Cranium. Spine (without CV1–2), sacral vertebrae 1–2, partial left and right pelves. Right ribs and some left, manubrium. All long bones, partial hands and feet
Evidence for execution: hands tied behind back?
Assigned period: 11th to 12th C. by association

SK1325 [Gr.1324]
Age: 23–57 years, Mature Adult   Sex: Male
Orientation: South-west
Posture: Supine. Extended, hands behind back
Human remains: 75+%. Most of skeleton present
Evidence for execution: hands tied behind back?
Assigned period: 11th to 12th C. or later by association

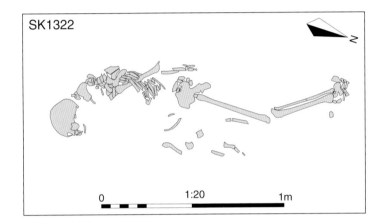

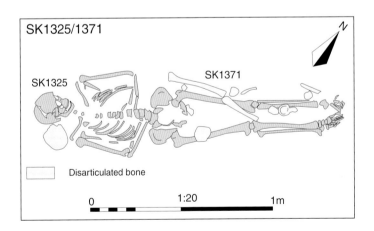

SK1327 [Gr.1332]

Age: 45+ years, Older Adult   Sex: Male
Not illustr.
Orientation: Not known
Posture: Cranium on left side
Human remains: 0–25%. Cranium and maxilla
Evidence for execution: decapitation?

SK1328 [Gr.1332]

Age: Adult, Adult   Sex: Male
Not. illust.
Orientation: Not known
Posture: Not known
Human remains: 0–25%. Cranium
Evidence for execution: decapitation?

SK1328b [Gr.1332]

Age: Adult, Adult   Sex: Male?
Not illust.
Orientation: Not known
Posture: Not known
Human remains: 0–25%. Frontal and parietal, partial temporal
Evidence for execution: decapitation?

SK1329 [Gr.1332]

Age: Adult, Adult   Sex: Male
Not illust.
Orientation: Not known
Posture: Not known
Human remains: 0–25%. frontal bone only
Evidence for execution: decapitation?

SK1330 [Gr.1296]

Age: Less than 25 years, Young Adult   Sex: Male?
Not illust.
Orientation: Not known
Posture: Disarticulated cranium - found prone at feet of SK1297
Human remains: 0–25%. Posterior cranium
Evidence for execution: decapitation?
Assigned period: 11th to 12th C. by association

SK1331 [Gr.1311]

Age: Adult, Adult   Sex: Male??
Not illust.
Orientation: Not known
Posture: Not known
Human remains: 0–25%. Right humerus and scapula
Assigned period: 11th to 12th C. or earlier

SK1335 [Gr.1334]

Age: 50–86 years, Older Adult   Sex: Male
Orientation: South-west
Posture: Skull under torso on right side. Hands in front
Human remains: 75+%. Most of skeleton present
Evidence for execution: Hands tied in front? Decapitation?
Assigned period: 11th to 12th C. or earlier

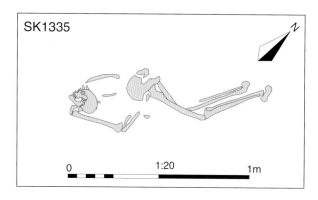

SK1338 [Gr.1337]

Age: Adult, Adult   Sex: Male?
Orientation: Not known
Posture: Not known
Human remains: 0–25%. Left femur (prox 2/3), right femur shaft, left tibia distal, right tibia shaft. Left and right feet.
Assigned period: 11th to 12th C. or later

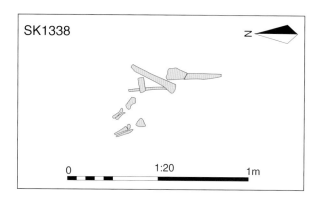

SK1344 [Gr.1343]

Age: 30–34 years, Prime Adult   Sex: Male
Orientation: South-west
Posture: Supine. Extended
Human remains: 0–25%. Right pelvis, left acetabulum. Sacral vertebra 1, LV5. Left femur, tibia and fibula. Left talus calcaneus
Assigned period: 10th to 12th C. by association

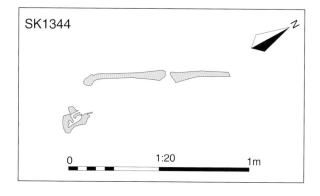

SK1346/7 [Gr.1284]

Age: Less than 10 years, Older Child   Sex: Indeterminate
Not illust.
Orientation: South?
Posture: Not known
Human remains: 0–25%. Arm and feet only of non-adult
Assigned period: 11th to 12th C. or earlier??

SK1349 [Gr.1348]

Age: 18–20 years, Young Adult   Sex: Male
Fig. 3.16
Orientation: South
Posture: Supine. Extended. Arms folded up across upper chest.
    Skull placed upright at base of right ribs
Human remains: 75+%. Skeleton mostly present except feet
Evidence for execution: Decapitation

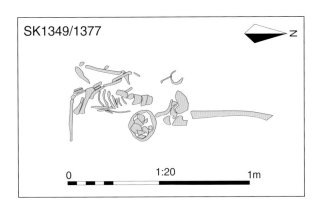

SK1352 [Gr.1351]

Age: Adult, Adult   Sex: Male?
Orientation: West
Posture: Supine. Extended
Human remains: 50–75%. Partial left pelvis. Left leg. Right distal
    half femur, right tibia and fibula. Left foot, right partial. Left
    clavicle, frag. scapula and left hand

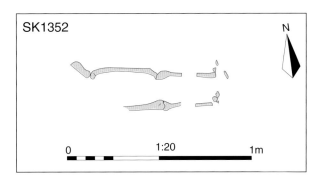

SK1355 [Gr.1354]

Age: 45+ years, Older Adult   Sex: Male
Fig. 1.6
Orientation: Not known
Posture: Partial skull adjacent to right leg of SK1356. May be
    associated?
Human remains: 0–25%. Frontal cranium, maxilla and left
    mandible
Assigned period: 11th to 12th C. or later?

SK1356 [Gr.1354]

Age: Adult, Adult   Sex: Male??
Fig. 1.6
Orientation: South-west
Posture: Extended lower right leg and foot
Human remains: 0–25%. Lower right femur, tibia, fibula and
    foot
Assigned period: 11th to 12th C. or later

SK1357 [Gr.1354]

Age: Adult, Adult   Sex: Male??
Fig. 1.6
Orientation: South-west
Posture: Supine. Lower legs and feet only. Extended. 2x crania lie
    on top of tibiae (SKs1358 and 1359)
Human remains: 0–25%. Right distal femur, tibia, fibula and
    partial foot. Left 2/3 distal tibia, fibula and partial foot
Assigned period: 11th to 12th C. or later

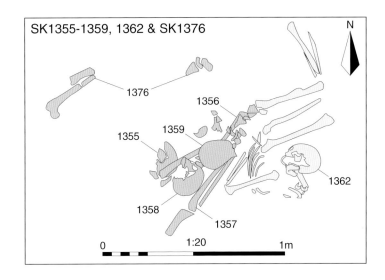

SK1358 [Gr.1354]
Age: 18–25 years, Young Adult   Sex: Female
Fig. 1.6
Orientation: Not known
Posture: Not known. Skull on right side above SK1357 legs
Human remains: 0–25%. Cranium and maxilla
Evidence for execution: decapitation?
Assigned period: 11th to 12th C. or later?

SK1359 [Gr.1354]
Age: under 21 years, Adolescent   Sex: Indeterminate
Fig. 1.6
Orientation: Not known
Posture: Not known. Upright cranium above SK1357 legs (maybe part of SK1357)
Human remains: 0–25%. Cranium
Evidence for execution: decapitation?
Assigned period: 11th to 12th C. or later?

SK1362 [Gr.1361]
Age: 18–25 years, Young Adult   Sex: Male
Figs 1.6; 3.9
Orientation: South-west
Posture: Right side, crouched position, with hands behind and skull placed on chest
Human remains: 75+%. Most of skull. Thoracic and lumbar spine with partial CV2–3. Manubrium, ribs. Right arm, left humerus, radius and ulna. Right leg, left leg present but only frag. of fibula. Right talus and calcaneus, left talus. Both hands
Evidence for execution: Hands tied? Decapitation CV2

SK1365 [Gr.1390]
Age: 20s years, Young Adult   Sex: Male
Not illust.
Orientation: Not known
Posture: Not known. Skull. on left side
Human remains: 0–25%. Skull and CV1 and 2
Evidence for execution: Decapitation. Cut-mark on mandible
Objects in grave: 1 sherd probable LIA pottery
Assigned period: 10th to 12th C.?

SK1368 [Gr.1367]
Age: 13–17 years, Adolescent   Sex: Indeterminate
Orientation: South-west
Posture: Prone. Hands behind back
Human remains: 75%. Most skull (except facial area). Spine, pelvis (minus pubis), sacrum, ribs, frag. sternum. Left arm, right arm except humerus. Right leg to top of tibia, left proximal and distal femur only, proximal tibia. Left and right carpals
Evidence for execution: Hands tied behind back?
Assigned period: 11th to 12th C. or earlier

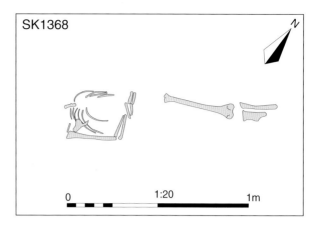

SK1368

0   1:20   1m

SK1371 [Gr.1370]
Age: 30–34 years, Prime Adult   Sex: Male
Not illust; parts shown with SK1253
Orientation: South-west
Posture: Not known. Skeletal elements scattered around the grave. Very roughly still anatomical location. Left femur appears *in situ* within original grave cut. Parts of SK1371 are in grave 1324 (SK1325)
Human remains: 0–25%. Left femur, tibia and fibula shaft. Right distal humerus and right proximal femur. Posterior cranium, both iliums. Two lumbar and one thoracic vertebra
Assigned period: 11th to 12th C. or earlier

SK1374 [Gr.1373]
Age: Adult, Adult   Sex: Indeterminate
Orientation: South
Posture: Supine. Extended
Human remains: 0–25%. Right tibia, fibula and foot. Left foot
Assigned period: 11th to 12th C. or earlier

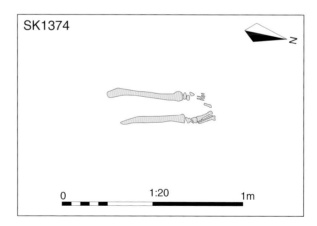

SK1374

0   1:20   1m

SK1376 [Gr.1354]
Age: Adult, Adult   Sex: Male?
Not illust.
Orientation: South-west
Posture: Supine. Extended
Human remains: 0–25%. Left proximal femur, left partial tibia and fibula. Left and right partial foot
Assigned period: 11th to 12th C. or later

SK1377 [Gr.1348]
Age: Adult, Adult   Sex: Male??
Illust. with SK1349
Orientation: Not known
Posture: Not known
Human remains: 0–25%. Left and right tibia. Right fibula and foot

SK1379 [Gr.1378]
Age: 35–45 years, Mature Adult   Sex: Female
Fig.8.5
Orientation: South-east
Posture: Prone. Hands to front crossed under chest. A disarticulated cranium (SK1380) adjacent to lower legs, confirmed as male, so not same individual
Human remains: 75+%. Cranium and partial maxilla. Thoracic and lumbar vertebrae. Pelves. Sacrum. Ribs. Right arm, left humerus, radius and ulna. Right hand carpal and metacarpal. Left hand some carpal and 1 metacarpal. Both legs. Right foot, left not as complete
Evidence for execution: Skull is absent, may be from later truncation or decapitation. Evidence too slim to be counted in the possible total of decapitations
Radiocarbon date: SUERC-74073   1026–1183 cal AD
    924 ± 30 yr BP
Assigned period: 11th to 12th C.
Isotope sample no: GU-44447 (local)

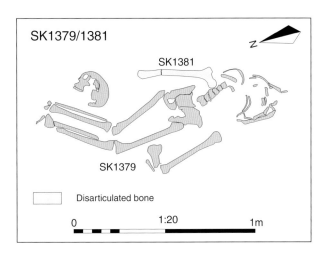

SK1381 [Gr.1378]
Age: Adult, Adult   Sex: Indeterminate
Illust. with SK1379
Orientation: Not known
Posture: Not known. Disarticulated right leg in backfill or over top of SK1379
Human remains: 0–25%. Right femur, tibia and shaft fibula. Some shaft of metatarsals
Objects in grave: Iron nail (no RA no.). Not illust.
Assigned period: layer 11th to 12th C. or earlier

SK1384 [Gr.1383]
Age: 20–27 years, Prime Adult   Sex: Male
Fig. 3.18
Orientation: South-west
Posture: Right side. Legs were probably bent up at knee. Mandible found separate to cranium
Human remains: 75+%. Skull, spine (without CV1). Sacrum, pelvis (left and right), ribs. Right arm, left humerus, clavicle, radius (all incomplete). Right hand (carpals and metacarpals). Both proximal femori
Evidence for execution: Second cervical vertebra has break across odontoid peg, ?evidence for hanging

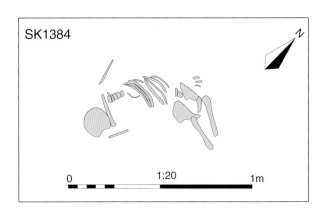

SK1386 [Gr.1388]
Age: Adult, Adult   Sex: Male?
Fig. 8.12
Orientation: Not known
Posture: Supine
Human remains: 0–25%. Left distal femur. Left tibia and fibula. Left talus
Assigned period: 11th to 12th C. by association

SK1387 [Gr.1388]
Age: 30–35 years, Prime Adult   Sex: Male?
Orientation: South
Posture: Prone
Human remains: 0–25%. Fifth lumbar vertebra. Sacrum, left pelvis. Left femur
Radiocarbon date: SUERC-74072   1025–1165 cal AD
    931 ± 30 yr BP
Assigned period: 11th to 12th C.
Isotope sample no: GU-44446 (local)

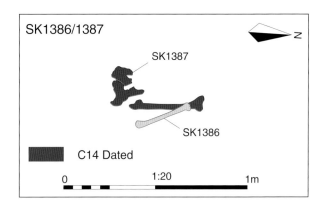

SK1391 [Gr.1390]
Age: early 20s years, Young Adult   Sex: Male
Figs 8.8; 8.12
Orientation: South-east
Posture: Prone
Human remains: 50–75%. Skull. Cervical spine. Half sternum, two ribs. Right leg. Left leg (but not fibula). Some right hand. Left humerus. Parts of feet
Evidence for execution: Hands were probably tied behind back from arm position. Odontoid possible fracture on second cervical vertebra may be evidence of hanging
Assigned period: 10th to 12th C. by association

SK1394 [Gr.1393]
Age: Adult, Adult   Sex: Indeterminate
Not illust.
Orientation: South-west
Posture: Prone
Human remains: 0–25%. Lower two thirds of femora and patella only
Assigned period: 10th C. by association

SK1396 [Gr.1341]
Age: 15–20 years, Adolescent   Sex: Male
Figs 8.8; 8.12
Orientation: North
Posture: Supine. Extended. Hands behind back
Human remains: 75+%. Most of post-cranial skeleton present
Evidence for execution: Hands tied behind back? Possible decapitation? May be later disturbance
Objects in grave: Knife handle, bone. Cat. no. 1, RA24, and iron frags. Near the left arm. 12th to 13th C.
Assigned period: 11th to 12th C. by association

SK1397 [Gr.1341]
Age: 25–30 years, Young Adult   Sex: Male
Figs 8.8; 8.12
Orientation: North
Posture: Supine. Extended with skull turned to left side. Left arm by side and right brought up across chest
Human remains: 75+%. Most of skeleton, except cranium facial and occipital only
Radiocarbon date: SUERC-74075   1020–1155 cal AD 962 ± 30 yr BP
Assigned period: 11th to 12th C.
Isotope sample no: GU-44449/GU-44462 (local)

SK1398 [Gr.1341]
Age: Adult, Adult   Sex: Male
Figs 8.8; 8.12
Orientation: Not known
Posture: Not known
Human remains: 0–25%. Cranium only (RA25) found next to SK1397 skull. ?belongs to SK1396, or is disarticulated in grave fill
Evidence for execution: decapitation?
Assigned period: 11th to 12th C. by association

SK21005 [Gr.21004]
Age: Adult, Adult   Sex: Indeterminate
Not illust.
Orientation: Not known
Posture: Not known
Human remains: 0–25%. Tarsals and 1 partial metatarsal only

SK21008 [Gr.21007]
Age: Adult, Adult   Sex: Indeterminate
Not illust.
Orientation: Not known
Posture: Not known
Human remains: 0–25%. Left parietal frag., left scapula frag.

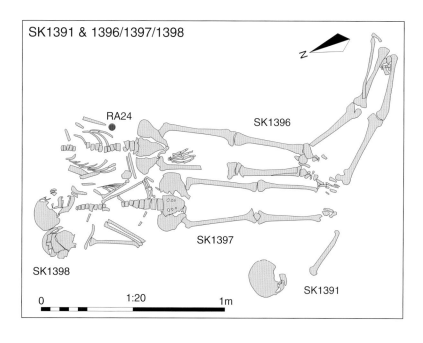

SK1391 & 1396/1397/1398

Chapter 3
Human Bone

by Sharon Clough

Introduction

Osteological examination and recording of the articulated human remains of 124 individuals was completed from the site at Weyhill Road, Andover. Recording and analysis of the disarticulated human bone was undertaken in order to determine minimum number of individuals, or the identification of further individuals.

Methodology

Samples

Samples were taken from 20 skeletons, in order to undertake radiocarbon dating (C14) and also to explore the isotopic ratios of strontium and oxygen, carbon and nitrogen, and sulphur. The long bones: femur, tibia and humerus, were preferentially selected, with 2–5g of material removed from the shaft of the bone. For strontium and oxygen isotopic analysis, the permanent second molar was removed. For the results see Healy and Jay (Chapters 5 and 6).

Skeletal methodology

All skeletal remains were examined and recorded, according to the standard methodologies (Brickley and McKinley 2004; Mays *et al.* 2018). Inventories of each skeletal element were made using presence/absence where appropriate, or as a percentage of each element. Long bones were divided into five sections. This detailed method has allowed for true prevalence rates to be calculated for pathologies, non-metrical and metrical conditions. The dentition was also thoroughly recorded, using the Zsigmondy system (Hillson 1996) and pathologies were recorded with reference to Dias and Tayles (1997), Brothwell (1981) and Ogden (2008).

For the completeness of each skeleton, an assessment of the percentage of the bones present (of the entire skeleton) was made, and divided into one of four categories: 0–25%, 25–50%, 50–75%, or 75+%. Completeness could be affected by a variety of factors including intercutting graves, truncation by later features and localised preservation.

Bone surface was assigned a grade, according the stages of preservation recommended by McKinley 2004 (grades 1–5+). This is important to note, as it affects observation of the more subtle bony changes in some pathological conditions. This may affect the true prevalence rates of the condition.

Fragmentation was recorded visually on a form. It has important implications for the quantity of metrical data, observation of pathologies, assessment of ancestry and age/sex.

The archive raw data will be available online DOI: https://cotswoldarchaeology.co.uk/publication/cotswold-archaeology-monograph 11/.

Due to small numbers, size and/or difficulties in accurately assigning some skeletons to a phase, the assemblage has been analysed as a whole. However, the discussion briefly examines individuals of known phase for similarities and differences. The phases are Late Saxon *c*. AD 850–1066; Norman, AD 1066–1154; and medieval, AD 1154–14th century. The cemetery potentially spans 500 years, and this is to be considered when examining the assemblage as a whole, where on average, there was a burial only every four years.

Age estimation

The ages of all individuals were assessed, using the methodologies given in Table 3.1. Multiple methods were preferred for each individual, and a final age-range given, based on the relative strength of each method. Age-at-death estimation methods for adult individuals are not 'fool proof', and many give very wide age-ranges from which the means do not fully reflect individual

Table 3.1 Macroscopic techniques used for age estimation

Pubic symphysis	Brooks and Suchey 1990
Auricular surface	Lovejoy *et al.* 1985; Buckberry and Chamberlain 2002 (used for older adults)
Dental attrition	Miles 1962
Cranial suture closure	Meindl and Lovejoy 1985
Sternal rib ends	Işcan and Loth 1984; Işcan *et al.* 1985
Epiphyseal fusion	McKern and Stewart 1957; Webb and Suchey 1985
Dental eruption	Moorees *et al.* 1963; AlQahtani *et al.* 2010

variation (Buckberry 2015). For the purposes of this report, each individual has been assigned to an age category detailed in Table 3.2. Consideration has been given to the work by Falys and Lewis (2010), and the recommendation by Buckberry (2015), that prior probabilities should be used for adults, so as such these categories represent a compromise. For the full details of each skeleton age-range for each method, the archive will be available, and the range and allocated category are detailed in the catalogue. However, this has meant that some individuals have been placed within the 'most likely' group. Further compounding the difficulties of age estimation was the incompleteness of the skeletons. The skulls were often absent, and the level of intercutting frequently reduced individuals to articulating long bones only. The dental attrition method developed by Miles (1962) (further refined by Brothwell 1981) was applied, since the current assemblage was comparable, but where this was the only method used it must be regarded with caution.

For non-adults, estimation of chronological age is generally more precise. Dental development, in particular, has been shown to be minimally affected by environmental factors (Elamin and Liversidge 2013). Where dentition was not available, long bone length

was used to gain an indication of the age-range. Tables developed by Maresh (1970) and Hoppa (1992) (based on an Anglo-Saxon sample) were used for the over-one-month ages.

The category of Adult was assigned to those individuals who had no age indicators other than that the bones present were all fully fused. The 'young adult' category was deemed to start at 18 years for the purposes of this report.

The limitation of adult ageing methods generally consigns all those over 45 years into one category, and does not reflect the true range of ages attained. Historical sources from this period (Cayton 1980) have found that kings and nobles lived to an average of 57.7 years (range 18–68+). The oft-quoted phrase 'three score years and ten' has been proved to be the model age at death amongst modern hunter-gatherer populations (Gurven and Kaplan 2007, 332), in that after 70 years you are more likely to die than live. It is likely that a good number died at or around this age, and perhaps older.

Sex estimation

Sexually dimorphic traits of the skull and pelvis were used to ascertain the sex of adult individuals (Ferembach *et al.* 1980): only adolescents with fully fused pelves were given an estimation for sex. Due to the heavy fragmentation of the skulls, estimation using these indicators was more difficult, and is well documented to be less reliable than the pelvis (Bass 1995). Metrical information was taken from known sexually dimorphic bones and confidently sexed males (Spradley and Jantz 2011). This analysis enabled a within-population range (known male measurement range) to be created, and this was applied to those un-sexed adults with preserved long bones (after Giles 1970).

Metrics

Cranial metrics were only possible on a limited number of crania, as these were nearly all fragmented. It is not recommended that metrics are taken from reconstructed crania, especially where fragmentation is severe (Buikstra and Ubelaker 1994, 70). This has prevented the use of morphological features to make accurate comparisons

Table 3.2 Age categories

Age range	Age category
0 – 1 month	Neonate
1 month – 1 year	Infant
1 year – 2 years	Young child
3 – 5 years	Mid child
6 – 12 years	Older child
13 – 17 years	Adolescent
18 – 25 years	Young adult
26 – 35 years	Prime adult
36 – 45 years	Mature adult
46+ years	Older adult
60+ years	Much older adult
18+ years	Adult

between and within skeletal populations, and in the assessment of ancestry.

The long bones were often fragmented, although unlike the crania, the post-mortem fractures were often only single and the parts refitted exactly. Long bones with only one break, and no obvious warping, were measured. Stature was estimated from the left femur, where available, and from another long bone where it was not (as stated in the results), with priority given to the bones of the lower limb over the upper, as these are a more reliable indicator of stature. The regression equations by Trotter and Gleser (1958, revised 1970) were used, and these have been proved to provide a fairly good fit to British white populations (Mays 2016).

Non-metrics

All individuals were examined for the presence of non-metrical traits. Those defined in Brickley and McKinley (2004) were scored for presence/absence and not observable. Where non-metric traits were observed, which were not in the list, they were noted only. These are likely to be more rarely occurring traits amongst British samples, and would have a very low true prevalence rate (TPR).

There is some debate has to how much genetic control these traits are under. Cranial traits were examined by Carson (2006), and it was found that there were large standard errors for those traits which appeared to have some heritability. This is in contrast to earlier studies, which suggested that some cranial traits were, to a degree, under genetic control (Berry and Berry 1967; Sjøvold 1984). Environmental factors may have an influence, as well as activity. Post-cranial traits in particular are more likely to be controlled by activity, and may well be expressions of enthesophyte-like reaction of the soft tissue.

In recording these individual variations, we were looking for the 'typical' for the population and outliers, as possible indicators of those taking part in different activities or those not from the locale. Much more research is needed into these traits and consistency in the recording, not just for presence/absence but the stage of the expression concerned (e.g. metopic suture residual, partial, full).

Enthesophytes

Recent work on the methods for recording entheseal changes (fibrous and fibrous cartilaginous) have attempted to standardise the degrees of expression (Henderson *et al.* 2016; Mariotti *et al.* 2007). The 'Coimbra method', while rigorous, is considered to be too detailed for a standard bone report. It did not identify any patterns when used on a population of known occupation, other than that which has been already established, that entheseal changes increase with age. The method proposed by Mariotti (*et al.* 2007) scoring three degrees of expression (Table 3.3) is more appropriate for the present context. The 23 recommended sites were reduced to the 12 most commonly found to have a degree of expression, with an option to note the other sites, but not formally scored.

Pathology

Skeletal pathology and/or bony abnormality were described, and differential diagnoses explored, with reference to standard texts (Ortner and Putschar 1981; Resnick 1995; Aufderheide and Rodríguez-Martin 1998; Waldron 2009). Where considered appropriate, the extent and range of pathology was explored by calculating crude prevalence rates (CPR, i.e. the number of individuals with a condition out of the total number of individuals observed), and true prevalence rates (TPR, e.g. the number of elements or teeth with a particular condition out of the number of elements or teeth observed). These were then compared with similar assemblages.

Preservation and completeness

The completeness of the recovered skeletons has a very considerable influence on the results and conclusions which can be gleaned from the remains, since specific areas of the skeleton are more useful for ageing and sexing, and if these are absent it becomes more challenging to interpret the findings or observe pathological lesions and non-metrics.

The intercutting of graves, as a result of the continuing use of the site over a period of time, meant that many skeletons were truncated. There were also several instances where the previous occupant of the grave had clearly been disinterred, replaced and then a good quantity of that individual included in the backfill. This has allowed more individuals to be identified than were actually fully articulated.

An articulated skeleton was defined by the articulation of one or more bones. A cranium was therefore articulated (they are formed from several bones), and is

Table 3.3 Grades of entheseal change

Grade	Definition
1	Faint or slight impression
2	The attachment site is well delimited, surface raised or depressed 1–3mm high development
3	Area well delimited and defined. Very raised or depressed, irregular or rugged surface. 3–5mm very high development

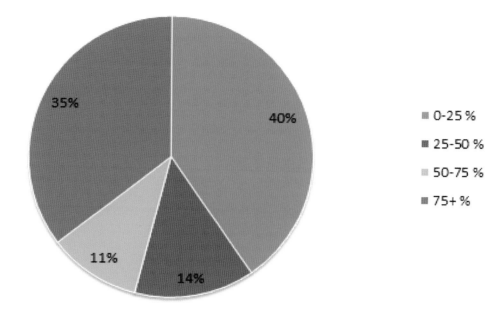

35%

40%

11%

14%

■ 0-25 %

■ 25-50 %

■ 50-75 %

■ 75+ %

Fig. 3.1   Percentage of completeness of articulated skeletons

a useful skeletal element, as it can provide an age and sex estimation. In addition to the articulated bones, where there was clearly one individual from disarticulated bone, this was also designated by a skeleton number. Some of these were identified at post-excavation stage, and as such have the designation 'a' or 'b'.

Bones which were allocated a skeleton number on site, but later were found to be completely disarticulated, were then included with the disarticulated material.

This work resulted in a calculated total of 124 skeletons, or individuals identified.

Vertical and horizontal truncation from later activity on the site also contributed to the removal of skeletal elements. In particular, the insertion of pipelines and geo-technical pits cut directly through articulated skeletons, entirely removing bones within the area impacted.

Accumulated disturbance has resulted in a large quantity of disarticulated bone being recovered from the subsoil, and this has been examined and is discussed further in the section.

Fig. 3.1 demonstrates that there were nearly as many individuals with more than 75% of the skeleton preserved as there were those with less than 25%. This large range of completeness has meant that observation for pathological and dental lesions was mostly limited to the 75+% group. In addition, those in the less-than-25% group were more likely to be only identified as adult, and not estimated for sex.

Bone surface condition was variable. The natural chalk substrate was free-draining and alkaline, and there was no evidence of coffins or other enclosing features to affect the burial environment. It is not known whether the dead were clothed or not, as only a few belt buckles

were recovered (Fig. 3.5), and these were not necessarily from clothing items. If the buried individuals were the result of judicial execution, careful treatment of the body, such as careful dressing, is unlikely. The positions of bodies within the graves suggest less than careful disposal. Clothing may have been removed (or as in Fig. 7.3, the individual hanged wearing only a loose shirt) as a final act of disrespect, or sold in compensation (the concept of *wergild*, or 'man payment' was prevalent at this time, the value of the clothing going some way towards paying the victim compensation), if it had a value.

These factors have all influenced the surface preservation of the bone. Fig. 3.2 shows mixed preservation across the burials: one third were grade 2, indicating only slight surface damage and allowing observation of most subtle surface changes. However, 20% were grade 4, which has severely affected the observation of pathology, as well as changes to the areas of the auricular surface and pubic symphyses, both needed for age estimation.

It is documented that, in later periods, hanged corpses were left above ground to rot. This would result in bones becoming exposed to the elements and wildlife. Bones may have become disarticulated when they became detached from the rest of the skeleton. There were no examples of bone surface-changes relating to the exposure of bone above ground. The only animal gnawing present was by rodents. This resulted in gnaw-marks on some bones (one articulated skeleton and one disarticulated). For articulated skeleton, SK1397, there was evidence of rodent burrowing removing surrounding bones. Therefore, animal gnawing was not evidence of corpses left above ground.

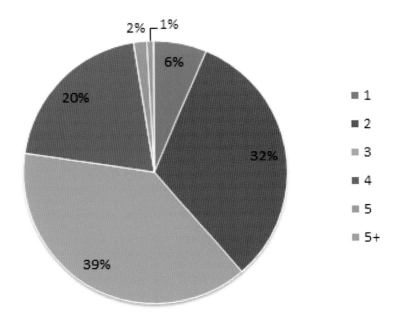

Fig. 3.2   Percentage of bone surface preservation (grade 1–5+ after McKinley 2004)

Demography

Of the 124 articulated skeletons, 108 were adult and 16 were non-adult (less than 18 years).

Table 3.4 shows the distribution of ages by group. The number of individuals across the age-ranges does not reflect the expected distribution (blue line) for this time-period (Fig. 3.3) (Wood *et al.* 2002). There are no children under six years, and the number of adults decreases with age. This age distribution, with a peak in the young adult and prime adult age-groups, is consistent with a 'deviant' cemetery, such as an execution site (Buckberry 2014).

The age distribution of those who commit crime (first

Table 3.4 Articulated skeletons by age category

Age range	Age category	Number of individuals
0 – 1 month	Neonate	0
1 month – 1 year	Infant	0
1 – 2 years	Young child	0
3 – 5 years	Mid child	0
6 – 12 years	Older child	2
13 – 17 years	Adolescent	14
18 – 25 years	Young adult	24
26 – 35 years	Prime adult	22
36 – 45 years	Mature adult	15
46+ years	Older adult	11
60+ years	Much older adult	0
Adult	Adult	36

offence) has not changed considerably over time. Crime increases in early adolescence, and peaks in the early to mid-20s age-range, and then begins to decline (Rocque *et al.* 2015). Age and crime has been studied since the early 19th century, and the relationship between age and crime is remarkably consistent over time. The age distribution from the Weyhill Road cemetery fits this established pattern, with the peak of incidence in the 18–25-years group. From this, we can infer that age of (first) crime distribution was the same in the period covered by the cemetery. It must be noted, however, that osteological ageing methods are not accurate to one year, and usually cover a range of possible years.

Similar mortality profiles were found in other 'deviant' burial sites. Ridgeway Hill, Dorset (Loe *et al.* 2014), Towton, North Yorkshire (Fiorato *et al.* 2000) and St John's College, Oxford (Wallis 2014) also had a greater proportion of young adults and adolescents. Ridgeway Hill and St John's were the only two to feature individuals of less than 16 years, and Weyhill Road and Towton had individuals over 45 years. The peak of mortality for Ridgeway Hill was 16–20 years; St John's 21–25 years; Towton 26–35 years; and Weyhill Road 18–25 years. Weyhill Road was therefore very similar to the first two sites (Ridgeway Hill and St John's). These were both considered to be massacre/execution sites representing a single event, where many bodies were disposed of in a short space of time; at Weyhill Road the evidence indicates burial over a long period as a series of separate events (see Chapter 6).

Examination of age-at-death distribution from nine identified execution cemeteries has also found a peak in the 18–25-years group (Mattison 2016).

In the pre-Conquest period, law codes suggest that 12

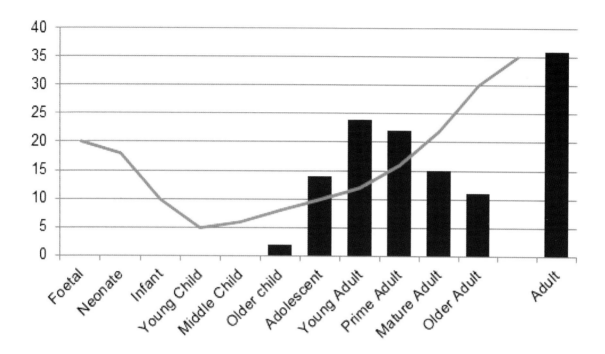

Fig. 3.3   Distribution of individuals by age category, with expected attritional profile line

years old was the minimum legal age of culpability. The 'older child' (6–12 years) age-group at Weyhill Road comprises only two individuals (although there may have been more – see 'Charnel or disarticulated human bone' below). These were both highly truncated graves, and therefore lacked the majority of skeletal elements, making more accurate ageing difficult (osteological ageing is always expressed as a range, since individuals grow at different rates). In this time-period, births were not officially recorded, and so each individual was required to remember and truthfully confess their age. Those accusing a child of crime (and sentencing) would rely on this testimony, and their individual discretion. It was also important that the accused understood right from wrong, and that they could be punished for misdemeanours. Evading the authorities, for example, clearly demonstrated guilt. It is therefore quite likely that children younger than 12 years will have fallen foul of the legal system. The current legal age of criminal responsibility is 10 years (England and Wales), although miscreants are treated as minors until aged 18.

Those assigned to the 'adult' age-group are unlikely to have more refined age-estimations, due to the lack of the relevant bones needed for more accurate ageing.

Of the 88 aged individuals, 40 were younger than 25 years at death (45.7%) and nearly 70% were under 35 years (62 individuals). This large cohort of young people has implications for the type and quantity of dental and skeletal pathology. Younger people have less joint disease, and less time for bony changes to develop (Waldron 2009). Buckberry (2014) suggests that the skew towards younger individuals should

be investigated, and perhaps the inadequacies of age-estimation methods, particularly in the older age-ranges, have biased the results. However, in ages up to 25 years, the skeleton is still fusing at the joints. This fusion is readily observable, and so it is unlikely that any of the individuals assigned to the 25-years-and-younger age categories are inaccurately placed. The age-at-death profile of this cemetery is clearly skewed towards younger individuals.

Sex estimation

Estimation of sex was possible for 100 individuals. Of these, three were female and the rest were male, or probable/possible male (Fig. 3.4). The three females comprised two articulated skeletons, and one isolated skull (SKs1105, 1379, 1358) (Fig. 3.5).

The females were identified from morphological differences in the pelvis and crania and have not been confirmed by aDNA or other method. SK1379 lay adjacent to disarticulated cranium SK1380 and it was initially assumed that they were the same person. The fragmentary nature of the cranium (SK1380) and poor preservation meant that the sexually dimorphic aspects were not clear. There were some teeth preserved in the maxilla and one was selected for determination of the presence or absence of peptides from the amelogenin isoform Y in the presence of amelogenin isoform X (Stewart *et al.* 2017). This test determined the cranium was male. On subsequent re-examination of the post-cranial skeleton SK1379 it was clear that the pelvis was very female and the other bones were petite and gracile. SK1379 was still considered to be female and the

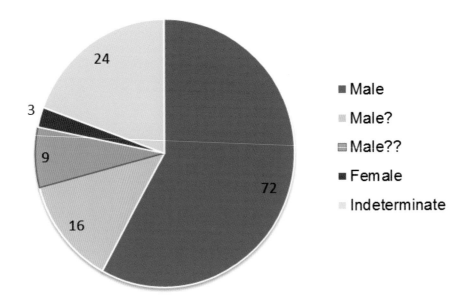

Fig. 3.4   Number of individuals divided by sex estimation

cranium SK1380 has been assigned to the disarticulated category.

A known bias in osteology is that males are sexed more readily than females (Weiss 1972). It is also standard practice not to attempt sex estimation until the pelvis has fused, and to be aware that adolescents and young adults do not necessarily develop the full masculine traits necessary for clear estimation as male, and that features can remain quite gracile (and therefore feminine). With such a large number of adolescents and young adults making up the assemblage, this was a factor in assigning probable and possible males (M?, M??).

The category of 'Probable male' was assigned to indeterminate adults who lacked a skull or pelvis (or both), but were sexed using metrical data (noted in inhumation catalogue). The measurements from long bones of firmly identified males were used to develop a range, mean and standard deviation for specific metrics. The femoral head longitudinal length, distal femur width, humeral head longitudinal, humeral epicondylar width and tibia length were all used. Where the indeterminate adults' metric fell within the standard deviation for that bone, it was assigned to probable male (M?). This work identified that previously considered probable males (by morphological features), had the smallest measurements of the femoral head and length of femur. SK1387 and SK1046 both had a femoral head-length of 42mm, the same as the females. SK1387 was also the shortest male, at 161cm. This puts in doubt the identification of SK1387 as male?. However, these gracile, petite bones may have appeared female, but the sacrum was curved and the ilium had male characteristics. SK1046 can be allowed for, as it was in the adolescent category and such young age may account for the small size. It is not

improbable that short, gracile males were amongst the population, and some degree of overlap between the sexes is to be expected.

The very high ratio of male to female, 32.3:1, supports the interpretation that this is an execution cemetery. Males consistently commit more crime than females, across both time and cultures (Carrabine *et al.* 2004). The reasons behind this are complex, and possibly relate to societies' regulation and limitation of women to the domestic sphere and the expected role of men and their masculinities (*ibid.*). Therefore, it would be expected to find significantly more men than women in an execution cemetery. In addition to this, Anglo-Saxon (and medieval) documents relating to the outcomes of legal proceedings for the punishments of crime suggest that, even in cases where women were found guilty of crimes normally resulting in capital punishment (death), this was not necessarily the outcome. Medieval law allowed women in shared-responsibility cases to plead that they were under the control of male perpetrators. Pregnancy was often used as a reason to avoid death, or death was to be inflicted in a different manner to male executions, including drowning, burning or being thrown off a cliff (Mattison 2016, 231). This would result in much lower incidence of females being hanged or decapitated and subsequently buried alongside male felons.

Other 'deviant' burial sites also lacked female individuals. None were found at Ridgeway Hill, Dorset; St John's College, Oxford; Towton, North Yorkshire; or Walkington Wold, East Riding of Yorkshire. Other proposed execution cemeteries included only small numbers of females, including: Dunstable, and Gally Hills, Bedfordshire; Castle Hill, Berkshire; Bran Ditch, Chesterton Lane Corner, and Wandlebury in Cambridgeshire; Meon

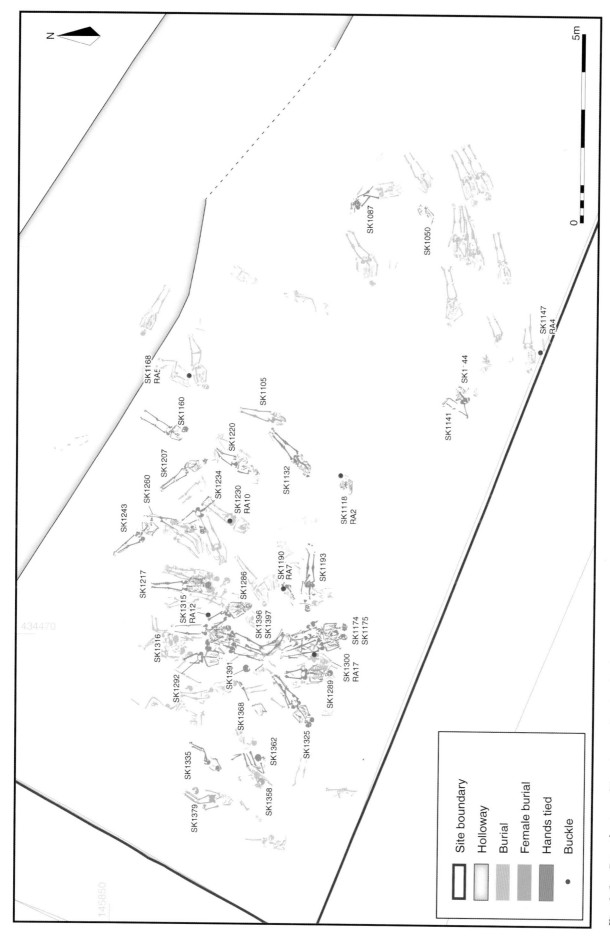

Fig. 3.5   Distribution of females, and individuals with hands tied or with buckles

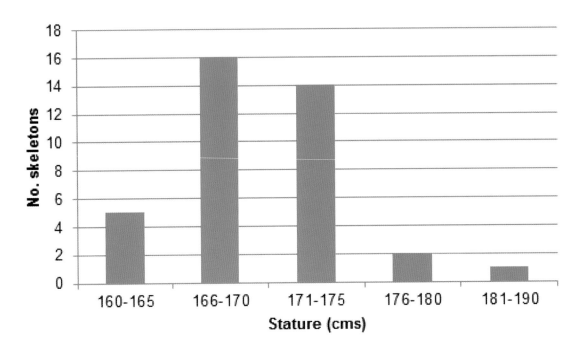

Fig. 3.6   Stature distribution of the males

Hill, and Old Dairy Cottage in Hampshire; Staines, Middlesex; Sutton Hoo, Suffolk; Ashtead, and Eashing in Surrey; Bokerley Dyke, and Roche Court Down in Wiltshire; and Guildown, Surrey (where re-examination has identified two, Mattison 2016) (Reynolds 2009a).

Metrics

Stature estimation was calculated for 38 males with complete left femora. The range was 161.13–181.12cm, with a mean of 170.77cm (Fig. 3.6). Only one female burial had a complete left femur, measuring 159.8cm.

The majority of individuals fell within a 166–175cm range. This gives the impression of a broadly similar group of people, perhaps inferring a similar genetic background and diet.

The stature achieved by the males is comparable, by mean and range, with those from other contemporary sites. As a group these do not appear to differ from other contemporary populations, either in terms of their genetic potential or the influence of health and diet on their final height. It is interesting, however, to note that the 'Viking' sites of Weymouth and St John's College both have greater mean heights and greater height within the overall range (Table 3.5). These sites concern individuals from northern Europe and Scandinavia.

Other limbs (considered less accurate) were used to estimate height in cases where the left femur was not available. These results are presented in Table 3.6. They are also within the range of heights for the period.

Table 3.5   Stature site comparison between Weyhill Road and broadly contemporary sites (cm)

Site	Sex	Mean	Range	Number of individuals	Reference
Mean for the period	Male	172	170–182		Roberts and Cox 2003
Weyhill Road, Andover 9th–14th century	Male	170.7	161.1–181.1	38	This report
Llandough mid-7th–10th/11th century	Male	169.57	156.71–186.66	151	Loe and Robson-Brown 2005
	Female	156.8	144.8–169.12		
Ridgeway Hill, Weymouth 10th to 11th-century execution site	Male	172.1	162.6–184.0	22	Loe *et al.* 2014
St John's College, Oxford AD 1002 massacre	Male	175.9	167.8–184.1	22	Falys 2014

Table 3.6 Stature calculated using long bone length where no left femur available (cm)

	Right femur	Left tibia	Radius (left & right)	Humerus (left & right)
Mean	169.12	179.45	174.644	174.57
Range	161.37–180.886	179.45	168.485–180.234	173.759–175.782
Number of individuals	10	1	4	4

Table 3.7 Post-cranial indices

Index	Mean		Range		No. of individuals	
	Left	*Right*	*Left*	*Right*	*Left*	*Right*
Platymeric	79.18	79.01	62.16–100	65.71–93.55	43	41
Platycnemic	74.76	74.16	64.71–89.29	60.53–89.29	33	37
Claviculo-humeral	45.4	43.5	40.3–51.2	38.2–46.3	9	8
Radio-humeral	75	74	71.21–78.43	70.91–79.06	15	17

Indices

Platymeric (flatness of the femur), and platycnemic (flatness of the tibia), indices are indicators of the shape of the femoral and tibial shaft. These shapes have been observed to change over time, and maybe caused by mechanical stress, habitual positions such as squatting or dietary deficiencies (Brothwell 1981).

Platymeric, flattened from front to back, was the average shape of the upper femur (Table 3.7). There were eight eurymeric (moderate shape) femori on the left side only. The assemblage from Ridgeway Hill had six (19%) individuals who were eurymeric, which is a very similar quantity.

There were two individuals with platymeric indices of 100 (stenomeria – in SKs1371 and 1074). Stenomeria (very rounded) is usually only found in pathological cases, and this appears to be the case in these instances. In SK1074, the left femur had a possible healed greenstick fracture, and periostitis on the tibiae. SK1371 did not have any apparent pathology to the lower limb, but soft-tissue pathology may not leave any indicators on the bone.

The tibia platycnemic index was on average eurycnemic (broad, wide). Seven left and nine right individuals were mesocnemic (moderately flat), with three right platycnemic (very flat). These results are comparable to other contemporary, and male only, assemblages.

Humeral indices

The brachial (radio-humeral) index expresses the relative length of the forearm to the upper arm, and the claviculo-humeral index is a useful indicator of the relative development of the thorax.

SK1286 had long clavicles at 158mm, which has a claviculo-humeral index of 51. This result stands out from the other individuals. There were two more with long clavicles, 159mm and 160mm, but the index was in proportion to the humerus. SK1057 had clavicle lengths of 158mm and 164mm, but these were unfused, so not included and they could also be part of a pathological condition. The average for the assemblage was 45 left and 43 right, with a range of 40–51 for left, and 38–45 for right (seven and nine individuals).

The claviculo-humeral indices are comparable to the Ridgeway Hill (mean 43.4) and Towton (mean 42.94) burial populations, which are other male-only assemblages from an active background.

The brachial index ranges were 71–78 for left and 70–79 for right, with averages of 74 left and 74 right (14 individuals).

Cranial metrics

Measurements could only be taken from seven crania. They were limited in number, because the majority of skulls were highly fragmented. Reconstruction, although possible, may have affected the measurements. Metrical data can be used in the assessment of ancestry, but the only skull complete enough (SK1297), lacked the complete set of landmarks needed to perform the analysis using CRANID6 database (Wright 2012).

Five crania were sufficiently well-preserved for the indices to be calculated (Table 3.8). Of these, three were mesocranic (average or medium) and two were

Table 3.8 Cranial indices calculated

Skeleton	Cranial indices	Ranges (after Bass 1995)
SK1251	75.6	Mesocranic 75–79.99
SK1250	74.4	Dolichocranic <75.0
SK1289	74.7	Dolichocranic <75.0
SK1325	77.1	Mesocranic 75–79.99
SK1335	78.1	Mesocranic 75–79.99

dolichocranic (narrow or long-headed). On SK1250, the sagittal suture was completely obliterated, while the other sutures were only closed, so this is possibly a case of premature fusion. It is therefore not surprising that this cranium was dolichocranic, i.e. long and narrow. The cranial height was also calculated for this skull, and it was 67.7 (chamaecranic, low skull), in contrast to the only other skull for which this was possible: SK1335, with a cranial height of 78.1 (hypsicranic, high skull).

In a period-wide study of UK assemblages (Jones 2014), it was found that the Anglo-Saxon period was most similar to the Iron Age in terms of craniometric features; both had narrow cranial vaults and short orbits, whereas in the medieval and post-medieval periods, the cranial vault became broader and the orbits lengthened. The mixed head-shapes between long and average from Weyhill Road fits with the time-period spanning the Late Saxon to early medieval periods.

There were no notable observations to suggest any individuals possessed facial or cranial features which were markedly dissimilar to the rest of the burial population.

Non-metrics

Post-cranial traits
The observable discrete traits on the post-cranial skeleton were scored as present/absent, and were noted as to whether the site was observable or not. The post-cranial traits are thought to be more influenced by activity and environment than the cranial (Mays 1998, 110). The mechanical factors acting on the lower limbs have been studied to observe the extent of influence over these traits. The third trochanter, for instance, maybe reflects the mechanical stress exerted by the *gluteus maximus*,

which will provide greater efficiency of contracture. The degree of genetic influence for these traits is unknown.

Table 3.9 details the non-metric traits which were represented by at least one example in the assemblage. Other sites were observed, but there were no instances of these traits. The most commonly observed trait was the calcaneal double facet on the right side, at 42% (36% on the left side). The second most commonly observed was the squatting facet on the lateral side of the distal tibia. Over 31% on the left side (24% on right side) of the observable assemblage displayed this facet. As the name suggests, this trait is associated with long periods of time, from a young age, spent in the squatting position. The habitual extreme dorsiflexion of the ankle joints leads to a formation of an anterior extension of the joint-surface on the lower end of tibia. This has been commonly found in the bones of groups who habitually squat, e.g. indigenous Australians. It was also observed in 70–80% of individuals at Wharram Percy (Mays 1998). There has been a suggestion that the trait may be hereditary, or that it may not be caused by activity (Brothwell 1981).

The presence of the sternal aperture, or foramen, of four out of 25 (16%) observable sternum is quite a high proportion. Only one out of 10 was found at Ridgeway Hill, and in a study of 1000 CT scans, only 4.5% had a sternal aperture (Yekeler *et al*. 2006). There is no evidence for an inclination for heritability with this trait, yet such a high number does suggest some degree of inter-relatedness.

Cranial non-metric traits
Cranial non-metric traits were considered to be under genetic influence, and have been used to study history and divergence of human populations (Berry and Berry

Table 3.9 Observed post-cranial non-metric traits

Post-cranial trait	Number observed/number observable (N/n) %			
	Left		*Right*	
Atlas facet double	4/33	12.12%	2/33	6.06%
Accessory transverse foramen	1/23	4.34%	1/23	4.34%
Femur third trochanter	3/47	6.38%	3/46	6.52%
Femur plaque	2/46	4.34%	5/46	10.86%
Femur exostosis in trochanteric fossa	2/47	4.25%	2/47	4.25%
Tibia squatting facet lateral	10/32	31.25%	9/37	24.32%
Humeral septal aperture	2/39	5.12%	2/45	4.44%
Patella notch	3/34	8.82%	4/33	12.12%
Calcaneal double facet	13/36	36.11%	15/36	41.66%
Calcaneal facet absent	2/36	5.55%	2/36	5.55%
Sternal aperture or foramen			4/25	16%
Other		Left clavicle foramen superior body		

1967). A study by Carson (2006) found no cranial traits which were statistically significant when examined against known pedigree. This is in contrast to previous work (Sjøvold 1984), which published the level of heritability for 20 common traits. As such, the use of cranial non-metric traits to examine possible familial relationships needs to be used with great caution. They should now be seen as an alternative to genetic markers when detecting outliers in groups and/or large familial groupings (Ricaut *et al.* 2010). Environment and activity are thought to have a higher influence than previously acknowledged.

The majority of crania were fragmented, which made observation of the traits more challenging. In addition, the calvarium was often preserved but the inferior areas were heavily fragmented.

Table 3.10 shows the cranial traits which displayed at least one expression amongst the assemblage. Further traits were observed for, but none were present.

Metopism, the retention of the metopic suture, which normally fuses in early life, was observed in four instances. This is the most commonly observed feature amongst the assemblage after the lambdoid ossicle. Lambdoid ossicles are frequently the most observed non-metrical trait, and as such have no particular significance.

On SK1174 and SK1250, the sagittal suture was completely obliterated. For SK1174, this is in contrast to the age of the individual, which was in the range of 22–27 years. Cranial sutures are thought to gradually fuse over time, so that by old age many are completely obliterated. Where one suture fuses completely before all the others, it is called premature fusion. When this occurs in childhood, it can affect the shape of the skull. In this instance, for SK1174, the cranial shape was not affected, but for SK1250 it was (see 'Cranial metrics', above). Cranial suture fusion-timing is extremely variable however; some sutures may never fuse, while others begin very early. As this may be an inherited trait,

it is discussed in this section on non-metric traits.

The low level of non-metric traits, and the narrow range of those observed, may suggest an un-diverse group. No traits were observed which would suggest someone from neither a different background nor any of the rarer traits (to be found in British populations).

Pathology

Congenital or developmental defects

Sacral defects

There were 15 individuals with sacral or lower spine congenital defects (Table 3.11). These conditions were all minor variations, which were unlikely to be have been known of by the individual. However, they may have been more prone to lower back problems and, as observed, more susceptible to joint disease.

Sacralisation of the fifth lumbar vertebra was observed in one individual. This condition occurs when the fifth lumbar vertebra is assimilated into the sacrum. It is a fairly common condition in approximately 17% of the modern population (Uçar *et al.* 2013). Lumbarisation of the first sacral segment was present in three individuals. This is less common, and occurs in approximately 2% of the modern population (Uçar *et al.* 2013). Both these conditions are likely to increase the incidence of joint disease in the spine.

Bifid first sacral vertebra was the most commonly observed defect (six individuals). A further two individuals were bifid along the entire sacrum (spina bifida occulta).

The exact cause of spina bifida is unclear. It is not known what disrupts complete closure of the neural tube, causing a malformation to develop. It is suspected that the cause is multifactorial, and that genetic, nutritional and environmental factors all play a role. Research studies indicate that an insufficient intake of folic acid in the mother's diet is a key factor in causing

Table 3.10 Observed cranial non-metric traits

Cranial trait	Number observed/number observable (N/n)			TPR %
	Left	**Right**	**Central**	
Metopism			4/39	10.2%
Coronal ossicle	1/20	1/20		5 and 5%
Lambdoid ossicle	28 ossicles seen on 13 individuals from 34 observable	30 ossicles seen on 13 individuals from 33 observable		38 and 39%
Ossicle at bregma			1/9	11%
Ossicle at lambda			2/20	10%
Parietal notch	1/4	2/4		25 and 50%
Other	SK1174 and SK1250 fused/obliterated sagittal suture			

Table 3.11 Congenital defects

Skeleton number	Area affected	Description
1056	Bifid sacrum from S1–S5	Double burial with SK1057. Spina bifida occulta.
1057	CV2–3 fused – Klippel-Feil syndrome	Block vertebra of upper cervical caused by segmentation failure. Type 2 Klippel-Feil syndrome. Other observations: clavicles very long, 158 and 164mm, still yet unfused at midline, therefore wide shoulders. Femur lengths 10mm difference.
1144	S1 inferior facets not fused to S2	Separation of S1–2 at facets, like lumbarisation. However, could be age-related as young individual, not yet fully fused.
1162	Six lumbar vertebrae	Lowest lumbar pedicle has additional bone extending to sacrum creating an articulation on the superior ilia. Stabilisation due to medio-lateral mild wedging on lowest lumbar.
1168	Bifid S1–2	
1174	S1 lumbarisation	S1 posterior arches not quite joined correctly and articulation with S2 is defined, partial lumbarisation.
1190	Bifid S1	Present but do not join.
1193	Lumbarisation of S1 and CV1 developmental defect	Full separation at body, left wing growth greater than right.
		Atlas transverse process left wider than right, accessory foramen on right side. Left side posterior arch ends with ?articulation.
	Rib segmental defect	Left rib, two head ends merged into one shaft.
1230	Possible sacralisation	S1 appears like an LV sacralised, but five lumbars present, so could be 6th.
1260	Bifid S1–5	Post-mortem damage prevents full observation. Spina bifida occulta.
1294	Bifid S1–2	
1300	Slight bifid S1	
1316	Bifid S1	Arches not quite fully fused.
1387	S1 incomplete lumbarisation	Posterior separation at inferior facets and arch. Anterior slight separations at body, but alae are fully fused.
1397	S1 bifid	

spina bifida and other neural tube defects, as well as resulting in an increased risk in first-degree relatives (Green 2002).

Notable individuals with developmental defects were SK1193 and SK1057.

SK1057 had congenital fusion of two cervical vertebrae (Fig. 3.7) a condition known as Klippel-Feil syndrome (KFS). Type 2 is classified as fusion of CV2–3. The rate of incidence for the condition is estimated as one in 42,000–50,000 live births, with females more commonly affected, and Type 2 the most common type (Driscoll *et al.* 2003). The condition can result in a short neck, low posterior hair line, with a limited range of motion and it may also affect the spinal cord and brain stem. It can also be mild, and may go unnoticed until later life, when symptoms develop or become worse. There is an extensive list of other possible abnormalities related to the condition (such as hearing impairment), but as these mostly relate to soft tissues, it would not be possible to state whether this individual was affected or not. KFS can be inherited.

Fig. 3.7   SK1057 Fusion of the second and third cervical vertebrae, known as Klippel-Feil syndrome

Fusion can also be caused by trauma or joint disease and so the diagnosis in this instance should be considered within this context.

In SK1193 (Fig. 3.8), the left ribs had separate head ends, but merged into one large shaft, resulting in fusion (synostosis). It could cause restrictive chest expansion. Rib fusion is also a symptom of KFS, but not diagnostic of it, and is also a feature of other syndromes. This individual also had lumbarisation of first sacral body, with the left alae greater than the right, and there was full separation at body. The first cervical vertebra (atlas) posterior arch on the left ended with what looked like an articulation, so was bifid. Cervical vertebra six had an accessory foramen through the transverse process, and on the left side of the seventh cervical vertebra there was a possible facet for a cervical rib.

The combination of these spinal defects suggests considerable developmental border shifting and segmentation failure while this individual was developing *in utero*. It is not known how the defects would have impacted on the individual in life, if at all.

Infection

There were four individuals with infection: two had periostitis, mild infection of the surface of the bone, and one had sinusitis, infection of the nasal sinus (plus another possible case, but not confirmed). One individual suffered from osteomyelitis, or bone infection (Table 3.12).

The periostitis was located in a common site on the tibial shaft (Roberts and Manchester 1995, 130). There is no evidence on either skeleton that this is indicative of a more systemic disease. It is notable that there were few individuals with periostitis (1.61% (2/124) CPR, 3.33% (2/60) TPR), and increase in age is clearly not a factor, as both individuals were in their 20s.

Sinusitis presents as thin, web-like bone growth

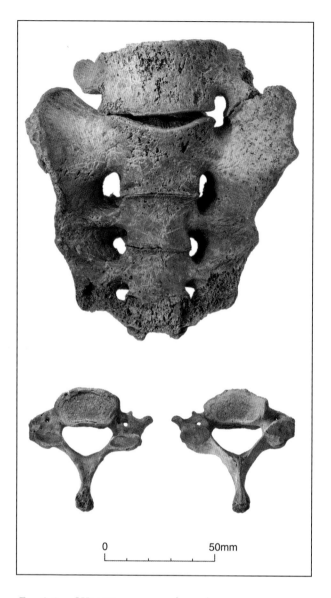

Fig. 3.8   SK1193 sacrum and vertebrae

Table 3.12 Skeletal elements affected by infection

Bone affected by:	Skeleton number	Comments
Periostitis		
Bilateral tibia and fibula	1074	Bilateral tibia mid-shaft new bone formation. Also left fibula active and healed periostitis distal shaft at interosseous margin.
Right tibia	1391	Right tibia mid-shaft striations and slightly swollen appearance of lamellar bone. Healed.
Sinusitis		
Right maxilla	1097	Isolated patch of web-like new bone growth in superior sinus level of M2.
Left maxilla	1286	Raised striations in sinus cavity, not web-like. Right side not observable. So not confirmed sinusitis.
Osteomyelitis		
Left femur	1362	Secondary to possible fracture mid-shaft femur.

on the nasal-cavity floor. It is the result of chronic inflammation of the paranasal sinuses, and an indicator of poor air quality (Roberts 2007). Despite the relative accessibility of the maxillary nasal sinuses, due to high fragmentation of the crania, only one case of sinusitis was identified. It is thought that open fires in small spaces would be the main cause of smoke inhalation resulting in sinusitis. Females sometimes have higher rates, due to historically gendered divisions of labour, resulting in women spending more time indoors. The predominance of younger individuals in the assemblage, and almost exclusively of male gender, has probably contributed to the low level observed.

SK1362 (male 18–25 years) displayed the only evidence of osteomyelitis, or bone infection. This skeleton exhibited extensive osteomyelitis of the left femur (Fig. 3.9), with necrosis (bone death, due to lack of blood supply) of both femoral heads, and subsequent osteopenic (loss of bone density) tibia and fibula. This individual would have been disabled by extensive bone loss to the femoral heads and prolonged infection (and assumed chronic pain). He was laid in the grave on the

Fig. 3.9   SK1362 Left femur osteomyelitis with necrosis of femoral head, right femur head necrosis and shaft with osteopenia

right side, bent over, and with the skull placed on the chest area and perimortem cut-marks evident on cervical vertebrae (see below) resulting from decapitation. The grave was truncated at the mid-section, so left and right pelves were absent, hence it was not possible to observe the effect on the acetabulum.

The left femur had a massive bony growth on the posterior shaft, extending by 21mm. This was a bony response to injury, and there was a slight angulation to the femur, suggesting a fracture, although this was not confirmed by radiography. Direct trauma is thought to be the most likely cause. A possible small sinus was observed, but extensive bony remodelling obscured observation. The distal femoral epiphyses were present, but the infection had not affected the patella or tibia. The femoral head on the left, and more extensively the right, was destroyed, particularly in the posterior neck area. Necrosis resulted in thin, web-like projections supporting the femoral head surface on the right side, with posterior areas almost completely destroyed. The anterior neck was not affected, and the head was flattened. The shaft of the right femur was thin, with much cortical bone loss. Both tibia and fibula were very thin, and with great loss of cortical bone. This would have been caused by lack of use of the lower limbs, not bearing weight and possibly by reduced blood supply. The destruction of the femoral heads suggests that blood supply may have been cut off or severely reduced (osteonecrosis or avascular necrosis). It would take from several months to years for the bone to have been reduced to this extent. In modern circumstances, this condition occurs more often in men than women, and more commonly in those aged over 40 years.

The extensive bone loss and osteomyelitis would have prevented the individual from weight-bearing on his lower limbs, so walking was impossible, and he was therefore physically disabled. It is notable that a clearly disabled individual was executed by decapitation.

Attitudes towards the physically disabled have been interpreted from Anglo-Saxon and medieval texts. Judicial mutilation was common practice, and the physical effect for those who received such punishments was generally lifelong suffering. Mutilation served as a permanent reminder of criminal status. This had an effect on wider society, whereby the disabled body effectively became associated with the criminal body (Metzler 2013). The notion that physical deformities were outward representations of inner sin was prevalent in church teachings. Disability was regarded as closer to the monstrous and the un-human. Such punishments reinforced this idea to the extent that disabled individuals would often go to great lengths to prove that they were not criminals, but that their injury had resulted from an accident. A person was more likely to be accused of crime if they were already disabled.

Skeleton SK1362 is therefore an example of 10th to 11th-century attitudes towards the disabled, as in his condition he was unlikely to have committed the crimes which, in a physically active person, would be likely to result in execution.

Joint disease

Joint degeneration and osteoarthritis is the most commonly observed and recorded pathology in this assemblage. This is also the case for many archaeological assemblages, and in modern populations.

Non-spinal joints

Fourteen individuals were affected with joint degeneration and/or osteoarthritis. Of these, six individuals had osteoarthritis of at least one joint (osteoarthritis is defined by presence of eburnation, and/or at least two of osteophytosis, porosity, and contour change, after Rogers and Waldron 1995). The number of individuals and the true prevalence rate per joint affected by osteoarthritis is presented in Table 3.13.

Table 3.13 Osteoarthritis by joint

Joint	Number of individuals	Left (n/N %)	Right (n/N %)
Shoulder	0	0/25	0/31
Wrist	1	0/33	1/34 2.94%
Hand	1	0/35	1/37 2.7%
Hip	1	0/46	1/48 2.08%
Knee	1	0/32	1/31 3.22%
Ankle	0	1/36 2.77%	1/32 3.12%
Rib	1	5/583 0.85%	5/593 0.84%
Elbow	1	0/34	1/38 2.6%

The cause of osteoarthritis (OA) is not known, but influencing factors are: age, genetics, sex, race, obesity, trauma and movement. Incidence and prevalence increase with age, and genetic predisposition is a large factor. From modern studies, obesity is highly correlated with knee OA. The most involved joints in modern populations are the knee, hip and hand (Waldron 2009). From the assemblage at Weyhill Road, there was only one incidence per joint. This is a reflection of the relative youthfulness of the assemblage, as incidence of osteoarthritis increases with age (Waldron 2009).

SK1101 had osteoarthritis in both ankles and the right wrist. The right wrist presented with erosive lesions to the capitate, scaphoid, lunate and second metacarpal proximal joint-surfaces. The lesions were small, smooth and around the joint-surface. The ankle joints (bilateral tali), had osteophytic bone growth extending superiorly, from the navicular joint-surface, and the navicular (ankle bone) had growth on the same joint-surface. The left first proximal pedal phalanx (big toe) proximal articular surface had osteophytic

growth around the joint-surface extending 3mm, and the right first metatarsal distal joint-surface had growth extending 5mm. Although these bone changes are not strictly defined as osteoarthritis, the bilateral nature and joints involved are suggestive of rheumatoid arthritis or some other osteoarthropathy. However, as the changes had not developed further, (the individual was only 30–39 years), it is not possible to precisely determine the causative factor.

Osteoarthritis as a result of trauma (included in Table 3.13) was identified on SK1118, which had healed fracture of the right distal radius. The osteoarthritis (eburnation) was to the right elbow (radial head) and right wrist (distal ulna). Further degenerative joint disease was seen on the bilateral rib facets, and one right rib had a healed fracture.

Osteophytes were observed lipping the joints of eight individuals (Table 3.14). These can be interpreted as degenerative joint disease in the early stages, or adaptation of the joint to stress. Osteophytic growth, as secondary to trauma, was identified on SK1146 and SK1397.

SK1146, a probable male (21–57 years), had fusion of right distal tibia and fibula (Fig. 3.10). The joint-surfaces of the cuneiforms had osteophytic lipping

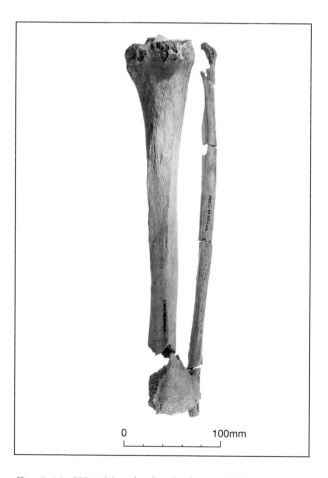

0   100mm

Fig. 3.10 SK1146 right distal tibia and fibula showing fusion

Table 3.14 Osteophytic growth by joint

Joint with osteophytes	Number of individuals	Left n/N	%	Right n/N	%
Hand phalanges	1	1/35 (hands), 532 (phalanges)	2.85, 0.19	0/37 (hands), 561 (phalanges)	0
Ribs	2	2/583	0.34	2/593	0.33
Shoulder	2	1/25	4	1/31	3.23
Clavicle-manubrium	1	1/44	2.27	1/53	1.88
Wrist	2	0/33	0	2/34	5.88
Carpal-metacarpal joint	1	0		1/34	2.94
Ankle/foot	1	0/36		1/32	3.1
Pelvis-sacrum	1	1/79	1.2	1/79	1.2

2–3mm and left navicular. First metatarsals presented with minor lipping. On the right wrist carpals all joint-surfaces were lipped by osteophytic growth.

On SK1397, a male of 25–30 years, left-hand proximal and intermediate phalangeal joints had porosity on joint-surfaces, and they had become irregular, with 1mm osteophytic growth around the joint margin. These changes are suspected to be secondary to trauma, especially given the young age at death of the individual.

Spinal joint degeneration and osteoarthritis

Thirty-seven individuals were affected with Schmorl's nodes (intervertebral disc herniation marks), spondylosis deformans (degeneration of the intervertebral disc - porosity on the vertebral body and/or marginal osteophytosis), or osteophytosis (extra bone growth around the perimeter of the vertebral body). These are all commonly observed conditions in archaeological and modern populations.

Schmorl's nodes

The presence of Schmorl's nodes on the vertebral bodies was recorded by the superior or inferior face. Table 3.15 has the total number of Schmorl's nodes per body (superior and inferior). There were 175 bodies in total, from 35 individuals (CPR 28.2%). This rate is similar to the one estimated for male and female CPR for the early medieval period, at 24.7% (Roberts and Cox 2003, 198).

As expected, most were observed in the lower thoracic area, TV8–TV12. There were a number in the lumbar vertebrae, and none in the cervical. There were 666 thoracic bodies observable, and 309 lumbar, and of these 130 thoracic had at least one Schmorl's node (TPR 19.5%) as did 38 lumbar (TPR 12.29%), with an overall true prevalence rate of 17.2% (thoracic and lumbar). This rate is also similar to that estimated for the early medieval period, 16.6% (Roberts and Cox 2003, 198). The prevalence rates for male-only assemblages, such as Ridgeway Hill at 35.7% TPR (81% CPR) and Towton (at 80% CPR) were significantly higher.

By age-group, the number of Schmorl's nodes appears

Table 3.15 Presence of Schmorl's nodes by vertebra

Vertebra	Total number of Schmorl's nodes (SN)		Number of vertebrae with SN TPR
	Superior	Inferior	
T4	1	1	1/53 – 1.88%
T5	3	4	5/52 – 9.61%
T6	8	11	12/55 – 21.81%
T7	12	16	17/58 – 29.31%
T8	20	17	21/57 – 36.84%
T9	19	15	20/57 – 35.07%
T10	19	19	20/59 – 33.89%
T11	20	18	21/61 – 34.42%
T12	20	16	21/60 – 35.00%
L1	13	8	13/62 – 20.96%
L2	9	4	8/60 – 13.3%
L3	6	3	6/61 – 9.83%
L4	6	2	6/63 – 9.52%
L5	4	0	4/63 – 6.30%
S1	1	0	1/62 – 1.61%

to peak slightly in the young adult and mature group, but with similar levels in the prime and older age categories (Table 3.16). The adolescents had the least. These results are similar to the findings by McNaught (2006), where she found that, contrary to earlier theories, Schmorl's nodes occur in the first two decades of life. Amongst archaeological populations, the rates were very variable, and work patterns are known to alter the levels and types of Schmorl's nodes.

Intervertebral disc disease or spondylosis deformans (SD)

The degeneration of the intervertebral disc is particularly associated with ageing. It is rarely seen in individuals

Table 3.16 Age distribution of Schmorl's nodes

Age-group	Number of individuals affected n/N %		Number of bodies affected n/N %	
Adolescent	3/14	21.42%	11/225	4.88%
Young Adult	11/24	45.83%	62/372	16.66%
Prime Adult	7/22	31%	32/318	10.06%
Mature Adult	6/15	40%	29/170	17.05%
Older Adult	5/11	45.45%	17/158	10.75%

below the age of 40 years, and very common in those over 70 years (Waldron 2009, 43). It is defined as pitting or porosity on the superior and inferior bodies of the vertebra and marginal osteophytes. These two bony changes are discussed separately, and then jointly.

The number of individuals with osteophytosis on at least one vertebral body was 10 (CPR 8.06%). This involved 52 instances (either superior or inferior body), or 35 bodies (Table 3.17).

Table 3.17 True prevalence of osteophytosis on vertebral bodies

Vertebra	Total number of bodies affected by osteophytosis		Number of vertebrae with SD – TPR %
	Superior	Inferior	
T2	1		1/45 – 2.22%
T3	0	0	0
T4	1	2	2/53 – 3.77%
T5	2	1	2/52 – 3.84%
T6	1	1	1/55 – 1.81%
T7	0	2	2/58 – 3.44%
T8	2	1	3/57 – 5.26%
T9	1	0	1/57 – 1.75%
T10	1	1	1/59 – 1.69%
T11	1	1	1/61 – 1.63%
T12	3	3	4/60 – 6.66%
L1	3	2	3/62 – 4.83%
L2	2	2	2/60 – 3.33%
L3	3	2	3/61 – 4.91%
L4	5	2	5/63 – 7.93%
L5	3	2	3/63 – 4.76%
S1	1		1/62 – 1.61%

The most extensive was 6mm, from LV4. This individual (SK1184) had TV11–LV5 involved, with each body having extensive osteophytic growth. The right hip of this individual had suffered some kind of trauma; the extreme osteophytic growth is likely to be a response to destabilising of the joints.

Table 3.18 True prevalence of porosity or pitting on vertebral bodies

Vertebra	Total number of bodies affected by porosity/pitting		Number of vertebrae with porosity/pitting -TPR %
	Superior	Inferior	
T2	1		1/45 – 2.22%
T3	0	0	0
T4	1	2	2/53 – 3.77%
T5	2	1	2/52 – 3.84%
T6	1	1	1/55 – 1.81%
T7	0	2	2/58 – 3.44%
T8	2	1	3/57 – 3.26%
T9	1	0	1/57 – 1.75%
T10	1	1	1/59 – 1.69%
T11	1	1	1/61 – 1.63%
T12	3	3	4/60 – 6.66%
L1	3	2	3/62 – 4.83%
L2	2	2	2/60 – 3.33%
L3	3	2	3/61 – 4.91%
L4	5	2	5/63 – 7.93%
L5	3	2	3/63 – 4.76%
S1	1		1/62 – 1.61%

Porosity on vertebral bodies affected nine individuals, with 27 inferior or superior bodies. This mostly affected the twelfth thoracic vertebrae (Table 3.18).

Four individuals had both porosity and osteophytosis (SKs1168, 1162, 1105 and 1260), which are the characteristics of intervertebral disc disease. These were all mature or older adults, confirming a general trend for the presence of porosity increasing with age (Rogers and Waldron 1995, 25). It is interesting to note that none of the cervical spine displayed either osteophytes or pitting. It is commonly found that the mid to lower cervical vertebrae are affected (Rogers and Waldron 1995, 27).

Facets

Six individuals had, between them, a limited number of spinal facets affected by porosity, osteophytosis or eburnation. These were distributed between the cervical, thoracic and lumbar vertebrae, with no particular pattern. There were 17 vertebrae facets affected (either superior or inferior or both), of the 1,122 vertebrae facets available for observation, or 1.51% (TPR).

There were only two instances of eburnation on one facet, involving one cervical vertebra and one lumbar vertebra. The remainder were osteophytosis, porosity or, occasionally, both.

Only three of the six had vertebral bodies affected as well (SKs1105, 1193 and 1112), and these displayed Schmorl's nodes and porosity.

It is interesting to note that SK1105, one of only two females with a post-cranial skeleton, was amongst the individuals with both body and facet spinal degeneration and osteoarthritis.

Metabolic

Cribra orbitalia

Pitting or porosity in the orbits was observed for six individuals; this involved five left orbits and six right (CPR 6/124 4.8%, TPR left 5/48 10.4%, right 6/49 12.2%). The crude prevalence rates were less than the 7.6% CPR of the combined data in Roberts and Cox (2003, table 4.11) for the time-period. They ranged from grades 1–4 (Stuart-Macadam 1991). It was once considered that cribra orbitalia was caused by iron-deficiency anaemia, but research suggests that it is a general indicator of metabolic distress (Walker *et al.* 2009), and used as a non-specific indicator of health stress in childhood. If nutritional deficiency was the cause of the cribra orbitalia, this could be caused by multiple conditions such as scurvy (vitamin C deficiency), rickets (vitamin D deficiency), anaemia (iron deficiency), vitamin B12 deficiency, folic acid deficiency, and these are often found to be co-occurring. The low prevalence of cribra orbitalia amongst the assemblage suggests that metabolic stress was not high in the population. Similar levels were observed at Ridgeway Hill, where this group were thought to be executed warrior Vikings.

Cribra femora

Porosity on the neck of the femur was observed for two male individuals, involving two left femurs and one right. Cribra femora is hypothesised to be due to magnesium deficiency (Miquel-Feucht *et al.* 1999), but more work is needed to determine whether it is part of the normal development process. It is predominantly seen in non-adults, as it is thought to develop during this period. It is therefore not surprising to observe this on SK1297, aged 22–34 years, and SK1396, aged 15–20 years.

Rickets (vitamin D deficiency)

A case of possible residual rickets was identified on SK1344. The 30–34-year-old male had slight anterior-posterior bowing to the mid-shaft of the left tibia (right not present). This bowing may have been caused by a period of rickets as a child. However, the plasticity of bone means that repetitive motion resulting in excessive muscle use can change the contour and shape of bone, so this possibility cannot be ruled out.

Entheseal Changes (EC) formerly called Musculo-skeletal Stress Markers (MSM)

In order to reconstruct behavioural patterns, such as occupations or activities, it was thought that EC could be used. However, recent research suggests that this is no longer tenable (Michopoulou *et al.* 2017). EC are thought to provide information on the ways in which a skeleton develops over a life-course (Milella *et al.* 2012). Given the young age demographic of the assemblage, and the fact that EC changes are considered to increase with age, then a low quantity observed would be expected. They were not scored (after Mariotti *et al.* 2007), where bones were not fully fused.

Despite the known correlation between age and increases in robusticity at attachment sites, two adolescent-aged individuals had grade 3 (after Mariotti *et al.* 2007) scores (SKs1046 and 1271). These were for the clavicle costoclavicular ligament and humerus pectoralis major. These attachment sites are involved in the motion of the arms, and stabilising the shoulder. The upper body muscle insertion-points featured largely in the scoring with the Achilles tendon site on the calcaneus the greatest for the lower limb.

There was no obvious pattern relating to side, limb or age, but a general impression of physically active individuals.

Trauma

Blunt-force trauma

Blunt-force trauma injury was identified on SK1371, a male of 30–34 years, comprising a depressed cranial fracture on the posterior parietal, adjacent and left of the sagittal suture at the level of the foramen (Fig. 3.11). The ectocranial surface had a sub-circular indentation 7mm deep, and measuring 24mm by 18mm in width, with rounded edges and smooth-walls. Endocranially, there was raised protrusion at the location, suggesting that it penetrated the inner table of the cranium, but there was no evidence of infection and the trauma had completely healed.

The location on the cranium could be from an accidental cause, or result from interpersonal violence. As the only example from a mostly male assemblage, this suggests a low level of violence amongst the population, and further supports the evidence that these are not individuals from a battle or other violence-related activity.

Osteochondritis dissecans (OD)

This is a condition of the joints which affects young individuals, especially in the first decade of life (Roberts and Manchester 2005, 121). The death of bone tissue (necrosis), from a lack of blood supply, results in a small defect on the joint-surface (Table 3.19).

A total of five individuals expressed OD, or a similar type of lesion on a concave joint-surface, sometimes called 'pseudo osteochondritis dissecans'.

The distal right femur (unfused epiphysis) of SK1086, on the medial condyle anterior surface, had a small area (18mm by 12mm) of osteochondritis dissecans. The knee is the most common site (80% of cases) (*ibid.*), and usually has an underlying traumatic aetiology.

SK1357 had a cortical defect placed centrally on the

Fig. 3.11 SK1371 skull showing blunt-force trauma injury

Table 3.19 Skeletons with osteochondritis dissecans

Skeleton number	Location of osteochondritis dissecans
SK1086	Right distal femur articular surface, medial condyle.
SK1352	Right talus convex surface for calcaneus small, 3mm, area of necrosis.
SK1356	Right calcaneal medial posterior articular surface, 2mm, area of necrosis (same as SK1357).
SK1357	Right calcaneal medial posterior articular surface and left first metatarsal proximal joint-surface.
SK1374	MT1 proximal phalanx joint-surface, not true OD, but small cortical defect (same as SK1357).

right calcaneal medial posterior articular surface. In addition, another cortical defect was observed on the left first metatarsal proximal phalanx concave surface. Although OD technically affects convex surfaces only, the first phalanx defect is commonly seen in archaeological material, and is considered to reflect an impingement of the blood supply to the big toe. This, in addition to the calcaneal defect, suggests excessive use of the foot.

Compared with other predominantly male skeletal assemblages, the rate of OD from Weyhill Road is very low at CPR 4% of individuals (CPR 0.8% for femur, TPR 1.61%, ankle 2.41% CPR, TPR 9.3% (3/32)). Ridgeway Hill had an overall CPR of 20%, with 2.8% and 3% for the TPR of the femur. It was also seen more commonly in the elbow than the knee. This assemblage is more comparable with a modern Royal Navy assemblage, and the high rates, especially relating to the upper body reflect a probable identification of the individuals as Vikings. A CPR of 1.5% for British

sites (Roberts and Cox 2003, 209–10), and at Wharram Percy (a deserted village site, dating from the Anglo-Saxon to the post-medieval periods) of 1.42%, are both much closer to the rates for Weyhill Road. This suggests a population with activity levels similar to that of a normal attritional cemetery.

Myositis ossificans, or heterotopic ossification
Myositis ossificans, or heterotopic ossification, is the physical dynamic of a deep bruise or haematoma calcifying and turning into bone. Calcified haematomas (or ossified haematoma) mostly occur when an individual sustains deep bruising and bleeding from a forceful blunt trauma to the muscle, or the periosteum of the bone.

These were observed on SK1286, a male of 25–35 years, and SK1357, a possible male (from metrical assessment). SK1362 had an excessive ossified haematoma on the left femur, and has already been discussed in relation to osteomyelitis and fracture.

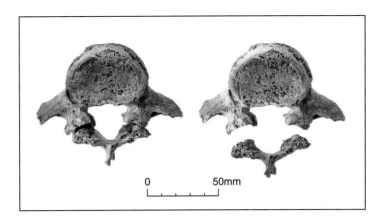

Fig. 3.12 SK1174 vertebrae showing spondylolysis

On SK1286, the right femur had ossification on the upper shaft lateral anterior. Smooth linear bone protruded from the surface, by 7mm, and was 43mm by 17mm in extent.

On SK1357, on the right tibia, the medial mid-shaft anterior side had smooth, raised bone protruding 3mm from the shaft surface, and measured 18mm by 5mm in extent. It was completely smooth and rounded, with discrete new bone growth. This individual had two cortical defects (see above), and excessive enthesophyte growth at the Achilles tendon attachment site, on the right calcaneus. In all, the right leg and foot appeared to have suffered considerable strain and trauma.

Spondylolysis

Spondylolysis is the result of a fatigue fracture resulting from biomechanical stress, when there has been hyperextension and torsion in the lower back (Merbs 1996). The result is a complete bilateral separation at the pars interarticularis, usually on the fifth lumbar vertebra. Between 2.3% and 10% of modern populations have spondylolysis. It is more common in males than females, and usually asymptomatic. This was observed for five individuals: SKs1101, 1174 (Fig. 3.12), 1294, 1316 and 1379 (female).

Of the fifth lumbar vertebrae available for observation, (63) 7.9% (TPR) had the separation (CPR 4%). It was not always across the arches at the pars interarticularis, but sometimes the separation occurred at mid-arch.

The crude prevalence rate overall for the period was 2.9% (Roberts and Cox 2003, 209), with a range from 0.6–10% (CPR), and 3.33% TPR for Ridgeway Hill (one instance); this suggests that there was a higher incidence of the condition at Weyhill Road. This population possibly had an underlying congenital weakness, or were partaking in activities which were more likely to cause this condition. In modern clinical settings, this condition is commonly seen amongst young men who participate in high-impact sports or physically demanding occupations (Jurmain 1999). This description appears to fit the profile of the individuals from Weyhill Road, and may contribute to the explanation for a fairly high incidence.

Os acromiale

Os acromiale is a condition where the acromial process fails to fuse to the spine of the scapula, which should otherwise occur between 18 and 20(5) years. However, since the assemblage comprised so many young adults, this has reduced the quantity for observation. Therefore, only one scapula could be confirmed as having this condition.

In SK1297 (22–34 years; likely 25–30 years), the left scapula was unfused at the acromial process. This individual was aged over 22 years, and should have had the joint fused, so the unfused part is a true identification.

Os acromiale was thought to have been caused by the long-term use from an early age of the long bow, as it was found frequently (13.6%) on the 'bowmen' from the Mary Rose (Stirland 1996). This link has now been reconsidered, and more recent work suggests a genetic causation (Hunt and Bullen 2007).

Fracture

Partial or complete break of the bone is the result of a traumatic event (Roberts and Manchester 2005). This may occur at the time of death (perimortem), before death (ante-mortem), and after death (post-mortem).

Presented in Table 3.20 are the observed healed fractures, which would have occurred at least six weeks before death. Generally, remodelling of the bone occurs over many years, and if the bone is not re-aligned correctly it will heal with some angulation. Age and sex impact on the quantity, type and location of fracture patterns observed across populations, and prevalence rates may imply certain activity levels and practices.

Radial fractures were the most common type of fracture from this assemblage, and distal radial fractures are the most common type of lower-arm fracture, and occur in approximately 16% of all modern clinical fractures (Rockwood *et al.* 2010). They are also amongst the most commonly seen in archaeological populations (Roberts and Manchester 1995, 75). They are caused by falling onto an outstretched hand. Clavicle fractures can be caused in the same way, or from a fall onto the shoulder or a direct blow. They are the most commonly broken bone in the human body, and occur more

Table 3.20 Healed fractures

Bone fractured	Skeleton number	Comment	TPR left	TPR right
Rib	1118, 1074	1074: 6 left ribs, 1118: 1 right, 9th	6/583 1.02%	1/593 0.16%
Radius	1118 (r), 1122 (l), 1193 (l), 1184 (r)		2/52 3.84%	2/58 3.4%
Ulna	1250 (r)	Nightstick	0/54	1/59 1.69%
Acetabulum	1294 (l) 1184 (r)	Un-united?	1/60 1.66%	1/59 1.69%
Clavicle	1174 (r)	Overlap	0/49	1/57 1.75%
Fibula	1146 (r)		0/55	1/57 1.75%
Phalanx	1141	Right distal	0/226	1/247 0.4%
Femur	1074 (l) (greenstick), 1362 (l)	1362: assumed fracture	2/63 3.17%	0/65
Sacrum	1209 (greenstick)	5th sacral & 1st coccyx fused at angle - rest of sacrum unfused	1/23 coccyx 4.34%	
Tibia	1250 (l & r), 1146 (r)		1/58 1.72%	2/57 3.5%
Thoracic vertebra	1074	Wedge	1/666 0.15%	
Cranial	1371	Parietal		

frequently in males and young people and children (Rockwood *et al.* 2010). Whilst it is easy to reduce the fracture, immobilising the joint is difficult while it heals for up to six weeks, so we see an overlap occurred for SK1174, which has shortened the bone. The implication here is that it was not possible to immobilise the arm for a sufficient period following the fracture incident.

A range of fractures from all areas of the body were represented. A study of medieval farming populations (Judd and Roberts 1999) found that, among the males, the most commonly fractured bones were the clavicle and fibula, while for females they were more likely to be the radius and ulna. Agriculture, along with construction and mining, are the top three most dangerous occupations. The multiple activities associated with farming means that non-fatal injuries (e.g. fractures) can occur on any part of the body. The prevalence rates from the Weyhill Road assemblage are low when compared to Raunds (Judd and Roberts 1999). A total of 12 individuals had at least one fracture (all male), comprising 9.6% CPR of total assemblage, whereas at Raunds it was 19.4%. At Raunds, there were nine clavicle fractures for males (23% of total), whereas at Weyhill Road it was one (9%). Conversely, Weyhill Road had higher numbers of radial and tibial fractures (both numbering three, 27% of total long bone

fractures), compared to two (9%) of each amongst the males at Raunds. A very different fracture pattern was found in the Ridgeway Hill assemblage, where nearly all fractures were to the lower limbs and feet. Wharram Percy (Mays *et al.* 2007) had a higher rate for males, at 22.3%, and ribs and vertebrae were the most common bones affected. The tibia is considered a rare bone to fracture amongst archaeological populations (Roberts and Manchester 1995), and yet there were three fractures at Weyhill Road, two of which are bilateral on the same individual (SK1250, Fig. 3.13). This individual also had a fracture to the right ulna, and it could be possible that all these fractures were caused at the same time, indicating a significant trauma event.

Interpersonal violence fractures were mostly absent; there were no fractured nasal bones for example. The blunt-force trauma already discussed on SK1371, with a healed depressed cranial fracture, is the only example that may have been caused by another individual. But equally this could have been caused accidentally.

There were two possible greenstick fractures; on the left femur of SK1074 (aged 19–24 years), and the fusion of the sacrum to the coccyx of SK1209 (aged 14–19 years). Both individuals were young, so the injuries sustained must have occurred whilst they were still growing. In SK1209 the fusion of the fifth sacral segment to the

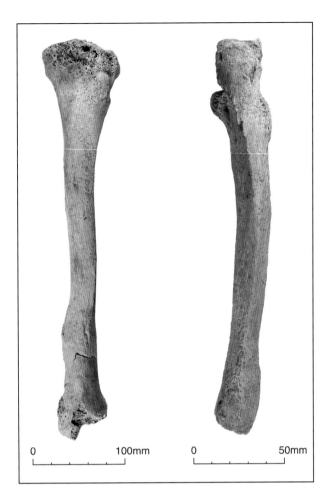

Fig. 3.13 SK1250 showing fractures to right ulna and left tibia

right side of the coccyx (with angulation) is noteworthy as the rest of the sacrum was still unfused due to the young age of the individual. It is likely that a direct impact, such as a fall onto a sharp object, while in the sitting position, could cause such an injury. In an adult, this probably would have caused a fracture to the bone, but the growth plates in the child were still present, and so the injury would have been a greenstick fracture, resulting in the fusion and angulation observed.

In SK1074, the upper shaft of the left femur had anterior-posterior bowing, and the shaft was rounded. The left side was not angulated in the same way, and was flattened anterior-posterior. As there was no callous on the bone, and in view of the young age of the individual, the bowing was not bilateral (indicating healed rickets) so a greenstick fracture is a probable explanation. This individual also had a wedge fracture to the twelfth thoracic vertebra, and the left ribs had an exaggerated angulation to them, different to the right, which may also represent healed greenstick fractures.

Two individuals exhibited trauma and possible fractures in the hip; these had both affected other skeletal elements and represented long-term injuries.

In SK1184, a male of 45+ years, with a right hip trauma, post-mortem damage prevented full observation. The acetabulum had been remodelled extensively, but the extensive fragmentation of the bone did not allow a clear interpretation. This individual was placed prone in the grave, along with a sheep skull. The right radius had a healed fracture, and all the bones were lightweight, indicating possible osteoporosis. The lower spine had extreme osteophytic growth and the auricular surface to the sacrum joint had an extension of bone at the superior aspect to the joint.

In SK1294, a male of 35–45 years, the left hip presented in three parts, due to a pseudo-articulation across the acetabulum and the posterior part of the left ilium (Fig. 3.14). The line was undulating, irregular and porous. The result was a new joint, a clean, articulating surface, with no sign of infection or much new bone growth. The sciatic notch was affected, changing the width, and bone growth extended into this area. The unaffected right hip had osteoarthritis, and the right shoulder had evidence for more joint degeneration than the left, which may indicate that the left was not used as much. In addition, the fifth lumbar vertebra on the right side, the pars interarticularis, was unfused, whereas on the left side it was mid-arch, so the stress fracture was uneven. The reason for the hip being presented in three parts may have been damage while it was still unfused, i.e. as a child, causing disruption to the growth plates, or congenital non-fusion. However, the undulating nature and lack of clean, neat lines would suggest a traumatic origin.

Perimortem sharp-force trauma – evidence for decapitation

A total of nine individuals had bony evidence for sharp-force trauma to the cervical vertebrae (Table 3.21; Fig. 3.15). A further individual had a perimortem cut-mark to the cranium (SK1174) which is considered evidence of hanging and not decapitation. There were other skulls (SKs1144, 1303, 1309/1310 and 1396) placed in the grave next to a body, but there was no evidence for cut-marks on the vertebrae, or the skull was entirely absent, with no room within the grave cut for it to have been articulated. These are assumed to represent decapitations.

Some skulls were found with no associated post-cranial skeleton (SKs1330, 1308, 1398, 1358, 1359 and 1380), and these may represent decapitations (for example SK1365 had cut-marks), but they may also represent remnants of earlier burials. A group of crania, or partial crania (SKs1327, 1328, 1329 and 1328b) were assumed to be from decapitations, and their close proximity suggests that they were possibly buried at the same time.

If all of the above are assumed to represent decapitations, then the total would be 23. This would place Weyhill Road as the assemblage with the largest

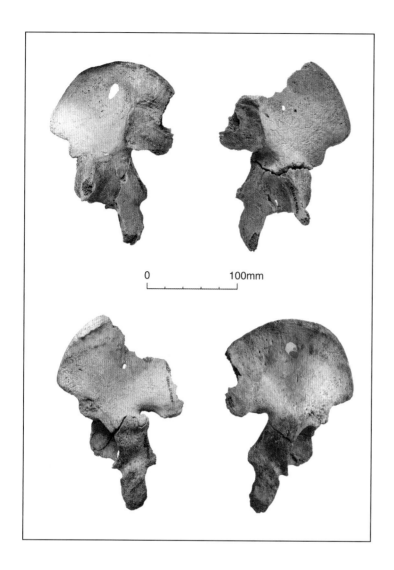

Fig. 3.14 SK1294 Left hip acetabulum with non-union possible fracture or damage to growth plate. Right hip not affected

number of decapitations from amongst all currently-known execution cemeteries. If only the individuals distinguished by cut-marks and cranial positions were counted, then there were as many as at Bran Ditch, Cambridgeshire (excavated in 1923, but with no published osteology report from the time).

Decapitations were largely performed with a heavy sword or axe; there were no 'professional' executioners at this time. Therefore, it is unsurprising to find evidence for perimortem trauma to other areas of the skeleton. In addition to the evidence for decapitation on the cervical vertebrae, there was evidence on four mandibles of a chop or cut-mark (Table 3.21). These comprised two on the right, and two on the left. These individuals also displayed evidence of cut-marks on the cervical vertebrae. Perimortem trauma to the mandible has been observed at other execution cemeteries, including Chesterton Lane Corner, Cambridge; Old Dairy Cottage, Winchester; Staines; Stockbridge Down, Hampshire and Walkington Wold, East Riding of Yorkshire. In such cases, the mandible is likely to have been affected if the blow was not accurately applied to the neck. The cervical vertebrae of SK1349 appear to

indicate that several attempts were made at decapitating the individual, with blows from the right side and the front (anterior) (Fig. 3.16). Mattison (2016), in discussing evidence for victims of judicial execution in the later Anglo-Saxon period, speculates that felons were held by their hair (head or beard) to render them sufficiently still to perform the execution with reasonable accuracy. The placing of a head on an execution block does not appear conclusively until AD 1450. Execution victims were also likely to be standing, or bent forwards/backwards, and a struggling victim would have made it difficult for the executioner to decapitate in one blow, as evident on SK1349.

It is also possible that, in cases where a single blow appears to have removed the head, this in fact took place shortly after death. It is very difficult to distinguish between decapitation as the actual cause of death and the removal of the head shortly after. Perimortem evidence refers to activity at around the time of death, and would therefore cover the removal of the head, either before or after.

The cut-marks were most commonly inflicted from the side, either left or right, and at the level of the third

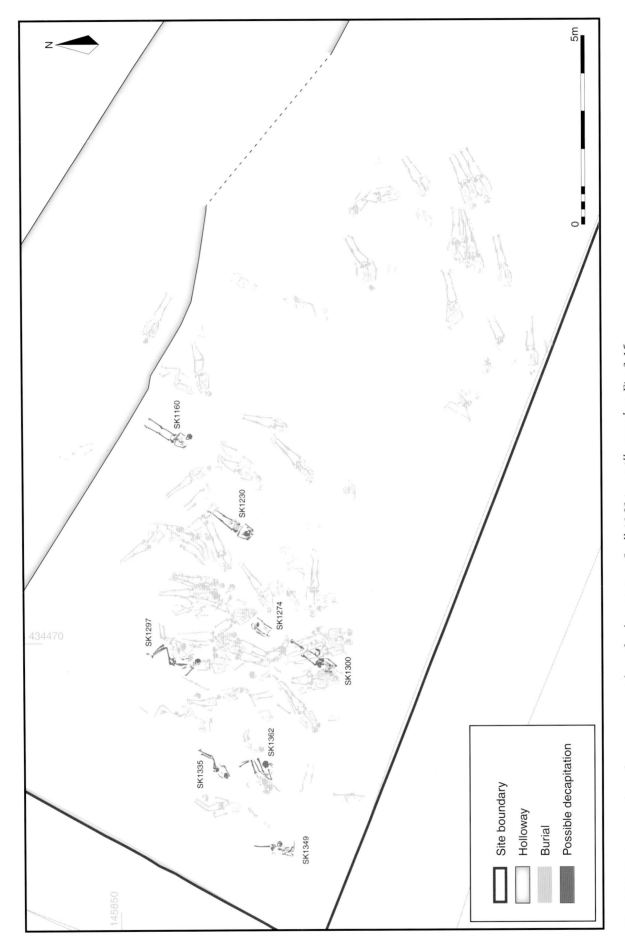

Fig. 3.15 Perimortem sharp-force trauma: evidence for decapitation. Scull 1365 is not illustrated on Fig. 3.15

Table 3.21 Perimortem sharp-force trauma – evidence for decapitation

Skeleton number	Cervical vertebra involved	Angle and location of wound	Notes
1160	CV3–4	Oblique inferior right facet CV3. Body of CV4 absent.	
1230	CV4	Oblique, inferior right facet removed and half the posterior arch.	
1274	CV?3	Single vertebra survives, oblique inferior left side of body.	
1297	CV3	Very small fragment of CV3, not possible to determine.	CV1–5 recovered with skull, with CV6–7 in with vertebrae. Only CV3 absent, except small fragment. So it is assumed that this is absent due to decapitation.
1300	CV6	Oblique, anterior body and left anterior facet.	Skull was placed by leg in grave with CV1–4 still attached. CV5 assumed to be involved, but absent.
1335	CV3	Oblique, superior posterior facet and right edge of body, left side entirely absent.	Right mandible cut-mark.
1349	CV1–2, CV3–4, CV5	CV1 right inferior facet slice and CV2 odontoid peg completely. CV3–4 partial slice from posterior affecting arch. CV5 severed through from anterior.	Right mandible cut-mark.
1362	CV2	Horizontal slice through the body, leaving only the odontoid process (or dens) and neck with a small amount of the superior body.	Left mandible cut-mark.
1365	CV3?	Inferred, only CV1 and 2 found with skull.	Left mandible cut-mark.

and fourth cervical vertebrae (Fig. 3.17, example of cut-mark on CV4, SK1230). This is consistent with the use of a sword, and cut-marks on the mandible suggest that the head was angled downward. The cut-mark to the left parietal on SK1174 may result from the removal of the hanged from the gallows. A study of an 18th-century gallows site in Germany (Wahl and Berszin 2013), found a similar cut-mark on the left parietal bone, and attributed it to the severing of the rope above the knot of the noose, while removing the hanged individual from the gallows.

Where groups of skulls were found collected together, these displayed no evidence for having been placed on a stake, or any long-term damage resulting from being above ground (other than absence of mandible). They were clearly deposited at a different time to their respective bodies, but no physical evidence of further treatment survived. Heads were used as conclusive evidence that sentences of execution had been carried out, or for collecting rewards, which may go some way to explaining their location.

Fracture due to judicial hanging

It is assumed that, where there is no evidence of decapitation, the burials at Weyhill Road were executed by hanging. Twenty-seven individuals were laid in the grave with their hands apparently tied at the front or back (Fig. 3.5). Although this is circumstantial evidence, and crossed arms or hands is a burial position adopted for some 'normal' Christian inhumations, the large number exhibiting this position, and many with hands at the back, strongly suggests that this represents the binding of the person concerned, and not a careful post-mortem positioning.

Contemporary images of judicial hanging depict victims with hands bound both at the front and back (Mattison 2016). Leaving the ties in place, while interring the executed individual, would have been another form of showing disrespect to the corpse.

There is unlikely to be osteological evidence for hanging, as this mainly affects the soft tissues of the neck. The 'hangman's fracture' refers to the dislocation of the posterior arch of the second cervical vertebra (or axis). This is rarely found in practice, even when executed prisoners are examined shortly after death. The hangman's fracture is therefore the exception rather than the rule (Waldron 1996). Further work on other known hanged individuals has identified fractures of the hyoid cornua, styloid processes, occipital bones, cervical bodies (C2) and transverse processes (C1, C2, C3,

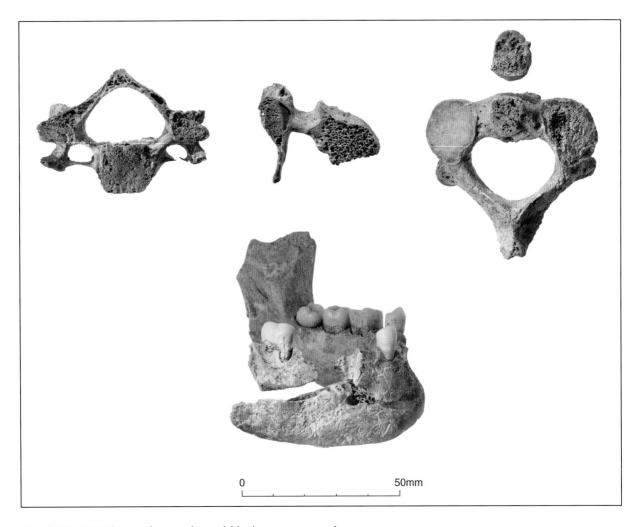

Fig. 3.16 SK1349 vertebrae and mandible showing cut-marks

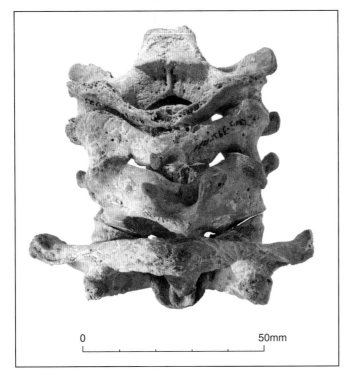

Fig. 3.17 SK1230 vertebrae showing cut-mark

C5) (Spence *et al.* 1999). In archaeological material, these bones and areas are often poorly preserved, and it is difficult to distinguish post-mortem damage and perimortem fractures.

The hyoid bone fusion, of the greater horn to the body, does not usually occur until the third decade of life. The incidence of fusion increases with age, so that 60–70% are fused by age 60 years (Scheuer and Black 2000, 164–5). Unfused hyoids are more flexible, and unlikely to fracture. In cases of strangulation, only a third had a fractured hyoid, and the fracture was observed in only 8% of hangings (Ubelaker 1992). The high proportion of young adults and adolescents in the assemblage severely precludes the likelihood of evidence of hyoid fractures. There were 22 partial (body or greater horn), or full, hyoid bones available for study, and none of these displayed any indication of fracture.

Only two individuals displayed possible evidence of hanging: SK1384 (20–27 years) and SK1391 (early 20s). SK1384 had been much disturbed by a later pipe trench running across the grave and the lower legs were also truncated. SK1391 was prone, with hands tied behind the back, but had suffered significant disturbance by later graves, and so neither individual was from a secure, undisturbed context. In both instances, the odontoid peg (and process, also known as the dens), on the second cervical vertebra had the appearance of being broken off.

On SK1384, the odontoid peg had an irregular break across, at an angle, displaying an uneven surface, of 'torn' appearance (Fig. 3.18).

SK1391 displayed a fracture of the axis vertebra across the odontoid peg, at an angle. This similarly had a rough, uneven surface, with no indication of bending to the edges of the bone. The atlas vertebra also had break on the anterior portion.

Odontoid fractures at this location are classified as type II (after Anderson and D'Alonzo 1974, classification types I–III), a fracture of the odontoid base. The mechanism of injury suggests a high-velocity force;

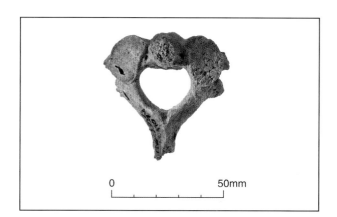

Fig. 3.18 SK1384 vertebrae showing an irregular break of the odontoid peg

clinical cases have included a fall (down a flight of stairs while drunk), motor vehicle accidents, and being struck on the head by a falling tree (Schatzker *et al.* 1971). Resulting injuries are not necessarily fatal, but are potentially lethal or result in grave neurological complications.

The identification of the fracture of the odontoid as a consequence of hanging has been identified in one individual (Spence *et al.* 1999), from a hanging in 1898. This individual was 17 years old, and the atlas-axis vertebrae had become dislocated, with the second cervical vertebra (axis) rotated through 40 degrees. The second cervical vertebra also exhibited the fracture-dislocation of the odontoid process. The trauma of the hanging had sheared the odontoid process from the body of the axis. This individual exhibited several developmental anomalies (cranial shifts) in the spine, and these are thought to have contributed to the separation of the odontoid from the body.

Factors affecting the process and physiological effects of hanging include type of rope, type of knot, location of the knot, length of drop and mechanism of release (direct fall, sideways). From the limited information available relating to Anglo-Saxon and early medieval hanging, a short-drop or running noose (victim hoisted up by rope already around the neck) would have been used. Gallows would have comprised a simple construction of two upright posts, with a cross-beam, or simply effected by dragging a rope across the branch of a tree. The victim then stood on the back of a cart or ladder, which was then removed. In both methods, strangulation is the cause of death, and unlikely to leave any lesions on the skeleton (Waldron 2009).

Given the number of variable factors involved in different types of hanging (discussed above), it is possible that circumstances were such that fracturing of the axis was possible, and the sheared-off odontoid pegs in the two skeletons described is evidence of this.

Perimortem trauma – evidence for mutilation

One individual, SK1240, had evidently been selected for exceptional treatment. This male of 35–45 years was laid supine and extended, with both lower arms bent at the elbow and across the body. The hands had been cut off and placed beneath the body in the area of the pelvis (so that the corpse's buttock area would have been directly above).

Osteological examination confirmed perimortem cutting and removal of the hands, as chop-marks were observed across the carpals. The right carpals' scaphoid, capitate and lunate had flat, neat slices cut entirely through the bone, which if the hand had been flat, would have been made vertically. The left-hand capitate slice was angled at 45 degrees, so the cut would have been angled towards the body if the hand was held pronated. The triquetral was also sliced in half. The cuts were made across the widest part of the hand, at mid-

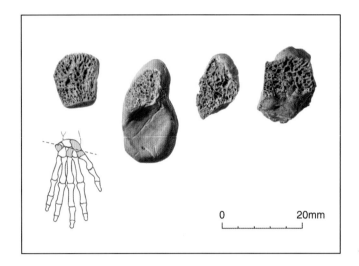

Fig. 3.19 SK1240 Bilateral amputation at the wrist. Right side scaphoid, capitate and lunate all demonstrate perimortem cut-marks

carpal level. There was no evidence of healing on the bone (Fig. 3.19).

Only two other execution cemeteries (Guildown and Sutton Hoo) allegedly had evidence for mutilation by removal of limbs, but neither of these could be confirmed, due to the antiquity of the examination of the bones in the case of Guildown and due to poor preservation in the case of Sutton Hoo. The amputation of body parts is known to have been recommended in Anglo-Saxon law codes, but not in addition to execution. The removal of a hand is prescribed as a punishment for producing counterfeit coins, perjury, or wounding someone while avoiding paying church dues. Theft was punishable by death, as it was regarded as a very severe crime, and only a few law codes prescribe loss of hand for theft. There is an interesting account from AD 1100, of death by 'piecemeal'. Thomas Dun had his hands chopped off at the wrist, before they then severed his arms at the elbows, and then at the shoulders. After this, his feet were reportedly cut off beneath the ankles, his legs chopped off at the knees, and his thighs cut off about five inches from his trunk, which, after severing the head, was burnt to ashes (*The Newgate Calendar*: Ex-Classics 2018). The various body parts were then displayed around the county.

Few osteological cases of the removal of hands are confirmed; one, possibly medieval in date, is from Ipswich, where the right hand of a male had been removed and the wound subsequently healed (Mays 1996). Another, possible 7th-century example, from the island of Tean in the Isles of Scilly, involved the removal and healing of the hand and foot (Brothwell and Møller-Christensen 1963). A recent discovery, from the 5th to 7th-century cemetery at Hinkley Point, Somerset (Clough, pers. comm. 2018), again involved the removal and healing of hand and foot.

Clear evidence of the amputation of both hands and burial with the individual is rare. What cannot be determined is the order of removal, i.e. before or after death, or indeed whether the individual concerned was hanged, or simply died from loss of blood after the amputation.

Other bony changes

Animal disturbance

Grave cut 1341 appeared to have been disturbed by animal burrowing. Some bones were absent, and gnaw-marks were observed on SK1397, on the upper third shaft posterior lateral left femur and left scapula lateral border. The tooth-marks appeared to be rodent-sized, although the few species which could burrow sufficiently deep and extensively include rabbits and badgers.

A number of ungulate species, including sheep and deer, will gnaw on bone (osteophagia), generally in response to nutritional deficiency (likely phosphorus). Many rodents (including rats) are known to gnaw on bones to sharpen and/or wear teeth. If soft tissue is still present, they will inevitably consume bone as they gnaw through the associated soft tissue (Pokines and Symes 2013).

Dental

There were 62 dentitions available for observation. As all individuals concerned had permanent dentition, with only the third molar as the un-developed tooth, and as only one female was present, the statistics have been merged. Table 3.22 shows the dental statistics for this assemblage.

Enamel hypoplasia is identified on teeth, as lines, furrows, grooves or pits. It is the result of disruption to the enamel during growth, and therefore represents periods of health stress experienced during developing years. This condition may be caused by periods of malnutrition, injury or disease. Of the 1,376 teeth available for examination, 93 adult teeth from 20 dentitions displayed at least one line of enamel hypoplasia (TPR 6.75%). This is a low level, and implies that childhood health was good, with little malnutrition or disease which would interrupt growth. This is a high

Table 3.22 The dentitions

	Number of teeth from 62 individuals	Percentage of the teeth/ alveolar affected (TPR)
Total permanent teeth erupted in occlusion	1376	
Total permanent teeth in sockets	1138	
Total number of sockets	1211	
Total adult lost ante-mortem	26	2.2%
Total adult lost post-mortem	73	
Total adult caries	61	4.4%
Total adult abscess	12	0.99%
Total adult calculus	480	34.8%
Total adult dental enamel hypoplasia	93	6.75%
Total adult socket with periodontal	21	1.73%
Total adult congenitally absent 3rd molar (unconfirmed)	29	16.2%

rate when compared with that at Ridgeway Hill (1.3%) and Towton (5%), but lower than the 7.4% calculated for the period (Roberts and Cox 2003, 187–8).

One individual exhibited gross enamel defects (SK1316), which affected the first molars. The defects covered the upper third of the crown, in the form of pitting and disruption to the cusps (cuspal enamel hypoplasia). The hypomineralisation of the molars would have occurred in the first three years of life, as the first molar develops in early childhood (crown development from 4–5 months to 1–2 years), and erupts around the sixth year. These defects would represent a significant growth disruption for a period of time. The aetiology is unclear, but preterm birth, poor general health and systemic conditions are all thought to be contributory factors.

Dental calculus (also known as tartar or mineralised plaque) is a layer of mineral deposits on the teeth surface, created by hardened dental plaque. Once present, it promotes further accumulation of dental plaque, causing inflammation of the gums, gum recession and gum disease, and exposes the individual to an increased risk of caries (Hillson 1996). It comes in two forms: supra-gingival and sub-gingival calculus (i.e. above and below the gum-line). Gum recession will also lead to tooth loss, and there is often a correlation between high levels of calculus and ante-mortem (before death) tooth loss. The rate of calculus in the population was 35% (TPR), from 52 dentitions. This is broadly comparable with an average for the period of 39.2% (TPR from four sites, Roberts and Cox 2003, 190–4).

Dental caries, or tooth decay, is directly related to carbohydrate consumption, and is seen to increase with the cultivation of starchy crops, with a more rapid increase after the later introduction of sugar from the New World. In the Anglo-Saxon-Norman period, the only sugars available were honey and fruit. Starchy

cereal crops in the form of wheat, oats, barley, rye were also consumed. Only 61 teeth present had caries at the time of death (TPR 4.4%). This does not include those teeth already lost to caries. The low level of caries recorded must be considered against the age profile of the assemblage. When examined by age, an increase in the number of individuals with at least one example of dental caries is clear (Table 3.23). The average rate of caries for the period was 4.2% (Roberts and Cox 2003, 190–1), and so the rate at Weyhill Road is very comparable.

Table 3.23 Number of caries by age-group

Age-group	Number of individuals	Total number of caries	Percentage of age-group
Young adult	5	15	20
Prime adult	8	13	36
Mature adult	6	15	40
Older adult	7	17	63

Evidence of dental attrition (tooth wear) was present in varying amounts. Severe enamel wear would leave the pulp exposed, and therefore render the tooth vulnerable to caries. Attrition is linked to grit in foods, particularly bread, which was the main staple of Anglo-Saxon (and later) diets. Two dentitions had possible extra-masticatory wear: the dental wear of SK1251 was much greater on the incisors and canines, which suggests use of the front teeth as a tool. The other individual's (SK1355) maxillary incisors had been worn down to the 'stumps', or had lost all the enamel. The degree of wear was much greater than that evident on the second incisors or canines. There was ante-mortem tooth loss of the second premolar and molars, which will have required the anterior teeth to be used for chewing. However, the mandibular teeth were not in such an affected condition; the first incisors were not as worn, which implies that they were not in occlusion with the upper incisors to result in such heavy wear. Abnormal dental attrition was observed at Ridgeway Hill, where 16 individuals exhibited evidence, mostly on the first molars (Loe *et al.* 2014).

Dental abscesses and periapical cavities

These have been combined for reporting purposes. These conditions are the result of infection entering the mandible or maxilla, usually through dental caries and decaying teeth. The subsequent accumulation of pus eventually creates a hole in the bone. If the infected tooth continues *in situ*, then the abscess will grow in size. Removal of the affected tooth will remove the source of the infection, and the abscess will then abate. Dental care at this time extended only to herbal cures and amulets. Abscesses or periapical granulomas were very rare in the assemblage; the low number (0.99% of alveolar) is linked to the low level of caries, where abscesses often originate. The young age of the assemblage has contributed to the low incidence of abscesses, as there was generally insufficient time for these to develop.

Dental non-metrics

Variation in dentition was quite limited. The most common observation was the congenital absence of the third molar (29 teeth, 12 out of 62 dentitions). Although not confirmed by radiography, this was recorded when there was clearly no room in the mandible or maxilla for any further molars, and there was no ante-mortem loss.

There was a low incidence of crowding or rotation of the teeth within their alveolar. This was present in three individuals, and usually affected the incisors and canines and premolars.

A further two individuals had a non-metric variation in the development of the tooth, with a third molar extra cusp on the lingual side and an enamel pearl on third molar mesial side. Retention of the right maxilla deciduous canine was also present on a third individual.

Chips were observed in the dentition of five individuals. These were mostly the upper (maxilla) first incisors, but also the lower left third molar and left maxilla premolars. These enamel chips can be attributed to a range of causes, including hard foods, using teeth as tools, physical combat, and accidents. In modern practice, they are more common in people who participate in sports. Given the youthful mortality profile of the assemblage, it is not surprising to find evidence of physical activity. Dental trauma, as it is better known, was present in quite a high number of individuals from Ridgeway Hill (CPR 77%, TPR 9.5%). At that site, it was argued that the majority were probably related to the act of decapitation. Cracks and

chips were also found at St John's College and Towton, and are relatively common in archaeological populations (Milner and Larsen 1991, 370).

Charnel or disarticulated human bone

A total of 38 contexts from grave fills recorded in the field as disarticulated, and 63 articulated skeletons, had additional bone with them. One feature appeared to be a charnel pit, and contained a large quantity of disarticulated bone (cut 1364, fill 1366). A large quantity of further bone was recovered from the subsoil (divided into two areas: 1004 and 1015) where it had become incorporated from later activity on site. Disarticulated bone was recorded in different ways, depending on the context. Where the bones were clearly from one disinterred individual and other bones continued to articulate, this was recorded as a skeleton. A complete skull or cranium was also recorded as a skeleton. Where it became apparent during the recording of articulated skeletons that more than one individual was present, an additional skeleton number was allocated. The same applied in those cases where an articulated cranial and post-cranial had been allocated separate skeleton numbers; if on further examination of archaeological recording and osteology these were considered to be from the same individual, these numbers were merged.

Where the context was deemed to contain multiple individuals, and where it was not possible to be entirely confident that any two bones originally articulated, these were recorded as disarticulated charnel. Each bone was examined individually, so that a minimum number of individuals (MNI) could be ascertained per context. It also allowed for the identification of 'missing' elements from the articulated individuals to be identified and re-united.

Context 1366

The fill 1366, of feature 1364, contained entirely disarticulated bone. This was in an area of highly intercutting graves, so it is not clear whether this was an intentional charnel pit, or simply an accumulation of material from other graves.

The number of fragments recovered from this context was approximately 293, and it represented a MNI of five adults and one child. The child was represented by pubis, calcaneus, left orbit, femoral head and tibia. The adults were represented by all areas of the skeleton. Some elements were unfused and therefore likely to be from adolescent or young adult individuals. There was one frontal bone, with a retained metopic suture. One sacrum had an articulating first sacral segment, probably a lumbarisation of the first sacral vertebra, as there was a pseudo-joint on the left ala. A maxilla had abscesses at the first molar level, the other teeth had enamel hypoplasia and quite heavy wear, suggesting an older individual.

Grave fills

Of the 77 grave cuts with human bone in the fill, 14 contexts contained at least one child (or non-adult) bone. The largest numbers were from contexts 1290 and 1298, which were the fills of graves 1288 (SK1289) and 1296 (SK1297) (and cranium 1330). SK1297 (fill 1298) cut through grave 1284, and contained the non-adults SK1347/46. It is therefore not surprising to find non-adult remains in the backfill of this grave. SK1316 cut through several other graves, which in turn cut 1284, which contained SK1347/46. The fill of SK1316 (1317) contained a right maxilla with teeth, from a child of 9–11 years, and it is suggested that this too is from SK1347/46.

The grave, 1288, of SK1289 contained a large amount of disarticulated bone in the backfill, of which some was non-adult. It was located at some distance from the other non-adults, so these disarticulated remains may be from another unidentified burial. It is worth noting that this backfill contained non-adult left and right tibiae, left and right femori, left and right humeri, right radius and ulna, all in matching pairs. The femur had a maximum length which aged to approximately 9.5 years (Maresh 1970).

Through carefully examining each context stratigraphically with the spatial relationships of skeletal parts, it is concluded that in all probability, the disarticulated material in grave backfills relates to the earlier, truncated grave, or the disinterment of the previous occupant. Therefore, the minimum number of individuals represented by this material would not significantly increase estimates of the overall, originally buried population of the cemetery. Where a large amount of disarticulated material was present in the grave fill, it appeared most probable that the grave had been substantially cut through an earlier grave.

As some individuals were only represented by articulating lower legs, feet, hands, cranium etc. and the backfill of the truncating grave contained a large amount of material of one individual it would be fairly safe to assume a relationship. For example, SK1381 (fill 1382), which cut grave 1378, was represented by only a right femur and tibia, after SKs1379/80 had cut through the grave. The backfill contained hands, feet, ulnae, fibulae, cranial fragments, ribs, left ilium, left mandible and two vertebrae, all of which might easily comprise the remainder of SK1381.

Pathologies

A number of pathologies were identified within the disarticulated bone recovered from 13 contexts. Similar to the articulated assemblage, these related to joint disease, fractures and metabolic disease, and included osteophytes on patella joint-surfaces, Schmorl's nodes, proximal first-foot phalanx pseudo-osteochondritis dissecans, cribra orbitalia and a femur bowed anterior-posterior (healed rickets?). There were healed fractures

of the left ilium (two instances in the articulated assemblage) and a distal tibia (three in articulated). A possible cut-mark was identified on a cervical vertebra (decapitation). Caries and abscess were observed on the dentition. Developmental defects were of a cleft atlas and bifid sacrum (S1–2 and 4–5).

Non-metric traits included the retention of metopic suture, of which three frontal bones were affected. A scapula foramen, and septal aperture on a left humerus, were also observed.

These pathologies and non-metric traits were observed in the articulated cemetery population, and add to the overall picture of its health. The healed, fractured iliac blade found in fill 1176 was a relatively uncommon bone to fracture. This fracture results from a high-energy impact, often in young people, and probably healed without too much assistance. In this period, it may have resulted from a fall from a height.

Contexts 1004 and 1015 – subsoil

The mixed charnel/disarticulated material recovered from the subsoil contexts almost certainly originated from some of the graves, as it was evident that the more shallow graves had lost skeletal elements to vertical truncation. Some may have derived from the repeated intercutting of the graves, or the modern service trenches which crossed the area. In such circumstances, it was only possible to determine the number of elements, and the minimum number of individuals they represented. Pathological lesions were observed, and have been described. Context number 1004 was given to the first part of the cemetery to be identified, where machining had removed all subsoil levels within the east part of the site. Context 1015 was given to the area containing the densest group of burials, close to the corner of the limits of excavation on the western side.

Approximately 758 fragments of bone were recovered from 1004, and 266 from 1015. In 1004 there was a MNI of 28 adults, and in 1015 there was a MNI of 6 adults and 1 child.

Context 1015

Within the disarticulated material from 1015, 20 bones from non-adults were recorded. Two articulated burials of older children had been identified from this part of the cemetery (SK1147a and 1346/7), and these bones may derive from these burials. The elements absent from these burials are amongst the disarticulated material. There are two ulnae (left and right); SK1346/7 had a left ulna and SK1147a had a right, so it is possible that these represent the 'missing' elements. It must be noted, however, that further hand-bones were found with SK1146, which were in addition to SK1147a and of a different size. So it appears probable that there was a third non-adult burial within this part of the cemetery, which has been entirely truncated away. This work highlights the value of examining the disarticulated bone, often overlooked, as this has revealed the presence of further non-adult remains.

Pathology and non-metrics

The pathology from context 1015 was vertebral and dental. There was, however, one maxilla with all anterior teeth lost ante-mortem (posterior was broken), so may have been edentulous. Two of the thoracic vertebral bodies had Schmorl's nodes. The non-adult right maxilla had caries on the second deciduous molar.

Context 1004

There were no non-adult remains amongst the dis-- articulated material from this context, and burials within this area to the east is mostly post-Norman in date. There were, however, a larger number of pathological bones.

Pathology

A number of dental pathologies were identified, including caries, abscess, calculus and enamel hypoplasia. These were present on three mandibular fragment dentitions and one maxilla. The maxilla had two large caries on the second premolar and first molar, with the first molar also displaying evidence of an abscess into the sinus cavity.

There were possible healed fractures identified on a radius (in additional to the four from the articulated assemblage), two vertebra bodies and fifth metatarsal. The two vertebral fragments had been heavily damaged post-mortem, so the pathology was not clear, but there was a large bony callous extending over the bodies on the left side and fusing them together, so while a traumatic origin is assumed, this may not be the only possible diagnosis. The fifth metatarsal is also assumed to have suffered trauma, as it presented with periostitis and a misshapen shaft, which were probably secondary to the fracture. The radius was a distal portion with slight angulation, which inferred a healed fracture. This bone is commonly broken in a fall onto an outstretched hand; in young people such falls may involve height or high velocity.

Periostitis was present on four bones: a fibula, two tibiae and fifth metatarsal (discussed above). This was all in a healed state.

The vertebral bodies had porosity, osteophytosis, Schmorl's nodes and intervertebral disc disease. There were two humerii, one with a malformed medial pro- trusion extending posteriorly, changing the shape of the ulna surface, and the other an ossification spur on the distal medial shaft. Both of these indicate some kind of direct trauma to the elbow area.

Non-metrics

A single sternal aperture was observed. This in addition to the four (of 25) observed amongst the articulated individuals, giving a total of five instances amongst the skeletal population.

Other

There were rodent gnaw-marks on a tibia shaft. Gnaw- marks were found on SK1397, so it can be assumed that this tibia came from the same area of disturbance.

Discussion of the skeletal assemblage

Condition/taphonomy

The surface preservation of the bones was variable, and fragmentation was generally high. Skulls had fragmented where they survived, which meant that cranial metrics were generally not possible. The extensive truncation of graves by other graves, and by later activity, has had the largest impact on the quantity of articulated human remains available for assessment. A large quantity of disarticulated human bone was recovered.

Number of individuals

As with most archaeological cemeteries, the entire extent and complete number of individuals interred at the Weyhill Road cemetery will never be known. Intercutting and later disturbance on the site has severely reduced levels of completeness of buried indiv- iduals. In addition, a confined location, in the corner of the development area, prevented the complete excavation of several graves, which could not be 'chased' beyond the limits of excavation. Therefore, the total of 124 identified individuals represents a minimum number and more probably lie under the present road. Examination of the disarticulated bone identified potentially 39 further Adult individuals. Amongst this material were a quantity of non-adult bones which, where estimated, belonged to the older child (6–12 years) age-range. Some of these are likely to represent further parts from already identified non-adults, but others may indicate an additional two children whose graves have been completely lost.

Demography

Reynolds (2009) characterises execution cemeteries predominantly by their geographical location, but also on the basis of body position and presence of other 'deviant' characteristics. However, precise dating, burial practice and the osteological evidence for execution and mutilation offer better evidence for these burial grounds. The demographic profile of the assemblage is a key piece of evidence. It is well established that young males commit more crime (and are therefore found guilty) than any other age or sex group. Therefore, it would be expected that an exclusive execution-only cemetery contained a high proportion of this group. In addition, women were not as commonly hanged, but where sentenced to death were more likely to be drowned, buried or burned alive, with pregnancy frequently cited as a reason for a lesser punishment.

The site at South Acre, Norfolk, had 36 females out

of 70 identifiable (from 136 graves) or 50%, and was identified as an execution cemetery (Wymer 1996). This is contrary to the findings at Weyhill Road. Problems of preservation at this site should be taken into consideration, but this high proportion of females to males, and the radiocarbon dates may throw some doubt on identification as an execution cemetery.

In contrast, the presence of only three confirmed females (two articulated skeletons and one cranium), from amongst the 124 individuals buried at Weyhill Road, enhances the evidence for an execution cemetery. Other skeletal assemblages which were predominantly or entirely male have been identified either as execution sites or battle-related (Towton – battle; Ridgeway Hill – Viking execution; St John's College - Viking massacre; Oxford Castle, 18th to 19th-century judicial hangings).

The age distribution from Weyhill Road, with a peak of incidence in the young adult (18–25 years) category, supports an interpretation as an execution cemetery. The age distribution does not follow the 'expected' pattern, and there were no young children present. In virtually all populations there is a much higher risk of dying at very young or very old ages. The peak in the young adult group, closely followed by prime adult (26–35 years) and reducing in the mature (36–45 years) and yet further in the older age (46+ years), is the complete opposite to the expected distribution pattern of age at death. As the burials were not all contemporary, single events involving battle, violence or disease may be ruled out, and premature death from execution is the most probable interpretation for this age-distribution pattern.

The presence of older children, in the 6–12-years age-range, appears at first to throw doubt on the exclusive use of the cemetery for executed criminals. The age of criminal responsibility in the Anglo-Saxon period was not fixed. Apart from issues pertaining to the accurate recording of people's ages, liability for crime appeared to depend on the individual child's understanding of right and wrong and the consequences of their actions. Those aged between 7 and 12 years appear to have been liable for criminal responsibility in some instances. This must have been a sufficiently common occurrence for King Athelstan, in *c.* AD 930, to raise the age of criminal responsibility from 12 to 15 years (Hostettler 2009). He was concerned that this was 'cruel', and that an excessive number were being killed below this age. How much influence this may have had on actual regional practices is not known, and it is worth noting that, in England, the judicial system continued to execute children accused of crimes into the early 19th century.

Physical attributes

The statures estimated from long bones fit the averages and ranges for this time-period. From this it is surmised that these individuals were not nutritionally-deprived or 'stressed' by pathogens as children, allowing them to grow to their potential. The lower limb indices and

cranial indices (Table 3.8) also place them firmly as typical of the general population for the period. The characteristics identified are not like those characterising the Viking assemblages (St John's College and Ridgeway Hill), or the battle site (Towton). This implies that the Weyhill Road burial population were not military or men used to regular fighting, or life on board a vessel.

The reconstruction of crania to observe varying cranial shapes and facial features did not identify any dissimilar individuals. They appear, metrically and non-metrically, to be a similar, relatively homogenous group, implying that they were all from a similar genetic background.

Pathology

The cemetery population revealed a variety of pathologies, but in general the skeletal pathological burden was low. This is partially a reflection of the high numbers of young adults present, as most commonly observed skeletal pathologies develop with increasing age.

In particular, the traditional skeletal indicators of 'stress': enamel hypoplasia, cribra orbitalia, periostitis, and other metabolic diseases, all have low prevalence rates compared to averages for the time-period.

Rates of accidental trauma, such as healed fractures and ossified haematomas were also low or average. This implies that the population were not exposed to trauma more than might be expected of a general population at this time. The tibia was the most commonly fractured long bone. It typically takes a major force to cause this fracture; in clinical cases this is often the result of a high-energy event, such as a motor vehicle accident (or period equivalent), or a low-energy injury sustained during sports. This would be expected of young, able-bodied individuals in this time-period. There were three tibia fractures, two of which were on the same individual, and involving both left and right sides. Fractures of the pelvis, by comparison, are relatively uncommon (especially for those under 60 years), and involve 3% of all adult fractures (Tile *et al.* 2003). Most pelvic fractures are caused by a traumatic, high-energy event, such as a car collision (or period equivalent), although in the elderly these may be caused by a fall. Two possible fractured pelves (SK1184 and SK1294), left permanent disruption to the hip joints, which would have affected the mobility of these individuals. This was evidenced in SK1184, by the bony remodelling around the acetabulum (this individual also had a right radius healed fracture), and in SK1294, where the right hip suffered from the additional use resulting from the inadequacy of the left. Although not physically immobile, these individuals would have had a noticeably different gait, and perhaps used a crutch or stick as an aid.

The disabling condition of chronic osteomyelitis, with necrosis of the femoral heads (and subsequent bone loss) in SK1362, meant that this individual was unable to walk. It was surprising to find an individual with this level of physical incapacity amongst those accused and found guilty of crime. However, within the context of contemporary society, with prevailing views on the criminal body, this is perhaps not so unusual. Hadley (2010) comments that execution cemeteries do not demonstrate evidence of significant physical impairment, yet at Weyhill Road there was at least one example of this, and if the hip fractures and Klippel-Feil cervical vertebrae individuals are included, there are further examples of physical deformities within the cemetery population.

Evidence of judicial punishment

Analysis of the human skeletal remains revealed nine examples of probable perimortem decapitation (plus one in the disarticulated material). Decapitation (as the cause of death, or after) is a key finding of execution cemeteries.

Decapitation as a burial rite is fairly common in the later Roman period (Tucker 2014), and these individuals are commonly found as fully extended inhumations, in the conventional manner, with the skull placed usually by the legs, or at the feet (*ibid.*). The key difference is the careful placement within the grave. The individuals who were found decapitated at Weyhill Road were not all carefully laid-out, and the skulls were in a variety of positions. There were also the apparently bound wrists, at front or back. The decapitation cut-marks were not consistent, and in four instances involved the mandible as well. The manner of decapitation appears to have varied, with cuts made from the side, front or back. The level of the cut-mark was mostly around cervical vertebrae three or four, but not consistently so. The importance accorded to proper burial in the later Saxon period was substantial, and by the 10th century churchyards were deemed the only place for a 'proper' burial (Hadley and Buckberry 2005). Post-mortem punishment was a further humiliation to the condemned, and brought further shame on their family. Despite Christian doctrine not requiring a complete body for the purposes of resurrection, or a particular location for mortal remains, the proper burial of an intact body was deemed necessary to ensure salvation of the soul. To be permanently excluded in this way from the rest of the spiritual community represented a further deterrent to committing crime.

The implication is that if a body was not carefully laid-out on a west–east orientation inside the churchyard, it was purposely excluded. Such exclusion had implications for the soul of the felon, and the shame it would bring on their family.

Some four individuals were also assumed to have been decapitated, although no osteological evidence survived. A further ten crania/skulls, also without osteological evidence of cut-marks, were found isolated from a post-cranial skeleton. It is possible that some of these isolated skulls, where only the cranium was present, may have been placed on display, prior to eventual burial. This

would have allowed the mandible and cervical vertebrae to become detached, due to degradation of soft tissues. There was no evidence of bone damage caused by impaling on a stake, for example; however, preservation of the inferior of crania was generally poor, so would not preclude display in such a manner. The display of severed heads, as a visible warning to others, was known to have been practised in earlier and later periods. It was stated in the 13th century that anyone could kill and behead fugitives resisting arrest, although they were obliged to hand over the head to the coroner (Duggan 2018).

Hanging

There are a few archaeologically excavated sites with confirmed evidence of executed prisoners having been hanged and then buried. These are all of post-medieval date, and usually of the 18th and 19th centuries. The evidence from these burials is of crudely dug graves, often too short, with mostly supine (but also on-side and prone) extended individuals. Hands were located very close together, over the waist or the pelvic area, interpreted as remaining tied together with rope from the hanging (Poore *et al.* 2009). If we assume that the same practice was adopted in earlier periods, then this comprises circumstantial evidence for hanging.

These findings mirror those from Weyhill Road, where 27 individuals displayed hands in a position that implied that they were still bound (front or back) at the time of burial. Some of the grave slots were too short, with the legs of individuals bent up, in order to fit in. Prone and side positions were also found, with a general impression of careless, hasty burial. The double burials were an exception, in that they were clearly laid-out together, in a manner which ensured that the arms overlapped.

Skeletal evidence for hanging was not expected (Waldron 2009, 167), and there was no preservation of the noose. Despite a lack of evidence of the 'hangman's' fracture of the second cervical vertebra, the shearing of the second cervical vertebra odontoid peg provided possible skeletal evidence of hanging. This type of fracture had been observed in one late 19th to early 20th-century judicial execution from Canada (Spence *et al.* 1999). This study demonstrated a variety of damage to the cranial and cervical bones, despite the general uniformity of the hanging technique. Only seven cervical fractures from 34 executed prisoners were observed in a study from 1992 (James and Nasmyth-Jones), none of which involved the odontoid peg. The evidence from Weyhill Road, for complete fracture of the second cervical vertebra odontoid peg due to hanging, is therefore a possibility. This type of fracture is seen in clinical cases, where the neck has been subject to extreme forces, and in one case associated with a hanging (Spence *et al.* 1999).

Amputation/mutilation

The perimortem removal of both hands of SK1240 is a rare find, and Reynolds (2009a) quotes only 14 known amputations in the Anglo-Saxon period from all cemeteries. This is possibly the only instance from Weyhill Road which can be confirmed osteologically. Mutilated corpses are reported from 14 cemeteries (37 cases) (Reynolds 2009a, 173). According to Mattison (2016, 268), few of these are confirmed osteologically, and some of the interpretations, particularly those from Guildown and Sutton Hoo, are doubtful.

The articulated nature of the hands, carefully placed into the grave first, with the rest of the corpse on top and with the amputated arms crossed, suggests a more considered burial than some of the others. As severed bone reacts in the same way both before and after death, the perimortem nature of the removed hands does not permit a full interpretation of events. The cause of the death of the individual may have been due to the amputation of hands, as this would sever the radial and ulna artery, which, if not cauterised, could result in fairly rapid death. If the cut was made cleanly, the artery may spasm and close-off with little bleeding. There is also a probability of hypovolemic shock; medical care and knowledge in this period were limited, and chances of dying therefore quite high. It is possible that this individual was buried in the execution cemetery, not simply because they were executed, but as the result of a judicial punishment. Alternatively, the removal of hands in *addition* to hanging may have been a further public humiliation. The mutilation of executed corpses is not unknown in this period, as punitive dismemberment offered a visible example of judicial power.

Several law codes mention the removal of hands. The late 7th-century laws of Ine invoke the loss of a hand or foot as a punishment option for theft. In other codes (such as Athelstan, r. 924–39, and Alfred, r. 871–99), a hand was required for theft from a church, but every other theft was punishable by death. Cnut (r. 1016–35) decreed the loss of both hands for wounding someone in the process of withholding payments to God, and one hand for perjury, and for the minting of false coin. Alfred and Athelstan both stated that the hand which committed the offence should be struck off. The law codes therefore provide possible scenarios for the removal of the hands, but offer no clarity as to why the individual concerned was buried in the cemetery with the rest of the judicially executed.

It is unclear how closely the written laws were followed in practice, and it is probable that the written lists codified existing traditions. The degree to which the application of the law was centralised in this period remains a matter of debate, and it is possible that the similarities observed between different execution cemeteries reflect analogous regional practices (Rabin 2014).

The double burials, those where it is clear that two individuals were interred at the same time, suggest that these individuals were jointly sentenced and executed. There were five burial pairs amongst the Weyhill Road assemblage, and four were radiocarbon-dated to either the 11th–12th century, or the 13th century. The skeletal evidence for the pairs indicated that they were all male and less than 35 years old. They were generally laid in supine position, with overlapping arms and/or shoulders. They were examined for skeletal similarities, and any suggestions of familial relatedness. The only pair to display similar skeletal traits was SK1056/SK1057. Both were young men, in their late teens to early 20s, and both had congenital spinal disorders. SK1056 had spina bifida occulta, a bifid sacrum along the entire length; this is usually caused by lack of folic acid during pregnancy, but also may be familial trait. Although there are not usually outward signs of this disorder, or complications, there may be occasional neurological complications, such as a tethered spinal cord, which could affect the legs. Minor, commonly found indications of this spinal cord problem include the skin over the defect being hairy, a fatty lump, a red or purple spot, skin tract, or skin with less colour. SK1057 had Klippel-Feil syndrome, which although rare, is also a congenital developmental disorder of the spine, and can co-occur with spina bifida occulta. The most common signs of the condition are a short neck, a low hairline at the back of the head and limited movement of the head and neck. Such an affected individual would probably have been regarded as 'different' to others; not disabled as such, but noticeably different.

Phasing was achieved for a good proportion of the skeletons, either through direct dating or by stratigraphic and common alignments. From the skeletal evidence, it was clear that there were no decapitations in the latest phase, of the 13th century. There were fewer in the 10th century (3), and more in the 11th–12th (7), with two phased as spanning the 10th–12th centuries. None of the double burials were decapitated. Both the female burials which could be phased were of the 11th–12th century, and interestingly, for SK1379 no skull was recovered so the individual may be assumed to have been decapitated, and SK1358 comprised a skull only, which may imply a further decapitation. The individual with the hands cut off (SK1240) was dated to the 10th century, which accords with the written law codes from this date.

Chapter 4
Artefacts and Faunal Remains

Metalwork
by Katie Marsden

Fourteen items of metalwork, all iron, were recovered from as many deposits, and comprised seven buckle elements, three nails, one fitting, one knife and one probably modern washer. A final item recovered from grave 1135 (fill 1136), was too corroded to identify to function. Of the group, 12 items were recovered from grave fills (Table 4.1), and the illustrated catalogue includes both the grave goods, and additional items of intrinsic interest from the assemblage. A similar range of buckles was recorded at the Portway cemetery, Andover (Cook 1985, 80). RA2, a buckle plate, is not illustrated, due to its highly fragmented state, but appears to be consistent with styles recorded at the site, and also at Portway.

Illustrated catalogue (Fig. 4.1)

1   Buckle with a 'D'-shaped frame. In its proportions, RA4 compares to examples from Stockbridge Down, Hampshire (Hill 1937, 250, plate I), which are dated to the Late Saxon and earlier part of the medieval periods (Goodall 2011, fig. 12.3, nos 3–5). RA4. Grave 1149 (fill 1147). Dimensions: length 45mm, width 40mm, thickness 5mm, weight 14g. See also Fig. 4.2.

2   Buckle with 'D'-shaped frame. The pin is broken, but present. Broadly dateable to the Saxon, or earlier part of the medieval period. RA17. Grave 1299 (fill 1300), located under pelvis. Dimensions: length 35mm, width 26mm, width 7.5mm, weight 10g.

3   Buckle with an oval loop frame. The frame is broken, missing approximately one third of the total, and the pin is missing. Oval buckles of this form commonly date to the Late Saxon period (Marzinzik 2003). RA10. Grave 1229 (fill 1230), located within pelvis. Dimensions: length 34mm, width 24mm, thickness 5mm, weight 3g.

Table 4.1 Metalwork from grave contexts

Context	Context description	Material	Date	Ct.	Wt. (g)	RA no.	Catalogue no.
1119	Grave 1117	iron	buckle	12	21	2	not illustrated
1133	Grave 1131	iron	nail	1	5	3	not illustrated
1136	Grave 1135	iron	object	1	28	0	not illustrated
1147	Grave 1149	iron	buckle	1	14	4	1
1169	Grave 1167	iron	buckle	1	5	5	5
1190	Grave 1189	iron	buckle	1	5	7	6
1238	Grave 1236	iron	nail	1	3	9	not illustrated
1230	Grave 1229	iron	buckle	1	3	10	3
1300	Grave 1299	iron	buckle	1	10	17	2
1315	Grave 1278	iron	buckle	1	18	12	4
1366	Possible charnel pit 1364	iron	swivel hook	1	6	22	7
1382	Grave 1378	iron	nail	1	4	0	not illustrated

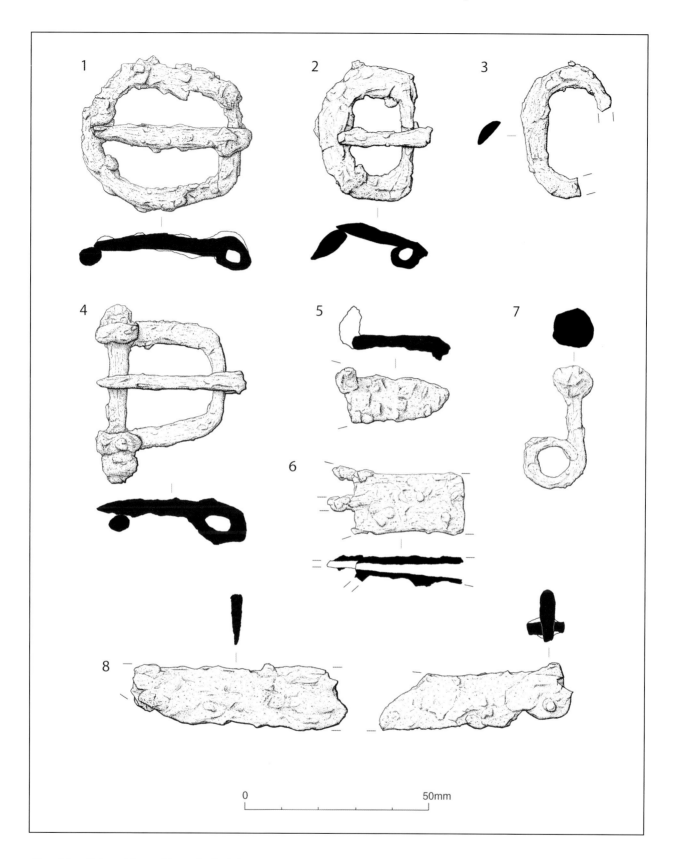

Fig. 4.1   Selected iron objects. Scale 1:1

RA4

0   50mm

Fig. 4.2   Buckle RA4

4   Buckle with rectangular frame and 'revolving arm'. This form of buckle is characterised by a large pin secured to, and freely moving around, the buckle loop, rather than attached to the strap bar. On this example, the strap bar terminates in large knops. Similar buckles are recorded from 11th and 12th-century deposits at Castle Neroche, Somerset and Southampton, Hampshire (Goodall 2011, fig. 12.7, nos 160–1). RA12. Grave 1278 (fill 1297). Dimensions: length 47mm, width 34mm, thickness 5mm, weight 18g.

5   Buckle, comprising single-piece plate with integral frame loop. The plate would have been secured to a leather strap by way of the iron rivet at the terminal. RA5. Grave 1167 (fill 1169). Dimensions: length 31mm, width 13mm, thickness 3mm, weight 5g.

6   Buckle, comprising probable 'D'-shaped loop frame, with separate plate folded over the strap bar and held together by two iron rivets. Both of these components are difficult to date closely. The leather strap remains mineralised between the plates. RA7. Grave 1189 (fill 1191). Dimensions: length 37mm, width 17mm, thickness 6mm, weight 5g.

Both catalogue nos 5 and 6 are difficult to date closely. Examples of this form include Marzinzik's Type II (2003), with examples known from Andover (*ibid.,* pl. 97, no. 1) proposed to date to the second half of the 6th century, and copper alloy examples dateable to the medieval period (Egan 1991). Iron buckles of this form, with later dates, include examples from Upton, Gloucestershire, dated to the late 13th and 14th centuries (Goodall 2011, fig. 12.4, no. K40).

7   Swivel fitting. Swivel fittings attach to chains to afford a freedom of movement to whatever was attached to them, and suggested attachments include harness straps and cauldrons (Goodall 2011, 302). Given the nature of the burials, it is possible that the swivel hook was a component in a limb restraint used on the occupant of the grave. A similar swivel was found with a chain link fragment and ankle shackles in a grave at Greyfriars, Oxford (Hassall *et al.* 1989). Similar examples have been recorded from Goltho Manor, Lincolnshire (and elsewhere), dated to the 12th cen-

tury (Beresford 1975, fig. 41, no. 107). RA22. Possible charnel pit 1364 (fill 1366). Dimensions: length 33mm, width 17mm, thickness of shank 6mm, thickness of head 11mm, weight 6g.

8   Knife, comprising a rectangular strip in two fragments. The dimensions and triangular cross-section are similar to knives of the medieval period (Goodall 2011, e.g. fig. 8.16), although the item is too fragmentary to attribute form with confidence. A rivet is present at the break on one fragment, possibly for attaching an organic handle. RA1. Disturbed ground layer 1004. Dimensions: length 110mm, width 15mm, weight 16g.

Coin
by Katie Marsden

(For photograph, see burials catalogue SK1220)

1.   Coin. Silver penny of Aethelred II (AD 978–1016), first-hand type, minted by Aelfstan at Exeter, and dateable to AD 979–85. It is equivalent to North (1994) no. 766. RA8. Grave 1219 (fill 1221). Dimensions: diameter 19mm, weight 1g.

Worked bone
by Katie Marsden

(Figs 4.3, 4.4)
Knife handle, comprising two bone fragments and an associated iron element. The handle is hollow and circular-sectioned. The central hole is man-made, although the maker may have exploited a natural cavity in the bone; the species cannot be identified. Faint rilling (circumferential incisions) are visible to the body of the longer piece, some incomplete, in that the ends of the incisions stop short of joining. The iron element is rod-like, measuring 18mm by *c.* 2mm diameter. The two bone pieces do not join, but ultimately belong to the same object, and the relationship with the iron element is unclear. As it was recovered partially within the main body, it could represent part of the tang of the knife blade. A similar handle recovered from Colchester (Crummy 1988, fig. 75, no. 3083) features a decorative narrowed collar between the main body, and a rounded terminal. It is probable that this narrowed collar formed a weakness in the handle, and has consequently broken along these constrictions and been lost. The object was recovered from a grave that had experienced truncation, so this breakage and loss is not surprising. Comparable examples are also known from York, dateable to the 12th and 13th centuries (MacGregor *et al.* 1999, fig. 927, no. 7722). RA24. Grave 1341, situated near the left arm of skeleton 1396. Dimensions: (main body) 66mm length, 11mm diameter; (terminal end) 8mm length, 10mm diameter; (iron rod) 18mm length, *c.* 2mm diameter. Combined weight: 4g.

Socketed handle, probably from a knife. Grave 1120 (lower limbs and lower arm and hand of skeleton

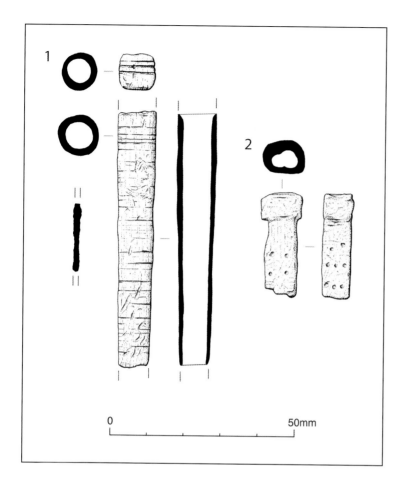

Fig. 4.3   Worked bone objects. Scale 1:1

Fig. 4.4   Worked bone object RA24

1122). The bone was originally circular in section, but the shaft has been squared. The handle terminates in a rectangular expansion at one end, and a break at the other. The surface is pitted through wear and damage, but circular indents are visible as decoration on one face of the shaft only. It is possible that further decoration was present, but is now obscured by wear. The indents are arranged in two lines of three, with a third line comprising two indents only, located just below the rectangular expansion. A similar handle, made from an antler tine, from Coppergate, York, is dateable to the mid 10th century (MacGregor *et al.* 1999, fig. 927, no. 7724). The simple form of the socketed handle and decoration could, however, suggest a wider date-range. Dimensions: length 27mm, width 11mm, thickness 9mm, weight 1g.

Pottery
by Kayt Hawkins

The small ceramic assemblage comprised eight sherds (55g), and encompassed prehistoric, Late Iron Age/ Early Roman and medieval material (Table 4.2). Count, weight, fabric and, where possible, form, were all recorded to provide a basic record as per recommendations by Barclay *et al.* (2016). Considerable plough disturbance was observed on site, which may in part account for the

Table 4.2 Quantification of pottery assemblage: sherd count and weight (g) by fabric and context

Period	Context	Fabric	Count	Weight (g)
Late prehistoric (probable Late Iron Age)	1029 (posthole 1028)	Flint-tempered	2	1
	1392 (grave 1390)	Flint-tempered	1	2
?Prehistoric	1060 (Ditch A, 1059)	Sand-tempered	1	2
Late Iron Age/early Romano-British	1012 (Ditch B, 1011)	Sand- and grog-tempered	1	31
	1119 (grave 1117)	Sand-tempered	1	2
	1136 (grave 1135)	Sand- and grog-tempered	1	14
Medieval (11th to 13th centuries)	1172 (post-pit 1171)	Sand/flint-tempered	1	3
Total			8	55

low sherd weights and poor sherd condition observed within the assemblage.

Late prehistoric

Flint-tempered sherds were retrieved from two features; posthole 1028 (fill 1029) and grave 1390 (fill 1392). The combined weight of these undiagnostic fragments was just 3g, and therefore identification to period is somewhat tentative. Given the noted soil disturbance in the area of excavation, combined with the condition of these sherds, they are most probably Late Iron Age in date and, therefore, residual occurrences. The same applies to a single, reduced-fired, sandy bodysherd, retrieved from grave 1117 (fill 1119).

Late Iron Age/Early Roman

The only diagnostic sherds recovered comprised two jar rimsherds; one from a sand- and grog-tempered everted rim jar (fill 1136 of grave 1135), and one from a necked, cordoned jar (fill 1012 of ditch 1011).

Medieval

A small and abraded sherd, predominately sand-tempered, could be of later prehistoric date, although it does potentially show similarity to 11th/12th-century fabrics in the region (Cotter 2011). From post-pit 1171 (fill 1172), a single, hard, sand- and flint-tempered sherd, with an oxidised surface, is more typical of the 11th to 13th centuries (*ibid.*; Vince *et al.* 1997).

Animal bone
by Dr Philip L. Armitage

Introduction

A total of 56 hand-collected animal bones from six contexts (four graves and a single post-pit), were submitted for study. For the purposes of quantifying the numbers of identified specimens present (NISP), where fragments of the same bone elements that had either been broken post-deposition/*in situ* (in antiquity) and/or during excavation/post-excavation handling, were able to be refitted together, these were counted as single NISPs.

Four mammalian species were identified, using the author's modern comparative osteological collections, and with reference to published works (Boessneck *et al.* 1964; Halstead *et al.* 2002; Lawrence and Brown 1973). These were: cattle *Bos* (domestic); sheep *Ovis* (domestic); house mouse *Mus musculus*; and wood mouse *Apodemus sylvaticus*.

Preservation and methodology

The sheep bones exhibit a high degree of fragmentation/breakage, owing to their brittle condition resulting from leaching/erosion following burial. Surface markings on the bones from context 1202 (grave 1183) have resulted from root etching. Measurements (in mm) were taken on selected elements, using a Draper dial calliper (graduated 0.02mm); following the system of von den Driesch (1976). Determinations of sex, age and stature estimates were made, using standard zooarchaeological methodology and formulae.

Description of the species

Bones from the mice were recovered from fill 1130, of grave 1128. A single lower left third cattle molar was

Fig. 4.5   SK1036 and sheep skeleton ASK1042 showing south-western edge of site and modern disturbances

identified from context 1244, the fill of grave 1242. Based on the wear-stage (b = classification of Grant 1982), this tooth came from an animal aged *c.* 30 months at time of death. In addition, a third phalanx (toe bone) from a sheep was found in fill 1172, of post-pit 1171. The mice are not considered to represent deliberate inclusions, and are not discussed further, although details can be found in the archive. The cattle

tooth may also have been unintentionally deposited. The sheep bones are of more significance due to their context, and are described below.

Part of an articulated sheep skeleton (ASK1042) had been placed on left leg of SK1036 (grave 1037, Fig. 4.5). It comprised 42 identified elements, including vertebrae, ribs, pelvic bones, and right and left upper leg bones (see Table 4.3). The skull and lower jawbones,

Table 4.3   Context 1042 – Animal Bone Group: Parts of a sheep skeleton

Bone	Right		Left		Measurements (mm)
thoracic		11			
lumbar		4			
sacrum		1			
rib		15			
scapula	1		1		GLP 30.3 LG 22.7 BG 18.6 SLC 18.7
humerus	1		1		GL 125.3 Bp 32.9 SD 13.8 Bd 26.9
radius	1				Bp 28.0 SD 14.7
ulna	1				SDO 19.2 DPA 22.8 BPC 16.2
innominate	1		1		depth medial rim acetabulum 3.0
femur	1		1		
patella		1			
TOTALS	**6**	**32**	**4**	**42**	

Notes: Measurements follow system of von den Driesch (1976)

as well as lower limb bones/feet, are not represented in the submitted material. All epiphyses of the limb bones are fused, apart from the proximal humerus, which is in the final process of fusing. As reviewed by Zeder (2002, 92), various authors studying bone fusion in sheep have found the proximal humerus to be the latest-fusing bone at 30 to 42 months, while all other bones are generally fused by 30 months. The withers height in this animal, when alive, is estimated from the greatest length (GL = 125.3mm) taken on the humerus (method of Teichert, referenced in von den Driesch and Boessneck 1974); revealing a stature of 53.6cm: comparable to the size of modern Soay ewes (see Clutton-Brock *et al.* 1990, 50). Recognition that this Weyhill Road sheep was female is based on anatomical features in the innominate bone: 1) the depth of the medial rim of the acetabulum (3.0mm); and 2) presence of a sharp ilio-pectineal ridge

(criteria of Armitage 1977, 76–81). None of the sheep bones shows signs of either butchery or skinning.

Three identified elements, the incomplete skull and lower jawbones of a sheep (context 1202) were associated with skeleton 1184 (grave 1183). The cranium is very broken up/fragmented, with the largest intact piece from the right side, which includes the attached horn core. Based on the morphology and appearance of this horn core, the animal is identified as a female, with a horn type similar to ewes in modern unimproved/primitive sheep breeds; including the Danish Gotland (Hatting 1983, 128) and the Soay (Armitage 1977, 83–4; Armitage in Clutton-Brock *et al.* 1990, 17). According to the eruption/wear-stage in the mandibular cheek teeth (stage E), the animal was aged between two to three years at time of death (criteria of Payne 1973).

Chapter 5
Radiocarbon Dating and Chronological Modelling

by Frances Healy

Radiocarbon dating

Twenty samples from articulated burials (16% of the identified individuals) were submitted for radiocarbon dating, selected to cover the spatial and vertical spread of the burials (Fig. 5.1). Their stratigraphic relations are noted in Table 5.1 and shown in Figure 5.2. Simple calibrated date-ranges for individuals extend from the 8th to the 14th centuries cal AD (Fig. 5.3).

All the samples were measured by the Scottish Universities Environmental Research Centre, East Kilbride. Gelatin was extracted from bone and ultrafiltered, before combustion, graphitisation, and dating by Accelerator Mass Spectrometry (Dunbar *et al.* 2016). The laboratory maintains continuous programs of internal quality control. It also takes part in international intercomparisons (Scott 2003; Scott *et al.* 2007; 2010).

Chronological modelling

The relevant principles and method are described elsewhere (e.g. Bronk Ramsey 2009; Bayliss 2009; Buck and Juarez 2017). In essence, Bayesian analysis brings together radiocarbon dates and other information relating to them (in this case primarily the stratigraphic relations between burials) by expressing both as probability density functions. The combination of different kinds of information permits more precise age estimates than the dates alone would, as well as the calculation of parameters which are not directly dated, such as the start, end and duration of a phase of activity.

The model employed here incorporates the stratigraphic relationships shown in Figure 5.2. It has been defined in OxCal v.4.3 (Bronk Ramsey 1995; 1998; 2009; Bronk Ramsey *et al.* 2010; Bronk Ramsey and Lee 2013), using the internationally agreed calibration curve for terrestrial samples from the northern hemisphere (IntCal13; Reimer *et al.* 2013). Calibrations have been

calculated using the probability method (Stuiver and Reimer 1993). Once the probability distributions of individual calibrated results have been calculated, the program attempts to reconcile these distributions with the other information incorporated in the model by repeatedly sampling each distribution to build up a set of solutions consistent with the model structure. This process produces a posterior probability distribution for each sample's calendar age, which occupies only a part of the calibrated probability distribution. In the illustrations in this text the posterior density estimates are shown in solid black and the calibrated radiocarbon dates from which they have been sampled are shown in outline. Highest Posterior Density intervals output from the model are rounded outwards to five years and are cited in *italics* to distinguish them from simple calibrated date ranges.

Statistics calculated by OxCal provide guides to the reliability of a model. One is the individual index of agreement which expresses the consistency of the prior and posterior distributions. If the posterior distribution is situated in a high-probability region of the prior distribution, the index of agreement is high (sometimes 100 or more, e.g. Fig. 5.4: *SUERC-74071 [A:104]*). If the index of agreement falls below 60 (a threshold value analogous to the 95% significance level in a X^2 test) the radiocarbon date is regarded as inconsistent with the sample's calendar age. Sometimes this merely indicates that the radiocarbon result is a statistical outlier (more than two standard deviations from the sample's true radiocarbon age), but a very low index of agreement may mean that the sample is redeposited or intrusive (i.e. that its calendar age is different to that implied by its stratigraphic position), or that it is contaminated with extraneous carbon. Another index of agreement, Amodel, is calculated from the individual agreement indices, and indicates whether the model as a whole is likely, given the data. In most applications, this too has a threshold value of 60.

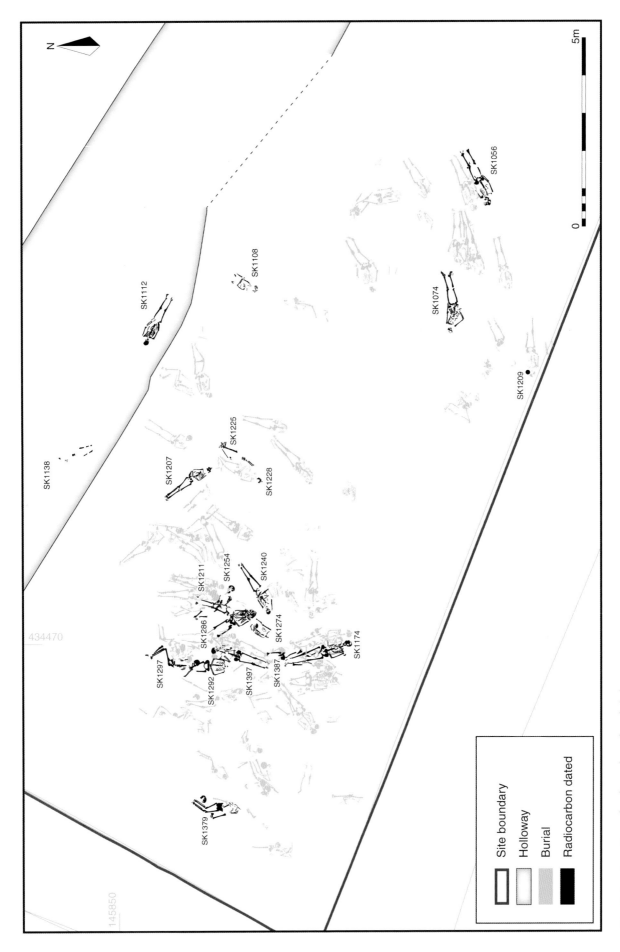

Fig. 5.1 Location of radiocarbon-dated skeletons

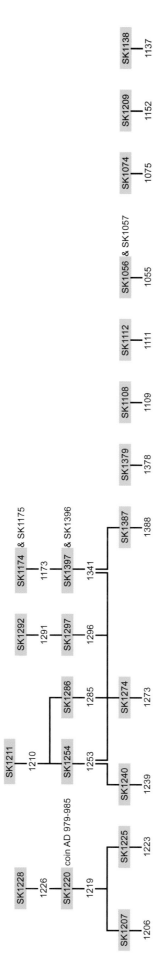

Fig. 5.2   Stratigraphic matrix of radiocarbon-dated burials and SK1220

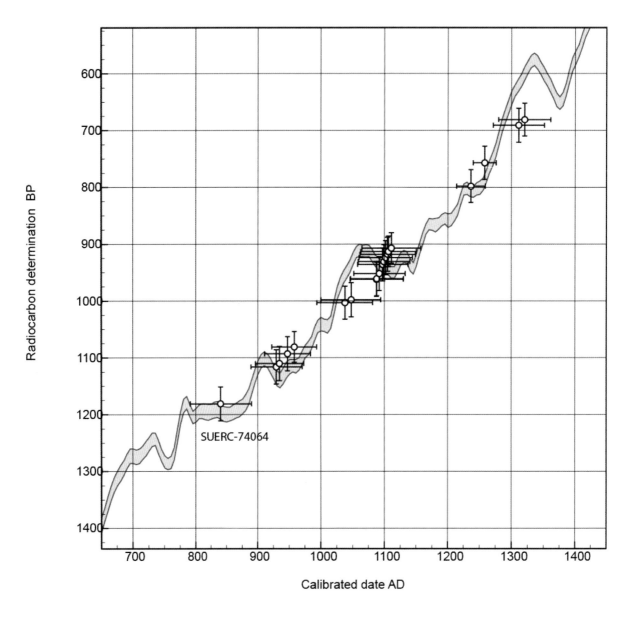

Fig. 5.3   Radiocarbon dates for the Weyhill Rd, Andover burials plotted on the IntCal13 calibration curve (Reimer et al. 2013), showing the date for SK1112 (SUERC-74064)

Practicalities

The calibration curve

The shape of the radiocarbon calibration curve for this period is unfriendly. All but six dates fall on one of three plateaux, in the 9th, 10th and 11th to mid 12th centuries cal AD. This makes their calibrated age-ranges wider than they otherwise would be and tends to bunch results together (Fig. 5.3). The most affected is the date for SK1112, which falls on a particularly flat stretch of curve effectively occupying the 9th century cal AD (Fig. 5.3: SUERC-74064). If this date is accurate, SK1112 is the earliest dated burial, since all the other dates avoid this plateau. SK1112's calibrated age range spans more than 200 years, so that the young man in question could have died at any time between the 8th and the mid 10th century cal AD (Table 5.1). In other words, the burial could be substantially earlier than the others and potentially unrelated to them, or it could be close to them in time, separated by the shape of the curve. The $\delta^{13}C$ and $\delta^{15}N$ values for SK1112 cluster with those for others from the cemetery (Jay, Chapter 6), so that a dietary offset is unlikely to account for the earliness of the date. There remains the possibility that SUERC-74064 is a statistical outlier, one of the 1 in 20 radiocarbon results where the age of the sample lies outside the 95% range of the measurement (Bayliss *et al.* 2013, 56). In the main model presented here, SK1112 is treated as part of the cemetery, on the grounds of its proximity to the other burials and the

Table 5.1 Radiocarbon dates. The calibrations in the 'Calibrated date range AD 2σ' column are calculated by the maximum intercept method (Stuiver and Reimer 1986) and are cited as recommended by Mook (1986): rounded outwards by 10, since the standard deviations are all over 25. They thus differ slightly from the calibrations shown in Table 2.2 which were calculated by the probability method. Those in the 'Highest Posterior Density interval cal AD' column are derived from the model shown in Figure 5.4. All samples are of articulated human bone

Laboratory no.	Sample	Material	Context	Radiocarbon age yr BP	$\delta^{13}C$ ‰	$\delta^{15}N$ ‰	C/N ratio	$\delta^{34}S$ ‰	Calibrated date range AD 2σ	Highest Posterior Density interval cal AD (95% probability)
SUERC-74061	SK1056 ASW16-1056a	R femur of young adult male	Grave 1055, beside SK1057	691 ± 30	−20.0	9.1	3.0		1260–1390	1260–1305
SUERC-78126	SK1074 ASW16-1074	L fibula proximal fragment of young adult male	Grave 1075	757 ± 29	−19.6	10.2	3.2		1220–1290	1220–1285
SUERC-74062	SK1108 ASW16-1108a	R femur of young adult male	Grave 1109	1116 ± 30	−19.9	10.3	3.1		870–1000	885–995
SUERC-74064	SK1112 ASW16-	R femur of young adult male	Grave 1111	1181 ± 30	−20.0	8.4	3.0		720–960	850–980
SUERC-78128	SK1138 ASW16-1138	Femur fragments of young adult ?male	Grave 1137	1003 ± 29	−20.0	9.4	3.2		980–1120	980–1050 (76%) 1080–1125 (15%) 1135–1155 (4%)
SUERC-74082	SK1174 ASW16-1174a	L femur of young adult male	Grave 1173, beside SK1175. Stratified above SK1397	998 ± 30	−19.7	8.3	3.0		980–1120	1085–1160
SUERC-74065	SK1207 ASW16-1207a	R femur of adolescent ?male	Grave 1206. Stratified below SK1220	961 ± 30	−19.8	8.0	3.0		1010–1160	1020–1155
SUERC-78127	SK1209 ASW16-1209	L humerus distal shaft of adolescent male	Grave 1152	681 ± 29	−19.5	9.7	3.2		1270–1390	1265–1310
SUERC-74077	SK1211 ASW16-1211a	L femur of prime adult male	Grave 1210. Stratified above SKs1254, 1286	913 ± 27	−20.1	9.2	3.2		1030–1210	1070–1210
SUERC-74063	SK1225 ASW16-1225	R radius of adult ??male	Grave 1223. Stratified below SK1220	1093 ± 30	−19.4	10.3	2.9		880–1020	895–1015
SUERC-78122	SK1228 ASW16-1228	L clavicle medial body of adolescent	Grave 1226	798 ± 29	−19.8%	12.3	3.2		1180–1280	1185–1280
SUERC-74066	SK1240 ASW16-1240a	R femur of mature adult male	Grave 1239. Stratified below SK1254	1081 ± 27	−19.7	8.2	2.9		890–1020	895–930 (16%) 935–1020 (79%)
SUERC-74074	SK1254 ASW16-1254a	L femur of older adult male	Grave 1253. Stratified above SKs1240, 1274; below SK1211	952 ± 30	−19.8	8.4	3.0		1020–1170	1020–1155

Table 5.1 (cont.) Radiocarbon dates.

Laboratory no.	Sample	Material	Context	Radiocarbon age yr BP	δ¹³C ‰	δ¹⁵N ‰	C/N ratio	δ³⁴S ‰	Calibrated date range AD 2σ	Highest Posterior Density interval cal AD (95% probability)
SUERC-74071	SK1274 ASW16-1274a	R humerus of mature adult male	Grave 1273. Stratified below SKs1254, 1286, 1297, 1397	1110 ± 30	−19.6	10.3	2.9		880–1000	885–1000
SUERC-78121	SK1286 ASW16-1286	L scapula mid lateral border of prime adult male	Grave 1285. Stratified above SK1274, below SK1211	936 ± 29	−20.0	9.9	3.3		1020–1170	1025–1150
SUERC-74081	SK1292 ASW16-1292	L femur of young adult male	Grave 1291. Stratified above SK1297	907 ± 27	−19.7	9.0	3.1		1030–1210	1055–1210
SUERC-74076	SK1297 ASW16-1297a	R tibia of prime adult male	Grave 1296. Stratified above SK1274, below SK1292	918 ± 30	−19.5	8.5	3.1		1020–1210	1025–1155
SUERC-74073	SK1379 ASW16-1379	R femur of mature adult female	Grave 1378	924 ± 30	−19.9	8.4	3.1		1030–1190	1025–1170 (94%) 1175–1185 (1%)
SUERC-74072	SK1387 ASW16-1387	L femur of prime adult ?male	Grave 1388. Stratified below SK1397	931 ± 30	−20.2	8.0	3.0		1020–1170	1020–1115
SUERC-74075	SK1397 ASW16-1397a	R femur of young adult male	Grave 1341. Stratified above SK1387 and below SK1174. In same grave as SK1396	962 ± 30	−19.7	9.3	3.2		1010–1160	1035–1150

similarity of the burial position to that of some of the others.

An apparent interval between dated individuals at the turn of the 10th and 11th centuries cal AD may similarly be a product of the shape of the curve. A longer interval in the mid 12th to early 13th century cal AD is clear of any plateaux (Fig. 5.3).

Artefacts

A silver coin of Aethelred, issued in AD 979 to 985, from grave 1219 (Marsden, Chapter 4) is modelled as a *terminus post quem* for the burial of SK1220, using the After function in OxCal, because it pre-dates the underlying 11th to mid 12th-century cal AD burial of SK1207 in grave 1206 (Fig. 5.4: *SUERC-74065*). It must have been in circulation for some time before it was placed in the hand of SK1220.

The present model

A preferred model is shown in Figure 5.4. It has adequate overall agreement (Amodel 77). Where dates for an individual occur in more than one sequence, their Highest Posterior Density intervals are cross-referenced from the first sequence into the subsequent ones, already constrained from their first occurrence, e.g. Fig. 5.4: *=SUERC-74074*. This avoids modelling the same date more than once, and thus giving it undue weight in the model. All the Highest Posterior Density intervals are in turn cross-referenced into two chronological groups (Fig. 5.5), so that their durations and the interval between them can be estimated.

Results (Figs 5.4–5.6; Tables 5.2–5.3)

Burials would have begun to be made in the cemetery in *cal AD 820–965* (*95% probability*), probably *cal AD 870–940* (*68% probability*; Fig. 5.4: *start Weyhill Andover burials*). The last of the 9th to 12th-century burials would have been made in *cal AD 1125–1215* (*95% probability*), probably *cal AD 1140–1190* (*68% probability*; Fig. 5.5: *end Weyhill Andover 9th to 12th century burials*), after a period of *180–330 years* (*95% probability*), probably *205–285 years* (*68% probability*; Fig. 5.6: *duration Weyhill Andover 9th to 12th century burials*). An interval of *1–125 years* (*95% probability*), probably *40–105 years* (*68% probability*; Fig. 5.6: *end C9 to C12 burials/ start C13 burials*) elapsed before SKs1228, 1074, 1056 and 1209 were buried, between *cal AD 1185–1275* (*95% probability*), probably *1215–1260* (*68% probability*; Fig. 5.5: *start Weyhill Andover 13th century burials*) and *cal AD 1275–1365* (*95% probability*), probably *cal AD 1285–1320* (*68% probability*; Fig. 5.4: *end Weyhill Andover burials*). To these four directly dated 13th-century burials must be added SK1057, buried beside SK1056 in the same grave, and SK1148, buried immediately above SK1209.

In other words, burials were being made in the cemetery for *210–295 years* after the Conquest of AD 1066 (*95% probability*), probably *215–255 years* (*68% probability*; Fig. 5.6: *1066/end burials*). If the 13th-century interments are treated as a separate episode and only the 9th to 12th-century burials considered, then burials continued to take place for *60–150 years* (*95% probability*), probably *75–125 years* (*68% probability*) after the Conquest (Fig. 5.6: *1066/end C9 to C12 burials*). Table 5.4 shows the probability that each burial was earlier than each other burial and that it was earlier than the Conquest of AD 1066. Nine of the 16 dated 9th to 12th-century individuals have more than *50% probability* of being post-Conquest. These are SKs1254 (*60%*), 1297 (*60%*), 1286 (*63%*), 1207 (*66%*), 1379 (*75%*), 1397 (*85%*), 1292 (*94%*), 1174 (*98%*), and 1211 (*98%*). To these should be added SK1396, in the same grave as SK1397, and SK1175, in the same grave as SK1174.

Questions and alternatives

What if SK1112 (Fig. 5.4: SUERC-74064) did not form part of the cemetery?

If SK1112 is excluded from the model then the start of the cemetery becomes slightly later at *cal AD 860–980* (*95% probability*), probably *cal AD 900–965* (*68% probability*; Fig. 5.7: *start Weyhill Andover burials excl SK1112*). The medians of this and the estimate in the main model vary by only 28 years; the duration becomes slightly shorter, at *315–470 years* (*95% probability*), probably *335–415 years* (*68% probability*; Table 5.3: *duration Weyhill Andover burials excl SK1112*).

Could there have been an interval between the 9th to 10th and 11th to 12th-century burials?

If the burials grouped as 9th to 12th century in Figure 5.5 are split into a 9th to 10th-century group (SKs1112, 1108, 1274, 1225, 1240) and an 11th to 12th-century group (the remainder), then the estimated interval between them is *–20 to +90 years* (*95% probability*), probably *5 to 60 years* (*68% probability*; Fig. 5.6: *end C9 to C10 burials/start C11 to C12 burials*), so that there could have been an interval, although it may be at least in part a product of the shape of the calibration curve (Fig. 5.3). Alternatively, they could have overlapped.

How does the radiocarbon dating relate to the dates attributed to artefacts other than the coin?

The remaining artefacts were simple, functional objects and hence not very chronologically sensitive (Marsden, Chapter 4). Furthermore, a piece of personal gear, like a buckle, may not have been freshly made when buried.

One artefact came from the same grave as a dated skeleton, although the association between the two is unclear. This is a fragmentary socketed bone handle (RA24) of probable 12th to 13th-century date found with iron fragments in grave 1341, where skeleton

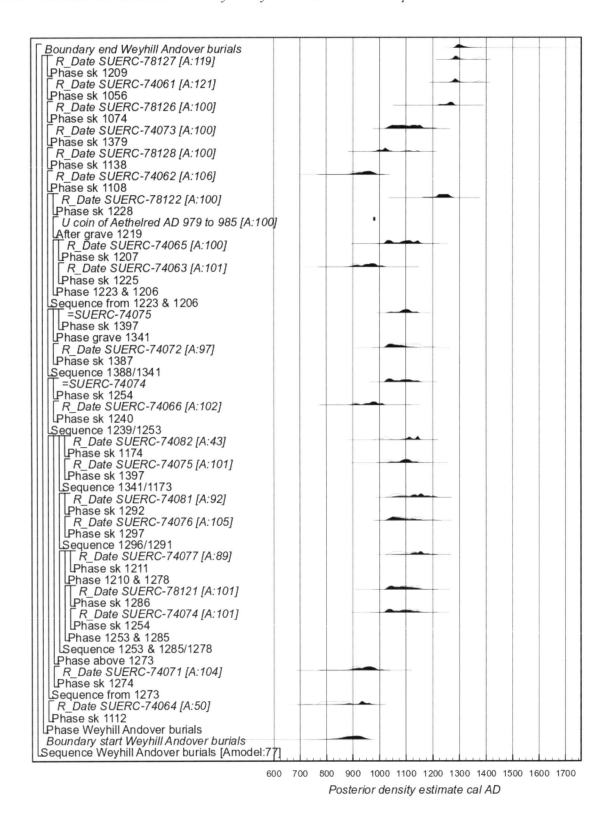

Fig. 5.4 Probability distributions of radiocarbon dates for the Weyhill Rd, Andover burials in a model incorporating the stratigraphic relations shown in Figure 1. Each distribution represents the relative probability that an event occurs at a particular time. For each of the dates two distributions have been plotted: one in outline, which is the result of simple radiocarbon calibration, and a solid one, based on the chronological model. The model is defined by the OxCal CQL2 keywords and the large square brackets down the left-hand side. A late 10th century coin of Aethelred is modelled as a terminus post quem for grave 1219, using the After function in OxCal, because it pre-dates the underlying 11th-12th century burial of SK1207

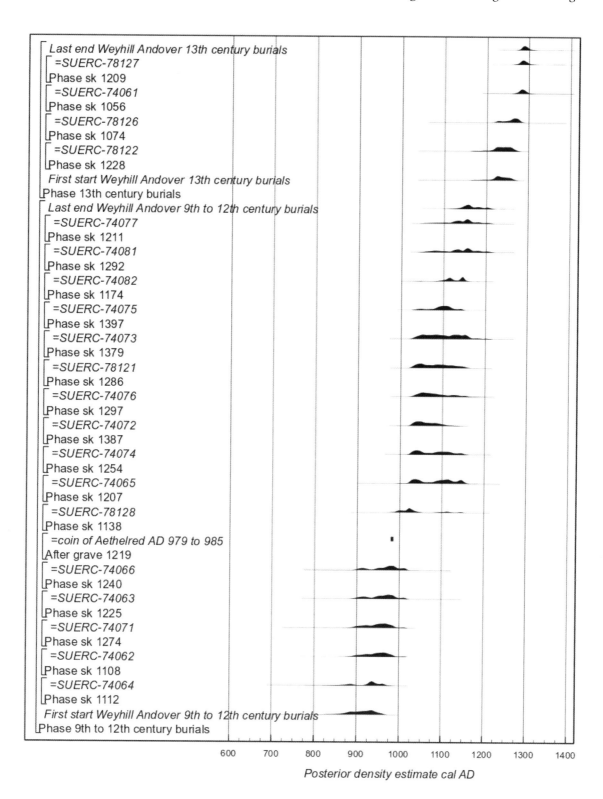

Fig. 5.5   Highest Posterior Density intervals for the Weyhill Rd, Andover burials, cross-referenced from Figure 5.4, attributed to two groups: 9th to 12th century and 13th century cal AD, for each of which start and end dates are estimated

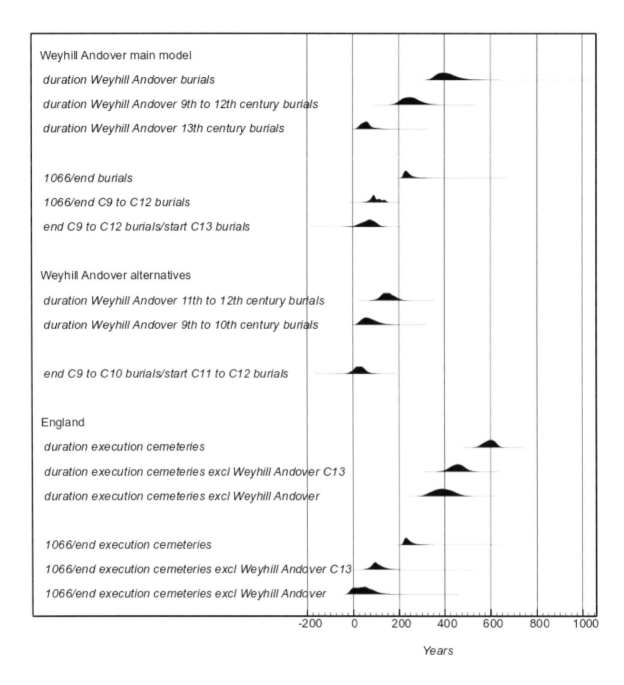

Fig. 5.6 Durations and intervals calculated by the models shown in Figures 5.4, 5.5 and 5.10 and from unillustrated variations on them

1397 is dated to *cal AD 1035–1150* (*95% probability*), probably *cal AD 1075–1125* (*68% probability*; Fig. 5.4 *SUERC-74075*). Otherwise, where artefacts were stratified above and/or below dated skeletons, their dates, or at least *termini post* or *ante quos* for them, can be estimated. All the results correspond to the typological dating of the objects. The relevant information is summarised in Table 5.5.

Could some of the dates be inaccurately old because of dietary offsets and could this affect the results?

Diet-induced radiocarbon offsets can occur if a dated

individual has taken up carbon from a reservoir not in equilibrium with the terrestrial biosphere (Lanting and van der Plicht 1998). If one of the reservoir sources has an inherent radiocarbon offset — for example, if the dated individual consumed marine fish or freshwater fish from a depleted source — then the bone will take on some proportion of radiocarbon that is not in equilibrium with the atmosphere. This makes the radiocarbon age older than it would be if the individual had consumed a diet consisting of purely terrestrial resources. Such ages, if erroneously calibrated using a purely terrestrial calibration curve will produce anomalously early radiocarbon dates

Table 5.2 Highest Posterior Density intervals for key parameters from the models shown in Figures 5.4, 5.5, 5.8, 5.9 and 5.10, and from unillustrated variations on them

Parameter	Highest Posterior Density interval cal AD 95% probability	Highest Posterior Density interval cal AD 68% probability
Andover main model		
start Weyhill Andover burials	*820–965*	*870–940*
start Weyhill Andover 9th to 12th century burials	*855–970*	*885–950*
end Weyhill Andover 9th to 12th century burials	*1125–1215*	*1140–1190*
start Weyhill Andover 13th century burials	*1185–1275*	*1215–1260*
end Weyhill Andover 13th century burials	*1270–1315*	*1275–1300*
end Weyhill Andover burials	*1275–1365*	*1285–1320*
Andover alternatives		
start Weyhill Andover burials excl SK1112	*860–980*	*900–965*
end Weyhill Andover 9th to 10th century burials	*950–1020*	*965–1000 (55%) 1005–1015 (13%)*
start Weyhill Andover 11th to 12th century burials	*985–1055*	*995–1035*
Execution cemeteries in England		
start execution cemeteries	*605–735*	*645–710*
end execution cemeteries	*1275–1365*	*1280–1320*
end execution cemeteries excl Weyhill Andover C13	*1115–1235*	*1140–1195*
end execution cemeteries excl Weyhill Andover	*1040–1185*	*1055–1140*
start Chesterton Lane Corner execution cemetery	*670–745*	*685–730*
end Chesterton Lane Corner execution cemetery	*790–895*	*820–875*
start Sutton Hoo group 1	*675–875*	*710–825*
end Sutton Hoo group 1	*955–1160*	*985–1075*
start Sutton Hoo group 2	*655–780 (89%) 790–805 (1%) 815–825 (1%) 835–875 (4%)*	*695–725 (16%) 735–775 (52%)*
end Sutton Hoo group 2	*905–930 (2%) 940–1060 (86%) 1080–1125 (6%) 1140–1150 (1%)*	*980–1035*
start Guildown Avenue	*770–950*	*775–795 (11%) 800–845 (26%) 855–905 (31%)*
end Guildown Avenue	*910–1020*	*960–1020*
start Old Dairy Cottage	*770–900*	*770–845*
end Old Dairy Cottage	*905–1015*	*940–995*
start London Road Staines	*685–890*	*715–745 (17%) 765–780 (9%) 785–870 (42%)*
end London Road Staines	*1045–1220*	*1090–1190*
start Walkington Wold	*650–730 (57%) 735–770 (38%)*	*660–690 (29%) 700–715 (6%) 740–770 (33%)*
end Walkington Wold	*900–920 (2%) 965–1035 (93%)*	*990–1025*

Table 5.3 Highest Posterior Density intervals for durations and intervals calculated from the models shown in Figures 5.4, 5.5, 5.8, 5.9 and 5.10 and from unillustrated variations on them

Parameter	Highest Posterior Density interval in years (95% probability)	Highest Posterior Density interval in years (68% probability)
Weyhill Andover main model		
duration Weyhill Andover burials	330–510	355–445
duration Weyhill Andover 9th to 12th century burials	180–330	205–285
duration Weyhill Andover 13th century burials	15–115	30–75
1066/end burials	210–295	215–255
1066/end C9 to C12 burials	60–150	70–125
end 9th to 12th century burials/start 13th century burials	1–125	40–105
Weyhill Andover alternatives		
duration Weyhill Andover burials excl SK1112	315–470	335–415
duration Weyhill Andover 9th to 10th century burials	15–140	30–95
duration Weyhill Andover 11th to 12th century burials	90–205	110–175
end C9 to C10 burials/start C11 to C12 burials	–20 to +90	5–60
Execution burials overall		
duration execution cemeteries	545–640	570–625
duration execution cemeteries excl Weyhill Andover C13	390–520	425–490
duration execution cemeteries excl Weyhill Andover	310–475	345–440
duration Chesterton Lane execution cemetery	75–195	105–170
duration Sutton Hoo group 1	120–420	190–340
duration Sutton Hoo group 2	130–400	220–330
duration Guildown Avenue	15–225	55–185
duration Old Dairy Cottage	40–225	100–200
duration London Road Staines	200–490	270–430
duration Walkington Wold	210–365	230–275 (31%) 290–345 (37%)

(Bayliss *et al.* 2004). Jay (Chapter 2) finds that the burial population overall had an omnivorous diet, probably without significant levels of aquatic protein. It is possible that freshwater, or even marine, resources contributed at low levels, such as for SK1228 or SK1225.

If SKs1228 and 1225 are modelled as having derived an arbitrary 10% of their protein from marine sources, using the Mix_Curves function in OxCal (Bronk Ramsey 2001), their individual date estimates become more recent, the medians varying by respectively 26 and 33 years from those estimated by the model shown in Figure 5.4. The medians of the estimated start and end dates for the cemetery are respectively only three years and 16 years more recent than those from the model shown in Figure 5.4. Dietary offsets are unlikely to have been significant.

Other execution cemeteries

Reynolds (2009a, 154–5) assembled and reviewed the radiocarbon dates then available for execution cemeteries, concluding that these sites began to be used perhaps in the second half of the 7th century AD, certainly in the 8th, and continued into the 12th century AD. Mattison, more tentatively, saw them starting possibly as early as the mid 7th century AD and continuing for an uncertain time after the Conquest of AD 1066 (2016, 225–9). An attempt is made here to model the dates now available. The 20 dates from the Weyhill site at Andover outnumber those from any other single excavation, the remaining substantial totals being 12 from Chesterton Lane Corner, Cambridge (Cessford *et al.* 2007) and nine from two cemeteries at Sutton Hoo, Suffolk (Carver 2005). These two groups of measurements are modelled independently (Figs 5.8–5.9) and the resulting key parameters are cross-referenced into an overall model together with those

Table 5.4 An ordering of individual burials from the model shown in Figure 5.4 in relation to each other and to the Conquest of AD 1066

Each cell expresses the % probability that the event in the first column was earlier than the event in the subsequent columns. It is, for example, 72% probable that SK1112 (row 1, column 1) died before SK1108 (row 1, column 2) and 100% probable that SK1112 died before AD 1066 (row 1, column 7).

	SK1112 SUERC-74064	SK1108 SUERC-74062	SK1274 SUERC-74071	SK1225 SUERC-74063	SK1240 SUERC-74066	SK1138 SUERC-78128	AD 1066	SK1387 SUERC-74072	SK1254 SUERC-74074	SK1297 SUERC-74076	SK1286 SUERC-78121	SK1207 SUERC-74065	SK1379 SUERC-74073	SK1397 SUERC-74075	SK1174 SUERC-74082	SK1292 SUERC-74081	SK1211 SUERC-74077	SK1228 SUERC-78122	SK1074 SUERC-78126	SK1056 SUERC-74061	SK1209 SUERC-78127
SUERC-74064 SK1112	-	72	74	80	85	100	100	100	100	100	100	100	100	100	100	100	100	100	100	100	100
SUERC-74062 SK1108	28	-	53	62	70	99	100	100	100	100	100	100	100	100	100	100	100	100	100	100	100
SUERC-74071 SK1274	26	47	-	59	67	99	100	100	100	100	100	100	100	100	100	100	100	100	100	100	100
SUERC-74063 SK1225	20	38	41	-	59	97	100	100	100	100	100	100	100	100	100	100	100	100	100	100	100
SUERC-74066 SK1240	15	30	33	41	-	96	100	100	100	100	100	100	100	100	100	100	100	100	100	100	100
SUERC-78128 SK1138	0	1	1	3	4	-	78	77	80	82	82	82	86	84	92	93	95	100	100	100	100
AD 1066	**0**	**0**	**0**	**0**	**0**	**22**	**-**	**41**	**60**	**60**	**63**	**66**	**75**	**85**	**98**	**94**	**98**	**100**	**100**	**100**	**100**
SUERC-74072 SK1387	0	0	0	0	0	23	59	-	63	66	67	68	77	100	100	93	96	100	100	100	100
SUERC-74074 SK1254	0	0	0	0	0	20	41	37	-	52	53	55	64	62	83	84	100	100	100	100	100
SUERC-74076 SK1297	0	0	0	0	0	18	40	34	48	-	51	54	63	64	82	100	88	100	100	100	100
SUERC-78121 SK1286	0	0	0	0	0	18	37	33	47	49	-	53	62	61	82	83	100	100	100	100	100
SUERC-74065 SK1207	0	0	0	0	0	18	34	32	45	46	47	-	59	54	75	79	85	100	100	100	100
SUERC-74073 SK1379	0	0	0	0	0	14	25	23	36	37	38	41	-	47	66	72	77	100	100	100	100
SUERC-74075 SK1397	0	0	0	0	0	16	15	0	38	36	39	46	54	-	100	79	87	100	100	100	100
SUERC-74082 SK1174	0	0	0	0	0	8	2	0	17	18	18	25	34	0	-	63	71	100	100	100	100
SUERC-74081 SK1292	0	0	0	0	0	7	6	7	16	0	17	21	28	21	37	-	53	99	100	100	100
SUERC-74077 SK1211	0	0	0	0	0	5	2	4	0	12	0	15	23	13	29	47	-	99	100	100	100
SUERC-78122 SK1228	0	0	0	0	0	0	0	0	0	0	0	0	0	0	0	1	1	-	22	78	99
SUERC-78126 SK1074	0	0	0	0	0	0	0	0	0	0	0	0	0	0	0	0	0	78	-	94	97
SUERC-74061 SK1056	0	0	0	0	0	0	0	0	0	0	0	0	0	0	0	0	0	22	6	-	58
SUERC-78127 SK1209	0	0	0	0	0	0	0	0	0	0	0	0	0	0	0	0	0	1	3	42	-

Table 5.5 Artefacts relating to dated burials

Artefact	Typological date (Marsden this volume)	Context	Relation to dated burials	Absolute dating
RA12 buckle	11th to 12th century	In grave 1278 (fill 1315)	Above grave 1285 (SK1286)	Later than SK1286, i.e. later than *cal AD 885–1000* (*95% probability*), probably *915–930* (*9% probability*) or *935–990* (*59% probability*; Fig. 5.4: *SUERC-78121*)
RA17 D-shaped buckle	Saxon or early medieval	In grave 1299	Above grave 1388, (SK1387) below grave 1341 (SK1397)	Estimated date of *cal AD 1025–1110* (*95% probability*), probably *1035–1085* (*68% probability*; distribution not shown), calculated as later than SK1387 (Fig. 5.4: *SUERC-74072*) and earlier than SK1397 Fig. 5.4: *SUERC-74075*)
RA22 swivel fitting	12th to 13th century	In grave or charnel pit 1364	Above grave 1341 (SK1397) and below grave 1173 (SK1174)	Estimated date of *cal AD 1075–1155* (*95% probability*), probably *cal AD 1105–1145* (*68% probability*), calculated as later than SK1397 (Fig. 5.4: *SUERC-74072*) and earlier than SK1174 (Fig. 5.4: *SUERC-74082*)
RA24 socketed bone handle	12th to 13th century	With iron fragments in grave 1341	In same grave as SK1397	SK1397 dated to *cal AD 1035–1150* (*95% probability*), probably *cal AD 1075–1125* (*68% probability*; Fig. 5.4: *SUERC-74075*)

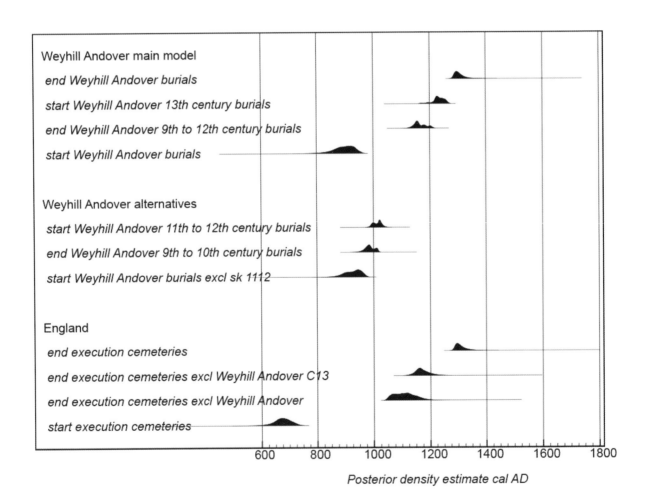

Fig. 5.7   Key parameters from the models shown in Figures 5.4, 5.5 and 5.10 and from unillustrated variations on them

Table 5.6 Radiocarbon dates from other execution cemeteries (Figs 5.8, 5.9 and 5.10). The calibrations in the 'Calibrated date range AD 2σ' column are calculated by the maximum intercept method (Stuiver and Reimer 1986) and are cited as recommended by Mook (1986): rounded outwards by 10, since the standard deviations are all over 25. Those in the 'Highest Posterior Density interval cal AD' columns are rounded outwards by 5. All samples are of articulated human bone except where otherwise stated

Laboratory no.	Sample	Material	Context	Radiocarbon age yr BP	δ¹³C ‰	δ¹⁵N ‰	Calibrated date range AD 2σ	Highest Posterior Density interval cal AD (95% probability)
12 Guildown Avenue, Guildford, Surrey. 3 out of 6 later Saxon burials excavated in 2016 from a cemetery extensively excavated in 1929, which included decapitated and bound individuals								
UBA-34822	SK 59	Bone from 26- to 35-year-old male	Grave 5, supine, crushed into slightly too small grave (Falys 2017)	1167 ± 34	Not yet published	Not yet published	770–980	770–970
UBA-34823	SK 64	Bone from 17- to 25-year-old male	Grave 9, supine, lower legs crossed, beside semi-articulated SK 65 (Falys 2017)	1096 ± 33	" "	" "	880–1020	880–1020
UBA-34824	SK 67	Bone from adult male	Grave 10, supine, legs spread, beside similarly positioned adult male, in turn beside space from which most of 3rd individual removed, leaving hands and a foot (Falys 2017)	1079 ± 34	" "	" "	880–1030	890–1020
Chesterton Lane Corner, Cambridge. 9 out of 10 articulated burials, 1 sample of semi-articulated bone, 2 of disarticulated bone. Excavation confined to area approx. 3.2m in diameter								
Wk-14893	Inhumation 1	R femur of young adult male, decapitated	Supine, in grave cut by inhumation 7 (Cessford et al. 2007, 205–6, illus 2–3, 6–7)	1226 ± 35	−20.2	-	680–890	670–780
Wk-14894	Inhumation 2	L humerus of adult male	Supine, in grave cut by inhumations 4 and 5 (Cessford et al. 2007, 206–7, illus 2–3, 6)	1196 ± 35	−21.0	-	710–950	685–755(47%) 760–835 (48%)
Wk-14895	Inhumation 4	Humerus, radius and ulna of adult male, decapitated	Supine, in grave cutting inhumation 2 (Cessford et al. 2007, 208, illus 2–3, 6–7)	1216 ± 36	−21.1	-	680–940	720–750 (6%) 760–885 (89%)
Wk-14896	Inhumation 5	Humeri, radii and ulnae of older subadult, ?male, decapitated	Supine, in grave cutting inhumation 2 (Cessford et al. 2007, 9, illus 2–3, 6)	1240 ± 35	−22.2	-	670–890	720–880
Wk-14897	Inhumation 6	Femora, R tibia and R humerus of older juvenile	Prone, hands and feet ?bound (Cessford et al. 2007, 210, illus 2–3, 6)	1233 ± 33	−21.1	-	670–890	685–865
Wk-14898	Inhumation 7	Femora of older subadult or young adult	Supine, in grave cutting inhumation 1 (Cessford et al. 2007, 210, illus 2–3, 6)	1301 ± 36	−21.1	-	650–780	690–780 (88%) 790–805 (2%) 810–830 (2%) 835–860 (3%)

Table 5.6 (cont.) Radiocarbon dates from other execution cemeteries

Laboratory no.	Sample	Context	Material	Radiocarbon age yr BP	δ13C ‰	δ15N ‰	Calibrated date range AD 2σ	Highest Posterior Density interval cal AD (95% probability)
Beta-151320	Inhumation 8	Supine (Cessford *et al.* 2007, 210, illus 2–3, 6–7)	R femur of adult male, decapitated	1230 ± 60	–20.1	-	670–890 (for weighted mean of 1240 ± 31 BP; T'=0.0; T'(5%)=3.8; v=1)	685–865 (for weighted mean)
Wk-14899			L femur of same individual as Beta-151320	1243 ± 36	–21.6	-		
Wk-14900	Inhumation 9	Supine, in grave cutting surface of Roman road and sealed by black earth (Cessford *et al.* 2007, 198–201, illus 2–3, 6)	Tibiae and fibulae of adult male, decapitated	1686 ± 37	–21.1	-	250–430	320–430 (54%) 455–475 (1%) 485–545 (40%)
Wk-14901	Inhumation 10	Supine, in grave cutting gravel surface which overlay other burials (Cessford *et al.* 2007, 215, illus 2–3, 6)	R humerus and femur of adult ?male	1193 ± 32	–20.6	-	710–950	815–905 (78%) 915–965 (17%)
Wk-15454	Burial group 12	Semi-articulated in grave with inhumation 3 (Cessford *et al.* 2007, 204, 208, 211)	Humerus, radius and ulna of adult ?female	1238 ± 36	–21.3	-	670–890	685–865
Wk-15452	Burial group 15	Unspecified	L humerus of adult, disarticulated	1156 ± 36	–21.0	-	770–990	765–895
Wk-15453	Burial group 16	Unspecified	L humerus of adult, disarticulated	1195 ± 34	–21.8	-	710–950	710–745 (9%) 765–885 (86%)
Old Dairy Cottage, Littleton and Harestock, Winchester. 4 out of 16								
OxA-12046	Skeleton 575	Grave 128, supine	Bone from adult male, decapitated	1088 ± 26	–18.8	-	890–1020	890–1015
OxA-12045	Skeleton 560	Grave 123, prone	Bone from young adult, ?male, decapitated	1163 ± 25	–18.5	-	770–970	770–905 (77%) 915–965 (18%)
GU-18215	Skeleton 576	Grave 129, prone	Bone from 10- to 12-year-old	1130 ± 30	Not yet published	Not yet published	770–990	775–795 (3%) 800–845 (6%) 860–990 (86%)
GU-19827	Skeleton 580	Grave 117, supine	Bone from young adult, decapitated	1170 ± 30	Not yet published	Not yet published	770–970	770–905 (81%) 915–965 (14%)
Oliver's Battery, Winchester. 3 out of >10. Only part of grave 4 excavated								
OxA-25745	AY 420 (7) individual 1	Grave 4, contexts 7 and 31, supine, overlying other, unexcavated burials (Russel 2016, figs 5–6)	L femur from adult male	942 ± 24	–19.2	8.2	1020–1170	1025–1155

Laboratory no.	Sample	Material	Context	Radiocarbon age yr BP	δ ^{13}C ‰	δ ^{15}N ‰	Calibrated date range AD 2σ	Highest Posterior Density interval cal AD (95% probability)
OxA-25679	AY 420 (30) individual 2	R femur from adult male, perimortem fractures, ?from fall from gallows	Grave 4, contexts 30 and 32, prone, fettered to individual 3, overlying other, unexcavated burials (Russel 2016, figs 5–6)	991 ± 26	–18.9	11.0	990–1150	990–1055 (64%) 1080–1130 (25%) 1135–1155 (6%)
SU-ERC-37908	AY 420 (6) individual 3	L tibia from adult ?male	Grave 4, supine, fettered to individual 2, overlying other, unexcavated burials (Russel 2016, figs 5–6)	991 ± 26	–18.9	11.6	990–1150	990–1055 (64%) 1080–1130 (25%) 1135–1155 (6%)
South Acre, Norfolk. 2 out of ≥119, some decapitated or bound								
HAR-10238	SAC1449	Bone from older subadult male	Skeleton 33, supine in grave cutting earlier one, outside probably Bronze Age ring ditch (Wymer 1996, 88, fig.45)	1150 ± 70	–21.9	–	770–990	710–750 (5%) 760–1020 (90%)
HAR-10239	SAC1305	Bone from older adult male	Skeleton 75, supine in grave cut into partly infilled probably Bronze Age ring ditch (Wymer 1996, 88, fig. 45).	1710 ± 90	–21.8	–	80–550 Excluded from model	–
London Road, Staines, Surrey. 3 out of 31								
AA-38407	Skeleton 226	Bone from indeterminate adult	Supine, hands ?bound (Hayman and Reynolds 2005, 219–20, illus 4)	1230 ± 40	–21.4	–	670–900	685–890
AA-38408	Skeleton 241	Bone from young adult	Supine (Hayman and Reynolds 2005, 219–22, illus 4)	960 ± 40	–21.50	–	990–1170	995–1005 (1%) 1010–1165 (94%)
AA-38409	Skeleton 277	Bone from young adult male, decapitated	Prone, head beside pelvis (Hayman and Reynolds 2005, 219, 222, illus 4, 6)	900 ± 40	–20.3	–	1020–1230	1030–1220
Sutton Hoo, Suffolk group 1. 5 out of 23, some possibly decapitated or bound, around possible gallows								
HAR-6800	Int 48, burial 17	Bone from young adult, ?male	F9, supine, head and shoulders vertical against N wall of grave (Carver 2005, 316, fig. 142)	1330 ± 80	–	–	570–890 Modelled as *terminus post quem* because possibly contaminated with consolidant (Ambers 2005, 54)	570–890
OxA-819	Int 32, burial 32	Bone from young adult	F109, prone, above a further prone body (Carver 2005, 323, fig. 145)	1200 ± 70	–	–	660–990	700–980

Table 5.6 (cont.) Radiocarbon dates from other execution cemeteries

Laboratory no.	Sample	Material	Context	δ ^{13}C ‰	δ ^{15}N ‰	Radiocarbon age yr BP	Calibrated date range AD 2σ	Highest Posterior Density interval cal AD (95% probability)
BM-3035	Int 32/F173 2526	Bone from young adult male	Burial 30, F173, supine, hands crossed over pelvis (Carver 2005, 323, figs 144, 147)	−21.7	-	960 ± 60	980–1220	900–925 (3%) 950–1160 (92%)
BM-2825	Int 52/ F34/1039/70–97	Bone from young adult	Burial 35, F34, supine, decapitated head on R arm (Carver 2005, 323, figs 145, 147, pl. 47:E)	−21.0	-	1250 ± 80	640–980	680–970
BM-3036	Int 52/F74 183–184	Bone from mature male	Burial 39, F74, kneeling, hands behind back (Carver 2005, 324, figs 145, 147)	−21.2	-	1070 ± 45	900–1020	875–1035
BM-3041	Int 32/F165 2277	*Betula* sp. charcoal	F165, post-pit, interpreted as part of gallows in centre of cemetery (Carver 2005, 324, fig. 148)	−26.0	-	1180 ± 50	680–990	715–745 (4%) 760–980 (91%)
Sutton Hoo, Suffolk group 2. 3 out of 17, some possibly decapitated or bound, at margin of pre-existing barrow								
BM-2865	Int 41/ burial 40/F152	Bone from young ?male	F81, on R side, legs flexed, feet ?bound, ?decapitated (Carver 2005, 334, fig. 150)	−21.3	-	1020 ± 45	900–1150	890–1055 (90%) 1080–1125 (5%)
BM-2824	Int 41/ burial 42/F148/1527/ 16056–8	Bone from adult male	Burial 42b, F148, supine, decapitated, beneath 2 prone bodies (Carver 2005, 334–46, fig. 150, pl. 49b)	−21.0	-	1320 ± 40	640–780	655–780 (89%) 790–805 (1%) 815–825 (1%) 835–875 (4%)
BM-3037	Int 41/F55 225–22548	Bone from adult	Burial 45, F154, extended	−23.4	-	1060 ± 50	880–1040	865–1050
Walkington Wold, Yorkshire. 3 out of 12, some decapitated								
OxA-10826	Skeleton 11	Human bone from articulated skeleton	In apparently multiple burial with nos 8, 12 and 13 (Buckberry and Hadley 2007, 312)	−19.8	-	1336 ± 34	640–770	650–730 (57%) 735–770 (38%)
OxA-12716		Disarticulated human humerus	With no. 13, in apparently multiple burial with nos 8, 11 and 12 (Buckberry and Hadley 2007, 312)	−19.6	-	1160 ± 25	770–970	775–905 (73%) 915–965 (22%)
OxA-12717	Skeleton 8	Human bone from articulated skeleton	In apparently multiple burial with nos 11, 12 and 13 (Buckberry and Hadley 2007, 312)	−19.4	-	1037 ± 27	970–1030	900–920 (2%) 965–1035 (93%)

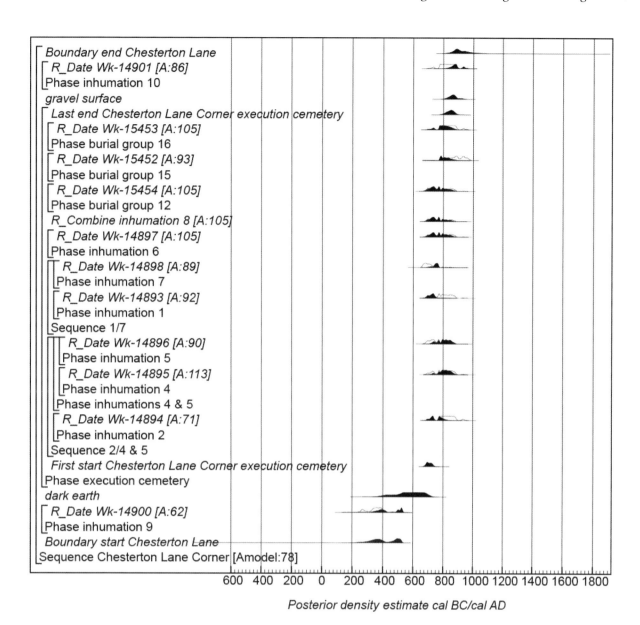

Fig. 5.8   Probability distributions of radiocarbon dates for the burials at Chesterton Lane Corner, Cambridge (Table 5.6), in a model incorporating the stratigraphic relations documented by Cessford (et al. 2007). The format is the same as in Figure 5.4

from the Weyhill site (Fig. 5.10), in order to avoid biasing the result with relatively large numbers of dates from just three cemeteries. It should be remembered that some of the measurements, notably those from Sutton Hoo, were made in decades when bone pretreatment was less satisfactory than it is now, AMS dating was unavailable, and errors were often wide. The dates and related information are listed in Table 5.6.

The dates from Chesterton Lane Corner, Cambridge are modelled following the reported stratigraphy. Inhumation 9, cut into a Roman road and overlain by a 'dark earth' deposit into which the graves of the cemetery were cut, is modelled as preceding the cemetery (Fig. 5.8: *Wk-14900*). Within the cemetery, inhumations

4 and 5 are modelled as post-dating inhumation 2, which they cut, and inhumation 7 is modelled as post-dating inhumation 1, which it cut. Inhumation 10, cut into a gravel surface which sealed the other burials, is modelled as post-dating the cemetery (Fig. 5.8: *Wk-14901*). A weighted mean has been taken of statistically consistent replicate measurements for inhumation 8 before incorporation in the model. Two dates for samples of disarticulated bone are modelled as contemporary with the articulated burials (Fig. 5.8: *Wk-15452, -15453*) because they are statistically consistent with the measurements for the eight articulated or semi-articulated samples from the cemetery as determined by a X^2 test (T'=10.3; T'(5%)=16.9; v=9; Ward and

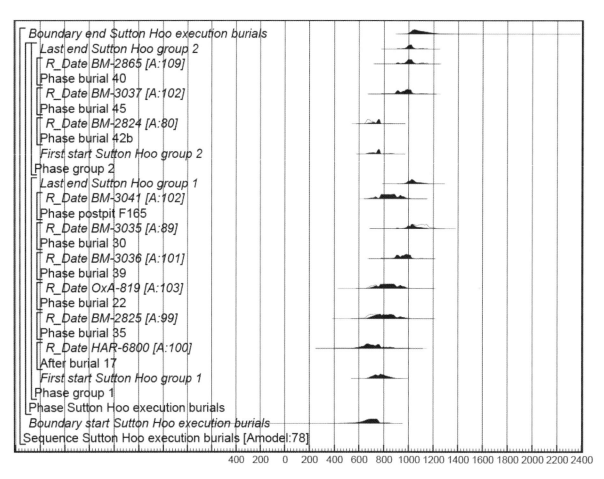

Posterior density estimate cal BC/cal AD

Fig. 5.9   Probability distributions of radiocarbon dates from two execution cemeteries at Sutton Hoo, Suffolk (Table 5.6). HAR-6800 is modelled as a terminus post quem for burial 17, using the After function in OxCal, because the sample may have been contaminated with consolidants. The format is the same as in Figure 5.4

Wilson 1978). The outcome is an estimated start date of *cal AD 670–745 (95% probability)*, probably *cal AD 685–730 (68% probability*; Fig. 5.8: *start Chesterton Lane Corner execution cemetery)* and estimated end date of *cal AD 790–895 (95% probability)*, probably *cal AD 820–875 (68% probability*; Fig. 5.8: *end Chesterton Lane Corner execution cemetery)*, with a duration of *75–195 years (95% probability)*, probably *105–170 years (68% probability*; Table 5.3: *duration Chesterton Lane Corner execution cemetery)*. It is impossible to tell whether this compact span is representative of the whole cemetery, since the excavated area was little more than 3.0m in diameter (Cessford *et al.* 2007, 197).

The results from the relatively few skeletons with adequate bone preservation at Sutton Hoo, have wide standard deviations, and the samples will have undergone less than optimal methods of bone pretreatment. The date for burial 17 in group 1 is modelled as a *terminus post quem* because the sample may have been contaminated with a consolidant which

would have made the result too old (Fig. 5.9: *HAR-6800*; Ambers 2005, 54). A date for birch charcoal from a feature interpreted as part of a gallows (Fig. 5.9: *BM-3041*) is modelled as contemporary with its context because birch is a relatively short-lived tree. For group 1, 23 burials clustered around the possible gallows, the estimated start date is *cal AD 675–875 (95% probability)*, probably *cal AD 710–825 (68% probability*; Fig. 5.9: *start Sutton Hoo group 1)* and the estimated end date *cal AD 955–1160 (95% probability)*, probably *cal AD 985–1075 (68% probability*; Fig. 5.9: *end Sutton Hoo group 1)*, with a duration of *120–420 years (95% probability)*, probably *190–340 years (68% probability*; Table 5.3: *duration Sutton Hoo group 1)*. For group 2, 17 burials around a pre-existing Saxon burial mound, the estimated start date is *cal AD 655–780 (89% probability)* or *790–805 (1% probability)* or *815–825 (1% probability)* or *835–875 (4% probability)*, probably *cal AD 695–725 (16% probability)* or *735–775 (52% probability*; Fig. 5.9: *start Sutton Hoo group*

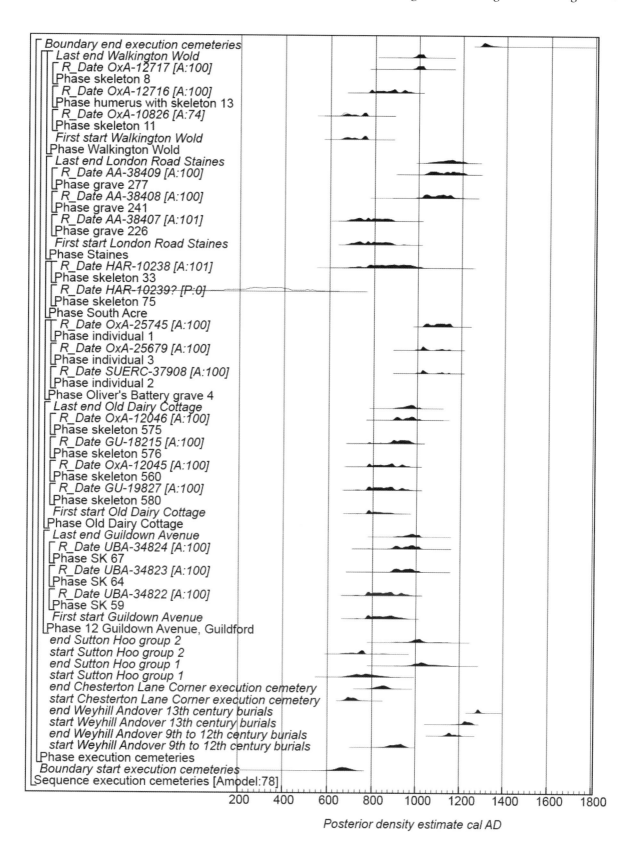

Fig. 5.10 *Probability distributions of radiocarbon dates for execution burials in England (Table 5.6) modelled by site. The start and end estimates for Andover, Chesterton Lane Corner and Sutton Hoo are derived from the models shown in Figures 5.4, 5.8 and 5.9 respectively. '?' denotes that HAR-10239, from South Acre, Norfolk, is excluded from the model. The format is the same as in Figure 5.4*

2) and the estimated end date *cal AD 905–930 (2% probability)* or *940–1060 (86% probability)* or *1080–1125 (6% probability)* or *1140–1150 (1% probability)*, probably *cal AD 980–1035 (68% probability)*; Fig. 5.9: *end Sutton Hoo group 2*), with a duration of *130–400 years (95% probability)*, probably *220–330 years (68% probability*; Table 5.3: *duration Sutton Hoo group 2*).

At South Acre, a 1st to 6th-century cal AD date for one of the burials cut into a barrow ditch is excluded from the model on the grounds that it either pre-dates the execution burials or is inaccurate (Fig. 5.10: HAR-10239?).

The overall result is an estimated start date of *cal AD 605–735 (95% probability)*, probably *cal AD 645–710 (68% probability*; Fig. 5.10: *start execution cemeteries*) and an estimated end date of *cal AD 1275–1365 (95% probability)*, probably *cal AD 1280–1320 (68% probability*; Fig. 5.10: *end execution cemeteries*), with an overall duration of *545–640 years (95% probability)*, probably *570–625 years (68% probability*; Fig. 5.6: *duration execution cemeteries*).

Discussion

The 13th to early 14th-century end date for execution cemeteries shown in Figures 5.6 and 5.10 depends entirely on the four 13th-century burials from Andover. If they are excluded, the end date drops back to *cal AD 1115–1235 (95% probability)*, probably *cal AD 1140–1195 (68% probability*; Fig. 5.6: *end execution cemeteries excl Weyhill Andover C13*) and the duration to *390–520 years (95% probability)*, probably *425–490 years* (Fig. 5.6: *duration execution cemeteries excl Weyhill Andover C13*). In other words, if the 13th-century burials at Andover are viewed as a separate episode, then the cemetery conforms more closely to the overall pattern.

Even with the 13th-century individuals excluded, however, nine out of the 16 remaining dated burials from Andover still have more than *50% probability*

of being post-Conquest (Table 5.4) and two further individuals share the graves of two of these. This is in marked contrast to the infrequency of such dates from other sites. When a comparable ordering exercise to that shown in Table 5.4 is performed on the dates from other sites shown in Figures 5.8–5.10 (excluding the pre and post-cemetery samples from Chesterton Lane Corner, the *Betula* charcoal date from Sutton Hoo and the Roman period date from Castle Acre), only three out of 35 individuals have more than *50% probability* of being post-Conquest. These are individual 1 from grave 4 at Oliver's Battery (*73%*; Fig. 5.10: *OxA-25745*) and skeletons 241 and 277 from London Road, Staines (*65%* and *81%* respectively; Fig. 5.10: *AA-38408, -38409*). A possible fourth is burial 30 in group 1 at Sutton Hoo. This is modelled as forming part of a single episode of activity with the other dated Sutton Hoo burials, and its resulting date estimate of *cal AD 900–925 (3% probability)* or *950–1160 (92% probability)* has only *26% probability* of being post-Conquest (Fig. 5.9: *BM-3035*). If, however, it was later than the other burials by a significant interval, then its true age could lie towards the recent end of its wide simple calibrated range of cal AD 980–1220 (2σ). Raising the number of probably post-Conquest burials at other sites from three to four would still leave a strong contrast between their frequency at Andover and elsewhere.

If the Andover results are removed completely from the overall model, the estimated end date for execution cemeteries becomes *cal AD 1040–1185 (95% probability)*, probably *cal AD 1055–1140 (68% probability*; Fig. 5.7: *end execution cemeteries excl Weyhill Andover*) and the estimated duration *310–475 years (95% probability)*, probably *345–440 years (68% probability*; Fig. 5.6: *duration execution cemeteries excl Weyhill Andover*). The cemetery at Andover seems to have continued in use exceptionally late. Fuller dating of other sites may modify this impression.

Chapter 6
Isotope Analysis

by Mandy Jay

Introduction

Isotopic analysis was of a sample of burials from the Weyhill Road cemetery (Fig. 6.1), with individuals dating mainly from the 9th through to the 13th century AD. Twelve individuals were analysed for oxygen isotopes from tooth enamel (2nd molars or premolars), with eight of these also analysed for strontium isotope ratios. Carbon and nitrogen analysis of bone collagen (cortical long bone) was undertaken on all twelve individuals, along with an additional eight human and two sheep bones, one of which was from a context overlying a burial and the second from a Saxon *grübenhaus*, at nearby Old Down Farm. Sulphur analysis of bone collagen was also undertaken on 15 of the human burials and both sheep. The purpose of the analyses was to consider mobility, diet and environmental factors for these individuals, some of whom had probably been decapitated, with some having their hands removed or tied back. All data were produced at the Scottish Universities Environmental Research Centre (SUERC) in East Kilbride, with the carbon and nitrogen data produced alongside radiocarbon dates. Their methods are described in Sayle *et al.* (2013) and Montgomery *et al.* (2009).

Two individuals (SKs1274 and 1297) have oxygen data which support immigration, and are consistent with a Scandinavian origin. SK1274 also has a strontium isotope ratio which is inconsistent with Andover. SK1211 has strontium data which are not consistent with the site, and may well be an immigrant, while SK1228 has a nitrogen value which is an outlier in the context of the group, and an oxygen isotope ratio which is suggestive of mobility, at least within Britain.

Non-specialist summary of analyses

Data obtained from the isotope analysis of skeletal remains reflect the chemistry of the food and drink consumed by an individual at the point of formation of those particular body tissues. This means that they can be used to produce a narrative which is directly relevant to an individual, or to a group of individuals. This usually involves consideration of mobility, migration, diet and local environment. The chemical composition of food and drink is tied to source locations in a variety of ways, and is affected by factors such as geology and climate; this is how mobility can be identified. There are many variables and potentially confounding factors involved in the interpretation of the data, and not all of them can be discussed in detail here. This section provides an overview of the most relevant points for each type of isotope analysis undertaken for this study.

Strontium isotope analysis of tooth enamel

Strontium isotope ratios are one of the main indicators used to provide evidence of geographical origin. Bio-available strontium mostly derives from the underlying geology on which the plants at the base of the food chain are grown. This means that isotope ratios are usually indicative of the rock present in the individual's home region. If the values obtained from the skeletal sample do not match those expected for the burial location, then mobility is indicated. The UK is a maritime region, which means that the effect of rainwater, which largely derives from seawater, should be taken into account, alongside both the geology and the possibility of marine salt deposition in coastal areas.

This study uses tooth enamel as the strontium isotope sample tissue, because it is highly resistant to diagenetic alteration. Enamel forms during childhood, with different teeth having different formation periods, and strontium is incorporated during that time without change during later life. The isotope ratios obtained therefore reflect the environment of food procurement during that childhood period. If the signal from youth is

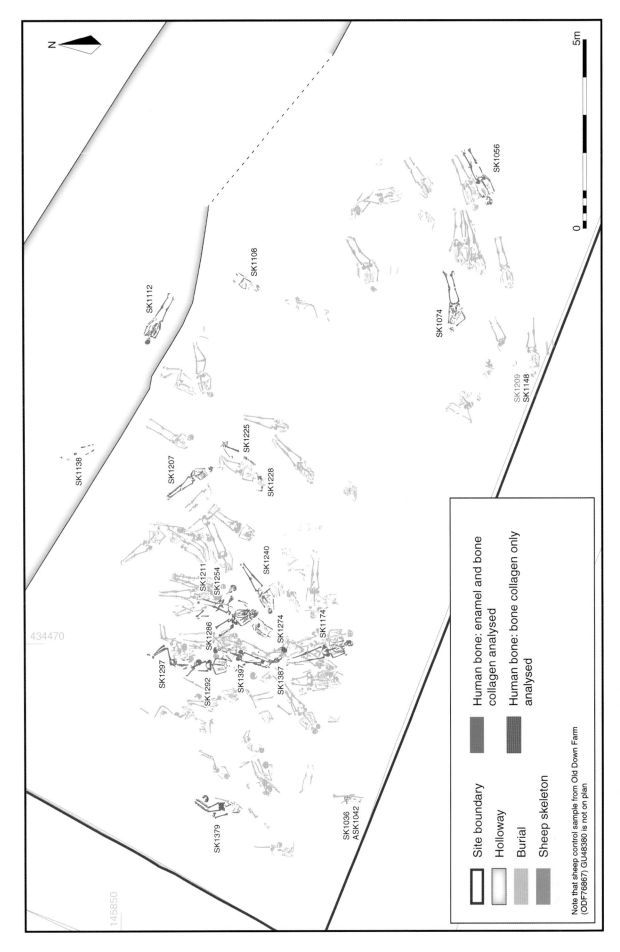

Fig. 6.1   Location of individuals from which isotope samples were taken

consistent with that expected from the burial location, then there is no evidence for mobility. However, if the values do not match, then it is likely that the person moved away from their original home region during or after childhood, or that their body was transported to the burial site after death.

Confounding factors include the possibility that an individual may have moved after childhood, lived away for a time and then returned to their original home location. In this case the movement cannot be identified from the enamel signal. Another possible scenario which would cause difficulty is where somebody moved between two locations where the geology was very similar. In addition, it is not only the movement of the person which must be considered; plants are the dominant dietary source of strontium, so if these were not obtained from the home location, such as where food was traded, or transhumance was practised, then this will also have an effect on the interpretation of data.

Strontium isotope ratios are given as $^{87}Sr/^{86}Sr$ values. Suggested sources for more detailed information about analytical techniques and data interpretation are Montgomery (2010), Evans *et al.* (2010; 2012) and Bentley (2006).

Oxygen isotope analysis of tooth enamel

Another isotope system widely used for interpreting mobility is oxygen. The isotope ratio data ($\delta^{18}O$ values), again from tooth enamel, mainly indicate the composition of ingested water, particularly drinking water, which can be sourced from rain or groundwater. There are many variables and error sources affecting these data, and they can be more difficult to interpret with precision than some other datasets discussed in this report, but can be particularly useful when used in a multi-isotope study, such as in conjunction with strontium isotope ratios.

A number of environmental variables, including latitude, altitude, distance from the coast, levels of precipitation, air temperature and season, can affect the oxygen isotope composition of precipitation. Geographical variation at higher latitudes is particularly governed by surface air temperatures, while a range of factors can cause differences in the values obtained from groundwater sources and precipitation, such as evaporation from surface water and recharge from rivers containing water from high altitude precipitation. Anthropogenic processes can also cause alterations in the isotope ratios, such as in cases where drinking water is boiled, or alcoholic beverages produced.

The $\delta^{18}O$ values obtained from tooth enamel will not precisely match those from the drinking water consumed, partly because some of the ingested water is also sourced from food. There is a direct relationship with the water values and a species-specific balance between the sources, with fractionation incorporated into the system. This relationship can be affected by a range of factors, such as the consumption of milk or blood, physiological factors such as disease or activity level, or the importation of food and drink from a different region.

It has often been the practice in earlier publications of $\delta^{18}O$ values to convert the data to environmental water values ($\delta^{18}O_w$), using equations which are particular to species. These water values are then compared with environmental surface water data mapped for those locations relevant to the mobility study. There are a number of different regression equations which can be used for humans and it is possible to introduce significant levels of error into the dataset by doing this. For this reason, researchers have more recently preferred to use unconverted $\delta^{18}O$ values in the context of British archaeological empirical datasets (e.g. Evans *et al.* 2012; Pellegrini *et al.* 2016). This is the approach taken in this study, although converted drinking water values have been provided for reference purposes.

When processing samples for oxygen isotope analysis, either a carbonate or a phosphate fraction can be used. This study uses carbonate, which requires a less technically difficult pretreatment of the sample, making it faster and less expensive. Suggested sources for more detailed information about the analysis and interpretation of $\delta^{18}O$ data are Evans *et al.* (2012), Lee-Thorp (2008), Lightfoot and O'Connell (2016), Pellegrini *et al.* (2016) and Pollard *et al.* (2011).

Carbon and nitrogen isotope analysis of collagen

The sample material for carbon and nitrogen isotope analysis ($\delta^{13}C$ and $\delta^{15}N$ values) is collagen, which is extracted from bone or dentine. The data are normally used to reconstruct dietary information, but they do have a connection to the environment and in a multi-isotope study they can be used in the interpretation of mobility as well. Basic summaries suggested for further reading are Sealy 2001, Lee-Thorp 2008 and Makarewicz and Sealy 2015.

The source of the carbon and nitrogen in the collagen is mainly dietary protein, unless nutrients are in restricted supply. One of the two isotopes being compared for each chemical element is usually taken up in preference to the other (fractionation), so that although the relationship between the food and the collagen sample is direct, the values will be different. There may also be differences between the values found in animal meat, milk and fat (i.e. animal food products) and those found in the animal's bone or dentine collagen, particularly for carbon. The food chain ultimately leads back to plants, and these are affected by climate and environmental conditions, so that the data can be used to interpret a person's connection with the location at a particular time and place. This is often done by using data from contemporaneous herbivores, which are assumed to be eating local plants, to consider the effects of the environment on those plants.

The main interpretative value of these data lies in three particular dietary relationships. These indicate levels of consumption of animal protein (trophic level), aquatic resources (particularly marine resources), and the photosynthetic pathway of the plants at the base of the food chain (C_3 or C_4). The $\delta^{15}N$ values are elevated between trophic levels, due to the fractionation in the system; they are usually around 3 to 5‰ higher in the consumer as compared to the collagen of an animal consumed (although this may be flexible, see O'Connell *et al.* 2012). The $\delta^{13}C$ values may also be elevated by around 1‰. Significant enrichments in both the ^{15}N and ^{13}C isotopes are seen when high levels of marine resources are consumed, with the relationship for freshwater aquatic dietary inputs being dependent on the particular local aquatic food web. It is important to be aware that other factors can also affect the values, including nutritional and physiological stress, and the consumption of breastmilk.

The main photosynthetic pathways of plants are labelled as C_3 and C_4. These different pathways result in $\delta^{13}C$ values which are significantly different in the plants, and thus in their consumers, with C_4 plants producing values which are higher. Temperate environments support mainly C_3 plants, and these are the indigenous resources available in northern Europe, with C_4 plants more usually found in warmer regions. The latter are not found in significant quantities in early Britain, although salt-marsh environments can support small quantities of C_4 halophytes. In archaeological studies, C_4 indications start to appear in the British food chain from the Roman period onwards, although at this early point the signal usually indicates migrants who have sourced their diet elsewhere. Millet, which is a C_4 plant, started to appear in continental European food chains from the late Neolithic onwards, either in the diet of animals, or directly consumed by humans. Broomcorn millet has been found in Roman Britain in small quantities, but is unlikely to have been grown here.

The importation of C_4 plants during the period covered by this study is likely to have been very limited. Sugar cane is C_4, but will not have been available to the majority of people. A C_4 signal in British samples at this time probably indicates immigration. The bulk of the ^{13}C present in collagen is from protein consumption, so it is important to be aware that an omnivorous diet will produce a signal which is weighted towards animal products and very small quantities of C_4 plant foods are unlikely to be visible from the consumer's bone collagen. If they are present in domesticated herbivore diets (e.g. millet or C_4 halophytes), it is possible that they will be more clearly visible in human samples.

Local environmental conditions, such as climate, salinity and manuring practices, affect the isotopes present in plants, and therefore the signals seen across the food chain. It is therefore difficult to interpret absolute values for individuals when variation is present in these factors through both time and space. 'Baseline' values for the contemporaneous local environment are therefore obtained in an ideal situation, in order to put human sample data into the best context. This is usually done by analysing animal samples, particularly herbivores, from the same location and time-period. It is not always possible to obtain appropriate samples, however, and in the case of this study, existing published comparative data have been considered for both humans and animals, rather than the animals specifically obtained from these excavations, although two sheep bones have been analysed, one from this site and the second from a Saxon context from a nearby Andover site.

Similar to the tooth enamel used for strontium and oxygen analysis, the formation timing of the sample is important. Bone collagen forms over a long period of time, and changes throughout life, with newly formed molecules replacing older ones. Turnover periods cannot be defined precisely, but they are much longer for adults than for infants or growing children, and for mature adults it is probable that a significant part of a cortical bone sample was formed during adolescence, so that the signal seen from such a sample reflects the averaged diet over many years (Hedges *et al.* 2007). Some parts of the skeleton turn over much faster, so that rib, for example, will reflect a period much closer to death than a cortical long bone sample (Cox and Sealy 1997). In a multi-isotope study such as this, it is important to be aware of these timing differences. Tooth enamel data is from childhood, while cortical long bone collagen samples reflect a much longer period, and the collagen may or may not have had sufficient time to equilibrate to a local dietary signal if an immigrant is identified.

Sulphur isotope analysis of collagen

Research into sulphur isotope analysis in archaeological skeletal material is at an earlier stage than that for carbon and nitrogen. There is a much less clear understanding of the full range of factors which may affect the data (e.g. Nehlich *et al.* 2010; Jay *et al.* 2013; Sayle *et al.* 2013; van der Sluis *et al.* 2016), and comparative datasets are smaller and fewer. Collagen contains only very small amounts of sulphur when compared to carbon or nitrogen, so that the analysis is technically more difficult and the analytical error to be expected is larger. Overall, therefore, it should be borne in mind that sulphur data may be less precise and more difficult to interpret, although research continues to develop our understanding. Inter-laboratory comparison may be more problematic for sulphur than for other isotopes, and the contentious issue of sample contamination and the requirement for ultrafiltration should be borne in mind (Bocherens *et al.* 2011; Nehlich, pers. comm.).

$\delta^{34}S$ values can reflect both environment and dietary constituents. There is a known 'sea spray' effect where the effect of marine sulphates can be reflected in dietary resources, so the proximity of the coastline to a site can be an important factor to consider, as can local geology (Richards *et al.* 2001; 2003; Nehlich 2015). Sulphur can also distinguish aquatic resource consumption, both marine and freshwater, particularly if $\delta^{15}N$ and $\delta^{13}C$ values are also available (Craig *et al.* 2010; Nehlich *et al.* 2010; 2011; Smits *et al.* 2010). As with carbon and nitrogen, animal 'baseline' signatures are invaluable for contextualising local environments, but in this case there is little fractionation in the system, so that no significant trophic level effect is expected (Webb *et al.* 2017); if the human $\delta^{34}S$ values differ from those of local animals, this may well be an indicator of mobility.

Samples were ultrafiltered for sulphur analysis.

Results and discussion

Table 6.1 shows details of the samples analysed, and the data are presented in Tables 6.2 and 6.3. The $^{87}Sr/^{86}Sr$ ratios range from 0.7081 to 0.7119 for eight individuals, while the $\delta^{18}O_{carbonate}$ values range from 24.2 to 27.6‰ for twelve individuals. $\delta^{13}C$ and $\delta^{15}N$ values range from 20.2 to -19.4‰, and 8.0 to 12.3‰ respectively for 20 individuals. The values for two sheep were both 21.7‰ for carbon, with 5.0 and 5.2‰ for nitrogen. For sulphur, the $\delta^{34}S$ values for 15 individuals ranged from 1.3 to 14.5‰, with the values for the sheep being 14.8 and 15.4‰.

Figure 6.2 shows the strontium and oxygen data plotted alongside comparative data from Weymouth in Dorset (Chenery *et al.* 2014), St John's College in Oxford (Pollard *et al.* 2012) and Old Dairy Cottage, Winchester (Warham 2011). The Weymouth and Oxford sites are mass graves dating to the late 10th or early 11th century AD, and hypothesised to represent raiding parties of Vikings captured and executed by local inhabitants, which may make them good comparatives for the decapitated and bound Andover burials. The Winchester site is an 'execution cemetery', where graves also contained decapitated and bound interments, and which contained a number of non-local individuals, based on the strontium data. This cemetery dates to the late 8th to early 11th centuries AD. The Winchester data are from strontium analysis alone, and some of the Oxford samples have only oxygen data available; these data-points are shown on the chart in randomly positioned linear arrays, to allow comparison.

The Winchester and Weymouth sites are on similar Cretaceous chalk geology to that at Andover, although Weymouth is much closer to the sea, and closer to Jurassic clay formations. The Oxford site is, in broad terms, affected by Jurassic geology bordering the chalk, the Thames floodplain underlain by the Oxford Clay, and is locally affected by limestones and sandstones.

Four of the eight individuals, for whom both strontium and oxygen data are available, fall within the ranges expected for a chalk location in Britain. The $^{87}Sr/^{86}Sr$ ratios lie between 0.7075 and 0.7092, which is the range expected for a chalk region with the seawater value at the upper limit, this being the source of a rainwater contribution to the diet (Montgomery *et al.* 2007). The $\delta^{18}O_{carbonate}$ values fall centrally in the range expected for Britain overall, based on the data from Evans *et al.* (2012). Two of these eight (SK1211 and SK1274) have strontium isotope ratios which are higher than the others (0.7119 and 0.7106 respectively), and outside the range expected for a general chalk location. The oxygen isotope ratio is well within the expected British range for SK1211, but outside of it for SK1274. This latter burial has combined strontium and oxygen data which are similar to those obtained from Weymouth and Oxford, who were postulated to be raiding Vikings from Scandinavia. These individuals are both male; SK1211 had no hands, and was buried with a large stone placed beside the right side of the head, while SK1274 is a possible decapitation, who was missing his cranium, with the mandible between his legs.

The final two of these eight have $^{87}Sr/^{86}Sr$ ratios, which fall within the chalk range, but they have $\delta^{18}O_{carbonate}$ values which suggest mobility. SK1297 has a low oxygen value (24.5‰) which puts him outside the range expected for Britain. He may also be a decapitated individual, having his skull positioned oddly and one of the cervical vertebrae apparently missing. While SK1228 still plots in the British section of the chart, this young person is at the other extreme (27.6‰), and is the only individual in the western, 'high rainfall' range. While it is possible that this individual is at the extreme of the range to be obtained from Weyhill, this is an indication that he/she may not have originated at this site when considered alongside the nitrogen data (see below), although if mobility is involved, this may well have been within Britain. It may also indicate unusual consumption, within the context of the Andover group, of a resource such as an alcoholic drink. The $\delta^{18}O$ value is very similar to those from Ringlemere in Kent, where the 5th-century AD individuals had higher than expected oxygen isotope ratios, and one of the possible reasons suggested for this was the consumption of processed drinks (Brettell *et al.* 2012).

Of the likely mobile individuals, SK1274 (879 to 1013 cal AD) is earlier in date than SK1297 or SK1211 (1030 to 1185 cal AD and 1033 to 1186 cal AD, respectively), and SK1228 is later (1187 to 1276 cal AD).

All four of the individuals for whom only oxygen data are available, without strontium isotope ratios, fall within the central range expected for Britain.

Figure 6.3 shows the strontium isotope ratios with the strontium concentrations for the eight relevant individuals, alongside comparative data from Weymouth and

Table 6.1 Details of samples taken for isotope analysis

ID	Details	Bone sampled	Tooth sampled	Oxygen	Strontium	Collagen: S	Collagen: C&N
SK1056	Skeleton 1056, Grave 1055. SUERC-74061, GU-44439/GU-44455. 691 ± 30 BP. Male, 17–22 yrs. Double burial with SK1057. Supine, extended. Arms to sides with left arm under SK1057 right arm. Spina bifida occulta.	Right femur	RM^2	✓	✓	✓	✓
SK1074	Skeleton 1074, Grave 1075. SUERC-78126, GU-46926. 757 ± 29 BP. Male, 19–24 yrs. Supine, extended, left arm by side & right arm flexed towards body wide, as if around something.	Left fibula	None	X	X	X	✓
SK1108	Skeleton 1108, Grave 1109. SUERC-74062, GU-44440/GU-44456. 1116 ± 30 BP. Male, <25 yrs. Only upper torso surviving. Supine, extended. Right arm extended & left arm bent at elbow 90 degrees across body, hand on right arm.	Right femur	LM^2	✓	✓	✓	✓
SK1112	Skeleton 1112, Grave 1111. SUERC-74064, GU-44442/GU-44457. 1181 ± 30 BP. Male, 16–21 yrs. Supine, extended, with arms down beside sides & hands in towards pelvis.	Right femur	RM^2	✓	✓	✓	✓
SK1138	Skeleton 1138, Grave 1137. SUERC-78128, GU-46928. 1003 ± 29 BP:Male, 18–25 yrs. Heavily truncated by modern feature.	Femur fragments	None	X	X	X	✓
SK1174	Skeleton 1174, Grave 1173. SUERC-74082, GU-44453/GU-44465. 998 ± 30 BP. Male, 22–27 yrs. Supine, extended with hands tied behind back, head tilted forward & to right. Adjacent to SK1175 (interred at same time). Possible evidence of being cut down from noose.	Left femur	LM^2	✓	X	✓	✓
SK1207	Skeleton 1207, Grave 1206. SUERC-74065, GU-44443/GU-44458. 961 ± 30 BP. ?Male, 15–17 yrs. Supine, extended, skull mostly damaged, hands tied behind back. Disarticulated humerus (SK1222) placed adjacent to right side of pelvis.	Right femur	RM_2	✓	X	✓	✓
SK1209	Skeleton 1209, Grave 1152. SUERC-78127, GU-46927. 681 ± 29 BP. Male, 14–19 yrs. Supine, extended, lower left side truncated. Arms crossed across body. Directly below SK1148.	Left humerus	None	X	X	X	✓
SK1211	Skeleton 1211, Grave 1210. SUERC-74077, GU-44451/GU-44464. 913 ± 27 BP. Male, 30–34 yrs. Supine, extended with left arm bent up over chest, but hands entirely absent. Large stone placed beside right side of head.	Left femur	RM^2	✓	✓	✓	✓
SK1225	Skeleton 1225, Grave 1223. SUERC-74063, GU-44441. 1093 ± 30 BP. ??Male, adult. Supine, extended. Only lower legs & lower right arm surviving *in situ*.	Right radius	None	X	X	✓	✓
SK1228	Skeleton 1228, Grave 1226. SUERC-78122, GU-46925/GU-48377. 798 ± 29 BP. Indeterminate sex, 16–19 yrs. Prone, axial skeleton only.	Left clavicle	LP_2	✓	✓	X	✓
SK1240	Skeleton 1240, Grave 1239. SUERC-74066, GU-44444/GU-44459. 1081 ± 27 BP. Male, 35–45 yrs. Supine, extended, with both lower arms drawn across body. Hands cut off at wrist level & placed separately underneath pelvis.	Right femur	RM^2	✓	✓	✓	✓

ID	Details	Bone sampled	Tooth sampled	Oxygen	Strontium	Collagen: S	Collagen: C&N
SK1254	Skeleton 1254, Grave 1253. SUERC-74074, GU-44448/GU-44461. 952 ± 30 BP. Male, 45+ yrs. Supine, knees bent up then truncated through, skull on right side & most of right torso truncated.	Left femur	RM_2	✓	✓	✓	✓
SK1274	Skeleton 1274, Grave 1273. SUERC-74071, GU-44445/GU-44460 and GU-48378. 1110 ± 30 BP. Male, 35–45 yrs. Supine, extended with feet truncated by grave 1253 & upper legs truncated by grave 1285. Cranium missing, but mandible & maxilla fragment between legs. Right arm down beside side, left forearm turned in across body. Hyoid found, ?decapitation. Possible cut on cervical vertebra, but truncation damage could have occurred in antiquity.	Right humerus	RP_2 / LP_2	✓	✓	✓	✓
SK1286	Skeleton 1286, Grave 1285. SUERC-78121, GU-46924. 936 ± 29 BP. Male, 25–35 yrs. Prone, hands tied behind back, lower legs truncated.	Left scapula	None	X	X	X	✓
SK1292	Skeleton 1292, Grave 1291. SUERC-74081, GU-44452. 907 ± 27 BP. Male, 25–29 yrs. Supine, extended, hands crossed across pelvis, skull missing (probably truncated by other grave) & lower legs truncated by modern cable. ?Hands tied.	Left femur	None	X	X	✓	✓
SK1297	Skeleton 1297, Grave 1296. SUERC-74076, GU-44450/GU-44463 and GU-48379. 918 ± 30 BP. Male, 22–34 yrs. Torso supine, legs flexed to right side, skull tilted forward to face left shoulder with mandible open. Left hand raised to left shoulder, but right arm truncated by grave 1337. Well preserved. SK1330 skull at feet. ?Decapitation – CV3 missing.	Right tibia	LM^2 / LP_2	✓	✓	✓	✓
SK1379	Skeleton 1379, Grave 1378. SUERC-74073, GU-44447. 924 ± 30 BP. Female, 35–45 yrs. Prone, arms crossed under chest, disarticulated leg bones (SK1381) placed on top, with male disarticulated skull SK1380 to east of legs. ?Decapitation – no osteological evidence, but no skull recovered.	Right femur	None	X	X	✓	✓
SK1387	Skeleton 1387, Grave 1388. SUERC-74072, GU-44446. 931 ± 30 BP. Male, 30–35 yrs. Partial pelvis, sacrum & left femur. Immediately beneath SK1386.	Left femur	None	X	X	✓	✓
SK1397	Skeleton 1397, Grave 1341. SUERC-74075, GU-44449/GU-44462. 962 ± 30 BP. Male, 25–30 yrs. Supine, extended with skull turned to left side. Left arm down by side & right forearm brought up across chest. Adjacent to SK1396, of which SK1398 may be the skull placed above right shoulder.	Right femur	RP^2	✓	X	✓	✓
Weyhill Road Sheep ASK1042	Sheep overlying SK1036, Grave 1037. GU-44454.	Innominate	None	X	X	✓	✓
Old Down Farm Sheep 867	Context 867. GU-48380.	Long bone	None	X	X	✓	✓

Table 6.2 Collagen isotope data

Sample ID	δ¹³C (‰)	δ¹⁵N (‰)	δ³⁴S (‰)	C:N (atomic)	C:S (atomic)	N:S (atomic)	S%	C%	N%
Humans:									
SK1056	-20.0	9.1	1.3	3.0	526	165	0.15	28.3	10.8
SK1074	-19.6	10.2	Nd	3.2	Nd	Nd	Nd	25.7	9.4
SK1108	-19.9	10.3	8.7	3.1	394	122	0.14	20.5	7.7
SK1112	-20.0	8.4	10.4	3.0	525	166	0.13	25.0	9.8
SK1138	-20.0	9.4	Nd	3.2	Nd	Nd	Nd	26.9	10.0
SK1174	-19.7	8.3	13.9	3.0	507	163	0.13	20.4	8.1
SK1207	-19.8	8.0	11.0	3.0	545	171	0.12	22.6	8.8
SK1209	-19.5	9.7	Nd	3.2	Nd	Nd	Nd	20.6	7.5
SK1211	-20.1	9.2	13.0	3.2	411	129	0.12	18.9	6.9
SK1225	-19.4	10.3	5.2	2.9	556	176	0.14	27.2	10.9
SK1228	-19.8	12.3	Nd	3.2	Nd	Nd	Nd	34.9	12.6
SK1240	-19.7	8.2	14.0	2.9	576	181	0.14	24.7	10.0
SK1254	-19.8	8.4	14.5	3.0	521	164	0.18	28.0	10.8
SK1274	-19.6	10.3	8.5	2.9	542	168	0.13	22.7	9.1
SK1286	-20.0	9.9	Nd	3.3	Nd	Nd	Nd	27.8	9.9
SK1292	-19.7	9.0	10.0	3.1	537	168	0.18	33.4	12.6
SK1297	-19.5	8.5	12.1	3.1	564	179	0.18	32.9	12.4
SK1379	-19.9	8.4	13.5	3.1	572	179	0.16	31.7	11.8
SK1387	-20.2	8.0	14.1	3.0	542	169	0.16	27.4	10.6
SK1397	-19.7	9.3	9.8	3.2	488	154	0.21	38.0	14.0
Sheep:									
1042	-21.7	5.0	15.4	3.0	607	190	0.14	26.6	10.5
867	-21.7	5.2	14.8	3.3	589	181	0.11	29.3	10.6

Notes:
1. All C:N ratios fall into an acceptable quality indicator range of 2.9 to 3.2. C% and N% values are within the ranges given by Ambrose (1990) and van Klinken (1999), but many are at the lower end of those ranges which can suggest the presence of inorganic matter in the collagen extract (van Klinken 1999). All C:S and N:S ratios fall within the acceptable ranges given by Nehlich and Richards (2009), although some of the S% data fall below the suggested range of 0.15 to 0.35%.
2. All collagen was ultrafiltered at SUERC for sulphur measurements.
3. All analyses were single measurements for carbon and nitrogen, with sulphur data either duplicated or in triplicate (mean averages shown in table), except for SK1254 which was a single measurement. Sulphur replication was in two separate runs and the mean of the maximum difference between replicates was 0.7 ± 0.5‰.

Winchester. In addition to the isotope ratio for SK1211 being inconsistent with a chalk location, his strontium concentration is higher than seen in the others, the closest being an individual from Winchester who is also an incomer to that site. Montgomery suggests that the concentration range usually seen as a result of mainland British diets is around 30 to 150ppm, although higher concentrations can be characteristic of populations inhabiting coastal environments represented by small maritime islands such as the Outer Hebrides and the Orkneys, where there is a tradition of using seaweed as fodder, fertilizer, and possibly food (Montgomery *et al.* 2014). In the case of SK1211, the concentration is 199ppm, while that for the Winchester individual is 164.

However, if a British maritime island origin were to be posited for SK1211, then a marine-dominated ⁸⁷Sr/⁸⁶Sr ratio would be expected, approximately in the range of 0.7092 to 0.7100. In this case, SK1211 has a ⁸⁷Sr/⁸⁶Sr ratio of 0.7119, which is higher than would be expected for this type of environment. It would be possible for a high strontium isotope ratio from bedrock (higher than 0.7119) to be mixed with a marine-dominated signal (below 0.7100), to produce a value on a mixing line which also produced a high, marine-dominated strontium concentration. This might be obtained from Britain (e.g. if coastal resources were obtained from a region of granite, such as might occur in Scotland, or in limited areas of western England, Wales or Ireland),

Table 6.3 Enamel isotope data

Sample ID	$^{87}Sr/^{86}Sr$ (enamel)	% Std error	Sr conc. (ppm)	Sr conc. error	$\delta^{18}O_{carbonate\_SMOW}$ (‰)	Calculated $\delta^{18}O_{phosphate}$ (‰)[2]	Calculated $\delta^{18}O_{dw}$ (‰)[3]
SK1056	0.7082	0.0014	99.3	0.1	26.3	17.5	-6.8
SK1108	0.7091	0.0015	85.7	0.1	26.4	17.6	-6.7
SK1112					26.4	17.6	-6.7
SK1174					25.9	17.0	-7.5
SK1207					27.0	18.2	-5.7
SK1211	0.7119	0.0014	199.1	0.1	26.2	17.4	-7.0
SK1228	0.7089	0.0014	100.4	0.4	27.6	18.8	-4.7
SK1240	0.7087	0.0012	56.2	0.1	25.9	17.0	-7.5
SK1254	0.7081	0.0013	80.4	0.1	26.4	17.6	-6.7
SK1274	0.7106	0.0014	85.0	0.3	24.2	15.3	-10.2
SK1297	0.7085	0.0012	48.5	0.2	24.5	15.6	-9.7
SK1397					27.1	18.3	-5.5

Notes:

1. Where no data are shown in table cells, no analysis was undertaken. Samples for which no enamel analysis was undertaken are not listed in this table.

2. The calculated $\delta^{18}O_{phosphate}$ values use the equation from Chenery *et al.* 2012 to convert from the measured carbonate values. These data are provided for the purpose of comparison with other published datasets.

3. The calculated $\delta^{18}O_{dw}$ values use equation 6 from Chenery *et al.* 2012 (based on Daux *et al.* 2008) to convert from the measured carbonate values. These data are provided for the purpose of comparison with other published datasets, but care should be taken in using them with environmental water value maps (Pollard *et al.* 2011).

although the $\delta^{18}O$ value is tending towards the 'low rainfall' eastern part of the British range, and this is not entirely consistent with what might be expected in the regions where higher strontium isotope ratios are to be found.

If SK1211 was from outside Britain, then the combination of a higher expected baseline $^{87}Sr/^{86}Sr$ value and the $\delta^{18}O$ value can be found in parts of Scandinavia and northern Germany which might be one of the most likely explanations for the values obtained for this individual (Price *et al.* 2014). South-western Norway and the southern tip of Sweden could provide similar values. Denmark and the area of northern Germany south of the Danish border would support the oxygen isotope ratio, but not necessarily a higher strontium isotope ratio (Frei and Price 2012; Lightfoot and O'Connell 2016), while moving further north or east into Sweden would lead to lower $\delta^{18}O$ values. It should be borne in mind that there will be other options further afield which can produce similar data.

The $\delta^{13}C$ and $\delta^{15}N$ values for bone collagen are shown in Figure 6.4, alongside the data for the two sheep analysed. These bulk data are consistent with an omnivorous diet without significant levels of aquatic protein (marine or freshwater), based on these limited sheep samples, if it is assumed that the sheep $\delta^{13}C$ value (the same for both animals) is at the extreme negative end of the variation expected if a larger group of sheep were to be analysed. Figure 6.5 shows comparative data

from St John's College, Oxford and Weymouth (for the humans only; no animals available from these sites), and from Berinsfield in Oxfordshire (where animals are also available) (Privat *et al.* 2002; Pollard *et al.* 2012; Chenery *et al.* 2014). The four groups of humans provide generally different spreads of data. The St John's College and Weymouth groups are hypothesised to be fighting men, possibly both of them with Scandinavian origins, with the likelihood that individuals were from different original locations and not from a single place (Pollard *et al.* 2012; Chenery *et al.* 2014). The Berinsfield population is dated to the 5th to early 7th centuries AD (i.e. earlier than the other sites), and is hypothesised to be largely local, although there are some immigrant individuals; the local geology is not based on chalk, as it is at Andover (Hughes *et al.* 2014). It is not to be expected that $\delta^{15}N$ baselines would be the same at these sites, given the number of variables, including geology, which will affect the locations. This is why contemporaneous herbivore data is used, wherever possible, to help define that baseline. It is reasonable, however, to compare the variation within the groups and the range of $\delta^{13}C$ values.

It is important to bear in mind that the carbon and nitrogen isotope data are from bone samples which produce values averaged over a lifetime, probably weighted towards adolescence. These values, therefore, include some element of equilibration with the British environment if immigrants have lived here for a while.

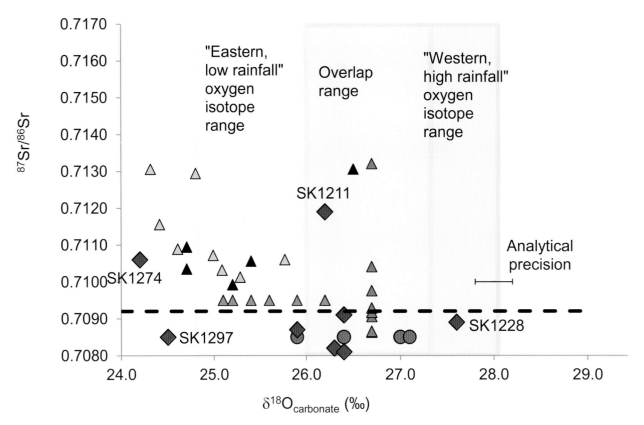

Fig. 6.2 $\delta^{18}O_{carb\_SMOW}$ (‰) values plotted with $^{87}Sr/^{86}Sr$ where available, and in a linear array where strontium or oxygen data are not available. Comparative data references are shown. The dotted line indicates the upper limit of the $^{87}Sr/^{86}Sr$ range expected for subsistence in a chalk region. The east and west vertical boundaries for the oxygen isotope ratios overlap in the centre area, which indicates a geographically undifferentiated signature for archaeological remains from Britain. The boundary values are taken from Evans et al. 2012, converted from phosphate values using the equation from Chenery et al. 2012, and are generally indicative of the 'high rainfall' region to the west and the 'lower rainfall' region to the east. They are based on data sets believed to be 'local' and the range is presented to 2 sd. Analytical precision error range for strontium isotope ratios is within symbol size

The strontium and oxygen isotope data reflect the enamel formation period during childhood, and so will not reflect this change over time, unless mobility was during childhood. Bearing this in mind, the $\delta^{13}C$ values for the Andover group are slightly higher than those for Berinsfield (mean -19.8 ± 0.2‰ for Andover, -20.1 ± 0.2‰ for Berinsfield), while the sheep samples from Andover are at the lower end of the range from Berinsfield (although the Andover sheep may be at one extreme of a range if more data were available). The generally lower $\delta^{15}N$ values for

both the Andover humans and the Andover sheep, when compared with the Berinsfield data, suggest that there is no significant, isotopically visible, marine resource consumption in the Andover group, as is also the case for Berinsfield (Privat *et al.* 2002).

The difference between the averaged $\delta^{13}C$ values for the Berinsfield humans and the herbivores is 1.4‰, which itself is relatively high for one trophic level, whilst at Andover, if the Berinsfield averaged herbivore value is used (to counter the fact that there are only

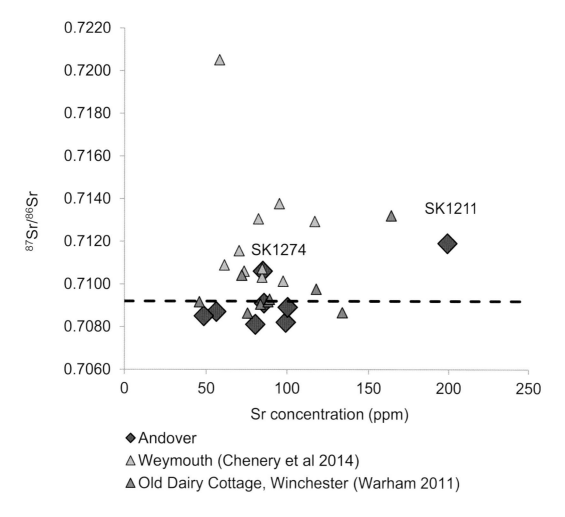

Fig. 6.3 Strontium isotope ratios plotted with strontium concentration, with comparative data. Analytical precision error range for these data are within symbol size

two sheep from Andover), the difference goes up to 1.7‰. It is as high as 1.9‰ if the Andover sheep are used rather than the Berinsfield animals. It is difficult to compare published absolute values precisely, because small differences may occur in laboratory procedures and calibration standards, but these data are suggestive of a diet which is not based entirely on British terrestrial resources. However, the direction of the shift in the $\delta^{13}C$ values is also not necessarily consistent with a Scandinavian origin, since a colder climate is more likely to lead to lower $\delta^{13}C$ values than higher ones (e.g. six sheep/goat samples from Neolithic Jutland and southern Sweden gave a mean of -22.2 ± 0.6‰ (Gron and Rowley-Conwy 2017), compared to -21.7‰ for the Andover sheep, and -21.5 ± 0.2‰ for the six Berinsfield herbivores). It must be considered, therefore, that the $\delta^{13}C$ values may be indicative of a diet which had some marine resources included, but which originated at a location where the baseline $\delta^{15}N$ values were significantly lower than seen at the other sites in Figure 6.5. Such a baseline has been found during the Iron

Age, for instance, in Hampshire (at Winnall Down and Micheldever Wood) close to Andover (Jay and Richards 2007). If they were migrants, marine resources need not have been included in the diet while the consumers were in Britain if they had lived here for a while; the signal could be from resources consumed before arrival in Britain, and averaged into the bone collagen over time. Another possibility might be that the resources consumed were terrestrial mammals which themselves had consumed marine resources, rather than that the marine foods were directly consumed. This is suggested by the domesticated herbivores from Viking Age and Early Christian Ridanäs on Gotland, Sweden (Kosiba *et al.* 2007). If this were the case, then the $\delta^{15}N$ baseline would not need to be significantly lower.

While marine resources in the food chain must be considered a possibility here, this explanation is not necessarily supported by the sulphur data (see below), because the individual with the highest $\delta^{13}C$ value (SK1225) has a low $\delta^{34}S$ value which is not consistent with the consumption of marine foods.

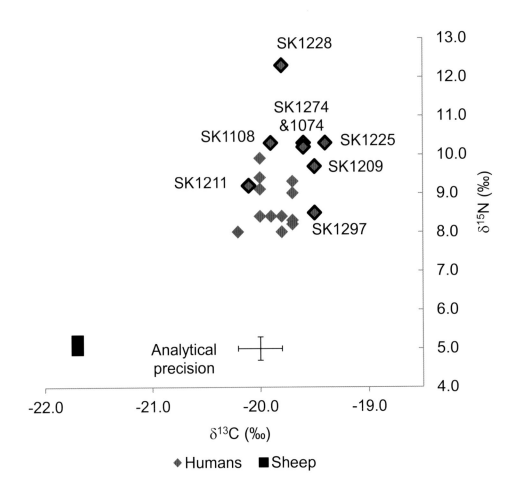

Fig. 6.4 $\delta^{13}C$ and $\delta^{15}N$ values for Andover humans and two available sheep

Alternatives would be that the food chain included some C_4 plants, that the origin location(s) were drier and/or warmer than might be seen for much of Scandinavia, or that a complex diet was consumed from a river valley environment (see discussion of sulphur data below for this final possibility). Millet is the main C_4 plant found in northern Europe at this time, but it is not found in Britain and is unlikely to have been present in Scandinavian food chains unless it had been imported. It has appeared at sites in early Denmark (e.g. Robinson 2003), so that it is possible for it to be in the food chain there, but is more likely found in Slavic populations (e.g. Reitsema *et al.* 2010; Reitsema and Kozłowski 2013). A more likely climate for enriched carbon isotope values would perhaps be more mainland temperate Europe, such as northern Germany, the Netherlands or Poland (e.g. McManus *et al.* 2013, although here the nitrogen isotope ratio baseline is too high, and Reitsema and Kozłowski 2013, where the $\delta^{15}N$ values are similar).

The individuals not consistent with an Andover origin (SKs1274, 1297, 1211 and possibly 1228) are marked in Figure 6.4. SKs1274 and 1297, both with $\delta^{18}O$ values

which indicate a colder environment such as Scandinavia, have $\delta^{13}C$ values which are towards the higher end of the range (-19.6‰ and -19.5‰ respectively); the other individuals with similar values are SK1225 (-19.4‰), SK1209 (-19.5‰) and SK1074 (-19.6‰), but there are currently no oxygen or strontium data for these. This suggests that whatever the higher $\delta^{13}C$ values indicate, the two likely immigrants are amongst those showing the signal most strongly. SK1211, on the other hand, has a carbon isotope ratio which is at the lower end of the range (-20.1‰), which suggests that he may have spent longer in Britain, or that he was not an immigrant with a similar collagen data pattern to the others. The latter possibility is less likely, given the high strontium concentration in the enamel.

SK1228 is the outlier of the Andover group in Figures 6.4 and 6.5, with a $\delta^{15}N$ value of 12.3‰ which makes them the only individual to overlap with the St John's College, Oxford, group in Figure 6.5. It is 2‰ above the next highest value at Andover, and well over 3 sd from the mean for the other 19 individuals (9.1 ± 0.8‰). The strontium isotope ratio for this individual is within the range expected for the location, although

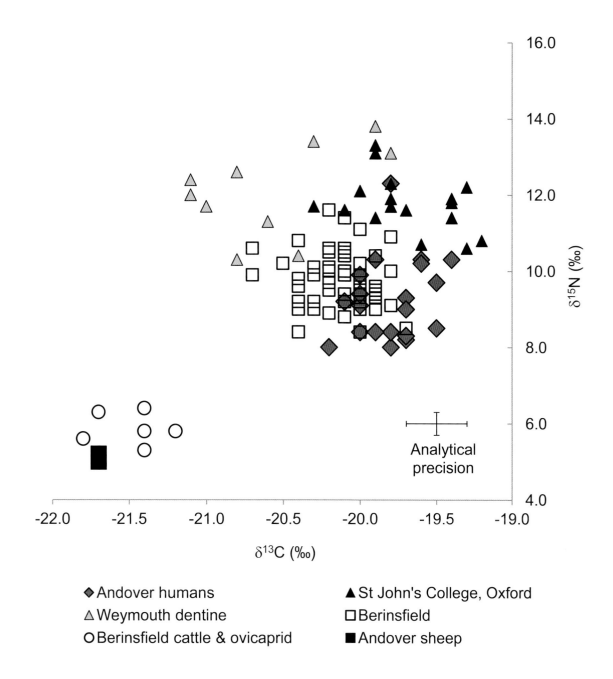

Fig. 6.5 δ¹³C and δ¹⁵N values for Andover humans and sheep plotted with comparative data from Weymouth (Chenery et al. 2014), St John's College, Oxford (Pollard et al. 2012) and Berinsfield (Privat et al. 2002)

the δ¹⁸O value is the only value within the range in Figure 6.2 to suggest a western, 'higher rainfall', region of Britain as an origin if he/she were not an immigrant. The combination of the absolute δ¹⁵N value (which is high for a British diet without significant levels of marine protein), together with the fact that it is unusual within the Andover group for both nitrogen and oxygen, suggest that this individual may well have been mobile, possibly an immigrant who was not present in Britain long enough to have equilibrated to the local diet. It is also possible that this individual had notably different dietary factors affecting him or her when compared to

the others at the site. One of the possible reasons for a high δ¹⁵N value is nutritional stress (e.g. Beaumont and Montgomery 2016) and it is possible that the higher δ¹⁸O value is related to processed liquid consumption. A combination of mobility and nutritional stress might also be involved, or there may have been other dietary differences (e.g. consuming more freshwater aquatic resources, or fowl). Certainly, this person is unusual in some way.

The sulphur data are plotted in Figure 6.6, along with some comparative data from Early Bronze Age cattle. The sheep from Andover have δ³⁴S values of 14.8 and

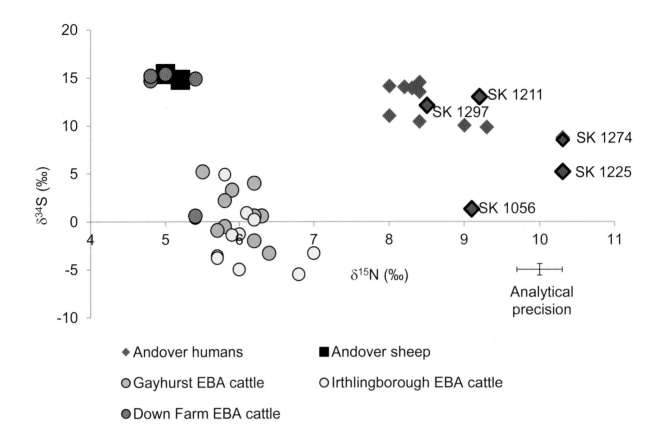

Fig. 6.6   δ¹³C and δ¹⁵N values for Andover humans and sheep alongside comparative data from cattle (Towers et al. 2011; Jay unpublished data)

15.4‰, which can be used as a baseline for the site if it is assumed that they were not brought into the area from elsewhere. This value is consistent with a chalkland region in southern England. The chart shows some Early Bronze Age cattle data from Down Farm, on Cranborne Chase, which is approximately 50km to the south-west and on chalk. The mean of four of the five animals shown is 15.1‰, and all four animals plot very closely with the Andover sheep. One of the Down Farm animals, however, has a much lower value, at 0.6‰. Other data plotted on the chart are Early Bronze Age cattle from Gayhurst (Buckinghamshire) and Irthlingborough (Northamptonshire), and these all have much lower values. These sites are central in England, and much further from the coast than either Andover or Down Farm. One explanation for these low sulphur isotope ratios at the central English sites is therefore that they are less affected by the 'sea spray' effect, which brings marine sulphates into the food chain closer to the coast.

An alternative explanation for the lower δ³⁴S values relates to the possibility that they can be obtained from food chains which include resources from freshwater floodplains (Nehlich *et al.* 2008). This would be related to the effect of the sulphates from the water on the environment from which the resources were obtained.

There has also been some contentious discussion about whether these low values are indicative of sulphur contamination of the collagen (Bocherens *et al.* 2011; Nehlich 2015). Nehlich maintains that ultrafiltration of the collagen sample separates out small sulphur contaminants (< 30kd), and that this produces purified collagen when the quality indicators are met (pers. comm.). It should, perhaps, be noted that the sulphur percentage content of the collagen from the samples in the Andover study are low, and that a number of them fall below that suggested as the ideal range of 0.15 to 0.35% for archaeological mammal bone (Nehlich and Richards 2009).

Bearing this in mind, there is a group of five individuals plotting very closely to each other for both the δ³⁴S and δ¹⁵N values (14.0 ± 0.4‰ and 8.3 ± 0.2‰ respectively): SKs1174, 1240, 1254, 1379 and 1387. None of these have data which are remarkable in other ways, and the sulphur values are similar to the sheep for the site. They are, therefore, consistent with the site for all of the data available.

SKs1274 and 1297, both of which are likely immigrants, based on the oxygen data, are highlighted in Figure 6.6. SK1297 has a δ³⁴S value, which is only a little lower than the 'local' group of five, at 12.1‰, while SK1274 has a value of 8.5‰, which is significantly lower. SK1211, the incomer based on strontium data, also looks quite similar to the 'local' group of five, with a δ^{34}S value of 13.0‰. As for the carbon and nitrogen data, the sulphur reflects a period of life after childhood, and can reflect equilibration to local site values and regional dietary patterns later on, so that the timing of movement is relevant. SK1211 may well have spent longer in the region, as is consistent with the carbon values.

SK1225 has a low δ^{34}S value (5.2‰), which is not consistent with marine resource consumption, so that the higher δ^{13}C values discussed above are not likely to be associated with marine foods, at least in this case. The lowest δ^{34}S value shown is for SK1056 (1.3‰); this individual does not have any other isotope data which are notable, and this value is comparable with the low comparative values shown for herbivores from Gayhurst and Irthlingborough. It is possible that at least some of the lower δ^{34}S values relate to movement within Britain, or to the consumption of resources which have come from a freshwater floodplain such as the local Test Valley system, which runs into Southampton Water. It is also possible that the variation in the δ^{34}S values outside the 'local' group of five is related to immigration from a variety of locations.

Conclusions

There are two individuals (SKs1274 and 1297) with δ^{18}O values which are consistent with an origin outside Britain, and which indicate a colder climate, such as Scandinavia or north-eastern Europe. The strontium isotope ratio for SK1274 confirms an origin away from Andover, while that for SK1297 is within the range for chalk. Both values can be found in many places outside Britain; they are at the low end of the range which might be found in Scandinavia, but such values are to be found, for instance, in Denmark (Price *et al.* 2014).

SK1211 has a ^{87}Sr/^{86}Sr value which is inconsistent with the Andover chalk, and also has a strontium concentration which is higher than expected for Britain unless dietary resources were heavily influenced by a maritime location, such as might be the case for island or coastal environments. The strontium isotope ratio is, however, higher than expected for a marine-influenced location, and this may indicate that the origin was on bedrock, with even higher values (older rocks, such as granites, present in Scotland and small areas of eastern England, Wales and northern Ireland), with a mixing effect bringing the enamel value down towards the expected range for a maritime environment.

Alternatively, this individual could have originated outside Britain; the δ^{18}O value is consistent with the British range, but also with Denmark and south-western Norway, although the argument for the combination of higher strontium isotope ratio and strontium concentration would make south-western Norway the more likely option of these two. The combined collagen values may indicate that this person had been in Britain for a significant amount of time before death.

The group overall has an ambiguous range of collagen values (δ^{15}N, δ^{13}C and δ^{34}S); the nitrogen isotope ratios are lower than expected for a diet which includes marine resources, whilst some of the δ^{13}C values suggest that these were included to a limited extent, either over the whole of life, or for migrants averaged into the signal from an earlier diet elsewhere. A southern English location could have provided a low δ^{15}N baseline, to which even the incomers mentioned above may have equilibrated if they had lived there for long enough; although the values for the sheep analysed from the Andover sites are not particularly low, it is possible that these animals were at the top end of the range available in the regional environment from which resources were obtained. However, the individual with the highest δ^{13}C value (SK1225) also has a lower δ^{34}S value than is expected for the site, and this is not consistent with marine resource consumption. Another possibility is that marine resources have entered the food chain indirectly, by being included in the diet of domesticated herbivores, in which case that is most likely to have occurred outside southern England. This combination of lower δ^{15}N, higher δ^{13}C and variable δ^{34}S values could also relate to resources being obtained to a varying extent from a riverine environment or floodplain, but not necessarily the direct consumption of either freshwater or marine fish, or else the variation in sulphur data might be indicative of immigration from a variety of locations.

The δ^{15}N value for SK1228 is notably higher than that seen for the rest of the group, and their δ^{18}O value is at the most positive end of the range seen from Andover. It is possible that this individual was an incomer to the site, in which case they would have originated from a warmer or wetter environment, perhaps similar to the south-west of Britain, although it is also possible that they were an immigrant. In that case, it is unlikely that the origin would be Scandinavia or north-eastern Europe, but more probably France or southern Ireland. If originating in Britain, they may have been consuming a diet significantly different to that seen in the rest of the group, and this may have involved nutritional stress and the consumption of processed liquids.

Chapter 7
The Medieval Background and Legal System

Medieval location and status

Andover Hundred

As mentioned previously, the Weyhill Road burial site lies towards the centre of a chalk ridge running east–west (Fig. 1.4). It is surrounded by a number of settlements, hamlets and manors, all within two to three miles of the site, and lies within the confines of the greater Andover Hundred and parish. A small number of isolated burials of possible Saxon or medieval date have been found accidentally during building works (for example, see 'burials' on Fig. 7.2). Andover itself lies to the east, and Weyhill to the west. To the north, the Anton river valley contains the dispersed settlements of Charlton, Foxcotte, Penton Mewsey and Ramridge, and to the south, the Pillhill Brook frames the settlements of Upper Clatford, Abbotts Ann, Monxton, Thruxton and Fyfield (Fig. 7.2).

Andrew Reynolds presents a discussion of the likely geopolitical landscape of the earlier period of the cemetery in the concluding chapter of this volume, but a few points are mentioned here. The place-name of Andover may be of Celtic origin (Grundy 1921, 84–6), meaning 'ash waters (streams)' (Coates 1989, 23). The settlement appears as *Andeferas* in 955 and *Andeferen* in 962 (*ibid.*), and in the *Anglo-Saxon Chronicle* in 994 (Swanton 1996, 128–9). Weyhill was not specifically mentioned in the Domesday Survey, but is documented from the 13th century as *Leweo*; in *c.* 1270 as *la Wou*; in 1318 as *Weo* and in 1379 as *la Wee* (Coates 1989, 174).

A church was recorded by the Domesday Survey for the manor of Penton Grafton, and is presumed to be the church at Weyhill. The church of St Michael and All Angels has a Norman chancel arch, while the chancel itself is of later medieval date (Historic England 2017). Penton Grafton was known in the 10th century as *Penintune* – 'Farm of the Penings' *(*Grundy 1927, 292–3). Knights Enham was first documented in 1086 as *Eanham,* but the name 'lamb homestead or village' suggests an earlier derivation, as Old English *ēan* means 'lamb' and *ham*, a village (Nottingham University

2018). Charlton was first documented in reign of Henry II (1154–89), as *Cherelton(e)* – 'Farm of the Free Peasants', although archaeological evidence shows that it was settled much earlier. Other Charltons mentioned in the Domesday Survey are satellite settlements of royal manors, and the free peasants from the Andover Charlton may have served to provide and store supplies for royal visitations or onward distribution (Russel 1985, 218).

Table 7.1 summarises information from the Domesday Survey of 1086 for certain local settlements. These settlements are of specific interest in view of their proximity to the execution site, and the possibility that residents might have served as jurors or indeed been from where the cemetery population was drawn. However, of those within the Hundred, only Monxton has preserved documentary records to suggest that it held rights of gallows.

The *Victoria County History* (VCH) has summarised the key facts with supporting documentary evidence (Page 1911c). Monxton has been identified with the 'Anne' of Domesday Book which the king held in demesne, and which one Ulveve had held as an alod (land owned absolutely and not subject to any rent, service, or other tenurial right of an overlord) of the Confessor. The manor was given to the Norman abbey of Bec Hellouin, by Hugh de Grandmesnil, which confirmed by later charters. When called to account in 1281 for exercising the privileges of view of frankpledge, gallows, tumbril, and assize of bread and ale without licence, the abbot claimed not only those rights on the manor of Ann de Bec (Monxton), but also *sac* and *soc, tol* and *theam, infangentheof* and all royal liberties and customs as given to the abbey by the charter of Henry II. Where a manor, or indeed a hundred, was in the hands of a religious order the highest estate official would be the chief steward. He would be in charge of the local manor bailiffs (see Morgan 1946, 53–7 for a description of this system at work).

The abbey of Bec Hellouin also held the nearby manor

Table 7.1 Landholding information before and after Domesday (information after Page 1911a–j)

Place	Overlord in 1066	Lord	Lord in 1086	Tenant in chief	Domesday
Abbotts Ann		Hyde Abbey often known as New Minster Winchester (St Peter), abbey of	Winchester (St Peter), abbey of	Winchester (St Peter), abbey of	30 households. 14 villagers. 12 smallholders. 4 slaves. 9 ploughlands (land for). 2 lord's plough teams. 7 men's plough teams. 3 mills. 15 exemption units
Amport (Over) Wallop	King Edward	Edric (the wild)	Hugh of Port	Hugh of Port	27 households. 7 villagers. 12 smallholders. 3 slaves. 5 ploughlands (land for). 2 lord's plough teams. 5 men's plough teams. 1 mill. 10 exemption units
Andover		King Edward (b. 1003–d. 1066)	King William	King William	62 villagers. 36 smallholders. 6 slaves. 3 freedmen. Meadow 18 acres. Woodland 100 swine render. 6 mills
Enham	King Edward	Alwin	Saeric	Saeric	
Foxcotte	King Edward	Free men, two	Ralph	Waleran the hunter	10 villagers. 13 smallholders. 3 slaves. 4 ploughlands (land for). 2 lord's plough teams. 4 men's plough teams
Fyfield	King Edward	Wulfeva (Beteslau)	William Mauduit	William Mauduit	17 households 10 villagers. 5 smallholders. 2 slaves. 5 ploughlands (land for). 1 lord's plough teams. 3 men's plough teams. 5 exemption units
(Weyhill with) Penton Grafton		Queen Edith (of Wessex) wife of Edward	Grestain (Sainte-Marie & Saint-Pierre), abbey of	Grestain (Sainte-Marie & Saint-Pierre), abbey of	37 households. 5 villagers. 27 smallholders. 5 slaves. 6 ploughlands (land for). 2 lord's plough teams. 3 men's plough teams. 1 church. 3 exemption units
Penton Mewsey	King Edward	Osmund (of Eaton)	Turold (nephew of Wigot)	Roger de Montgomery (Earl of Shrewsbury)	21 households 11 villagers. 7 smallholders. 3 slaves. 5 ploughlands (land for). 1 lord's plough teams. 4 men's plough teams. Meadow 5 acres. 1 church. 5 exemption units
Monxton	King Edward	Wulfeva (Beteslau)	King William	King William	11 households. 3 villagers. 5 smallholders. 3 slaves. 3 ploughlands (land for). 2 lord's plough teams. 2 men's plough teams. Meadow 2 acres. 1 mill. 10 exemption units
Quarley		Earl Harold	King William	King William	27 households. 4 villagers. 11 smallholders. 12 slaves. 4 ploughlands (land for). 1 lord's plough teams. 3 men's plough teams. 1 church. 5 exemption units

of Quarley, also in the Andover Hundred. Page (1911d) states that Earl Harold had held Quarley and by the time of the Domesday Survey of 1086, it was assigned to the Conqueror, although Maud of Flanders (his wife, who died in 1083), had given it to the abbey of Bec Hellouin. Like its neighbour, Monxton, the manor was in the charge of the Prior of Ogbourne (Wilts), the principal cell of Bec Hellouin in England, and is probably that 'Cornby', over which the abbot claimed royal liberties and customs in 1281. According to the Assize Roll of 1280, the prior exercised the rights of gallows, view of frankpledge, *infangentheof*, chattels of felons and fugitives and assize of bread and ale, in all his lands in Hampshire (Assize R. 789, m. 15 d).

It is worth noting, that the open field in Abbotts Ann parish closest to the Weyhill Road site, Enclosed by Act in 1774, was known as Gallows or Gallow Field in the 18th century (David Rymill, pers. comm.; Chapman and Seeliger 1997, 9, map 1). Abbotts Ann was held both before and after Domesday by the abbey of Winchester (St Peter).

The royal estate

The history of Andover itself has been much researched. Lavelle (2005) points to the likely presence of a large royal estate centred on Andover as demonstrated by references to official visits by kings and their councillors to Andover and Grateley, and to Queen Edith's association with Penton Grafton. Andover was mentioned in the will of King Eadred, in the mid 10th century; he bequeathed land in the area to the New Minster at Winchester. It has also been suggested (various, anon) that this estate was a hunting lodge rather than a high-status site (*villa regalis*, palace or royal enclosure), and no archaeological evidence has been found to support either claim. It is likely that, if present, any such buildings would have been timber-built. As summarised by Vinogradoff (1908, 323–9) royal estates could take a number of different forms. Some were little more than food production and storage units for collection by royal officers, or to directly supply the king's household for a set number of nights. In these cases, the reeve or bailiff might effectively be little more than a collector and storeman. In other cases, the royal estate may have been associated with groups of free tenants and a fully-realised manorial estate with jurisdiction and attached court.

The later Anglo-Saxon kings travelled around their kingdoms, supporting their retinues with locally provided food (customary dues or food rents, Reynolds 2009b, 75). It is known that Saxon kings visited Andover, possibly when *en route* from London to the south-west. Eadred's successor, King Edgar the Peaceful (r. 959–75) called a council of advisors, a *Witenagemot*, early in his reign (Yorke 1994, 90). He issued a law code from Andover (*II and III Eg*, which survives wholly or partially, in six manuscripts (Early English Laws (EEL) 2018)). Amongst other things, it sought to fix the price of wool ('and a wey of wool shall be sold for half a pound (120 pence), and no-one shall sell it for less (or more)' (Lloyd 1977, 1)). It may be noted that wool and cloth appear to have been important to the economy of Andover in both the medieval and early post-medieval periods (Hopkins 2004). The code also deals with church dues, judicial organisation and surety. It has often been referred to as the second and third codes of King Edgar, but these are now known to have been the ecclesiastical and secular parts of a single code issued at Andover (EEL 2018).

King Athelstan (r. 924–39) stopped at Grateley in *c.* 936–7, and Lavelle (2005, 156) suggests that his retinue, which might have totalled up to 400, could have been provisioned by an existing royal estate at Andover. Andover was also an assumed hundred meeting place, where Aethelred II's councillors assembled in 980. In 994, Olaf Tryggvason was confirmed by the Bishop of Winchester in the church of Andover, with King Aethelred as his sponsor (Garmonsway 1972, 128–9). This act completed a treaty with Olaf that ended a period of Norse attacks.

Kings, overlords and the borough of Andover

The victory of William at Hastings would soon have become known locally, as the new king quickly demanded the surrender of Winchester, which was at that time held by Queen Edith. Baring (1915, 36) suggests that William wasted the country that he passed through on his line of march, and the drop in value shown for some manors in the Domesday Survey 20 years after the Conquest may have been a result of this. He suggests that 'a string of manors, located at intervals of about ten miles, or a day's march, which suffered heavy but temporary loss of value between 1065 and 1067, may mark the line of his march, or a place where he stopped for a day or more… including Fyfield, west of Andover' (*ibid.*). There is no known Norman motte or castle in Andover, though the manor which was co-extensive with both the parish and borough was held by the king as lord paramount. The VCH (Page 1911a) states that, except during the few years (1215–26), in which it was in the hands of the half brother of King John, William Longespée Earl of Salisbury, 'it was always held by the burgesses, the bailiff being *ex officio* lord of the manor and the town clerk steward'.

Table 7.1 shows the sweeping changes of local landholding following the Conquest, with not only the overlord changing with the king, but also often of the lordship and main tenants. While Queen Edith was confirmed in her lands, the manors of the dead King Harold II and his brothers were divided amongst followers of William (Williams 1995, 10). Some native-born Englishmen were retained, or given posts. In 1102–3, for example, the hundred of Andover was commanded by King Henry I to enquire into the possessions of Andover Priory which had been appropriated by Alvric (Aelfric) reeve of Andover; the court met at the house of the former reeve Edwin. Both these reeves were English (Williams 1995, 103).

The manor of Andover was controlled by the burgesses of the borough of Andover. The bailiff was *ex officio* lord of the manor with the king as lord paramount. By the 16th century it is known that the bailiff was acting as coroner by right of unwritten law (Page 1911a). From at least the time of Henry II, a series of royal charters granted during the medieval period conveyed various rights to the town of Andover, in return for fees paid to the Crown. 'By his charter of 1213 [Cal. Rot. Chart. (Rec. Com.), 195], (King) John granted the out-hundred to the men of Andover, who ever afterwards held it of the king, paying fee-farm rent as for manor, hundred and vill'. Records also suggest that a court was held every Monday at Andover (Gross 1890, 341 cited in Page 1911a, 333), but when this began is unclear. A charter of 1256 gave privileges in respect of debt, forfeiture, inheritance and the hambling of dogs, and another charter of the same date granted the return of all writs touching the vill and hundred. An example from 1304 from Oxford (Salter 1912, 12) shows how an abjuror's forfeited goods were held by the town bailiffs, not the mayor, until such time as the king's representatives arrived. The bailiffs in this example were the direct representatives of the king's interests, which might have been the case in Andover.

Among the privileges granted by Queen Elizabeth in a charter of 1588, were a borough gaol, of which the bailiff was warden, plus goods and chattels of fugitives, felons and outlaws, return of writs, exemption from suit to county or hundred of the sheriff, assize of bread, ale and other victuals and fines for false weights and measures. She also granted a yearly view of frankpledge with court leet, and law days for the inhabitants of the borough, town and hundred. The leet was held at Easter and Michaelmas. At Easter, there were two separate courts, one at Andover for the 'in hundred', the other at Weyhill for the 'out hundred'. At Michaelmas, one court held at Andover was deemed sufficient. Later documentary evidence for Andover suggests that it followed the usual pattern for officers and courts. Although the charter from Elizabeth I was a new one, it may have reflected earlier rights and practices, as seen above, in the case of the reeve Aelfric convening a court in 1102–3. The records that survive from the Andover courts (see Phillips, Appendix 1) do not reflect the types of cases that would have led to capital punishment through the standard judicial system for the general area. The case for an Andover court which was capable of capital punishment remains unproven.

The origins of the borough gaol for Andover are not known. It may also have been that, particularly in the case of detention before trial, temporary arrangements were made, such as keeping suspects at the reeve's house or in a local church gaol until the bailiff, coroner or other court officials could be summoned. This might be more likely in a system where the local society (tithing, parish etc.) undertook to give surety, for the appearance of a suspect for trial (Harding *et al.* 1985, 3). Imprisonment as a punishment was known in England before the Norman Conquest for oath breaking in the 890s and for witchcraft sorcery and arson in the 10th century (Brodie *et al.* 2002, 10–11). At the Council of Whittlebury (*c.* 930) King Athelstan imposed prison as a punishment for juvenile thieves. A number of royal manors did have prisons, and as in post-Conquest

times, there may have been monastic prisons. By the early 11th century much of England was divided into shires with a sheriff who managed finance, justice and customs for the area. After the Clarendon Assize of 1166 sheriffs were responsible for building gaols, with the cost being met by the Crown. Most of these were in castles in the county town. The king's justices would travel to supervise the trial of those held in prison on suspicion of a serious crime – a process that became known as 'Gaol Delivery' (Harding *et al.* 1985, 5). Prisoners could be expensive to provide for and maintain, but the use of imprisonment as a punishment gradually became more common during the Middle Ages. There has been a view that throughout the Middle Ages prisons served mainly as places of pre-trial custody. Geltner (2006, 261) states, that 'Pugh (1968) has demonstrated clearly that punitive imprisonment was an articulated legal concept and a practiced penal measure in England throughout the high and late Middle Ages'. Likewise, although felonies were not, in theory, able to be punished by imprisonment, in practice 'many felons did find themselves in gaol in the Middle Ages' (Harding *et al.* 1985, 9). In addition to the sometimes long wait for a trial, others found that the option of an ordeal was no longer open after the Church withdrew its support for the practice in 1215 and for a time imprisonment was ordered instead for those suspected of serious crimes. Church courts were also likely to inflict prison for their own wrongdoers rather than capital punishment (*ibid.*, 9–10).

Adjacent hundreds

Also of local interest is the adjacent hundred of Wherwell. Bucknill (2003, 146–8) collates the jurisdictional evidence for the hundred. It was under the control of the Abbess of Wherwell, and at the eyre of 1279/80, the hundred jury of presentment had given evidence that the Abbess claimed, amongst other things, the right of gallows, *infangentheof* and *outfangantheof,* although without specific warrant. Bucknill suggests that Wherwell represented an old Anglo-Saxon hundred, grouped around a royal manor, with customs set up without written records. The Abbess successfully defended her claims, and enjoyed exemption from the normal hundred and shire courts. Her power appears to have been absolute within the hundred she controlled directly, but could not necessarily be used in outlying lands within other hundreds. For example, the Abbess had been found guilty during the reign of Edward I, of raising a gallows in Compton, Berkshire, without justification or licence. The Abbess claimed the right to seize chattels of fugitives of Wherwell: when Henry Harold killed his wife Isabel and fled to the church, the Abbess had her reeve seize his chattels to the sizable value of £35 4s 8d (Page 1911e; Power 1922, 104–5). It should be noted that the Abbess had control over Little Ann and Goodworth, areas within or next to Andover Hundred.

Other nearby powers known to hold the rights to gallows, included both Nether Wallop and Basingstoke. Nether Wallop is approximately 7 miles (11km) to the south-west of Andover. The VCH summarises key landholding information (Page 1911f). The chief manor of Nether Wallop had its origin in the estate in Wallop, worth £37 a year, which was granted by Henry II in 1177 to the monastery of Amesbury at the time of its conversion into a cell to the abbey of Fontevraud in Anjou. This grant was confirmed a number of times, between 1199 and 1281. In 1231, the prioress produced her charter from Henry II as evidence against a claim to the manor. In 1280, the prioress claimed pillory, tumbril, gallows and the assize of bread and ale in her manor of Nether Wallop. Although the jurors then declared they knew not by what warrant, six years later Edward I confirmed these rights when his daughter took the veil at Amesbury and added that of free warren.

Basingstoke, although further away, is of interest as, until the reign of John, the kings of England held Basingstoke as a demesne manor, and the sheriff accounted for its revenues with those of the other royal lands in Hampshire (presumably including Andover). Again, the VCH summarises key information (Page 1911g): 'When the fee-farm rent was granted to Edmund de Woodstock, … it appears that the men of the town resented the idea that he was in any sense the lord of their manor', and in 1330 'they declared, "Edmund had naught in the said town except the ferm" (rent for the land or an abode) … The bailiffs remained the king's bailiffs until they became the "bailiffs of the men of Basingstoke." They now had all the official business of the town in their hands, and the reeve is not mentioned after the middle of the 13th century. They were now, as before, elected yearly from among the men of the town, and their duties were to "hold the king's courts, and do whatever appertains to justice." The assize of bread and ale, the return of writs, the gallows and the pillory, which had been granted to the town by Henry III, were all under the control of the bailiffs.'

The position of Winchester

Winchester was an important seat of Saxon government, and later the shire centre for the king's justice. Felony trials were certainly held there. Winchester was also an old and established centre of clerical power, with the Old Minster being the Anglo-Saxon cathedral for the diocese of Wessex, and after William replaced Winchester's Saxon bishop, a large new cathedral was built in the Norman Romanesque style and consecrated in 1093. The bishops of Winchester were amongst the wealthiest and most powerful lords of medieval England. They possessed approximately 30 manors in Hampshire, and accumulated considerable wealth. As well as the hierarchical system of clerical courts (see Table 7.2), the Church as landowner became Lord of the Manor, and

might in that role have had traditional or granted rights over local judicial process. The Soke of Winchester, for example, had its own bailiffs, law officers and stocks, and jurisdiction over malefactors (Haggard 1965, 27). A Late Saxon or early Norman execution cemetery was found at Hillcroft (Oliver's Battery), on the western side of Winchester, near the boundary of the Buddlesgate Hundred, in the Soke, or Liberty, of Winchester. It contained at least four individuals, and produced radiocarbon dates spanning a period of AD 980–1170. That this was a judicial cemetery is strongly suggested by the two individuals who had been fettered together (the iron fetters preserved), and two large post-pits which were interpreted as possible evidence for the presence of gallows. Circumstantial evidence for the careless drop of a corpse from the gallows was also recovered in the form of an individual with multiple breaks to the legs and ankle (Russel 2016).

The law of the land and the hierarchy of courts

Introduction to the law

The nature of the Weyhill Road site requires some understanding of contemporary national and local legal frameworks. While it is unfortunate that the preservation of hundredal and other documentary evidence is generally quite poor for Hampshire, when compared with other counties, some local court documents are preserved by the Hampshire Record Office (Figs 7.1 and Appendix 1.1). Although the town court rolls were unlikely to provide clues for our cemetery, they were examined, as part of the project, to confirm that this was indeed the case (see Phillips, Appendix 1). While no examples of capital felony cases from Andover were found, nationally there are many surviving original rolls and transcripts of documents, from a wide range of types of court and geographic areas, many of which have been transcribed into English and published. Various hundred, court, eyre and coroners' rolls from the post-Conquest period have provided detailed testimony of actual events from comparable places.

In addition, there exists a very large body of work regarding the evolution, enactment and results of the emergent English legal system in the medieval period. This is not the place to review or repeat that work. However, in discussing the context of a medieval judicial cemetery, the legal framework has to be broadly understood, and certain aspects must be mentioned, as they are likely to be of relevance to the origins of the cemetery and its population.

During the period of use of our cemetery, laws were generally re-iterated and altered, rather than being subject to wholesale change, although the ways in which they were implemented changed repeatedly through time. Relevant information can be found in two extensive

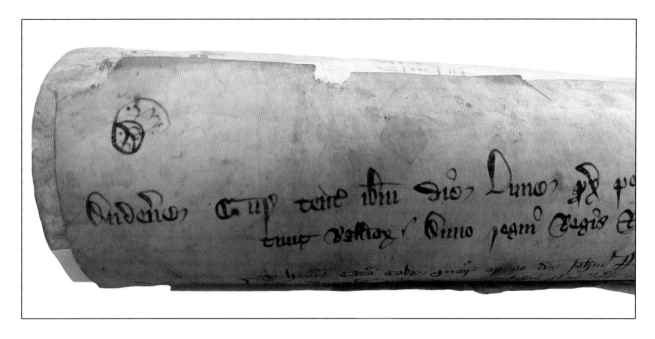

Fig. 7.1   Andover court roll 37M85/2/HC/14 In and Out Hundred Court roll 1387–1388.   Hampshire Record Office: Andover Borough Archive: 37M85/2/HC/14

reviews undertaken in the 19th century, namely the three-volume history of the criminal law of England by Sir James Fitzjames Stephen, published in 1883, and the somewhat more focused, two-volume work on the history of English law before the time of Edward I, by Sir Frederick Pollock and Frederick William Maitland, published in 1898. More recent reviews include Patrick Wormald's first volume (1999) of *The Making of English Law*, Musson (2009), and Baxter and Hudson (2014). Reynolds (2009a, appendix 1, 251–61) provides a hand-list of Saxon law codes relating to capital punishment) and Mattison (2016) mentions recent critical editions (print or digital) of law codes, from the 7th, to the early 11th centuries.

Elements of law codes from the times of the kings of Mercia and Wessex have survived, as have greater numbers from the later kings of all England. By the 12th century, collections and commentaries such as *The Treatise on the Laws and Customs of the Kingdom of England* (known as *Glanvill*) and the *Laws of Edward the Confessor* were available, and demonstrate the evolution of a considered approach to the laws of the land. From the 13th century, we also have both a text known as *Bracton*, and *Fleta* (an anonymous treatise). *Britton*, a French summary of the law of England, which was purported to have been written by command of King Edward, and *The Mirror of Justices* by Andrew Horn (or Horne), became available in the 14th century.

The king's law

From Early Saxon times onwards, the king's duty included keeping the peace. It also included law and order

in general, and the reduction of any, and all, potentially disruptive behaviour. At the beginning of the period of our cemetery, the mitigation of internal conflict was evolving from the kindred and private justice of blood feuds and *wergild* of the earlier Anglo-Saxon kingdoms. By the end of the period, the imposition of state-sanctioned fines and other punishments, both corporal and capital, were apparently increasingly motivated by the needs of local lords, overlords and the king, to maintain control of their vassals and to fill their coffers. At the beginning of the period, sentences could be mitigated by reference to the results of ordeals overseen by church representatives. As the period progressed, the process by which evidence was gathered, decisions made, and sentences carried out, was ever more tightly controlled and refined. Jury trials became the norm.

The limits to the power of the king and influence over criminal law, especially the differences in attitudes to theft and killing before and after the Norman Conquest, are discussed at some length by Lambert (2009). He notes an explicit differentiation in the pre-Conquest period between theft, with its strict prohibitions and lack of protection from punishment, and killing, which although threatening to the peace was dealt with according to circumstances (for example, *ibid.*, 203).

At the highest level under the Norman and later kings, the king's court or council, the 'Curia Regis', consisting of his tenants in chief, dealt with everything legislative, judicial and conciliar that was not merely local (Adams 1907, 12). Written charters (often granted for a fee paid to the Crown) could be, and were, granted to lords or certain places. These gave liberties from certain obligations and/or granted certain rights which, amongst other things, would raise income which would otherwise have accrued to the Crown. As also noted by Pollock and Maitland (1898, 494–5), 'only by slow degrees was larceny becoming a plea of the crown', with theft remaining a possible capital offence within the purview of local courts with *infangentheof* for some considerable time.

In practice, king's pleas could be heard in the presence of royal officials in the hundred and county courts (Carpenter 1996, 107). By the 1120s, Henry I sent judges (justices in eyre) travelling from county to county, to hold court, and this continued in various forms until the end of the 13th century. 'In the intervals between their visitations (in the thirteenth century, a customary seven years), it became increasingly common to appoint justices of assize, gaol delivery, and oyer and terminer, and these came to share with the eyre (and the bench and the court *coram rege*), the burden of dispensing criminal and civil justice in England' (*ibid.*, 108). 'For most of the 12th century, crown pleas were apparently determined, more or less as they arose, by the sheriffs or by local, county, justices' (Meekings 1961, 3). The eyre for the common pleas was a type of royal court held at intervals by the king's justices, normally in the town where the county court met. The crown justices dealt with deaths caused criminally, misadventure, felony cases and matters relating to the king's rights. That the court could secure profits of crown pleas for the king was important, but additionally, so was ensuring that the guilty were punished by appropriate sentences, in order to deter crime. This was despite there being a large number of cases with un-apprehended suspects, or persons not presented to the court. Some of these had escaped arrest or escaped from custody, whereas others had already had a judgement against them by a lesser local, or visitational court, or had been outlawed in the county court by an appeal, or abjured the realm (left the country under specific rules) (*ibid.*, 53–8).

From the 1220s, additional commissions were sent out to try felonies, in an attempt to avoid a backlog of prisoners awaiting gaol delivery (Musson 2001, 138). Despite increasing numbers of officials, commissions, eyres etc. the Statute of Winchester of 1285 stated that 'from day to day robberies, homicides and arsons are more often committed than they used to be' (Carpenter 1996, 111), and while 'this is impossible to prove' (Stubbs 1870, 464), it shows the perceived state of affairs at the time. Under Henry III, in 1273, systematic assize circuits were set up, although again these were subject to change through time (Musson 2001, 139).

The introduction of coroners, in 1194, allowed for an overview by the state of local procedures. See Hunnisett (1961, 9–12) for examples of irregularities resulting in fines for burial before the legal requirement of a coroner's view of the body. Coroners did not pass judgement, but could attend local courts which exercised the liberty of *infangentheof* in the absence of royal justice, as the hundred serjeant did prior to 1194. Whether this occurred regularly is a matter for conjecture, given the large case-loads of coroners. Although there were supposed to be four county coroners for each county, in 1204 Hampshire had only two (*ibid.*, 134). It should be noted that the presence of the coroner would ensure that the king received the appropriate fines, but was not designed as a curtailment of local rights and customs. 'Being the king's officers, but elected by the men of the county, the coroners formed a direct link between the Crown and the people, and a check on the intermediate lords' (Pollock 1899, 184).

The hierarchy of courts and power

A highly simplified explanation of the structure and workings of English medieval courts and the roles of employees of a developing legal system can be found in Table 7.2. While serious crimes would normally be expected to be dealt with at a county (shire) level, there were several mechanisms outside the simple judicial court structure, by which local manor (seigniorial or franchise) courts could have been allowed to deal with criminals. The increasingly strident claims made on behalf of the Crown were quite consistent with the lords of private jurisdictions having power of criminal justice extending in many cases even to life and death. Indeed, their exercise of such powers could be justified only by the highest theory of the king's power. It was because the king had them himself to begin with, that he could grant them to any lord whom he chose to favour. This occurred in practice when a landowner was able to prove by production of a written charter, or by claiming that they had inherited or 'ancient' rights, that they had the authority to deal with petty claims and serious crimes that had occurred on their land. These varied, but many, like the exemptions from certain fees and duties which sometimes accompanied them, led to material gain. They were therefore often highly sought-after and defended. These judicial processes explain how criminals could be executed locally, and thus become part of our cemetery population.

The Norman and early Angevin kings brought no law codes with them and between 1066 and *Magna Carta* there were relatively few new legislative acts, so the 12th to 13th-century legal system was built largely on pre-Conquest foundations (Poole 1951, 385). The Norman kings professed to rule by the law of Edward the Confessor, with few of their own additions. The so-called collection *The Laws of Edward the Confessor* was in fact produced and published during the Norman period, to underwrite the impression of continuity. They wanted to emphasise that innovations such as trial by battle were a small part of a system based on ancient custom. They retained the local system of administration through the hundred and the shire, and although attendance was supposed to be at the same time and place as in Edward

Table 7.2 Simplified courts structure

KING'S COURT
Curia Regis
Under William I royal tenants in chief both lay & ecclesiastical.
(KING'S RIGHTS & APPEALS. BOTH CIVIL & **CRIMINAL**)
Later delegated to various justiciars (Wm I – Henry II), commissioners and travelling courts:
1166–1300 Eyre
1305 Trailbaston

	ECCLESIASTICAL COURTS	LOCAL ASSEMBLIES	MANORIAL COURTS	
C O R O N E R ↓	(RELATING TO THE CLERGY OR OTHER SPECIFIC MATTERS)* Also a complex and stratified system	**SHIRE (County) COURT (CRIMINAL)** Presided over in Anglo-Saxon period by a Shire-Reeve and post-Conquest by a Sheriff	(CIVIL)* Presided over by the local lord under delegated authority from the king or under feudal (seigniorial) responsibility for limited area Sometimes known as 'Courts Leet'	C O R O N E R ↓
	* Unless the religious house or bishop had *Infangentheof* (the right of the lord of the manor to try and to punish a thief caught within the limits of his demesne) or other rights, such as the right to erect gallows, pillory and tumbrel for the punishment of malefactors	**HUNDRED and / or BOROUGH** for towns. (PRIVATE AND PETTY CRIMINAL MATTERS) Sheriffs held bi-annual tourns or meetings of the hundred court. The hundred was collectively responsible for various crimes committed within its borders if the offender were not produced. (Frankpledge) (Tithing). The (hue and) cry had to be raised by the inhabitants of a hundred in which a robbery had been committed, if they were not to become liable for the damages suffered by the victim. In Anglo-Saxon period a Reeve (*Gerefa*)/ town-reeve	Three types: **Honour** - chief tenants. May also have acted as a (local) court of appeal for lower manorial courts Baron - for free tenants of one manor Customary – for unfree tenants – later, most common (Manor reeve or bailiff) * Unless the lord had *Infangentheof* (the right of the lord of the manor to try and to punish a thief caught within the limits of his demesne) or other rights to punish.	
		Small local meetings Vill / tithe		

the Confessor's time, people could be exempted, and many hundreds fell into the hands of church or private landlords (*ibid.*, 386). Wormald suggested 'that the only unquestionable change in twelfth century English law was in the nature of the evidence for it' (1999, 142). The pressure at all levels for written records of their undertakings, continued throughout the period. Henry I made new statutes on coinage and theft, and Henry II introduced new laws that he called assizes (Poole 1951, 385). There were far-reaching changes and growth in the administration of justice during the reigns of Henry I and II, through their instructions to ministers and judges (*ibid.*, 386–7).

Hundred courts

Early meeting places and their possible use for holding Saxon hundred courts and their relationship to punishment cemeteries are discussed by Reynolds (Chapter 8) in his concluding remarks. The hundred courts could represent a local jurisdiction, as many were not directly controlled by the king. Wormald (see Baxter and Hudson 2014, 210) summarised the ownership of the private hundreds pre-1066 thus: '74% are in safe ecclesiastical hands; and, of the remaining 34, 25 "belong" to King Edward's wife or in-laws, while just six are "owned" by other lay noblemen and three to abbeys under their patronage. This is all as much as to say that, marginal though hundredal jurisdiction seems to have been, it was rarely left in hands other than those a king could easily trust'. By 1316, of 628 hundreds, 388 (nearly 62%) were in private hands (*ibid.*).

During the earlier part of the use of the Weyhill Road cemetery, the hundred court would have been organised by the reeve and the hundred '*serviens*' or serjeant. It then became the responsibility of the sheriff during most of the later part of the period under discussion. However, in practice, it was organised by the hundred bailiff. The bailiff was held accountable by the local lord and the sheriff, and was the equivalent of the hundred serjeant. Interestingly, Hunnisett (1961, 6) sets out how a number of the roles previously undertaken by the hundred serjeant have been subsumed into the role of the coroner, but not all. In a royal manor, the 'king's bailiff' may have held greater delegated or customary powers, and Cam (1930, 178) suggests that the king's bailiff might act without the presence of a coroner. She gives an example from 1279 where, in a royal hundred, a king's bailiff held the court and controlled the king's gallows. Stephen (1883, 129) gives an example of a king's bailiff from 1290, one Bogo de Nowell from Montgomery Castle, who complained that one of his (the king's) men had committed a murder and fled to a nearby hundred, where he was hanged. His complaint, which was that the murderer should have been handed back into his own hundred for execution there, was upheld. The lack of direct documentary evidence for Andover does not preclude the possibility that a king's bailiff held comparable power in the local area.

In a later example, Gross (1896, 107) gives a case overseen by a town bailiff acting under the devolved authority of a bishop. In 1382, in the presence of the coroners at Salisbury, one John Down was appealed for having feloniously stolen two coverlets worth 6s 8d, 2 sheets (2s), a carpet (6d), a towel (6d), a curtain of thread (4d) and a blanket (6d). The accused was convicted at Salisbury before John Gowen, bailiff of the liberty of the Bishop of Salisbury, and was hanged. He had no goods or chattels.

Local courts

The feudal courts (manorial and other seigniorial courts) of the 12th century could be expected to deal with virtually all types of case, except those specifically reserved for the king. The range of subjects covered by a local court could vary considerably, depending on the nature of the power invested in the lord in question, and their willingness to press the issue. Throughout the 12th and 13th centuries, the reigning monarchs and local

overlords tested these boundaries as they represented important local and national income streams. Vinogradoff's work (1892, 354–96) brings together in some detail the inner workings of the local manor court. The tenants, both free and not free, from subsidiary hamlets and farms, were bound to attend. If specifically summoned, their appearance was required by the next day, even if the summons arrived at midnight. The courts were normally held in the manor hall, but there are examples of courts held elsewhere, such as the local abbot for the manor of Stoneleigh (Warks.), who had proved that he held a long list of franchises (Salzman 1951), and had a house built especially. This was a far from one-sided representation, as both freeholders and villains attended, and cases could be effectively brought and decisions made by the community. Such courts would have been of an altogether more intimate and customary nature.

The balance between the lord and the people

In the 13th century, and beyond, the great lords, including those of large religious houses, still attempted to enforce their rights to hold feudal courts wherever they could. The arguments came down to questions of power and money. Prosecution led to fines, which in some cases could represent a considerable portion of a local landowner's income. Edward I's reign (1272–1307) started with a special commission into local customary rights across the kingdom. Pollock and Maitland (1898, 579) contains the quote that summary local justice was 'ridding England of more malefactors than the king's court could hang'. This is with reference to the thieves caught in the act: '*Handhaben* or *bakbarend*' in the words of Bracton quoted in Stephen (1883, 126–7) as 'in actual possession of stolen goods'. Although this period coincides with the possible end of use of the Weyhill Road cemetery it must be assumed that burials of malefactors continued elsewhere.

Jurisdictional limitations and boundaries, while in some cases very complex, should have been well known to all parties as inquests could often require the presence of jurors from adjacent tithings, parishes, manors or hundreds. For example, in 1362, a dead man was found in the high street in the parish of St Giles, in Oxford (Salter 1912, 42). A joint inquest was held, with representatives from the parish of St Giles, where Richard Bruns was sheriff, the parish of St Mary Magdalen, the tithing of the Abbot of Cseney, who had a manorial court in Walton Street, and the village of Walton, which was held by the Abbess of Godstow who had a manor in Walton itself. In view of these potential conflicts of interest, other settlements are discussed below, where they demonstrate possible similarities in the manner in which they were governed, or the mechanisms by which our cemetery might have been used.

Throughout the many procedural and local variations to the legal system the king and his local representatives continued to have a vested interest in making the enforcement of law all-encompassing and profitable. For example, chattels of convicted felons and of proved fugitives were forfeit to the Crown, unless a liberty-owner had been granted the right to take them. Any land belonging to convicted felons and fugitives escheated to the overlord, who might be the Crown (Pugh 1978, 27). By the end of the 13th century, the Crown had attempted to take decisive control of the criminal process (Maitland 1889, li–liv) although, as noted above, this was the culmination of a series of legislations and procedural refinements. In the 13th century, additional felonies reserved for the crown courts included wounding and wrongful arrest and detention (Carpenter 1996, 105–6).

However, the ultimate responsibility for ensuring local stability and compliance with socially acceptable standards continued to rely on the tithing or frank-pledge system of self-policing by mutual consent. While local communities would have been all too aware that reported crimes and accidents could result in fines or other punishments to those immediately involved, any non-reported crime or failure to intervene at the appropriate time could lead to larger fines for the whole community, when or if the truth came out. On the other hand, they would also have been aware that they could influence, and in some instances drive the results of, a civil or criminal case. This was because they were collectively responsible for the reporting of any initial actions against irregularities, and increasingly in the form of witness juries, for giving character references and statements of events.

This level of involvement by the community, in a stable area where the king's representative was trusted, or at least thought to be not too corrupt, would have helped to maintain the peace in general while still allowing state functionaries to gather taxes and fines. It should be noted that the community would, in effect, be encouraged to actively catch and hold any individual who could be considered obviously guilty. This included both the hue and cry, where the criminal might be caught red-handed or in possession of stolen goods, and also instances where outlaws or the abjured guilty were found and recognised. In all these cases, although the hoped-for outcome was a bloodless chase and restraint, it was accepted that resistance could end in death during the attempted capture.

The legal profession and the rise of functionaries

From the very end of the 12th century, there was what one might fairly call a legal profession, taking fees for its expertise. The status of physical infirmity in relation to ordeals, and the more complex question of mental infirmity, both chronic and traumatic, was hotly debated in relation to culpability. Culpability in relation to both age and sex were also topics of inquiry. The severity of sentencing, and the accepted age of maturity, were

debated and changed during the period. It is also to be noted that attitudes were changing with regard to the status of women in law, in that a wife could be cleared of a felony in which she had participated, on the grounds that she was obliged to act as her husband demanded.

There was also, during the medieval period, an increasingly large cast of characters who could hold judicial power on behalf of God and King. Locally, at the start of the period, this power was held by the local lord and/or bishop, who would hold court at regular intervals and also tour their lands. Some of the local magnates or prelates would hold land which came with devolved powers attached, whereas in other areas the king's representatives would have greater powers to intervene and override local custom. In all cases, some of the roles would be devolved to, amongst others, archdeacons, deacons, chancellors and official principals for the clerics, and to reeves, sheriffs, hundred serjeants, bailiffs and coroners for the laity. The church and civil courts were supposed to act in concert and deal with all aspects of social dispute at differing levels of courts, which were held at increasing intervals in reverse relationship to the severity of the problem. Some of these functionaries, such as sheriffs and bishops, as well as coroners and sheriffs, were also supposed to provide checks and balances to each other's powers. Morris (1927) and Hunnisett (1961) set out the interlocking powers and privileges of the sheriffs and coroners for the period in question. The coroners acted on behalf of the king and were, therefore, figures of local authority in their own right. At the start of the period of interest, the sheriff held pre-eminent power, but was often absent, as many of them held more than one shrievalty, or also held other posts within the king's court. Although in 1166 the Assize of Clarendon increased the powers of the sheriff over criminal cases (Morris 1927, 115), by the end of the cemetery period the power of the sheriff had declined, and he was replaced annually, his role and powers much reduced.

Church courts

Although it was said that in William I's time the 'church confined itself to causes touching the rule of souls' (Poole 1951, 201), by the reign of Henry II, jurisdiction of the clergy was still widespread and influential. They could not pronounce a sentence of blood, and although they could imprison people they rarely did, due to the cost of maintaining prisons (*ibid.*), but see below. Such circumstances could give rise to jurisdictional anomalies, as the Church authorities would be unwilling to cede primacy to a secular court in cases involving clerks. The Oxford coroner's rolls provide examples of overlapping spheres of influence between the town and the religious teaching orders. Where the laity might face execution, people claiming to be clerks and other low-level ecclesiastics, could instead face imprisonment or fines. A number of examples occur in the records of coroners' inquests from Oxford, for example in 1302, a baker died of wounds received from two clerks (Salter 1912, 16). One clerk was arrested and held in the town prison, whereupon the chancellor demanded he be released to be held at the chancellor's prison. The clerk was subsequently released by the church authorities, and disappeared. Another record relates how a drunken brawl between clerks, in a beer tavern, resulted in a death and murder conviction (*ibid.*, 8). The convicted clerk was handed over to the Bishop of Lincoln, who was expected to hold him in the bishop's prison at Banbury for two to five years or more.

Religious orders could also be, in effect, lords of the manor, and as such would maintain a local manorial court which could administer the same levels of justice as any equivalent lay baronial court. Quite frequently, a 'monastery had ordinary powers of justice over its tenants in the manor courts but the *Dominus* also might have "*sac* and *sol, tol* and *theam, infangentheof* and gallows and other liberties", so had the *Domina*, the nun'. It was, from the owner's point of view, an ordinary commercial asset (Coulton 1927, 53–4).

Power (1922, 103–4) says that, in addition to the manor rents, 'the position of a religious community as lord of a manor gave it the right to various other financial payments. Of these, the most important were the perquisites of the manorial courts. These varied … according to the extent and number of liberties which had been granted to any particular house'. The abbey of Syon (founded in Middlesex in 1415), for example, had far more liberties than most, including view of frankpledge, leets etc., plus assizes of bread, ale wine, weights and measures. 'They had all the old traditional emoluments of justice, which lords had striven to obtain since the days before the conquest, *soc, sac, infangentheof, outfangentheof,* waif, *estray*, treasure-trove, wreck of the sea, *deodands*, chattels of felons and fugitives, of outlaws, of waive, of persons condemned, of felons of themselves (suicides), escapes of felons, year day waste and estrepement and all commodities, forfeitures and profits whatsoever. They had the right to erect gallows, pillory and tumbrel for the punishment of malefactors'.

The Hampshire eyre roll of 1249 deals with crimes related to violent robbery in the pass (path through woodland) of Alton, that were tried at Winchester. An edited and translated account (Clanchy 1978) allows an insight into the complex legal processes of the 13th century, the power of the church, the hundred jury system and likely punishments. In a time when crime was rife, notorious criminals could possibly escape death by turning king's evidence against their associates (becoming an 'approver'), or accusing others. People said by jurors to be guilty, could be hanged, outlawed, and relieved of goods and chattels for harbouring or confederacy with outlaws, or for not 'raising a hue', having seen outlaws. Other accused prisoners paid large fines by their own, or someone else's, surety. At least two clerks accused of

harbouring outlaws refused to answer to the court. The Bishop of Winchester's official claimed them both. The jury said that John Clerk of Hartley Wintney (*ibid.*, 57) was not guilty, although his companion was to be taken into custody because he did not 'raise the hue' when he fell in with the outlaws, Thomas Clerk of Priors Dean (*ibid.*, 59), accused with two others. He was said by the jury to be guilty; he was a married man and the sheriff was ordered to take his land into the hand of the king, and he was committed to the Bishop of Winchester's gaol as a convict. One of his fellow accused was found guilty, and the other acquitted. Some prisoners, such as Henry Clop, managed to escape; having escaped from custody of the vill of Bishops Waltham, the vill was seen to be answerable for the escape. Henry fled to St Swithun's Church, where he admitted that he was a thief and swore an oath to leave the country for ever ('abjured the realm'), leaving the Bishop of Winchester answerable for the value of his chattels (*ibid.*, 56). The Benedictine monk and chronicler Matthew Paris (d. 1259) implied that jurors could be corrupt, and the eyre roll seems to corroborate this. John Boarhunt, one of twelve jurors, was convicted of stopping other jurors telling the truth, but although he was to be taken into custody for his crime, he later paid a fine of 40 shillings 'of his own surety' suggesting that he was a man of some means (*ibid.*, 56). There were problems with obtaining guilty judgements from juries, as their verdict was 'essentially a collective statement about the accused's reputation by local men of property, who might conceal crimes committed by people of their own class. No stranger, particularly if he were a poor vagrant, would willingly submit to trial by jury' (*ibid.*, 35–6). An earlier Law Code of Henry I (r. 1100–35) had stated that, if the body of a murdered man was discovered, then the hundred, the reeve and the neighbours would assemble, and that the body, whether identified or not, would be kept raised on a hurdle for seven days with logs burning around it at night (Downer 1996, cited in Daniell 2002, 254). However, the murder of a stranger in the pass of Alton appears to have raised little interest amongst the locals. The roll says 'who killed him is not known. No Englishry, so a murder [fine]. The vills of Alton, Medstead and Chawton did not come in full to the inquest' (Clanchy 1978, 55).

The Church and burial

The Church set out its own guidance on who should be excluded from Christian burial. At one extreme was Archbishop Wulstan of York (d. 1023), who believed that any who were ignorant of the creed and paternoster were not good Christians and so were not worthy of rights such as burial in consecrated ground (Foxhall Forbes 2013, 1). Specific rules were laid down for the clergy as well as the lay people. Canon 2 from the Council of London held in 1075 under Archbishop

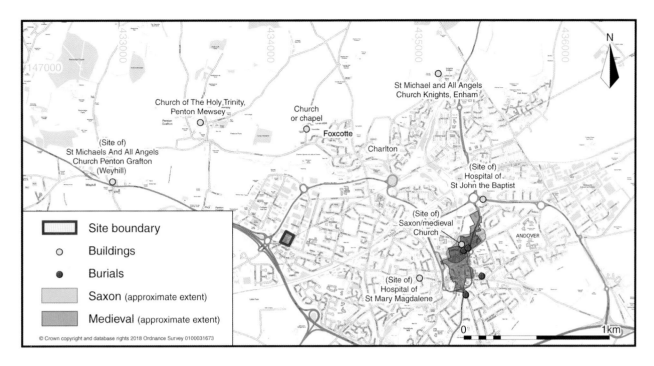

Fig. 7.2   Saxon and medieval Andover area

Lanfranc contained a restriction for monks. 'If anyone be discovered at death to hold any property without licence (aforesaid) and shall not restore it before death, confessing his sin with penitence and grief, let not the bells be tolled for him … nor let him be buried in the cemetery' (Gee and Hardy 1914, 55). The canons of the Lateran Councils tended to reserve the threat of exclusion from Christian burial grounds to specific transgressions and/or failure to confess. The Second Lateran Council of 1139, in canon 14, forbids jousts and tournaments and refuses a church burial to any who die as a result of such activities. Canon 18 from the same council prohibits church burial to arsonists. The Fourth Lateran Council of 1215, in canon 3, refuses the sacrament and Christian burial to heretics and to any supporters of heretics. Canon 21 threatens to bar parishioners from entry to the church and Christian burial if they fail to attend confession at least once a year.

Excommunication was used as a weapon to ensure good behaviour and the local priest could refuse his services to the dead and their family if an individual died unforgiven, thereby refusing to allow a burial under church auspices. Roger of Wendover gives an example of an unknown soldier who died in 1217 at a battle at Lincoln, as an excommunicant who was buried at a crossroads (Giles 1849, 396). He also relates a shocking story which resulted from the instruction by a town priest to the family of an excommunicated usurer to bury the body outside the town where two roads met (*ibid.*, 532). An example from the other end of the social spectrum is that of Gaveston, the favourite of King Edward II, whose headless body was left in the hands of some Oxford Dominicans who 'dared not bury it in consecrated ground as Gaveston had died excommunicate' (McKisack 1959, 27).

One further complication with the Church which arose during the period of the cemetery was the Interdict of 1208 to 1212, when the relationship between King John and Pope Innocent III reached an impasse over the selection of new archbishops (Poole 1951, 442–8, 456–7). The general Interdict was followed and strengthened by the excommunication of King John. This allowed a threat of deposition and invasion to force the surrender of the king. During the period of the Interdict the services of the church were severely curtailed. A letter of 1208 from Pope Innocent III to the bishops of London, Ely and Worcester sets out that priests were allowed to visit the sick, hear confessions and commend souls but would not be following the corpses of the dead as they would not have a church burial (Gee and Hardy 1914, 74). The Chronicle of Melrose states that there were no masses held or communion for the dying, or burials (Stevenson 1856, 149–50). Roger of Wendover wrote that the bodies of the dead were carried out of the towns and cities and buried in roads and ditches without prayers or attendance of priests (Giles 1849, 246). If it were not for the continuing evidence for execution amongst the 13th-century population of the Weyhill Road cemetery and the lack of empty graves from which corpses had been retrieved, the inhabitants of Andover could have been using the cemetery as an emergency measure.

Even as late as 1352, Archbishop William Zouche of

York (d. 1352) proclaimed that 'according to canonical sanctions ecclesiastical burial is not to be denied to those hanged on the gallows, as long as they died penitent' (Summerson 2001, 131), which in turn suggests that ecclesiastical burial was not always the case, especially for non-penitents. It is possible that he showed understanding because he himself had an early brush with the law if he was the same William la Zouche 'who, with other clerks, was accused before January 1328 of breaking into the house and stealing the sheep of the prior of Charley, Leicestershire' (DNB 1885–1900). On 14 May 1329 he received protection on going abroad with the king. Zouche had also in 1349, when there was pressure on cemetery spaces due to the plague, showed great activity in consecrating new cemeteries.

Forest Law

There were territories not far from the town of Andover which would have provided another source of income to kings, under Forest Law. The Anglo-Saxon rulers took steps to protect their hunting reserves, and pre-Conquest local land owners included 'Waleran the Hunter', so while Forest Law was new, protection of hunting grounds had existed earlier. The nearby Forest of Chute was first mentioned in 1156, as 'the Forest of "Witingelega" and the brails of Andover and "Digerley" (Doiley or Doyley, Hants), and as 'the Forest of Chute' in 1215, and a 14th-century inquisition referred to 'the forest of Chute in the hundred of Andover' (Crittall 1959a). Given its location adjacent to the Forest of Chute, one of the changes regarding land-use which would have been felt in the Andover area would have been the introduction of *Forest* (both the word and the Law), by William I. Kings had owned, and probably hunted on, land around Andover long before the Conquest. It has been a generally held view that Anglo-Saxon kings exercised no more sporting rights than any other landowner, although Flight (2016, 311) has argued that the Anglo-Saxon and Norman aristocracies both hunted in much the same way, and that hunting was legally restricted to the ruling classes long before 1066. Forest Law may have been further developed in England, rather than being transposed from the Continent (Green 2013). What is certain is that Norman kings asserted their right to keep deer on other people's land, and to set up forest officialdom and courts to protect them. The forests' products, and the fines and amercements arising from their protection, were a source of revenue, as evidenced by a document of 1130 (Winters 2018). Afforestment was continued by Henry I (r. 1100–35), and the encroachment of forest legislation was also a way of controlling the power of the nobility, which was eventually curtailed by *Magna Carta* in 1216 (Rackham 1986, 131; 2006, 119). It can be supposed that these changes influenced the lives of ordinary rural people. It has been noted that, during 'the upheaval of Stephen's reign, when "wild animals … which before had been most scrupulously preserved in the whole kingdom … were now molested in every quarter, scattered by chance-comer and fearlessly struck down by all" ' (Winters 2018 citing the *Gesta Stephani*, (Potter 1976, 3)). It is not clear whether people turned to the forest for food due to disruption of normal harvests or other supplies, or due to a lack of usual supervision and control.

While Norman punishments for infringing the rules might involve mutilation or death, the Angevin kings normally used imprisonment and heavy fines. More than a hundred men were fined for forest offences in Hampshire in 1176, in sums ranging from 500 to half a mark, and totalling £2,093 10s (Poole 1951, 33–4). By the reign of Edward I, imprisonment was used to enforce aspects of Forest Law.

Due process and capital punishment. How might the Weyhill Road cemetery come to be populated?

As previously mentioned, the power to hold trials and, when necessary, order the death penalty, was strictly controlled, and transferred only to a select few. In Hampshire at the beginning of the period, we would expect the Earl and the Bishop to have held this right, which in turn could be transferred downwards to selected substitutes. Winchester would have been the natural seat of decision-making for capital trials, and as would be expected, evidence has been found for execution cemeteries in the vicinity. See, for example, Oliver's Battery (Russel 2016). The evidence from Andover, therefore, needs to be linked to a more localised or different process. A local manorial lord and/or the king's bailiff from Andover are more likely originators of the cemetery.

The various court, hundred, eyre and coroners' rolls do provide a number of examples of less-centralised deaths via legalised processes. Morris (1927, 119) noted that theft at county courts and others was handled in various counties according to diverse customs. An irregularity was recorded for 1234, when the men of Gretton in Northampton were pardoned for raising a gallows on which two outlaws were hanged because the king's Constable of Rockingham had ordered them to do so (*ibid.*, 234). Relatively few records of private courts survive, and the hangings they sanctioned were not regularly presented at the eyres. Stephen (1883, 128–9) notes, from the records of hundred rolls, that private gallows had become common, as he puts it 'the usurpation of franchises had gone to extraordinary lengths', and that of the 35 gallows recorded for Berkshire, 12 were from the hundred of Newbury alone. Later records of private punishments are much harder to come by. Given (1977, 93) suggests that by the 13th century 'the old communal courts, which in the course of the 12th century had been deprived of their rights to try capital crimes, seem to have only rarely attempted to reassert their old prerogatives. One person was hanged in a county court and two in hundred courts'.

Duggan (2018, 196–206) cites the 13th century as the time when English kings attempted to realise their claims to a monopoly over the punishment of crime, through administrative and procedural developments. This included control over rights of *infangentheof* which might or might not include rights to possess a gallows. He gives 13th-century examples of gallows raised without the king's permission being knocked down, and also of failure to exercise the right, resulting in the right reverting to the Crown. Permission was now also required to renew or replace old gallows.

The medieval document *The Court Baron* presents a blueprint for the holding of local courts. It contains examples of presentations for thieves and receivers of goods caught by hue and cry (Maitland and Baildon 1890, 65–7 and 73–4). The expected end result in an open and shut case would be hanging or abjuring. Pollock (1899, 182–3) discussed cases where a crime was 'too manifest for any formal proof to be required'. He stated that, 'for more than a century after the Conquest, and much later in some local jurisdictions, the stern rule of the popular courts against open and notorious crime held its ground. A criminal taken red-handed was not entitled to any further defence or trial before the king's justices, whether he were a murderer with his bloody weapon, or a robber with his stolen goods, "seised" as men then said "of the murder or theft," so that the fact was undeniable before the lawful men who apprehended him. As early as Athelstan it is stated that thieves seized in the act will not be spared. This was deliberately confirmed as late as 1176 (Assize of Northampton, art. 3, S. C. 151), and the jurisdiction, as long as it existed, remained with the county court, save in the case of crime specially reserved for the Crown'. Murder was often incidental to theft or housebreaking as there was nothing more to be lost by adding murder to robbery, already a capital offence. If the crime was admitted or witnessed, the criminal could be summarily hanged, not for the murder, which was not within the county court's jurisdiction, but for the manifest theft, which was. The same rule was applied by the king's judges to manslaying, down to the middle of the 13th century. It was not necessary that the judgement should be rendered immediately, but only that the damning circumstances of the offender's arrest should be promptly recorded by good witness. In the Gloucestershire eyre of 1221 there were 330 homicides presented, which led to 14 hangings and one mutilation, and 100 men who were not produced were outlawed, and a further 166 crimes attributed to persons unknown (Carpenter 1996, 112). Summerson (1996, 126) notes that although Gloucestershire was not directly involved in the civil war of 1215–17, it probably contributed to the crime rate recorded at the eyre.

Outlaws were liable to arrest on sight, and could be killed if they resisted arrest or fled, as was also the case for returning abjurers. In his study of 13th-century homicide, Given (1977, 208–10), presents examples of abjurors being beheaded, but suggests that many may have been allowed to escape. One who did not escape was Adam Roules who in 1248 abjured the realm at Ludlow but was found making his way back to Shropshire. The hue was raised and he was arrested and beheaded (Summerson 1996, 124–5). Summerson (*ibid.*, 123–6, 135–42) said that if an individual was summonsed to appear at court and failed to appear at four successive sessions of the county court, they could be declared outlaw at next session. As Pollock and Maitland noted (1898, 580) outlawry was 'still the law's ultimate weapon'. Hunnisett (1961, 49–50) deals with coroner's view of bodies of outlaws, fugitives and straying or returning abjurors pursued and beheaded 'as by law they should', noting that the heads were sent to the county gaol. He presents evidence for outlaws being decapitated, and at the time of Richard I (r. 1189–99) a 5s bounty for an outlaw's head was paid to serjeants by royal writ (*ibid.*, 67–8). In 1288, the villagers of Sompting (Sussex) were fined because when they captured an outlaw, they took him into custody (from which he escaped) rather than beheading him as a fugitive (Summerson 2001, 124–5). Hunnisett (1961, 67) suggests that by 1355 summary execution of outlaws was exceptional. There is a documented example from 1322, for Northamptonshire, of an abjuror being beheaded after leaving the king's highway to flee across the fields towards the woods (Gross 1896, 75–6). The head in this case was sent to the king's castle at Northampton.

How common was capital punishment?

The Gloucester eyre of 1221 covered nearly an 18-year period, and showed an average homicide rate of 20 per annum (Summerson 1996, 125). In comparison, the eyres of Buckinghamshire, Essex and Surrey for the 1230s, show averages of 9–10 per annum (*ibid.*). The civil war of 1215–17 had probably contributed to the crime rate, in that stable areas, with good road systems and nearby prosperous towns, would attract the footloose, needy and ambitious, with added numbers of people fleeing more troubled parts. The various woodlands surrounding Andover could have been used to hide wanderers and evildoers. An example is given from Gloucestershire, where criminal bands were encountered. Eleven criminals were hanged at once at one eyre, which showed a local willingness to deal with whole bands (*ibid.*, 130). Given, in his study of 13th-century homicide (1977, 106), points out that homicide committed in the course of a robbery was a major phenomenon. As theft was punishable by death, in the isolation of the countryside during a theft from a

Table 7. 3 Summary data from Wiltshire eyre of 1249 (after Meekings 1961, 95)

Crime	Numbers accused	Number of persons			
		Verdict		Verdict	
		Come (present)		Absent	
		Guilty	Not guilty	Guilty	Not guilty
Arson	1	-	1	-	-
Burglary	3	-	2	1	-
Consorting with and harbouring thieves	30	4	20	4	2
Homicide	35	1	23	10	1
Larceny	205	15	60	109	21
Poaching	1	-	-	1	-
Totals	275	20	106	125	24

house, a decision to leave no witnesses might be made. He shows that, while a simple homicide might not result in a successful pursuit or indeed a guilty ruling, cases of combined theft and murder were more likely to result in a successful pursuit. The danger to isolated communities from bands of robbers was greater and recognised as such by those most likely to be victims. Meekings (1961, 95) gave data (Table 7.3) summarising cases types and verdict results, from the Wiltshire eyre of 1249. In the same eyre, 17 murderers, 28 thieves, two coiners and two other criminals had abjured the realm (*ibid.*, 53).

The local organisation of executions

As Summerson (2001, 123–31) notes, many local authorities had the right to execute judgements of death, raise gallows by old, approved and used custom, or special grant and licence of the king or his forebears. The organisation of executions varied, according to whether the gallows employed was in private or royal hands. Those in private hands had probably greater variation, in that the tasks of guard, carpenter, ladder keeper and hangman, would have to be locally agreed, as and when required. Free tenants in some hundreds would have to undertake the burden of providing secure premises to hold thieves, guard them and eventually hang them, as required by the details of their tenancy agreements (Cam 1930, 176). The abbey of Stoneleigh (Warks.), founded in 1155, had four bondmen who held land by a number of services such as ploughing and reaping but also by the making of gallows and the hanging of thieves (Page 1908). In 1270, four tenants of Newenham Abbey (Devon), in return for their tenements, provided the following services - one conducted the prisoner to the gallows, one put the gallows up, one supplied the ladders and one performed the hanging (Carpenter 1996, 118). Although tenants with these duties acted as assistants

to the local hundred bailiff, abbot's proctor or other representative of the overlord, they were not appointed by the delegated authorities. In these cases, the duties were bound to the tenancy and therefore could create a hereditary burden for a local family. That family would

Fig. 7.3   The Gibbett of Montfaucon. A contemporary woodcut illustration with the opening lines of François Villon's Ballade des Pendus, from one of the earliest editions of his poems, published in 1490 (De Vere Stacpoole 1914)

then provide another strong element for the case for local continuity of custom and location. It was also possible for some tasks to devolve to aggrieved parties or strangers. 'It was not unknown for a condemned man to be left to hang in solitude, to be later cut down by passing strangers' (Summerson 2001, 130). In the king's courts the roles were undertaken by obligations set down to specific right-holders. During the 12th century, the terms *carnifices* and *suspensores* are mentioned, which may suggest a more professional class of worker.

Other sources of contemporary information

In addition to the written records of court procedures and cases, there is also a body of illustrative evidence for the period. Many of the examples come from religious works where, although the subject matter is far-removed from events taking place around Andover, the portrayal of dress and equipment is of a contemporary nature. The Eadwine (Canterbury) Psalter for example, is profusely illustrated with scenes of hunting, ploughing, spinning and other aspects of rural life, as well as the expected range of judgements, resurrection, baptism and hell. Winchester at this time was a major production centre for manuscripts for the ecclesiastical centre, and to supply the demands of royal administration (Chedzey 2003). This became an important local industry from the 9th to the 16th centuries.

A Hampshire Curia Regis or eyre roll, of 1249 (appeal of approvers; The National Archive (TNA) Ref: KB 26/223), is famous for having the only known, contemporary illustration of a rare documented case of 'trial by battle'. A sketch also shows the gallows located on a mound or a hill, as a simple pair of upright posts, each with a forked end, and a timber cross-piece (Clanchy 1978), complete with occupant, with hands tied behind his back. Another image of a man hanging from similar gallows (though without the landscape), can be found as an historiated initial 'C'(rimen) from an illuminated English parchment codex, a general encyclopedia in two volumes, inscribed by James le Palmer, of *c*. 1360–*c*. 1375 (MS Royal 6 E VI f. 444, British Library 2018). A sumptuous, but rather gruesome, later 15th-century illustration shows decapitation, drowning and hanging. The gallows (again sited on a hill) comprise two upright posts, with the cross-piece supported by corner braces (Riisøy 2015, 55; fig. 1). The other common source of contemporary illustration is marginalia which, among all the mainly fantastical, metaphorical and whimsical subjects, does show small vignettes of violence, robbery, hanging, decapitation and burial.

Other somewhat unexpected sources hold some tantalising glimpses of expected and possibly common behaviour. The early 12th-century *Leges Henrici Primi* (Laws of Henry I) has a short section which sets out the proper course of events following a death caused in self-defence or during a feud (Lambert 2009, 60). Amongst

the rules concerning the victim's belongings and due notification processes, the body is to be laid on the ground with the face towards the west and the feet to the east. Even under these temporary circumstances the body is to be respected with the traditional alignment. Another vignette comes from a ballad published in the 16th century but possibly of earlier origin, *Adam Bell, Clym of the Clough, and William of Cloudesley* (Sargent and Kitteredge *c*. 1904, 244–54). In this, the sheriff at Carlisle provides a 'ladde' to get the measure of the victim prior to the hanging. This appears to imply both a fairly rough and ready sizing up for the grave and a desire to have the process well under way with no waiting, concomitant with a lack of grave side ritual and the potential for 'short' graves.

> And Clowdysle hymselfe lay redy in a carte,
> Fast bounde bothe fote and hande,
> And a strong rope aboute his necke,
> All redy for to be hanged.
>
> The Justyce called to hym a ladde;
> Clowdysles clothes shoulde he have,
> To take the measure of that good yoman,
> And therafter to make his grave.

Contemporary prose and poetry, both secular and religious in subject matter, helps to round out our picture of both the mundane and inner lives of the local population throughout a period of great change. The surviving Icelandic sagas allow one view of the early medieval world. The major protagonists often represent the remnants of the Viking invaders, 'the great northern army' etc. of the Anglo-Saxon Chronicles. They were a source of fear and loss, both physical and financial, for the kingdom of Wessex. The saga of Egil (Pálsson and Edwards 1976) for instance is a tale of a man who was a noted killer of men. He showed no great respect for kindred, his local community or even the various overlords he met. While acting as a mercenary in England under the control of King Athelstan, he received a preliminary form of baptism for commercial gain. When Egil eventually died of old age, he was laid to rest with his weapons under a mound. His body was later moved to a church, and then subsequently re-interred on the edge of the church graveyard. In spite of his dubious personal history and criminal past, his family's continuing influence allowed his body an acceptable burial.

The compilations known collectively as the *Anglo-Saxon Chronicle* provide a chronological framework in some detail, and include a number of episodes which occurred around and within the Hampshire area. Various works such as *The Court Baron* (Maitland and Baildon 1890), and the *Gerefa*, serve as templates for the proper form of procedure for a manorial steward or a reeve in the normal course of his estate management duties. These records of physical events are also brought to life by the surviving copies of Anglo-Saxon and medieval illustrated calendars, such as *The Labours of the Months*. Whether these served as mnemonic aids for holy days, or simple illustrations of the changing seasons remains debatable, but nonetheless they do show a sequence of standard, everyday tasks in fine detail (Shepherd 2010).

The perceptions and beliefs of the general public are touched upon in Riviello's work (2017) on the nature and significance of exile, by reference to examples of Old English poetry. The author expounds on the absolute division between the stability and safety represented by the community and the constant danger and chaos suffered by the outcast. This is apt when considering the status of the abjuror and also the outlawed, and how they may have viewed themselves and been viewed by others. These examples are balanced by the homilies or verse and prose sermon texts, which set out proper forms of behaviour for all good Christians. As well as exhorting all to love God and their fellow men, they also set out the torments to come, of hunger, thirst, fire and frost etc., which will overcome all oath-breakers, traitors, thieves, unjust judges, unfaithful stewards and other felons who fail to repent.

Chapter 8
Discussion

Introduction

The local topography is not dramatic, but the site does lie on a low spur, and this prompts the question of whether there would have been a line of sight from Monxton in the south, or from Andover to the east, particularly if a gallows had been erected there. It may be noted that the boundaries and nature of Chute Forest to the north-west, Finkley and Harewood forests to the east and the Thickets of Ann to the south at the time of the cemetery's use are not clear, although Chute Forest is mentioned in contemporary records (Chapter 7). Shore (1888, 41) suggested that, throughout the Anglo-Saxon period, and far into the Middle Ages, north Hampshire retained a generally forested character. Saxton's 1575 map depicts a heavily-forested Chute to the north of Penton, around Appleshaw and Enham, and Norden's map of 1607 shows a few trees to the north and west of Weyhill. The presence of substantial prehistoric monuments and a number of Roman villas in the immediate vicinity of the site suggests, however, that open, cleared areas were of a long-standing nature and that the forests were already heavily managed.

The geography and characteristics of Anglo-Saxon execution cemeteries have been recognised through various 20th-century excavations (for example, Hill 1937; Liddell 1933), which have been collated and defined (Reynolds 2009a), and further augmented in recent years. Andrew Reynolds identified a total of 27 excavated examples of possible execution cemeteries (*ibid.*, 152, fig. 39), of which Meon Hill, Stockbridge Down, and Old Dairy Cottage, Winchester are closest comparators (Fig. 8.1), with Roche Court Down, Bokerley Dyke, and Old Sarum slightly further away. Alyxandra Mattison (2016) has suggested a reduced selection of execution cemeteries, at nine locations (Bran Ditch and Chesterton Lane Corner, Cambridgeshire; Guildown, Surrey; Meon Hill; Stockbridge Down; Old Dairy Cottage, Winchester; Staines, Middlesex; Sutton Hoo, Suffolk; and Walkington Wold, Yorkshire). To

this may be added Oliver's Battery, Winchester (Russel 2016). Mattison (2016) has reviewed the evidence in the light of further excavation results and looking in particular at the Norman period. The local historical-geographic context (Fig. 8.2) is discussed in detail by Andrew Reynolds below.

Type of cemetery

With the exception of interments at battlefield or massacre sites (Fiorato *et al.* 2000; Loe *et al.* 2014; Wallis 2014), executed felons in burial grounds associated with places of execution (Buckberry and Hadley 2007), or occasional finds of infant burials in settlements (Rahtz 1969; Chapman 2010), archaeological evidence in the later medieval period for burials or other deposits of human remains outside formal cemeteries is rare (Gilchrist and Sloane 2005, 73).

While there are some similarities in the cemetery population and burial rites, normative medieval cemeteries generally show different patterns to those at Weyhill Road. An example, from a contemporary Hampshire community, might be the church and settlement at Hatch Warren, Brighton Hill South, Basingstoke (Fasham and Keevil, 1995), where nine graves were recorded within the church itself, including a probable grave of a priest (a mature adult male buried with a pewter chalice and paten and an iron buckle). Another, earlier grave, of an immature male, was accompanied by two silver farthings of Edward I (minted 1280–1300). The churchyard was found to contain at least 258 graves, of which 37 were excavated, revealing at least 46 individual burials. There were a number of double burials and several graves had been re-used, and intercutting of graves was common. The age profile of the excavated cemetery population (52) makes an interesting contrast to that of the Weyhill Road cemetery, in that a high proportion of children (21), and juveniles (10), compared with adults (16) and unknowns (5) was recorded (Waldron 1995, 143).

For example at Raunds, which provided a radiocarbon

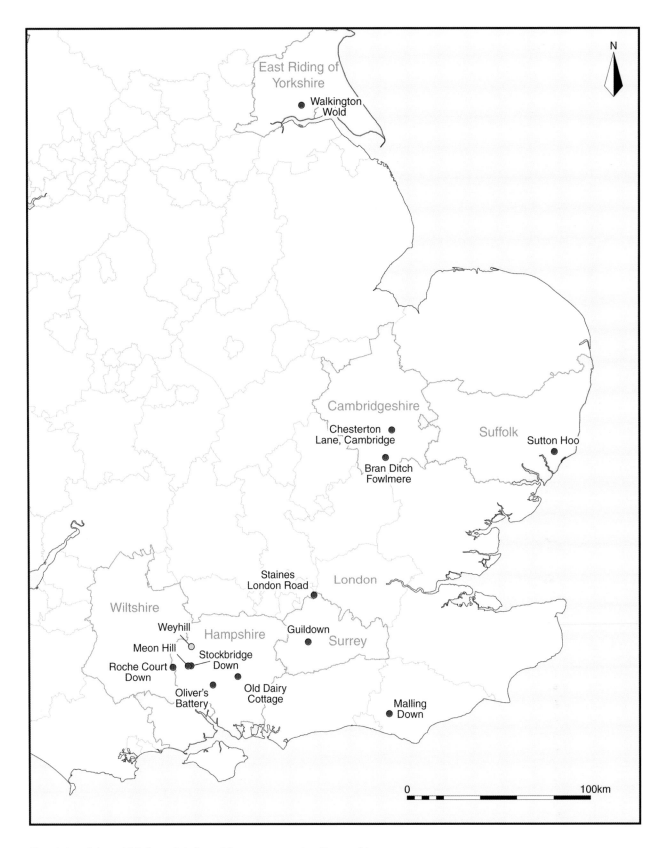

Fig. 8.1   Selected likely judicial punishment cemeteries discussed in text

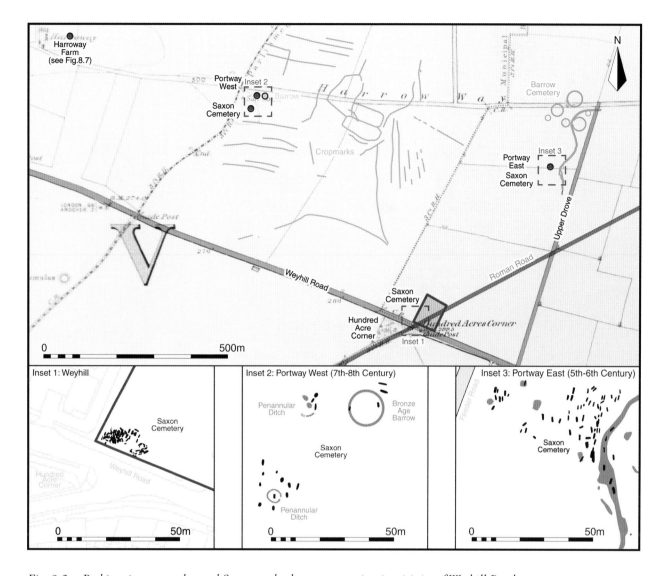

Fig. 8.2   Prehistoric cropmarks, and Saxon and other cemetery sites in vicinity of Weyhill Road

date-range of 978–1040 cal AD to 2, the complete cemetery of 361 inhumations could be assumed to represent a much wider spectrum of the potential local burial population. The graves were within an enclosed churchyard, aligned west–east, in rows, and the burials were in supine positions, without grave goods. This is a good example of the expected, normal, small community cemetery, which chronologically overlaps with the first stage of burial at the Weyhill Road site.

We can therefore define, with confidence, what our cemetery is not. Altogether clearer, or definitively different, evidence would be required to be able to include this cemetery among the classes of standard field cemeteries. Nor is it, as far as we can discern, within consecrated ground, a massacre or plague cemetery, a burial ground for the recognisably disease-afflicted, religious or ethnic subsets, or indeed a punishment cemetery of specifically Anglo-Saxon date.

The Church and cemeteries

The churchyard burial as 'normal' emerged in the later 7th century, for members of religious communities, royalty and some members of the laity, but was not considered to be standard social practice until the 10th century (Hadley 2010, 103; Cherryson 2005, 211–17, 227–34). These burials were largely west–east-aligned, supine and unaccompanied by grave goods. Other changes in burial practices between the 7th and 9th centuries included burial grounds which were more closely integrated with settlements, including within the burgeoning towns, or *wics*; cemeteries located next to churches and minsters and, by the early 8th century, the emergence of identifiable execution cemeteries, containing high proportions of 'deviant' burials. Normal burials in settlement contexts appear to have peaked in the 8th century, and fallen-off substantially in the 9th, when other burial grounds were perhaps giving way to the already-growing practice of minster and, later, local churchyard burial (Sofield 2015). Reynolds (2009a, 68–89, 159–77) defined 'deviant' burials to include prone burial, decapitation, amputation, binding of limbs, post-mortem display of the body, and the covering of the body or grave with numerous or heavy stones. He had found that roughly 1% of burials in 5th to 7th-century cemeteries were deviant (*ibid.*, 94, 97–151). Hadley (2010, 107) suggests that unusual burial treatment is more likely to be seen in the burials of males, and that execution cemeteries would necessarily contain a higher proportion of younger adults, i.e. 15–30 years at death, who were more pre-disposed to engage in the kinds of behaviour that would result in them being excluded from normative burial. While other types of non-normal burials are noted – including 'single incident' mass graves (the Ridgeway, Weymouth and St John's College, Oxford being examples: Loe *et al.* 2014; Wallis 2014), nothing in the current cemetery suggests the type of incident which resulted in those grave sites.

The extent of the cemetery

The original size and extent of the Weyhill Road cemetery cannot now be known with any certainty and, as discussed previously, there is no doubt that the recorded number of individuals represented by the articulated remains is an under-representation of the original total of burial events. An unknown number of shallow burials may have been lost and, similarly, some of the earliest burials may have been destroyed by later use. However, it is possible to suggest that the total extent of the burial ground is unlikely to have been very much greater than recently uncovered, with the proviso that, although we have a probable north-eastern boundary, it is clear that burials extended beyond the current site edges to the south and east. Figure 2.7 shows the reconstructed grave outlines, and suggests that the overall pattern is distinctly focused either on the position of the gallows, or perhaps on the line of the old Roman road, and shows little sign of expansion. We can, therefore, anticipate that the minimum number total of 124 skeletons has not been significantly reduced from the original burial population. Some 63 articulated skeletons had additional bone with them, and vertical and horizontal truncation had clearly taken place. This pertains to graves near the edge of the cemetery, such as grave 1167, which had been cut by 1161 (Fig. 8.3) but also, particularly, those in the central area.

Internal elements

Archaeological features within the cemetery may be divided into three distinct elements: the boundaries, the holloway, the Roman road and ditches; the evidence for structures (post-pits); with the third element comprising the graves themselves. The remaining pre-cemetery and undated features have been discussed in Chapter 2.

Fig. 8.3   SKs1162 and 1168, graves 1161 and 1167

Boundaries and structures

The first group highlights a number of problems relating to function and containment. The majority of the ditches recorded on the site relate to earlier periods than that of the cemetery. Although there is no direct relationship between any of the graves and the elements which made up the Roman road, it is possible that its central *agger*, if it still existed in the early medieval period, may have influenced the position and alignment of some of the graves. Only the holloway (Ditch D) represents a feature which could be interpreted as both contemporary and, most probably, forming a distinct edge to the cemetery. A usable cart track would have been a necessity in some seasons for the transportation of bodies. The positioning of graves adjacent to an area of earlier Roman activity might equally reflect the use of an area which at the time had little use for other purposes (Quensel-von-Kalben 2000, 227). A limited number of graves can be seen to be situated either parallel or perpendicular to the alignment of that feature. Even here, modern disturbance had obscured relationships between the holloway and the two closest burials.

The second element comprises the post-pits. It is reasonable to consider these as indicative of structures, but any further interpretation of their function presents challenges. Documentary evidence confirms that both beheading and hanging were relatively common forms of judicial punishment. The former might leave no archaeological record beyond skeletal evidence, and the latter could have been carried out using a tree or a makeshift structure such as a cart. (The tail or the shafts of upraised carts are also known to have sometimes been used as mobile flogging-posts). As noted elsewhere, hanging is more difficult to identify osteologically than decapitation (Clough, Chapter 3). There are many later images and descriptions which suggest that the use of substantial wooden gallows was normal practice. These would have required sturdy, ground-fast uprights, probably with bracing struts. The post-pits recorded on the site were substantial features, and at least one has been shown to lie within the main sequence of grave-digging. Some evidence for both post-pipes and packing was recovered. A substantial post and pit would have been required to raise either gallows-posts or a gibbet.

The pattern made by four of the post-pits may be interpreted to suggest two pairs of gallows (see Fig. 2.13). One of the pairs, 1280 and 1276, is then tied to the life of the cemetery by reference to post-pit 1276 which is within a stratigraphic sequence of graves (Figs 2.15 and 8.9). The end of the sequence is dated by skeleton 1211 (Fig. 8.10) to a radiocarbon date of 1033–1186 cal AD (95.4%; SUERC-74077) and the start with skeleton 1240 to a radiocarbon date of 895–1017 cal AD (95.4%; SUERC-74066). The other pair, 1265 and 1171, had no physical relationship to any of the graves, but the single fill of post-pit 1171 contained one sherd of pottery dateable to the 11th to 13th centuries. From the foregoing we cannot say whether these pairs were contemporary or successive. If, however, gallows were a permanent fixture on site we could reasonably expect there to have been a number of replacements over the centuries. The juxtaposition of these two possible gallows with the heaviest concentration of graves on the site suggests a focal point, which in turn could suggest why some grave orientations can not otherwise be explained by reference to the holloway or a standard west–east alignment. This, unfortunately, is in danger of becoming a circular argument and should be treated with caution.

Reynolds (2009a, 158–9) notes a number of punishment cemeteries where two or more post-pits presumably for gallows have been recorded, with the paired posts located approximately 3m apart. These examples include Stockbridge Down and Sutton Hoo. The excavator at Stockbridge Down described two circular-plan holes, about 2ft (0.6m) in diameter and 3ft (0.9m) deep, and situated about 8ft (2.4m) apart, each with sharply cut sides and filled with very loosely packed chalk, free from flints (Hill 1936, 352). Two immediately adjacent features at Oliver's Battery were identified as possible post-pits, although both had been truncated, one by a grave and the other by a modern water trench. Feature 38 was 0.9m in diameter and included fragments of human bone within the fill, and feature 40 was at least 0.75m in length and 0.20m in width (Russel 2016, 95). At Guildown, a group of four large postholes of approximately 2ft depth was thought by Bird (2018a, 4), to represent a gallows.

It is known that some gallows were erected specifically for some hangings, whereas others were permanent structures that needed upkeep. Locally, records attest that, in 1515, Richard Skett, a farmer of the manor of Monxton, claimed expenses for 'timber and labour used to construct a pair of stocks (16d), and for making and setting up a pair of gallows (6d)' (Coldicott 1998, 24). We may assume that, *The Exeter Book* example notwithstanding, bodies would normally have been removed as soon as possible (indeed sometimes before the felon was actually dead (see Chapter 7)). The message conveyed by the very presence of a permanent gallows or gibbet, readily visible from nearby roads, would have been clear to locals and travellers alike, as the outward sign of a local lord's powers.

Possible single-post settings have been recorded at two cemetery sites (Gally Hills, Surrey and Crosshill, Notts), although they are noted as being possibly of later date than the burials there (Reynolds 2009a, 158–9). An undated lone posthole (1125) at Weyhill Road might perhaps have held a gibbet post, as gibbets were often placed on parish boundaries and on highways, and in places of high visibility. There is no physical relationship between this single, undated feature and the small group of burials in the south-east of the site, potentially of 13th-century date, which may have been positioned with reference to it. The Oxford English Dictionary suggests an early 13th-century derivation for 'gallows', from the Old French *gibet,* and suggests that gibbet was originally synonymous with gallows, but was later used to signify an upright post with a projecting arm, from which the bodies of criminals were hanged in chains or irons after execution. A late 10th-century document cited by Russel 2016 (The Fortunes of Men from *The Exeter Book*) suggests that a man's body would hang on a wide gallows, while ravens feasted on the corpse. The distinction between gallows and gibbet may be a modern one. Indeed, the so-called 'Halifax Gibbet' was in fact an early guillotine, in use up to 1650 (Midgley 1789, 393–439). Its earliest manifestation is of unknown date, but was designed to replace the uncertainties of manual decapitations in Halifax, which were undertaken on behalf of the local lord who exercised rights in the town to execute thieves, from at least 1286 onwards.

In the post-medieval period, the normal form of gibbet was a tall wooden post, often specified in the sheriffs' cravings documents to have a height of 30 feet or more - with a cross-beam at the top, from which was suspended a short chain attached to an iron cage containing the body of the criminal (Tarlow and Dyndor 2015). However, the post-execution punishment of gibbeting was never the most widely practised post-mortem punishment, and even at its peak in the mid 18th century was a comparatively rare occurrence. A review of documentary evidence from later periods (1752–1834) suggests that there were marked differences in the frequency of hanging in chains. In the counties of Sussex, Essex, Gloucestershire and Hampshire, for example, five or six gibbetings might sometimes occur within a decade, whereas in Cornwall there were none at all during the whole period, and many counties had fewer than five gibbetings over an eighty-year period (*ibid.*). Most criminals were executed at a customary place of execution, often on the edge of a town, where all executions, and often other public corporal punishments such as whipping, took place. Between 1720 and 1830, 198 people were hanged on specially-erected scaffolds at the scene of their crime (*ibid.*). It is also known that, in the medieval period, some executions similarly took place at the scene of the crime.

The purpose of a gibbet was to leave the corpse visible long after death. A gibbet would have had distinct, long and short-term effects on the surrounding area, with the spectacle, smells and macabre atmosphere associated with it. The siting was intended to maximise the impact of retributive and deterrent justice enacted on the body, but such punishment had longer-term consequences, in attaching the communal memory of social vengeance to the enduring features of the landscape (Poole 2008). It should be pointed out that there are any number of other interpretations possible which could explain the presence of a single undated post-pit. Another possibility in keeping with the idea of a visible punishment concept is that of a whipping post. See Reynolds (2009a, 22, fig. 4), for the reproduction from an 11th-century manuscript showing that form of restraint.

The Annals of the Church of Winchester (Stevenson 1856, 377) provides an example from 1259 when justiciars were present in Winchester for the tearing to pieces of Walter of Scoteneye and subsequent hanging of the body in a gibbet. Matthew Paris (Giles 1852, 139) gives an example from 1238, where a man who confessed to plotting to kill the king was torn apart by horses, beheaded, the body in three pieces was dragged around the city and finally hung in a gibbet.

The evidence for decapitation from the site, while strong, also suggests a degree of inefficiency with examples of multiple cuts to the cervical vertebrae and mandible. The dated examples were from the 10th to the 12th centuries. There were no securely dated examples from the 13th century, although one example, SK1144, a possible decapitation, was from the general area of the suspected 13th-century group to the east of the site. Some medieval marginalia show executioners using a sword single-handedly with kneeling victims, hands tied behind their backs, and again partly restrained with the executioner's spare hand in the hair. The executioners are depicted sometimes as men and sometimes as man-sized anthropomorphic animals, so a degree of artistic licence may be present.

The graves

The third element comprised the graves themselves. As previously noted, the graves exhibit a wide range of alignments (Fig. 2.7), some of which could have been influenced by the holloway, the route of the Roman road, the possible gallows and gibbet features and possibly by a late attempt at a vaguely standardised pattern of head to west or south-west. Table 8.1 compares alignments for execution cemeteries as compiled by Reynolds (2009a, 157–8) with the dataset of 1,557 burials used by Cherryson (2005, 70–3) for her study of Wessex burial practices *c.* AD 600–1100, and the data from Weyhill Road. As can be seen from the comparative percentages, the three most common orientations remain the same across the datasets. Cherryson's population is from a wide collection of sites from published examples in the Wessex area, and while it does include executions, can be considered as the expected baseline, with a pronounced head-to-west bias. Reynolds' execution cemetery dataset retains head-to-west as the most popular alignment but shows a greater degree of variation than the general population. The Weyhill Road group shows a preference for head either to south-west or to south, over head-to-west, and also contained a higher relative percentage of south-east orientations than either of the other

Table 8.1 Grave alignments: Weyhill Road compared with other datasets

	Cherryson 2005 %	Reynolds 2009a %	Weyhill Road %
W–E	81.6	25	19
SW–NE	10.7	12	30
S–N	4.8	16	28
N–S	0.8	8	2
NW–SE	1.3	7	4
SE–NW	0.3	4	10
E–W	0.4	3	2
NE–SW	0.3	2	4
Other		1	n/a
None recorded		22	

groupings. This may be a function of the length of time the cemetery was in use, in that the nearest focal boundaries or points of reference could have changed both physically and in local significance over the centuries.

It is difficult to comment on the overall form of the Weyhill Road graves as a group, as many have been obscured by the overall loss of original ground levels and by a high degree of intercutting. However, while it is evident that some graves were cut to reasonable depths, and with relatively generous dimensions, many appear to have been shallow and mean in their size. While the corpses were at least buried, this appears to have been accomplished with a minimum of effort and a general lack of respect.

Multiple burials

Fifteen of Reynolds' proposed 27 execution cemeteries included multiple burials (11 had 41 double burials). Evidence suggests that the majority of the Weyhill Road bodies were interred as single events, although the presence of double-width graves with two occupants, and the presence of normal-width graves with more than one occupant, could be indicative of multiple executions and burial. There were five examples of wide graves holding two occupants side by side and a further two normal-width graves with two occupants placed one on top of the other. The historic record attests to executions of groups of convicted felons, and the intermittent holding of courts might have made this more likely. Double burials are recorded at Stockbridge Down (Hants), Old Dairy Cottage, Winchester, Roche Court Down (Wilts), Guildown (Surrey), Staines, and Sutton Hoo (Reynolds 2009a, 270). Triple burials are reported from a number of sites (*ibid.*) and at least four individuals were present in part of one grave at Oliver's Battery, Winchester (Russel 2016, 89), two of whom had been fettered together. Some care should be taken with assumptions about multiple burials, although as a re-examination of the evidence from Walkington Wold (Yorks) using radiocarbon dating has shown, 'the so-called "triple grave" was reopened for further burial on at least one occasion' (Buckberry and Hadley 2007, 323). Crangle (2015, 114 and 139–41) suggests that by the later 12th century and onwards multiple burials where the second body is placed on top of, sometimes with a thin dividing layer of soil, the primary burial, is predominant, rather than the wide grave with side-by-side occupants. The Weyhill Road examples would appear to bear this out in that the double-stacked graves occurred within the area most likely used during the 13th century, with one, SK1209, the primary burial in grave 1152, radiocarbon-dated to the 13th century.

Treatment

The physical evidence for execution from Weyhill Road is set out above (Clough, Chapter 3). Much of it is mirrored by similar examples at other such cemeteries, and Reynolds (2009a, 266–71) has summarised the existing evidence in his hand-list of select burials from execution cemeteries.

A number of skeletons at Weyhill Road were found without their heads in the expected position, and there were a number of isolated crania, although as Buckberry and Hadley (2007, 316) point out, this does not in itself provide proof of decapitation. This would particularly be the case in a cemetery such as this, with a high degree of disturbance and truncation. A minimum of 10 (9 from graves with one from the disarticulated material) and maximum of between 23 and 25 (depending on how the evidence is interpreted), of the 124 articulated skeletons at Weyhill Road would appear to have been decapitated. At Walkington Wold, a far greater percentage (between 30.8 and 84.6) of individuals buried had been decapitated than at the comparable sites cited by Hayman and Reynolds (2005), for example, 19% at Staines and 4% at Guildown (Buckberry and Hadley 2007, 323–4). A large proportion of the individuals at Chesterton Lane Corner had evidence of cut-marks on vertebrae, mandible or skull (Cessford *et al.* 2007, 204). Decapitations were noted at Guildown (two individuals (Bird 2018b) and a third (skeleton 207) was identified (Mattison 2016, 538)); two definite and two likely decapitations from Stockbridge (Hill 1937, 253–6); five decapitations from Meon Hill (Tildesley 1933, 137–9); and approximately ten from Roche Court Down (Porter 1977, 101–2). None of the Anglo-Saxon skeletons from Old Dairy Cottage retained the skull in the normal position (Wessex Archaeology 2007, 11).

A substantive number of people in the Weyhill Road cemetery were buried with their wrists tied and/or face-down. See, for example, SK1322, who had been buried on his right side, with tied hands (Fig. 8.4). Tied hands are often regarded as circumstantial evidence of hanging (Cessford *et al.* 2007, 205). A number of other bodies had also been buried on their sides. Similar examples are found locally at Stockbridge Down and Old Dairy Cottage, and further away at, Staines and Sutton Hoo (Reynolds 2009a, 266).

The high incidence of tied corpses may relate to thievery cases, in that suspects caught in the act were often presented to the authorities with the stolen goods bound to them. Perhaps this was a symbolic gesture as well as practical, intended to prevent escape and undue struggling. Reynolds (2009a, 89) observed that in past societies, prone burial was applied 'across the spectrum of gender, age, and wealth, and it is likely that the rite had different motivations but with a common desired effect.' Arcini suggested that criminals and prisoners were amongst the most likely groups of people to be buried face-down (Gardeła 2015, 115) and that prone burial 'indicates the collective and unconscious conception as to the treatment of people who deviated

Fig. 8.4   SK1322 on his side and hands tied

from the perceived norms of society. There may of course be several underlying causes depending on the specific historical context, yet there is a clear pattern indicating that prone burials were used for those who were different' (Arcini 2009, 197). A recent study of contemporary prone burials in Poland also argues for 'a very strong possibility that some prone burials may represent suicides or criminals (especially those buried in marginal locations and with tied limbs and/or decapitated), while others could have been laid face-down to signal an act of penance' (Gardeła 2015, 117). The latter interpretation has been noted with regard to monastic churchyards (Gilchrist and Sloane 2005, 154). Tied burials have, however, been noted from other execution sites, including, for example, one from Chesterton Lane Corner (Cambridge) (Cessford *et al.* 2007, 204), and a possible 23 from the large cemetery at Guildown (Bird 2018b). Locally, examples also come from Meon Hill, Stockbridge Down and Old Dairy Cottage (Reynolds 2009a, 267). Two decapitated individuals at Roche Court Down also had tied wrists (Porter 1977, 101–2).

The female SK1379 (Fig. 8.5), who is assumed to have been decapitated as no skull was recovered, is a rarity. Only three of the 100 skeletons identifiable to sex at Weyhill Road were female. Small numbers of females have also been found in other probable punishment cemeteries, including at Bran Ditch (Fowlmere, Cambs),

Chesterton Lane Corner, Cambridge, and Sutton Hoo in the eastern counties, Staines (Middlesex), at other Hampshire cemeteries (Meon Hill, and Old Dairy Cottage), and also at Roche Court Down, Wiltshire (Reynolds 2009a, 268–9). Abjurers or outlaws were probably the most likely criminals to be beheaded rather than hanged, and there is only limited documentary evidence for females in these categories. A study of osteological evidence for decapitation, from 30 skeletal assemblages of 6th to 16th-century date in Ireland, produced 68 individuals with evidence of decapitation, and of those which could be sexed, 55 males and seven females were identified (Carty 2015, 1–2). In 1312 Gaveston, King Edward II's favourite, was beheaded. In the subsequent negotiations between the king and the barons, the barons argued that the death was legal as Gaveston had been previously designated an outlaw and enemy of the king thereby allowing him to be beheaded as a traitor (McKisack 1959, 27).

Grave goods

The small number of finds from graves in the Weyhill Road cemetery is entirely consistent with both Late Saxon punishment cemeteries (Reynolds 2009a, appendix 3.14) and with medieval cemeteries in general (Gilchrist 2012, appendix 13). When the small single nails, which may have been accidental inclusions, are removed from

Fig. 8.5   SK1379 Female, assumed to have been decapitated as no skull was recovered. Rare as there is limited documentary evidence for female abjurers or outlaws. Skull 1380 belongs to a male

consideration, the few iron objects found within graves are mainly buckles. These are as likely to have had a functional use as to have been deliberately included as 'grave goods', and may represent items of apparel or of restraint. Geake's (1997, 79) study of grave goods from an earlier period showed that, although the majority of small buckles acted as belt fasteners, the variety of positions on the body in which they have been found demonstrates that they were multipurpose, serving to fasten the straps of knife scabbards and bags etc. (cited in Stoodley 2006, 71). Gilchrist's classification of goods from 67 normative medieval burials showed buckles to be the most commonly found objects worn on the body (2012, 283). Illustrations of hangings often show people wearing only shirts or tunics (see Fig. 7.3). Their belongings and clothing would have been forfeit, and the value of the objects, if not the objects themselves, would have provided part-payment to the Crown or lord. In a punishment cemetery context, it is possible therefore, that the crude buckles may well have been used with straps, to restrain people. Although intrinsically difficult to date, small D-shaped iron buckles may be of 10th to 14th-century date (Chuter, pers. comm.). Examples of such buckles have been found at Stockbridge Down, Meon Hill, and Malling Down, Sussex (Hill 1937, 250, plate 1; Liddell 1933, 153–4; Reynolds 2009a, 119; and Chuter, *ibid.*).

Also recovered, from grave 1219, a single silver penny of Aethelred II (AD 978–1016) was dateable to AD 979–85. Aethelred II promulgated laws that included capital punishment including *I Aethelred 4.1*, proclaimed at Woodstock before 1013: 'If he has no surety, he shall be slain and buried in unconsecrated ground' (Reynolds 2009a, 257). He also paid large sums to stop Viking raids, and large numbers of such coins are found in hoards in Scandinavia (Wallis 2014, 37). Later silver pennies of Edward the Confessor (indicating a mid 11th-century date) have been found from three probable punishment cemeteries. At Meon Hill, a single coin was found just beyond the extended fingers of a skeleton (Liddell 1933, 154), and the six from Stockbridge Down were found 'tucked in the armpit' of a skeleton (Hill 1937, 249). At Guildown, a single coin of Edward the Confessor 'of about the year AD1043, was found buried with three skeletons that were over, and partly displacing, an earlier triple burial which had itself completely broken up and displaced a 6th-century burial' (Lowther 1931, 2).

The two worked bone objects recovered from Weyhill Road graves are believed to be handles, possibly from knives, and may similarly have been hidden in the clothes of the corpse, or deliberately deposited at burial. One was situated near the left arm of SK1396, and the other from grave 1120 (SK1122). In neither case was an iron blade preserved. Worked bone objects are occasionally found in medieval graves (Gilchrist 2012, 283), but knife handles are unusual; were these perhaps

domestic or broken items, or weapons hidden in the desperate hope of escape?

Two individuals in the Weyhill Road cemetery had apparently been deliberately buried with articulated parts of sheep. SK1036, a ?male of 14–20 years old, had the remains of a two- to three-year-old ewe (ASK1042; grave 1037; Fig. 4.5) lying over his left leg. The partial skull and lower jawbone of a two- to three-year-old ewe (ASK1202) had also been placed on top of the prone body of a 45+ years male, SK1184 (grave 1183). Given the scarcity of 'grave goods' at the cemetery, and the lack of animal bone generally, it is assumed that the sheep parts were deliberate depositions.

The finding of sheep skulls in punishment cemeteries is not common, but is also not without local parallel. At Stockbridge Down, the skull of a hornless sheep was found tucked in on the left side of the face and neck of a skeleton (Hill 1937, 251). Although no other sheep bones were found at that site, the bones of a large dog (without the skull) lay between the skull and the left thigh of a different skeleton, and a few bones, possibly representing another large dog, were found among the loose bones that lay above several other skeletons. The excavator suggested that the inclusion of the dogs indicated punishment for poaching in the fairly nearby Royal Forest. He suggested that it was improbable that the men were executed under Forest Laws in either Saxon times or during the reign of William I, but that they might have been so executed in the times of William Rufus (1087–1100) or Henry I (1100–35) (*ibid.*, 257–8). At Old Dairy Cottage, four neonatal lambs had been placed across the knees of a decapitated male in Burial 565 (Reynolds 2009a, 172). A further possible animal burial was noted at Sutton Hoo, where an inhumation burial was buried immediately adjacent to a cow burial, and may have been contemporary.

There are a number of possible reasons for these inclusions. Might the person concerned have been convicted of stealing sheep? Between 1741 and 1832, sheep stealing was specified as a capital offence (although the most usual punishments were imprisonment and transportation, rather than death). At that time, sheep stealing was typically committed by men, usually working in groups of two or three, though a few, very rare cares of women executed for this crime are documented (Clifford 2018). There is, however, an old English proverb of unknown origin, 'Hanged for a sheep as a lamb, As good be.' This was first recorded in the 17th century, which shows that it was regarded as a serious crime at a much earlier date, and it seems likely that in the Saxon and medieval periods this would have been dealt with under 'theft'. Another later saying was that 'One sheep follows another'. 'So one thief, and any other evil doer, follows the ill example of his companion' (Ray 1737, 314). The possibility that animals buried with individuals are a sign of conviction for bestiality has also been previously raised (Reynolds 2009a, 172).

Social and spiritual implications

Although the people buried in this cemetery were clearly regarded as unfit for churchyard burial, the lamb or sheep features significantly in Christian iconography. The Agnus Dei, or Lamb of God, is depicted in churches, such as the Anglo-Saxon church of St Mary, Breamore, on the east bank of the River Avon, seven miles south of Salisbury, and on graves - often of children, where it signifies innocence (CMS 2018). People would have been familiar with John 1, 29, 'Behold the Lamb of God, which taketh away the sin of the world'. Could the sheep parts have been placed in these graves as a sign of guilt, or as a plea of innocence?

We have argued that the Weyhill Road cemetery resulted from judicial punishment. A possible alternative for excluding the dead from a normal cemetery might have been phenomena of superstitious practices intended to prevent the dead returning from the grave to trouble the living. As Gilchrist (2008 and 2012); Thompson (2002), and others have pointed out, religion and superstition were everyday preoccupations of the time, so their possible relevance to the burial practices recorded here cannot simply be dismissed. It should be noted that, throughout the period of use of this cemetery, there were significant changes in religious doctrine, and the emergence of beliefs such as the concept of purgatory etc. The contemporary religious connotations of, and reactions to, death during our period of interest have been summarised in two recent works. The earlier part of the period is dealt with by Thompson (2002), and was a time when the transition from pagan Saxon traditions to Christian forms was in its final stages. The concept of sudden death, or bad death, presented some problems for the religious community (*ibid.*, 35–6 and 170–7). Specific spiritual crimes had been defined which would lead to individuals being excluded from the community after death, and the Weyhill Road cemetery is a good example of this ideology in action. While it is apparent that a number of religious leaders promulgated their strongly-held beliefs regarding ideal practice, there appears to have been considerable variation in its actual implementation. For the later part of the period,

Schell (2011) considers the prevalent forms of religious observation, especially associated images and music from Books of Hours, and other documents, from 1250–1500. She has shown that the process of death and burial had become much more strictly formalised and ritualised by the Catholic Church by the end of that period. Although, as Foxhall Forbes (2013, 30) points out, 'What people believed was determined to some degree by personal choice and decision as much as it was governed by local circumstances including place-bound beliefs and practices, or affected by the views of the local religious and secular authorities'.

The wealth of secular information gleaned from preserved court records, can be combined with known religious works from the period. Contemporary translations of the Bible, homilies, decretals and other treatises on canon law, all serve to offer an insight into the beliefs driving the actions of people at this time. Limited survivals of poetry, and incidental illustrations from various sources, mainly marginalia, also help to bring the contemporary picture to life. In some instances, they describe in detail the potential train of events that could lead to desperate actions, and the finality of a grave in a judicial cemetery. It should also be noted that writers of the time, and their audience, would have considered the grave to represent more of a staging-post than a final destination.

Two examples of apparently deliberate, peculiar treatment of the dead by the inclusion of objects in the grave were noted at Weyhill Road. Various beliefs known to be contemporary with the use of the cemetery might have permitted such practices, and these have been the subject of recent study. They include a wish to subdue the 'dangerous dead', and a wish to 'heal or transform the corpse, to ensure its re-animation on judgement day, and to protect the dead on their perilous journey through purgatory' (Gilchrist 2008, 153). In one case (SK1211; Figs 8.6; 8.10), a large stone was placed close to the right side of the head, and a second, somewhat smaller stone appears from site photographs to have been on the other side of the skull. Isotopic analysis (GU-44451/GU-44464) suggests that this individual, SK1211, was not of local origin, as his strontium data were not consistent

Fig. 8.6 SK1211 Single example from the cemetery of possible use of stones

with those of the area surrounding the site, and suggest that he was an immigrant. A radiocarbon date of 1033–1186 cal AD (SUERC-74077) was obtained for this individual. In the second case, a long bone from another body had been placed across the neck of SK1193 (of 10th-century or later date), who was buried with his hands tied behind his back.

None of the objects in graves at Weyhill appear to potentially represent magical offerings or amulets, such as the waist-bags, boxes, fossils, or Roman coins occasionally found elsewhere in medieval graves (*ibid.*, 121). Gilchrist showed that natural materials, such as animal teeth or fossils, were only occasionally included in normative cemeteries (2012, 283). Animal teeth were found in a number of 13th to 15th-century graves at Whithorn, which contained both cattle teeth and white pebbles (*ibid.*, 136, 138–9). A single lower left, third cattle molar was identified from context 1244, the fill of grave 1242, SK1243 in the Weyhill Road cemetery. No particular association with the body was recorded, and it may have been an accidental inclusion, although the site is noteworthy for a lack of animal bone generally.

Blair (2009) suggested that, in the Early Saxon period, there was a fear that certain people would return after death – presumably revenants or re-animated corpses rising from their graves. Belief in revenants was widespread in medieval northern and western Europe. Revenants were usually malevolent, spreading disease and physically assaulting the living (Gordon 2014). Textual accounts of revenants in England are known, though they may represent a more ancient strand of folklore (Simpson 2003). Bartlett (2002, xxix) gives an example from Geoffrey of Burton who related a tale of two possible revenants in Drakelow, (Burton on Trent) whose bodies were exhumed with the permission of the bishop. Their heads were cut off and the bodies were replaced in the graves with their heads between their legs as part of the solution.

Beresford (2012, 7) notes a wider cultural practice, of rocks being placed on top of the body, and this may offer an explanation for the stone(s) at Weyhill Road. However, Gilchrist and Sloane note that 'head support stones' – comprising one or two blocks of stone, with one on either side of the skull, were used in a small number of medieval graves, including in a few cemeteries of religious houses. The number and types of stone used varied, and they suggest that the meaning of this rite is hard to discern (2005, 137–9). Similar finds were recorded from local punishment cemeteries. At Roche Court Down, the excavator noted that a layer of heavy flints had been placed on each corpse (Reynolds 2009a, 147). Individual 7 had been 'packed down by flints', and No. 5 had been 'blocked by flints' (Porter 1977, 101–2). At Meon Hill, a large flint boulder had been placed across the back of one skeleton (Liddell 1933, 135), and at Sutton Hoo, one had been covered with a plank (Reynolds 2009a, 172). It may be noted that, at

Chesterton Lane Corner, the single Roman individual recovered (No. 9) had had a large stone placed on the left kneecap and a smaller one over the right, which the excavators suggested had been symbolically intended to weigh the body down (Cessford *et al.* 2007, 198). In addition, two of the Middle Saxon individuals (Nos 1 and 6) were also noted as having apparently deliberately-placed material (a fragment of quernstone and two stones and a large tile, a flint cobble respectively), which might represent further indications of 'weighing down' (*ibid.*, 206, 210). No local parallels have been found for the apparently careful placing of a long bone across the neck of a corpse, although at Old Dairy Cottage, one burial lay under a heap of human bone (*ibid.*).

Citing Blair (2009, 552), Beresford (2012, 14) suggests that it is possible that prone and decapitated burials did not represent executed felons, but the 'dangerous dead' brought from elsewhere. This cemetery would have been the type of place to remove the dangerous dead to, rather than away from, but there was no evidence to suggest the transfer of partially decomposed remains from elsewhere. Nor was there evidence apparent for the deliberate removal of occupants from graves as a result, for example, of a successful trial to regain possession of a corpse to have it re-buried in consecrated ground (another practice for which there is documentary evidence). Loose bones could have been the result of that ultimate sign of disrespect to an individual, leaving the body to rot unburied. Matthew Paris (Giles 1854, 116) gives an example of the body of an executed parricide left to be disposed of by the dogs and birds of prey. The very limited signs of animal damage to the disarticulated bone from this assemblage suggest that this form of display was unlikely here.

Crangle in her study of medieval post-depositional funerary practices (2015, 107) notes that 'at many sites disturbance was avoided where feasibly possible'. She makes the point that intercutting of graves does not precisely mirror that of the disturbance of the burial, so interments within the grave could be undisturbed. She also notes differences between types of disturbances to graves between the earlier and later medieval periods (*ibid.*, 155ff). At Weyhill Road there was evidence of considerable disturbance through a combination of successive grave-digging in a limited area and on differing alignments, and post-cemetery destructive factors. However, it should be noted that in a number of cases, later graves appear to have stopped at the level of previous burials. There were also two small, irregular features, which were interpreted as possible charnel pits. The first of these (1364) contained bones from a minimum of five different adults and one child, and a second (1332) small, shallow irregular feature contained cranial remains representing four individuals. Both features were in areas of highly complex, intercut graves. It is not clear whether feature 1364 was an intentional charnel pit, or simply a hollow containing an accumulation of material from other disturbed graves. However, the fact that only cranial-material was found in 1332 suggests that this fill was a deliberate deposit. There is good documentary evidence for the rewards offered for the removal and presentation of the heads of outlaws to the authorities, and this provides a possible reason for this accumulation of severed heads and their later disposal, separately from their bodies.

Chronology

The date-range for a Weyhill Road tradition

The 20 radiocarbon dates from the Weyhill Road cemetery, although selected to cover the overall spatial and vertical spread of the burials, are not sufficiently precise to link any individuals or groups to specific historic events or known characters. As Cessford (2015), notes, burials typically represent a continuum of individual events, rather than discrete phases of activity. We can, however, suggest possible patterns here.

Simple calibrated date-ranges for the 16% sample, from the total of interred individuals, extend from the 8th to the 14th centuries cal AD (Table 2.2). Chronological modelling of the results (Healy, Tables 5.1–5.4), suggests that the earliest date, that for SK1112 (SUERC-74064), falls on a particularly flat stretch of the radiocarbon calibration curve effectively occupying the 9th century cal AD. If this date is accurate, it is the earliest dated burial. However, SK1112's calibrated age-range spans more than 200 years, so that the young man in question could have died at any time between the 8th and the mid 10th century cal AD. Even with a conservative interpretation of the radiocarbon dates we can confidently place the duration of use of the cemetery from at least the 10th to the 13th centuries. Despite the disadvantages of the radiocarbon calibration curve for this period, and the resulting widely calibrated date-ranges, the evidence for both pre and post-Conquest burials is compelling.

Currently, we can suggest that there were three main successive phases of use: the 10th century and immediate pre-Conquest period, the later 11th century and 12th century, and lastly, a culminating period of use in the 13th century. Whether these phases represent one continuous sequence within a single enduring regime, or represent a communal memory of a single place with a particular use re-utilised over generations, as required, is not known at this stage. The chronological sequence introduced in Chapter 2 is the result of combining the radiocarbon sequence with the stratigraphic and spatial groupings. Both Daniell (2002) and Craig-Atkins (2017) emphasised the lack of accurate dating for execution cemeteries, that might be 'obscuring the timescale across which 11th-century changes to "deviant" burial practices occurred'. Cherryson (2005) summaries the data for burial practices in Wessex for the

7th to the 12th centuries and highlights the problems inherent in the dating of predominantly unfurnished burials. Her addition of two new radiocarbon samples for Old Dairy Cottage demonstrated the value of these dates and the need for more (Cherryson 2005, 215, 224, 315 and 322). The 20 radiocarbon dates from articulated burials at the Weyhill cemetery add greatly to the corpus of absolute dates from execution cemeteries, and these results both confirm and challenge aspects of current thinking. As Craig-Atkins (2017) states, where radiocarbon evidence is available, 'it is clear that the floruit of execution cemeteries is firmly within the period from the 7th to the 10th centuries'. Compared with other dated cemeteries, the Weyhill cemetery seems to have continued in use to an exceptionally late date.

The date-range of the cemetery was a time of considerable significance for the evolution of the English state. The cemetery continued to serve a local need, while the relative spheres of influence of various royal houses, groups of nobles and competing religious bodies evolved. The feudal system itself culminated, and adapted to pressures of commercial development. The physical continuation of the cemetery mirrors the continuing local coherence demonstrated by the survival and growth of the grass-roots organisations implied in the development of hundreds, tithings, parishes, hamlets and, of course, the town of Andover itself. Andover and its hinterland both show evidence of continuity of the major landowners and tenants, and of the developing power of the borough as a commercial base which was partially independent of old feudal interests.

A historical-geographical discussion
by Andrew Reynolds

Besides its remarkable range of internal features and topographical setting, the Weyhill Road cemetery inspires a wider consideration of its socio-political and historical-geographical setting. The first issue worthy of comment is the marked longevity of the cemetery. While the national pattern indicates a broad date-range for such sites between the late 7th and 8th centuries and the 12th century (Reynolds 2009a, 154–5; Healy, this volume, Chapter 5), the Weyhill Road sequence is the only site where a suite of C14 determinations of sufficient number, tempered by the capacity for Bayesian statistical analysis facilitated by intercutting graves, demonstrates in the context of a single site a long, and indeed longer, chronology than that revealed to date for any other comparable cemetery. A possible start date during the 8th century is commensurate with that from several other sites (Reynolds 2009c), while the latest dates indicate that burials continued to be made at the site into the 13th to early 14th century AD (Healy, Chapter 5). Given the difficulties of calibrating C14 dates during the medieval period, however, it remains possible that the entire Weyhill Road sequence might be bracketed between the 9th and 12th centuries if the late burials are seen as a separate group interred at the site after an interval.

The key point of interest for the present discussion is that the date-range encompasses a raft of fundamental step-changes in the nature of social organisation across a period of time that bore witness to: 1) the formation of the Anglo-Saxon kingdom of Wessex between the 6th and 8th centuries out of a series of smaller 'tribal/familial' territories – the variously called *regiones*, notably referred to by Bede, and more lately as 'small shires' following the analysis of local territorial arrangements in this region by Bruce Eagles (Eagles 2015); 2) the emergence of a unified kingdom of England during the 10th century and the regularisation of local government that ensued; and 3) the emergence of an increasingly urbanised and organised society in the 12th and 13th centuries. The Weyhill Road evidence, therefore, can be assessed against developments in the spatial organisation of power that occurred between the 8th and 13th centuries as a reflection of large-scale processes in local microcosm.

The spatial organisation of power

The first task is to assemble the evidence for the various elements that formed focal points for social organisation across the Anglo-Saxon period, although restrictions of time and space preclude a comprehensive analysis. The Anglo-Saxon judicial system in particular, involved several elements (confinement at royal estate centres, judgement at assembly sites, ordeal at minster churches and punishment, which, if capital, took place at execution sites), while the 12th and 13th centuries witnessed increasing centralisation of judicial affairs in relation to the marked urban expansion that occurred during this period in tandem with modifications to the way that judicial matters were conducted (see Chapter 7). Although this contribution focuses mainly on the Anglo-Saxon material, it is likely on the basis of wider landscape studies that the framing of the landscape in terms of the basic settlement pattern as it persisted into the later Middle Ages and after was largely in place by the time of the Domesday Survey of 1086. The formation of local estates that became fossilised as ecclesiastical parishes by the 12th century, however, was a process that probably began in the 9th and 10th centuries and was ongoing across the period of the Norman Conquest into at least the 12th century.

The principal elements that formed social systems during the Anglo-Saxon period varied in their details and nature across time, but in general they can be characterised as: 1) settlement-related; 2) burial-related; 3) cultic/religious; 4) economic; 5) conciliatory. The evidential base for these features includes archaeological remains, written evidence and place-names, while in many instances several functions might be found at either the same spot or close together.

In the pre-Christian period (5th to 7th centuries), Categories 1 and 2 find strong archaeological correlates in the Weyhill area. Evidence for settlement is known, for example, at Old Down Farm (6th century), Charlton (?later 5th to 7th century) and Foxcotte (which appears to run into the middle Anglo-Saxon period) (Davies 1980; Dacre and Warmington 1977; Russel 1985).

From about AD 600, the archaeological record of lowland Britain reveals the first evidence for elite settlement and an allied polarisation of wealth in society at large. At least on the basis of grave goods, this aspect is evident between the two Portway cemeteries noted below (Stoodley 2006, 76). Indeed, one of the key type-sites for elite settlement in southern England is that at Cowdery's Down, near Basingstoke, just over 30km due west of Weyhill (Millett with James 1983). It provides a snapshot of the style of accommodation of local elites during the period of the formation of (in varying degrees) autonomous local communities occupying valley-based territories in the long wake of the breakdown of the pattern of settlement and authority of the Late Roman period. We should expect similar residences to that found at Cowdery's Down in the Weyhill area, perhaps at Andover itself where 6th/7th-century pottery has been recovered (Campling 1989), while the known sites at Charlton, Old Down Farm and Foxcotte likely represent the kind of small-scale farms that became increasingly dependent on elite settlements as the 7th and 8th centuries progressed. These sites perhaps demonstrate a relatively early 'fixity' of the local settlement pattern, which persisted into the Middle Ages and after.

Burial sites (Category 2) are known at Portway East (5th to 6th century AD) and West (early 7th to mid 8th century AD) (Cook and Dacre 1985; Stoodley 2006) (Fig. 8.2). A further cemetery (Fig. 8.7), a group of at least six burials with heads to the west, was recovered under rescue conditions in the 1980s *c.* 1km ENE of the Weyhill Road site (Scott 1988). These burials appear not to have been associated with any kind of church or chapel and are undated apart from an iron knife found in Grave 3, a feature common to Christian field cemeteries of the 7th to 9th centuries in England (Blair 1994, 69–73) prior to the foundation of parish churches (see below).

During the course of the later 7th and 8th centuries and the conversion to Christianity the landscape came to feature so-called minster churches, often with large royal endowments, with associated cemeteries (Blair 2005). It seems that the church at Andover was one of these minster churches (Hase 1994, 54, 58 and 63–5) and thus we can add a further Category 2 and 3 site to the Weyhill area. With the establishment of parish churches across the landscape of most of England by the 12th century, the locations of cemeteries became fixed and persistent in the long durée.

Category 3 sites have proved largely, but not entirely, elusive in the archaeological record for the pre-Christian

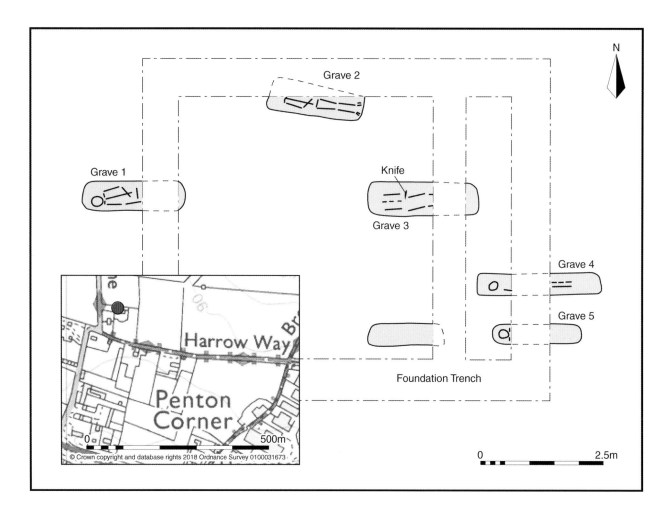

Fig. 8.7   Harroway Farm cemetery plan

period more widely (see for example Blair 1995), with place-names providing the best source of evidence, particularly in the form of *wēoh* and *hearg* place-names (Semple 2007; 2013), of which Weyhill belongs to the former group and the Harroway potentially to the second, the name of the latter perhaps a reflection of the fact that the route passes Stonehenge (Reynolds and Langlands 2011) and also potentially Weyhill. The word *wēoh* means 'holy place, idol, altar', arguably but not exclusively of the pre-Christian period (Semple 2013; Eagles 2015, 131), but perhaps likely to be, given that the known examples have nothing explicitly Christian about them. Names of this type crop up in a clutch of the very earliest English land charters, for example in Middlesex (AD 767) (Sawyer 1968, cat. no. 106), Surrey (AD 685–7) (*ibid.*, cat. no. 235) and also, possibly, in Hampshire (AD 685–7), where *Besingahearh* 'the sanctuary of the Besingas (possibly "the people of Basing")' features in a charter (*ibid.*, cat. no. 235), although an identification with Basing is apparently not watertight (Eagles 2015, 146, no. 114).

If the church at Andover was indeed an early minster, then its foundation is likely to have seen the end of the use of the suggested pre-Christian shrine at Weyhill. It is possible, therefore, that it was during this episode of religious change that the Weyhill locale became imbued with negative connotations and became used for the burial of execution victims and other social outcasts as the geography of burial and religion in the area changed across the conversion period. The earliest dates for the Weyhill cemetery and the latest dates for the Portway West cemetery are entirely consistent with such a process. Other cult sites of the Christian period more generally included wells and roadside shrines, but these lay beyond our consideration here.

The economic basis (Category 4) for the social group who inhabited the Andover area need not concern us here beyond noting two aspects: 1) the general tendency in the region towards valley-based territories, whether at the scale of the region, hundred or local estate, whereby territorial entities exploited the full potential offered by downland and vale-type landscapes (Bonney 1976; Williamson 2013); and 2) the existence of the Weyhill Fair, a major socio-economic event further commented upon below.

The origin of Anglo-Saxon assembly sites (Category

5) is a difficult question to address, but several models can be proposed. In some cases, they appear to have begun life in the context of communal burial sites where communities would have come together on a frequent basis (Williams 2002; Reynolds 2018) - in our area potentially the Portway East or West cemeteries as noted above. In others they may have begun in the context of cult sites, given that a number of English hundreds can be shown to be named after figures or phenomena with pre-Christian cultic significance (Meaney 1995; Baker 2019).

It is well known that assembly sites often featured mounds, as did many early Anglo-Saxon cemeteries, utilising either pre-existing Bronze Age mounds (as at Portway East and Portway West) or with newly built ones (as at Portway West). We do not know whether either of the Portway cemeteries served such a function, but it is a possibility between the 5th and 8th centuries as such sites represented key nodes where communities would have come together on an all-too-frequent basis. It is also a matter of interest that the later of the two Portway cemeteries also comes to an end in the 8th century and it is perhaps during this time that any assembly-related functions performed there were trans-located to Weyhill at a spot adjacent to the execution cemetery. Later evidence reveals assembly sites for both the Domesday 'out' hundred (i.e. beyond the jurisdiction of the borough of Andover) at Hundred Acre Corner at the site of the Weyhill cemetery as well as at (presumably) Andover for the inhabitants of the Domesday borough, but also for gatherings of the very highest status as evidenced by the place of promulgation there of a law code of King Edgar (r. 959–75), and two meetings there in the reign of King Aethelred (r. 978–1016), with his witan in 980 and for the drawing up of a peace treaty with the Vikings in 994 (Clutterbuck 1898, 123–4; Lavelle 2005, 158–9). Ryan Lavelle has written on the location of the law-promulgating assembly at Grateley, 8km west of Andover but within the hundred, where King Athelstan gathered with his witan (AD 925x30), emphasising the importance of Andover as a key locale in the late Anglo-Saxon period and one evidently with sufficient resources to support the king, his personal retinue and other leading figures for the duration of such a major event (Lavelle 2005). Caution must be exercised in terms of assuming a direct correlation between an assembly site and a place-name, but there seems little doubt that Hundred Acre Corner at Weyhill was indeed the meeting place for the 'out hundred', while Andover and district hosted a raft of gatherings of the greatest political import.

The coincidence of an assembly place with one of outcast burial is most unusual, but not unknown. Possible execution burials at a documented Anglo-Saxon assembly site have been excavated at Wandlebury, near Cambridge. The Wandlebury site is an Iron Age hillfort where excavations on several occasions have revealed

several unusual, but undated, burials. The disposition of the remains invites parallels with Anglo-Saxon deviant burials, while the location itself is referred to in late 10th and mid 11th-century sources as the site of judicial gatherings as 'the assembly of the nine shires' in the latter source; in other words a site of major social, political and legal gatherings (Hart 1966, 42; Harmer 1952, 349, no. 79; Reynolds 2009a, 111–13). The site lay on the boundaries of three hundreds and adjacent to a Roman road. The celebrated Weyhill Fair which existed by the Middle Ages, is also worthy of comment here (Page 1911j). Although the origin of this event remains unknown, it is possible that its beginnings lay in the pre-Conquest period and that its location was inspired by a combination of excellent communications by road and a strong sense both locally and regionally of Weyhill as a long-lived meeting place. While the fair occupied a large area and its focus appears to change over time, the locale in general clearly attracted large numbers of people during the Middle Ages and before. A possible parallel is Wiltshire's Tan Hill Fair, an event first mentioned in 1499 (Letters 2005b; Crowley 1975, 29), but which existed before that date. Significantly, the earliest reference to the Tan Hill Fair notes that it met at the *Ceorlbeorgh*, a toponym of Old English origin meaning 'hill or barrow of the peasants' and a name perfectly suited to an early medieval assembly site (Pollard and Reynolds 2002, 254).

Territoriality

A second line of enquiry is that of local territorial formation and the extent of changes that took place over time to the limits of land units, especially in view of the relationship of the Weyhill site to local boundaries. Local administrative districts that developed out of the formative *regiones* and small shires noted above – hundreds and estates – are generally seen as products of the hand of elites bringing formal modes of social organisation to local districts. Although this latter notion is much debated, archaeological evidence for unusual burials and their role in the dating of territorial boundaries is of a high quality in Hampshire more widely. This body of material has a significant bearing on the matter of how the Weyhill cemetery fits into a broader hierarchical pattern of such sites and the emergence of fixed territorial entities at different scales (Reynolds 2009a, chapter 5).

We are fortunate that the region surrounding Weyhill – north-eastern Hampshire, west central Wiltshire and western Berkshire – has received detailed consideration with regard to its territorial history (Reynolds 2005; Eagles 2015). Place-names and Anglo-Saxon written sources facilitate an otherwise unusual depth of analysis, although the question of territorial origins, chronology and socio-political setting nevertheless leave many issues open-ended, foremost among these being the earliest phases of these units and the background from which they emanated, be they Romano-British in essence, tribal/familial in origin in the setting of post-Roman reconfigurations of power, or impositions foisted upon local people by emerging elites controlling increasingly large regions in the setting of kingdom formation in later 6th, 7th and 8th-century England. All of these trajectories are possible and, if anything, the picture revealed by combining archaeological, historical and place-name evidence suggests combinations of these situations, even within local micro-regions. While there is a tendency for territorial boundaries to cut across Romano-British sites in certain cases in this region (Reynolds 2005), thus indicating a fundamental re-configuration of territorial patterns, it may well be the case that the basic pattern of valley-based settlement noted above reflects the manner in which the Romano-British countryside was organised. Indeed, the name Andover appears to be derived from an earlier name for the River Anton, Ann, 'a derivative of the British *dubro-* "water, river" ' (Ekwall 1970, 10). Such a name highlights the river-valley focus of the land unit, while the pre-English element of the name indicates linguistic – and perhaps territorial - interchange between pre-English (Brittonic) and Germanic speakers in the area.

Drawing on the widest possible body of evidence, Bruce Eagles' work on Anglo-Saxon territorial formations in the Andover region proposes social groupings occupying valley-based areas of an extent in most cases larger than those of the late Anglo-Saxon/Domesday hundreds. The principal complication here is again the relative complexity of the formation of individual local units. In some cases Domesday hundreds might equate to early 'tribal/familial' holdings – the case of Kinwardstone Hundred (assessed at a huge 196½ hides) just over the county border in Wiltshire might be just such an instance (Reynolds 2005) – but in other cases the earlier territories appear larger than the Domesday hundreds as Eagles proposes for Andover (Eagles 2015, 139–40, fig. 1). The first reference to Andover is found in the will of King Eadred (AD 951x55) (Sawyer 1968, cat. no. 1515) drawn up at some point between 951 and 955. The document refers to the *Andeferas*, 'the Andovers', a territory that on various grounds (detached parts of hundreds within other hundreds and adjacent counties, namely Wiltshire) Eagles suggests originally comprised a 'small shire' including the hundred of Welford to the west and parts of Broughton to the west and south.

Land units that emerged as 'tribal/familial' territories in the 7th and 8th centuries – and possibly earlier during the 6th century – in this region steadily fragmented, particularly from the 10th century onwards (Eagles 2015, 138), as a function of kings granting lands to local lords, a process that set in chain the pattern of churches, manors and villages that went on to become widespread across the lowland English landscape.

Comparing the list of Domesday vills in the hundred of Andover with the number of parishes by the 19th century shows that the process of local territorial fragmentation was ongoing across the 11th century, the Norman Conquest and the production of the Domesday Survey, but the number of 19th-century parishes largely corresponds to those of the 12th and 13th centuries and thus the settlement pattern established during this period was one that largely persisted until the present. The growth of Andover itself into a prosperous medieval town is demonstrated by written sources that reveal its relative prosperity in relation to other towns in the district (as discussed in Chapter 1).

Interestingly, the boundary upon which the Weyhill cemetery lay (that between the Domesday borough of Andover and Foxcotte), takes a marked deviation to the east from an otherwise more-or-less straight NNE–SSW course – presumably to take in the site of the 'out hundred' assembly place and the execution cemetery (Figs 1.4 and 1.5). If the location of Hundred Acre Corner can be accepted as precisely locating the assembly place, that then situates the meeting place and execution site immediately adjacent to each other but on either side of the boundary line.

Wider study of execution cemeteries in Hampshire (known by excavated remains or from references in charter boundary clauses) places all known sites on boundaries, a view confirmed by recent research and further archaeological discoveries as at Oakridge (Basingstoke), Oliver's Battery, Winchester and Weyhill (Reynolds 2013, 708, fig. 5; Cole *et al.* forthcoming; Russel 2016). The same location characteristic can be observed with regard to assembly sites (Pantos 2003) and thus the relationship of the Weyhill cemetery and the 'out hundred' assembly site are likely to have been at least partly motivated by a pre-existing boundary, but perhaps one that was modified in its course to provide a degree of spatial distinction between the 'clean' space for public assembly and the 'unclean' space for deviant burial.

Discussion

It is abundantly clear that the locale of the Weyhill cemetery remained as a fixed place for the burial of execution victims and other social outcasts across a period punctuated by social and political change from the local to the 'state' level. This aspect allows for a developed understanding of the pace and rhythm of change against degrees of persistence in the medieval landscape.

On the basis of the brief survey of the local evidence presented above, it is possible to suggest three main phases of organisational and territorial development in the area around the Weyhill site, with the place of execution and burial proving to be one of the few constants across this period of otherwise marked social, political and economic change.

Period 1 (5th to 8th centuries): a local tribal/familial territory on the scale of that proposed by Eagles existed with neighbouring districts of a similar order of magnitude. Local communities – such as those living at Old Down Farm – exploited valley-based land units, utilised community cemeteries such as those at Portway East and West, and punctuated their territory with other locales of cultural significance such as the shrine that ultimately lent its name to Weyhill, the place and local district. Weyhill may also have been an assembly place at this period on the basis of place-name and archaeological studies elsewhere (Meaney 1995; Reynolds 2018).

Unusual/deviant burials were made at community cemeteries during this period, often at the margins of such sites, as revealed at Portway West where a possible prone burial (Grave 17) and two possible decapitation burials in the same grave (Grave 3) led Stoodley to perceptively predict an execution cemetery close by (Stoodley 2006, 65, fig. 2; 78).

Period 2 (8th to 10th centuries): the period during which the kingdom of Wessex took shape as a large-scale political entity reduced the status of former tribal/familial territories to that of constituent parts of a larger whole. It is likely that many of these territories remained in the hands of various branches of what became the West Saxon royal house and their retainers or as possessions of major churches. The emergence of elite residences was followed within a generation or two by the foundation of major churches, possibly including the likely minster at Andover. In some cases it appears that minster parishes (*parochiae*) fossilised the extents of tribal/familial territories, but grants of land to monasteries by kings were often smaller and it may be that fragmentation on this scale led to the creation of land units of the scale later explicitly known as hundreds. It is in this context, it seems, that the Weyhill cemetery came into being; at some time during the formation of the early West Saxon kingdom, as opposed to a place of execution and burial in the setting of a local autonomous polity even though justice itself was almost certainly meted out a local level and by local officials. In this sense it can be argued to be a classic case of formalised and imposed judicial practice in the context of and as a function of the increasing geographical extent of a political territory (Reynolds 2013).

It is of particular interest that the cemetery lay not on a kingdom boundary – as do the other four execution cemeteries with 8th-century origins (Reynolds 2009c) – nor on the ('out hundred') boundary of what later became the hundred of Andover. Instead, the cemetery lay in the centre of its district, but nevertheless on an internal boundary which by at the least the 11th century was that of the 'in hundred' of the Domesday borough of Andover. It might be argued in the case of the Weyhill cemetery, however, that the draw of the site here was in part the former cultic association of the locale, and

perhaps also its function as an assembly site by this time, the latter being unproven but likely. A further pull with regard to the location of the cemetery must have been the pattern of roads in the locality, although it is interesting to note that the cemetery lay within the curtilage of the Roman road between *Calleva* (Silchester) and *Sorviodunum* (Old Sarum) (Figure 1.7) indicating that the Roman road was not maintained to the NE of the cemetery but that it was to the SW. A holloway appears to have developed to form the NE limit to the cemetery and broadly reflects the line of Weyhill Road and, further north, the line of the Harroway.

Period 3 (10th to 13th centuries): this period saw the development of the pattern of villages and towns that persisted throughout the Middle Ages and beyond. Court meetings will have persisted at Weyhill beyond the Norman Conquest, but very likely became relocated into Andover itself as that centre grew in importance in line with a general tendency for administrative functions to coalesce during the 12th and 13th centuries. It appears that, despite broader changes to the spatial organisation of judicial power that took place at this time, Weyhill continued as the locally recognised locale at which to bury social outcasts, although whether they were formally sanctioned executions or persons who had otherwise contravened social norms is unknowable – a combination of the two motivations is possible.

People

The question then remains, who were these people? In terms of the prevailing religious mores of the time, burial in unconsecrated ground at a distance from the settlements represented the lowest form of three main divisions of burial-type available. The most acceptable to both man and God, and by the end of the period concerned overwhelmingly the expected version, was that of burial with full Christian rites, within a delimited and consecrated church burial ground. The second, for the burial of the spiritually dubious, was a simple, restricted rite, located as close to the edge of the approved burial area and the rest of the parish population as possible. The third saw the disposal of the social and spiritual outcast, and as mentioned there were a number of reasons for representatives of the Church to be unwilling to bury an individual in consecrated ground.

In the secular world, as we have seen in Chapter 7, there were a number of routes by which any individual who found themselves at odds with their peers or masters could face legally-sanctioned death. Such routes varied, and were refined during our period of interest, but they can be roughly divided into three strands. The route probably preferred by the Crown could be the most complex. The accused, having been identified, restrained and passed through the lesser courts, would then await the coming of the higher court. That court would then pronounce the king's justice, and execution would take place. For our purposes, two aspects make this a less likely route for our site. The legal procedure might occur at irregular and long intervals, and crucially ought to have taken place in the regional seat, Winchester. While some criminals in later periods were sentenced to be executed at the place at which the crime took place, or to have their corpses exposed locally, this does not seem to be the most likely explanation for their eventual burial outside Andover.

Two other, more local mechanisms were also available. Some landowners, both secular and religious, held the power to execute criminals within their own land-holdings. These trials would not have resulted in the death penalty in great numbers, but could have resulted in a steadier stream of executed dead requiring disposal at a local level. The third strand is the death of outlaws or abjurers 'in hot blood'. The death of abjurers who had not followed the prescribed road for leaving the realm, i.e. people who had previously been declared outlaws and criminals caught in the act, could occur at the hands of the local tithings, and be legally accepted. Any resulting requirements for burials would also require prompt local resolution. These two potentially locally-occurring processes are likely mechanisms by which the need for, and organisation of, this cemetery was maintained over a period of around 400 years. The status of Andover as a royal estate, with the possibility of the presence of a king's bailiff acting in place of the lord of the manor, supports this theory.

The next question relates to who was most likely to run foul of the law, and why. Given's 1977 study, based on homicide rates derived from 12th-century examples in eyre rolls, suggests that, in a rural area, where the ties of the immediate group, parish, village or tithe were strong, and the lord's court was well-run and approachable, the homicide level was relatively low. Nonetheless, examples of homicide between relatives and of individuals from the same and different villages did occur. Homicide is only the most obvious of the crimes to which a death

penalty could be attached. The most numerous category was that of thieves, taken locally and most likely of local origin, thereby allowing rights of *infangentheof* to apply. It is interesting that the numbers for decapitations for thievery in Halifax, although for a later period (1542–1650) give a rate of about one every two years (Midgley 1789). These are not altogether dissimilar to the rates possible for Weyhill Road.

While local records provide no known and named executed criminals from Andover within this study period, there is one Andover man whose name is preserved in court documents. William of Andover, who had been arrested and detained as a prisoner at Havering, confessed to the coroner of Essex that he was a thief, a burglar of houses and a murderer. He appealed (see glossary) a number of others, who he accused of being in a band who robbed and killed a merchant, stealing £20-worth of goods. He also claimed that the same group killed five unknown merchants at Woolmer, in 1288–9 (Gross 1896, 129). From the example of William, it seems that, in common with the upper classes of king, councillors, lords, bishops and judges who maintained a peripatetic lifestyle, visiting their various estates, some of the criminal class likewise travelled the countryside in search of profit.

We can also glean information from the human remains themselves. For example, Fig. 8.8 shows a complex group of 11th to 12th-century burials. It includes three, relatively young men, the grave of only one of whom, SK1397 (grave 1341) is visible on plan (Fig. 2.19). Isotopic analysis suggests that this man was local, and a radiocarbon date (SUERC-74075) of 1020–1155 cal AD was obtained. He had at some point suffered a probable trauma to his left hand, and some of his bones had been gnawed by rodents after his death. The second is one of the few individuals with skeletal evidence of hanging (SK1391, grave 1390) who was buried prone and with his hands tied. The third, SK1396, was 15–20 at the time of his death, and a knife handle was found in his grave (1341).

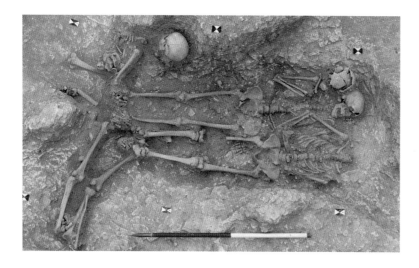

Fig. 8.8 SK1397 (grave 1341; bones gnawed, probable trauma of left hand), SK1391 (grave 1390; one of the few 3 individuals with bone evidence for hanging, prone and hands tied) and SK1396 (grave 1341)

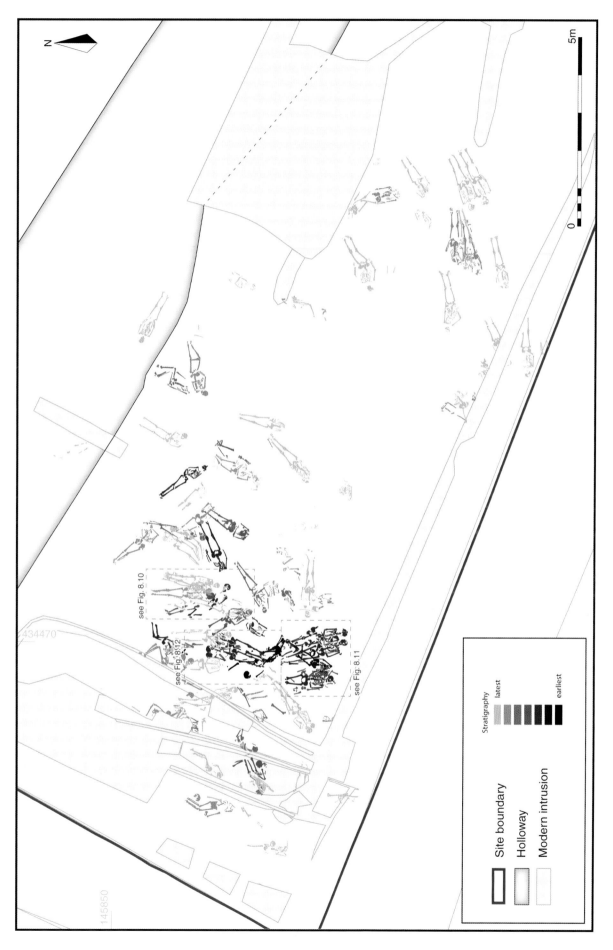

Fig. 8.9 Overall cemetery plan key to close-ups of dense area of 11th to 12th-century burials

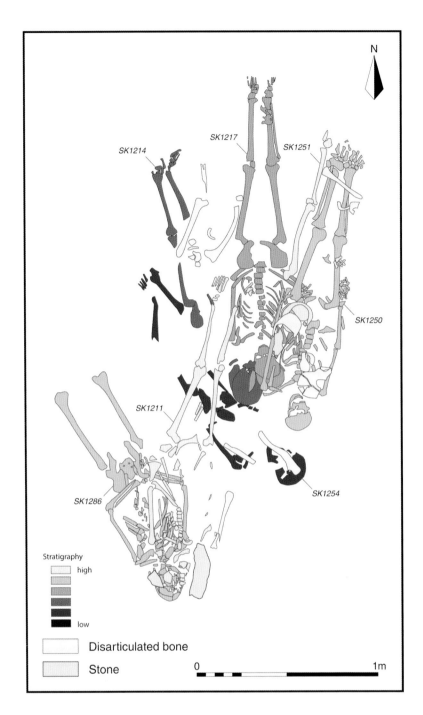

Stratigraphy

high

low

Disarticulated bone

Stone

0   1m

Fig. 8.10 SKs1211, 1214, 1217, 1250, 1251, 1254, 1286, and disarticulated material

Another man, SK1362 (18–25 years old), had suffered from an extensive bone infection, and would have been physically disabled (Figs 1.6, 3.9). He had been decapitated (perimortem cut-marks were evident on the cervical vertebrae), and placed in the grave on the right side, bent over, with the skull placed on the chest area. One pair of burials (Fig. 2.9) had similar skeletal traits, suggesting familial relatedness (SKs1056 and SK1057). The two young men, in their late teens to early 20s, both had spinal congenital disorders and SK1057 may have looked 'different' to others, although he would not have been disabled. Another pair (SKs1174 and 1175, Fig. 8.11) were both buried with their hands behind their backs, one facing upwards, with another face-down,

probably in the 11th to 12th century (SUERC-74082, 985–1152 cal AD), and at least one of them was a local man (GU-44453/GU-44465). The group of 11th to 12th-century burials shown in Fig. 8.12 shows the complexity of stratigraphy in the main area of the cemetery, with a number of intercutting burials, two of which were radiocarbon-dated to the 11th–12th centuries (SK1292 SUERC-74081, 1036–1205 cal AD and SK1397 SUERC-74075, 1020–1155 cal AD). Again, these were all male, and isotopes, where tested, again suggested that they were local.

Whilst the isotope evidence from the site demonstrates that not all of the members of the cemetery population were local to Andover, it is suggested here that it is

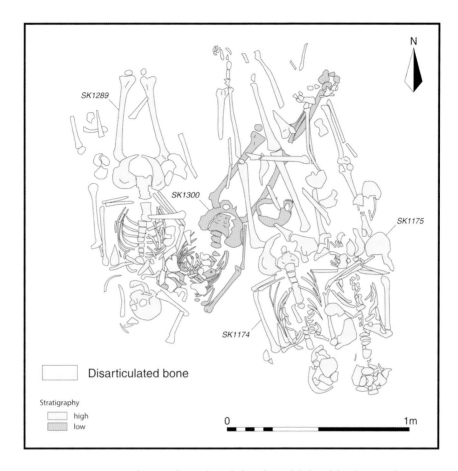

Fig. 8.11 SKs 1174 and 1175 buried with hands tied behind backs, one face-up, one face-down (and SKs 1289 and 1300 plus disarticulated material), 11th to 12th century

likely that the numbers represented by the cemetery population can be explained by the likely rate of executions inflicted on felons in the local area, without recourse to additional large-scale external groups, such as might be the case during periods of civil war or economic hardship. If such was the case, then the victims of criminal acts, the criminals themselves and the responsible tithings and/or juries would nearly all have come from the local area. Most of the actions, motivations and past histories between the main actors in these local dramas would have been known to the community, either at first hand or through word of mouth. In the case of raised hue and cry, or organised searches for local malefactors, any resultant 'death while escaping' would most probably have been the end result of such a communal effort. Even in cases convicted in a court, a death penalty was likely to have been the result of a previously-agreed decision by the juries, on both the guilt of the individual and the willingness of the community to sanction, or even connive at, a judicial death. Many of these burials would, with some likelihood, have been the end result of a purely local affair, which took place amongst the families resident in the Andover area.

In a mainly agricultural, and at times very physical, society, the readily available sharp-edged tools for personal and professional use provided ready weapons, which in combination with the stresses of a seasonally-vulnerable lifestyle, would naturally lead to occasional accidents (as reported in coroner's rolls), and violence both within, and between, small communities. These stresses were, in the main, controlled and suppressed by the presence of a strongly-regulated and continuously monitored sense of collective responsibility maintained by the local lord or lord's representative. This was strengthened by the widely-understood teachings of the Church on matters of individual responsibility and generally-accepted Christian values, reinforced by the threat and promise of hell or paradise for all. There can be no doubt that there was both the local will and the ability to execute anyone judged by the community to be sufficiently dangerous to that same community. The Statute of Winchester of 1285 (13 Edward I, c.1–6), in its first section, put forward the case that robbery, murder and arson were becoming more commonplace, and that the guilty were going unpunished. Section six then laid down the obligation of every man between the ages of 15 and 60 to bear arms, ready to keep the peace, including those who have no land and less than 20 marks in goods, who were still expected to possess swords, knives and other small arms.

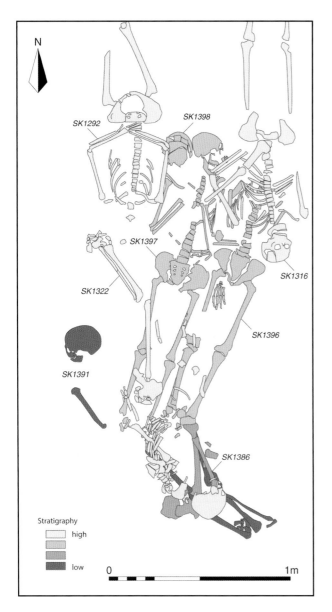

Fig. 8.12 The complex stratigraphy of 11th to 12th-century burials SKs1292, 1316, 1322, 1386, 1391, 1396, 1397 and 1398

It is probable that some local families held land with duties attached, which required them to organise all aspects of a well-run and successful execution, up to and including the maintenance of gallows, and grave-digging. There were, however, other groups during the medieval period who maintained a vested interest in the care and maintenance of cemeteries for those executed by law. We do know of at least one religious institution in Andover, the hospital of St John the Baptist (see Chapter 1), present from 1247 to 1536, whose members prayed for the souls of those buried in 'the un-consecrated ground' described as 'adjacent' (Bennett 1931). Is it possible that these brothers and sisters of the hospital might have been responsible for the later group of more orderly burials of 13th-century date at

the Weyhill cemetery? This author is unsure whether this was entirely unrelated to the Order of St John, the Knights Hospitallers, which had an interest in collecting the bodies of the executed for burial, and some of whom possessed dedicated burying grounds. The Hospitallers were one of several new religious orders who arrived in Hampshire during the 12th century (Beard 2005, 178). They had John the Baptist as patron (Cockburn *et al.* 1969), and appear to have been first introduced to England in the reign of Henry I, circa 1100 (Wadmore 1897, 232). 'Their seal ... shows St. John the Baptist standing under a canopy, pointing with his right hand to the Paschal Lamb supported on his left arm' (Cockburn *et al.* 1969). Hospitaller foundations were commonly called St John or St Mary (Gomersall and Whinney 2007, 85). By the late 12th century, 'all preceptories of the Order could have had graveyards, in which, in return for material benefits conferred upon the order, people of various sorts could find burial' (Pugh 1981, 571). For example, in 1299, Hospitallers took the corpses of two hanged men to St Margaret's Church (probably St Margaret in Combusto), Norwich. Skeletons from this graveyard included people who had been buried with their wrists tied behind their back, buried face-down or in the 'wrong' orientation (Gilchrist and Sloane 2005, 73–40). By the 15th century, the Hospitallers buried not only those who were, in some form, members of their order, but many others also (Pugh 1981, 572). It is known that there were Hospitallers operating relatively locally, as the Winchester hospital of St Cross was placed under the custodianship of the Knights Hospitaller between 1151 and 1204, before being returned to the rule of the bishops (Gomersall and Whinney 2007, 85). Beard (2005, fig. 1) suggests that, amongst their Hampshire estates, the Hospitallers held land at Andover, Nether Wallop, Over Wallop, Amport and Thruxton, although 'most of their donors were obscure figures, who gave only small amounts of land, and ... their holdings placed them well down the list of Hampshire foundations' (*ibid.*, 184). In the late 13th century, John de Evinely held land of the Knights of St John of Jerusalem within the hundred of Andover, but the precise location of this is not known (Page 1911i, 333).

Hadley concludes that those males who had met a violent end could be buried in distinctive locations (2010, 112), and also gives examples of evidence of people with apparently fatal wounds who were found in otherwise normal burial grounds. A variety of responses might be available, which were perhaps dictated by the specific circumstances of the death, and the subsequent reactions of both the authorities and local communities. There is evidence, therefore, that general population cemeteries could be inclusive, and perhaps that the Weyhill Road cemetery represented a complementary component. The existence of this cemetery may well suggest that variant burials in otherwise normative cemeteries in the core Wessex area might simply represent the various communities' reactions to untimely deaths, be it death by violence, accident or the sudden illness of otherwise blameless individuals. By contrast, other classes of people deemed by the church to be undeserving of God's mercy would be physically excluded, and they continued to be so treated well into the 13th century near Andover.

Research

This cemetery is apparently the result of local tradition and the continuity of rights and privileges within the immediate area of Andover. It should not, therefore, serve as a direct model for other parts of the country. However, it is likely that other variant examples could be awaiting discovery within Anglo-Saxon and medieval Wessex.

Further research, especially involving larger sampling strategies for radiocarbon dating, across all forms of later Anglo-Saxon and early medieval cemeteries together with the use of museum-curated samples from sites excavated previously, should prove informative. In this instance archaeological research can be used to help inform ongoing debates and research threads concerning early medieval state-building, religious reform, legal evolution and social structure already well-served by written records. There remain further questions that additional targeted sampling of the Weyhill Road skeletons could address in the future. For example, the sampling of both individuals, or the second individual, in some graves identified as double graves could be undertaken to determine whether the radiocarbon dates obtained overlapped at a 95% confidence level or if, by contrast, if they suggested a re-opening of the grave.

Finding that there were 'isotopic aliens' in the Weyhill Road cemetery population is not surprising, as Stuart Needham (2014, 221) says, 'there will always have been some elements of society who travelled much and/or afar', citing war-bands, religious specialists, traders and leaders as possible examples. We know, for example, that as early as the Late Bronze Age 'Scandinavians' and 'Southern' individuals were buried on the Isle of Thanet, Kent. The nature of the burials and the radiocarbon dating has shown that the burials were not the kind of mass burials resulting from a massacre or battle. Given the Viking raids from the 9th century, and the fact that by at least the early 10th century, Swedes, Danes and Norsemen were founding towns and settling in England (Wallis 2014, 37), we might expect to find individuals in the cemetery from Scandinavia or north-eastern Europe. The individuals identified as having these traits (SKs 1211, 1274 and 1297) have 10th-century and 11th to 12th-century dates. With the influx of soldiers and new landowners following the Norman Conquest and medieval trade, a 13th-century individual (SK1228), possibly from France, amongst the Weyhill Road dead,

might also have been expected. What this does tell us is that foreigners do not seem to have been judged differently by the local authorities, and certainly did not receive preferential treatment. These results add to the growing body of data which will eventually help us to corroborate existing data on the proportion of incomers in medieval England. It will be more difficult to assess the proportion of truly settled immigrant people from those just passing through, given Andover's position on the road network, the proximity of the popular Weyhill Fair and the closeness of the expanding ports of Southampton and Portsmouth. Considering the difficulties travellers might have experienced in finding people to stand surety for them, the relatively low proportion of 'foreigners' in the present sample is interesting. Extending isotopic sampling across later Anglo-Saxon and early medieval cemeteries might help us to achieve a greater understanding of local social and economic situations, and alter our existing perceptions.

Another significant contribution to research was the opportunity to test the isotopic values of one of the Late Saxon or medieval sheep from the Weyhill Road cemetery, against a sample from a sheep from the nearby Saxon settlement at Old Down Farm. There is currently a dearth of local, published comparative data, and the similarity of the results demonstrates that the Weyhill Road sheep was raised locally, and allows us to establish a baseline local isotopic profile for sheep against which other samples can be compared.

As the osteological evidence has shown (Clough, Chapter 3), the cemetery population from the Andover cemetery at Weyhill Road was overwhelmingly young, male and reasonably healthy at the time of their death. As such, the osteological analysis can add information from only a limited demographic section of the population, and is not as useful to the broader search for evidence for patterns of health and disease in Andover, as we do not yet know where the rest of the inhabitants were buried (Craig-Atkins 2017). We also cannot explain the presence of executed criminals by reference to environmental stress, in spite of there being recognised short periods of social disruption throughout the existence of the cemetery. However, the general lack of indications of severe biological stress in this cemetery population is in itself of some interest. As Craig-Atkins and Buckberry state: 'It is apparent from the case study presented here, and from the small number of other studies of later Anglo-Saxon cemetery populations, that the investigation of social and biological status has great potential to illuminate the motivations behind burial rites. It can be demonstrated that early Christian burial was not egalitarian, and that there is clear evidence for social stratification in the burial rite. This pattern is supported by the osteological record, which reveals that individuals who suffered more biological stress were often those commemorated by less elaborate burial, and visa versa' (2010, 22). In contrast, while our cemetery holds a specific subset of the general population, which might be expected to have come from the generally disadvantaged, this does not display significant biological stress markers. The beliefs of the religious thinkers of the time seem to be vindicated, as the executed were believed to have taken conscious individual decisions to commit crimes, i.e. to sin, rather than being forced into actions by their circumstances.

In contrast to the somewhat equivocal evidence for stress, the more brutal and obvious evidence for decapitation from our sample leads us to assert that headless corpses represent direct evidence for a judicial process, probably from both formal execution after trial, and the more immediate decapitation of an outlaw brought to local justice. They should not, therefore, be considered as outliers, or evidence for 'deviants' suggestive of some form of magical or superstitious rite to appease or control the 'dangerous' dead. The Weyhill Road dead would not have been seen as victims per se, but the end-products of accepted and acceptable judicial process. The real victims of crime, and there are large numbers of violent deaths attested in the historical records, might well show up as 'deviant' burials in contemporary church-organised cemeteries, where they did in fact continue to be an accepted part of the religious and social community.

The cemetery came to light under watching brief conditions (see Fig. on back cover), and was undertaken under a commercial rather than a research premise, so despite the commissioning of some primary documentary research on Andover records, there is scope for further documentary research. With the sheer volume of material, including transcribed and translated records and early studies of the law, made available online, this is now easier than it would have been even a few years ago. We have been able to review a large amount of documentary data relating to the law, and records of actual legal cases, but this represents only an initial appraisal of all available resources.

The burgeoning field of research into Saxon and medieval funerary practices continues to result in the publication of conference papers, research theses and popular books. There is a wealth of secondary research readily available, including a steady stream of more regionally-focused information from local historians,

such as the articles published in the *Proceedings of the Hampshire Field Club* (*Hampshire Studies*). We hope, therefore, that our contribution will prove useful to a wide readership.

We have not undertaken primary research in archives of large local landholders such as Winchester College. This project has provided an opportunity to attempt a preliminary integration of the archaeological record with written sources. It has allowed us to identify potential mechanisms behind our cemetery but not, so far, provided actual written testimonies or identified the individuals in the cemetery or the people who put them there. Other sources may come to light, and those with greater knowledge of documentary records may be able to make better use of them.

Concluding remarks
by Andrew Reynolds

One of the more interesting debates in medieval studies more recently has been to investigate the interfaces between local social organisation and the capacity of local people to organise their own affairs and the degree and depth of the influence of elites upon localities (Davies 2006; Routledge 2015, 19–27). Broadly speaking, execution and outcast cemeteries of Anglo-Saxon origin appear to cease functioning by the close of the 12th century. Such a chronology for the end of these sites fits well with what is understood as a widespread top-down reform of legal practice and procedure in the 12th century under King Henry I and King Henry II.

In common with execution sites elsewhere, the location is classic as the site lay on a boundary and at a nexus of long-distance routes of communication. The Weyhill Road cemetery in its earliest phase perhaps reflects the earliest pattern of social organisation observable in local districts of the 7th and 8th centuries at places such as Sutton Hoo, Thwing and Yeavering, where social/religious/political functions tended to be distributed within a small area (Reynolds 2009c; Manby 1985; Hope-Taylor 1977). The evidence from Weyhill Road, however, also reveals continuities at a local level in terms of the spatial organisation of judicial power from the early Anglo-Saxon period into the later Middle Ages.

Appendix 1: Analysis of Local Early Medieval Sources

By Rebecca Phillips

Methods

In order to identify and investigate documentary sources that could set the archaeological finds from Weyhill Road in their relevant historical context, a brief desktop survey was undertaken of the medieval court sources relating to Andover. This was followed by the examination of relevant printed (transcribed) and original documents at the Hampshire Record Office in Winchester. Several types of local records dating to before AD 1400 were considered. These included: Gild Rolls, Civic (hundredal) Court Rolls for the town of Andover, a view of Frankpledge and Andover Manor Court Rolls (Winchester College). The latter were not examined, as the Winchester College Archivist (Suzanne Foster) was able to confirm that although the College held property in Andover town centre as well as at Foxcotte/Charlton, it did not own property on the Weyhill Road.

Many of the hundredal court rolls have been badly damaged in the past, either by water, which makes the writing very difficult to discern, or by years of poor storage or handling, leading to large tears and missing areas of some documents. Our best efforts have been used to read the remaining text, and the results are described here. Parts of documents were only identified, transcribed or translated where they were of direct relevance to crime and punishment or death. Eight of the fifteen original Andover civic court (hundredal) rolls were analysed and reported on. An effort has been made to ensure that both the earliest, latest and a range of the available dates have been reviewed.

Results

Secondary sources

The Curia Regis is the 'Crown Court' and was the highest court in the land until the 13th century. It dealt with all matters coming to the king's attention, whether legislative, judicial or diplomatic. The records of this court between 1199 and 1242 have been transcribed. These printed transcripts were found to be available on the library shelves at Hampshire Record Office, and the indexes were searched to identify any entries relating to Andover. Sixteen volumes were checked, and only seven entries were found indexed against Andover. These entries were reviewed for evidence of executions and death. Six of the seven entries relate to property disputes (three specifically connected to non-possession of supposed dower property by widows), and the remaining item related to debt. There is therefore no evidence in these records that sheds light on the cemetery.

Primary sources

Gild Rolls

A single sample Gild Roll was checked to verify the description given in the VCH (*Victoria County History*; Page 1911a). This Gild Roll (37M85/3/GI/10, Morespech roll, 1311-1321-1322, 1347-1347-1348) confirmed that the gild rolls record matters of gild membership, and some commercial and mercantile agreements, but no information relating to crime and punishment was found.

Hundredal Rolls of the Civic Courts

The VCH describes the contents of these rolls thus: 'The entries refer for the most part to pleas concerning debt, land, transgressions, bloodshed, trespass, battery, theft, breaking the assize, carrying off the toll (*pro tollonio asportato*), raising hue and cry, &c' (Page 1911a).

The following rolls were examined:

37M85/2/HC/1 and 2 1272–1273	In and Out Hundred Court roll
37M85/2/HC/3 1275–1276	In and Out Hundred Court roll
37M85/2/HC/5 1277–1279	In and Out Hundred Court roll
37M85/2/HC/8 1281–1282	In and Out Hundred Court roll

37M85/2/HC/13 1305–1307	In and Out Hundred Court roll
37M85/2/HC/14 1387–1388	In and Out Hundred Court roll
37M85/2/HC/15 1394	In and Out Hundred Court roll

The following hundredal rolls have not yet been reviewed but it is expected that their contents would be much like the rolls HC1–13:

37M85/2/HC/4 1276–1277	In and Out Hundred Court roll
37M85/2/HC/6 1278–1280	In and Out Hundred Court roll
37M85/2/HC/7 1279–1281	In and Out Hundred Court roll
37M85/2/HC/9 1281–1283	In and Out Hundred Court roll
37M85/2/HC/10 1283–1285	In and Out Hundred Court roll
37M85/2/HC/11 1286–1287	In and Out Hundred Court roll
37M85/2/HC/12 1304–1305	In and Out Hundred Court roll

37M85/2/HC/1 and 2
In and Out Hundred Court roll   1272–1273
These two rolls are the earliest identified, and the cases relate mainly to disputes between individuals, debts and disputes about property. It was found that the transgression cases are not given in greater detail, so it is not possible to determine what the nature of the transgression was. The first roll includes records of 56 courts held during this single part year. A court was held every Monday, with two separate records being found for many of the courts. While each membrane of the roll runs chronologically, the membranes do not run in sequence overall.

There were no entries relating to crime and punishment identified, aside from occasional references to raising the hue and cry. There were at least three jury lists found.

37M85/2/HC/3
In and Out Hundred Court roll   1275–1276
This roll was not found to contain any significant information for the purposes of this research.

37M85/2/HC/5
In and Out Hundred Court roll   1277–1279
The most notable feature of this roll was the extensive lists of essoins presented to each court. It did not shed any light on the history of the cemetery.

37M85/2/HC/8
In and Out Hundred Court roll   1281–1282
This roll was not found to contain any significant information for the purposes of this research.

37M85/2/HC/13
In and Out Hundred Court roll   1305–1307
This roll followed the same basic nature as those described above. A sample court was chosen, and the nature of the cases dealt with was quantified. There were: two cases of debt; three of hue and cry; three of people not appearing in court; two of taking and detaining property; two of trespass; five of carrying off the toll; and two of concealment.

There were no significant cases relating to crimes or information relevant to the cemetery found in this roll.

37M85/2/HC/14
In and Out Hundred Court roll   1387–1388
(Figs 7.1 and Appendix 1.1)
This proved to be the most interesting of the rolls. It consists of ten membranes, with the weekly courts being recorded. It is significantly later than the majority of other hundredal rolls consulted, and has significant differences. It has useful marginal notes to the types of cases or outcomes. Many are marked px meaning that the case was held over to the next (proximo) court. These have therefore been skipped in our review of the document.

This roll was unusual, as it is the only one in which entries relating to bloodshed were found. The details of these are given in Table A1.

The fine for bloodshed was always annotated as 6d. It is not clear whether this was simply a particularly violent

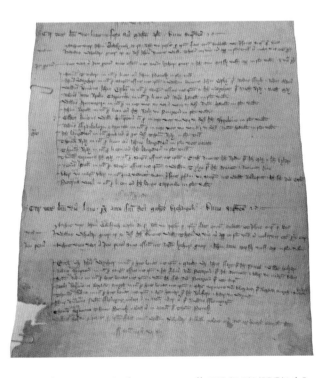

Appendix 1.1   Andover court roll 37M85/2/HC/14 In and Out Hundred Court roll 1387–1388 (detail) Hampshire Record Office: Andover Borough Archive: 37M85/2/HC/14

year, or whether, in the intervening 82 years between HC/13 and HC/14, changes had occurred to the type of cases within the remit of the hundredal court. It is noticeable from this roll that the reports of violence vary on a seasonal basis, with high points around both Christmas and Easter. It might be inferred that this was due to the pleasures and strains of the festivities. It is also interesting to note how a few individuals and their households are responsible for much of the bloodshed.

37M85/2/HC/15
In and Out Hundred Court roll   1394
This roll consists of a single membrane, with courts held on: Monday next after the feast of St Valentine, in the 17th year of Richard II's reign (16 Feb); Monday next after the feast of St Matthias the Apostle (2 Mar); Monday next after the Feast of St Gregory the pope (16 Mar). All three entries relate to the same property case. This therefore adds nothing to the cemetery story.

View of frankpledge
37M85/2/FP/1　View of frankpledge　1379–1380
This single membrane for 1379–1380 is badly damaged, and has lost almost half of the text. There is an unusually long case in 1380, concerning an innkeeper selling excessively against the statutes. No evidence could be deciphered relating to deaths or executions.

Conclusions

Although it has not proven possible to review all the court rolls in the available time, those which have been reviewed indicate that these sources do not refer to committing offenders for trial by touring crown magistrates. Although they indicate the social conditions in Andover during the 13th and 14th centuries, they have not included mentions of the cemetery or of execution.

Table A1: Detail from 37M85/2/HC/14: *In and Out Hundred Court roll 1387–1388*

Date	Case
Monday after 7 July, 20 July, Last Monday in July, Monday after 1 August, 10 August, 24 August, Monday after 29 August, Monday before 8 September, 14 September	Inquiry into bloodshed between John Wycher and William servant of John Estby (twice)
20 July, Last Monday in July	Fine given – Wate Michel for bloodshed with William servant of Roger Wallop
20 July	Inquiry into bloodshed between John Wyneman and Reginald Tonker
Last Monday in July	Fine given – John Wyneman for bloodshed with Reginald Tonker
Monday after 1 August	Inquiry into bloodshed between Nicholas servant of John Fletcher and John servant of William Nugge
10 August	Inquiry into bloodshed between Joan wife of Radulph Skyrell and William son of Stephen
10 August	Fine given – Nicholas servant of John Fletcher for bloodshed with Thomas servant of William Nugge (twice)
Monday after 15 August	Fine given – John Lange for bloodshed with John son of Richard Petigon
Monday after 15 August	Fine given – Joan wife of Stephen Muleward for bloodshed with William son of Stephen Muleward
Last Monday in July, Monday after 1 August, 10 August, 24 August	Inquiry into bloodshed between two Extravens
24 August	Fine given – John Muleward of the Mersh for bloodshed with John Brasyare
24 August	Fine given – Joan wife of Gilbert Taile for bloodshed with John son of Gilbert Helyare
24 August	Fine given – Joan wife of Gilbert Taile for bloodshed with Joan wife of John Tankard
Monday after 29 August	Fine given – John Extravens for bloodshed

Table A1 (cont.): Detail from 37M85/2/HC/14: *In and Out Hundred Court roll 1387–1388*

Date	Case
21 September	Fine given – John Wycher for bloodshed with William servant of John Estby (reciprocal fines given)
21 September	Fine given - Thomas servant of John May for bloodshed with Edith servant of John Brode
21 September	Fine given - Richard Hodett for bloodshed with William Tylye
Monday before 29 September	Fine given – Rob Shupton for bloodshed with John son of Richard Petigens
29 September	Inquiry into bloodshed between Thomas Frenie and John his servant
29 September, Monday after 6 October, Monday after 13 October	Inquiry into bloodshed between John Blakeborne and Thomas Hampton
Monday after 6 October	Inquiry into bloodshed between [Rad'ne] Cole and Thomas Swan
Monday after 6 October	Fine given – Thomas Frenie for bloodshed with John his servant
Monday after 13 October	Inquiry into bloodshed between John Duydy and Joan daughter of Richard Estbury
Monday after 13 October	Fine given – Rad'ne Cole for bloodshed with Thomas Swan
Monday after 13 October	Fine given – John servant of Alexander Smyth for bloodshed with Reginald servant of Thomas Bray
28 October	Inquiry into bloodshed between William servant of Roger Wallop and John Mul'
28 October	Fine given – Thomas Carter servant of Thomas Bray for bloodshed with John Bray
28 October	Fine given – Thomas Tanner for bloodshed with John Bray
28 October	Fine given – John son of John Vykar for bloodshed with John son of John Monsort
28 October	Fine given – John son of John Monsort for bloodshed with John son of John Vykar
Monday after 1 November	Inquiry into bloodshed between William servant of Roger Wallop and John Myleward ate Merysh
Monday after 1 November, Monday after 6 November	Inquiry into bloodshed between Alice wife of John Vyar and Malena de Wyght
Monday after 1 November	Inquiry into bloodshed between Joan servant of Richard Conhurd(e) and Joan servant of [unreadable name]
Monday after 1 November	Fine given – Edith Gaumbon for bloodshed with Joan Montagu
Monday before 16 November, Monday after 16 November	Inquiry into bloodshed between Margaret wife of John Cawlyn and John Trente junior
Monday before 16 November	Fine given – John Trente for bloodshed with Margaret
Monday after 16 November	Fine given – Malena de Wyght for bloodshed with Alice wife of John Vyar

Table A1 (cont.): Detail from 37M85/2/HC/14: In and Out Hundred Court roll 1387–1388

Date	Case
25 November	Inquiry into bloodshed between Agnes wife of William Wyt and [unreadable name]
25 November	Fine given – Margaret wife of John Cawlyn for bloodshed with John Trente junior
25 November	Fine given – Edith Gumabon for bloodshed with Joan Montagu
25 November	Fine given – Thomas Wychegar servant of H Blok for bloodshed with John Parker
29 September, Monday after 30 November, Monday after 8 December, 25 December	Inquiry into bloodshed between John Monsort and an unidentified individual
Monday after 8 December, Monday before 21 December, Monday before 25 December	Inquiry into bloodshed at home of Richard Hosteler
Monday before 8 December	Fine given – Margaret wife of Andrew Benneby for bloodshed with John Pouchemaker
Monday after 13 December	Inquiry into bloodshed between John Bray, Thomas servant of Thomas Bray
Monday after 13 December	Inquiry into bloodshed between Thomas Tanner servant of Thomas Bray and John Bray
Monday after 13 December	Inquiry into John Blakeborne and Thomas Hampton
Monday after 13 December	Inquiry into John son of John Mounsort and John son of John Vykar
Monday before 21 December	Fine given – John Leche for bloodshed with Thomas Cato Conk
Monday before 21 December	Fine given – Tithing of Wynch' for concealing the bloodshed between John Mounsort and John servant of Robert H'
Monday before 25 December	Inquiry into bloodshed between Andrew Shoppe and Radulph servant of John Penesy
Monday before 1 January	Inquiry into bloodshed between Andrew Shoppe and Radulph servant of Peter
Monday before 1 January	Fine given – Richard Hosteler for bloodshed with Margaret wife of John Laurens
Monday before 1 January	Fine given – Alice servant of Robert Montyng for bloodshed with Anice daughter of John Reynolds
6 January	Inquiry into bloodshed between Andrew Shoppe and Radulph servant of John Penesy
6 January, 13 January	Inquiry into bloodshed between Christian servant of John Potter and John servant of William Iremonger
6 January, 13 January	Inquiry into bloodshed between John servant of Nicholas Flemyng and William son of William Kadynton
13 January, 20 January	Inquiry into bloodshed between Simon Souper and Joan his servant
13 January	Fine given – Andrew Shoppe for bloodshed with Radulph servant of John Penesy
20 January	Fine given – John servant of William Iremonger for bloodshed with Christeman servant of John Peter

Table A1 (cont.): Detail from 37M85/2/HC/14: *In and Out Hundred Court roll 1387–1388*

Date	Case
20 January	Fine given – Edith Gamubon for bloodshed with John son of Richard Petigon
Monday after 2 February	Fine given – John Laurens for bloodshed with Richard Hosteler
Monday after 2 February	Fine given – Margaret wife of John Laurens for bloodshed with Richard Hosteler
Monday before 24 February	Inquiry by tithing of the Priory into bloodshed in their tithing by and to whom
Monday before 12 March, 13 April	Inquiry into bloodshed between Agatha and Joan
Monday after 12 March	Fine given – John Croliebois for bloodshed with Roger Lycher
Monday after 25 March	Fine given – William servant of Robert Osward for bloodshed with John Pynyng
First Monday in Lent	Fine given – Agnes wife of Richard Cowhurd for bloodshed with Joan her servant
First Monday in Lent	Fine given – Thomas Spede for bloodshed with Thomas servant of John May
After Palm Sunday	Fine given – Christina servant of John Potte for bloodshed with Thomas servant of John Potte
After Palm Sunday	Fine given – Alice Gewell for bloodshed with Robert servant of John Oyare
After Easter	Inquiry into bloodshed between Margaret daughter of Thomas Conto Conq and Agnes daughter of John Bykar
27 April	Fine given – Agatha wife of John Wycher for bloodshed with Joan Extraven
Monday before 17 May	Inquiry into bloodshed between William Lane and John Blakeborne
Monday before 17 May	Inquiry into bloodshed between John Pyket and John Pyctel
Monday after 17 May, Monday before 26 May	Inquiry into bloodshed between John Monsort and Joan servant of John Hayward
Monday after 17 May	Fine given – John Monsort for bloodshed with John May
Monday before 26 May	Tithing of Alderman le Grand present a case of bloodshed between Richard May and John Monsort, and are given time to verify the case
Monday after 26 May	Fine given – John Montfort for bloodshed with Richard May
Monday after 26 May	Fine given – Ut Pouchemaker for bloodshed with Alice servant of Robert Mychell
Monday before 11 June	Fine given – John Montfort for bloodshed with Joan servant of John Hayward
Monday before 11 June	Fine given – Katerina wife of William Kerner for bloodshed with Christian servant of [unreadable name]
Monday after 11 June, Monday before 24 June, 29 June	Inquiry into bloodshed between John Lytelsmyth and William servant of Edward Spircok

Table A1 (cont.): Detail from 37M85/2/HC/14: In and Out Hundred Court roll 1387–1388

Date	Case
Monday after 11 June	Fine given – Joan wife of Will Cosham for bloodshed with Alexander son of Roger Wallop
29 June	Inquiry into James servant of Alexander Smyth and John Blake
29 June, Monday before 7 July	Inquiry into bloodshed between William servant of John Estby and John Wycher
Monday before 7 July	Fine given – John Blake for bloodshed with James Smyth
Monday after 7 July	Fine given – William Iremonger for bloodshed with Thomas ate Mede his servant
Monday after 7 July	Fine given – Robert servant of Richard Conhurde for bloodshed with William Cosham
Monday after 7 July	Fine given – Robert servant of Richard Conhurde for bloodshed with Joan wife of William Cosham

Appendix 2: After the Cemetery

Not all local settlements thrived continuously during the medieval period, as demonstrated by excavations at the site of the deserted medieval village of Foxcotte, to the north of the site (Fig. 1.1). The earliest documentary reference to the settlement is in the Domesday Book of 1086 (Russel 1985). Although no archaeological features were excavated that were of proven Saxon and Norman period date (6th to 12th centuries AD), building remains of 13th to 14th-century date were recorded. The settlement appears to have grown in the 13th and 14th centuries, before gradually shrinking in the later medieval period, with the 'general deterioration in the climate and the concomitant fall in population accelerated by the Black Death and other plagues, probably responsible for curtailing the growth' (Russel 1985, 219). For example, plague in the diocese of Winchester in 1348–9 resulted in up to 56% mortality amongst the beneficed clergy of Andover (Shrewsbury 1970, 91). It is probable that local lay people suffered equally.

Grant (2009, 183) suggested that the population in Andover in 1603 was 1,308; by 1676 it had increased to 2,175 (up 66%) and by 1811 it was 3,367 (a 55% increase between 1676 and 1811). There appears to

have been only limited settlement growth beyond the town's probable medieval core *(ibid.,* 186; fig. 3), although Grant notes that some of this growth might have been accommodated in the hamlets of the rural parts of Andover.

In broad terms, most of this expansion was of late 18th-century and/or early 19th-century date, piecemeal, and located on the periphery along existing routes *(ibid.,* 197). By the 19th century, Andover borough and parish had a fairly substantial population (3,304 in 1841 and 4,748 in 1821), and an annual rental value in 1815 of £8,975. Weyhill, by contrast, had only 408 in 1821, while its annual rental value was not recorded (House of Commons 1831, 231, 237).

That a long-forgotten punishment cemetery was in agricultural use, and owned by the Baronet is perhaps a measure of how little life had changed for the ordinary man. The years following the end of the Napoleonic Wars witnessed economic hardship, political unrest, overpopulation, unemployment and the introduction of new technologies. Agricultural depression led to suffering amongst many, including small farmers and rural labourers, and eventually led to widespread disorder (Hobsbawm and Rudé 2014; Afton 1987,

237). At a time of rural poverty and unrest, Sir John was against relaxation of the corn laws (Salmon and Spencer 2009); although a speech reported in *The Times* (1826) shows that he was aware of the privations of the rural poor and said 'It is melancholy to see the poor devils with scarcely a rag to their backs' (*ibid.*).

Surviving documents show that punishments were hard. 'There is also one individual petition (Moses Brackstone, of Andover, carrier, prisoner's father and undersigned by four people, John Lellaude, bailiff, George Thompson and John Godden, justices and W N Pedder, minister of Andover) on behalf of Moses Brackstone, 27 years, convicted at the Hampshire Lent Assizes at Winchester in March 1821, of fowl stealing (stealing poultry). Grounds for clemency: his father is 65-year-old widower with nine children, who are all in respectable service and employ, led astray by others, contrition and good conduct during confinement. Initial sentence: seven years transportation. October 1824, Sept 1825' (National Archives HO 17/34/128).

The Swing revolts, a series of revolts, or agricultural risings, broke out during the winter of 1830. Between the 19th and 22nd of November, there was an outbreak of riots, which locally lasted several days. This included the breaking of agricultural machinery and demolishing of equipment at Tasker's Waterloo Foundry, at Upper Clatford. The 19th of November saw riots, wage-demands, extortion and arson (amongst other local disturbances) in Andover, with further outbreaks there on the 21st and 22nd. Weyhill also saw riots and extortion (on the 22nd), and arson on the 23rd (Afton 1987, 249–52). The Andover magistrates wrote to the Home Secretary saying the whole town and its neighbourhood continued 'in a state of the greatest agitation and alarm'

(Hobsbawm and Rudé, 2014, 118–19). Such was the local unrest that regular troops such as the 9th Lancers, were detached to various places in Hampshire, Wiltshire and Somersetshire, to assist in keeping order among the agricultural population (Reynard 1904, 35). After order was resumed, the government appointed a Special Commission (rather than local magistrates) to try prisoners in certain counties, Hampshire amongst them. The first Special Commission opened in Winchester, in December, 1830, and was later viewed as particularly harsh in its judgements (Hobsbawm and Rudé 2014, 258). Several of the offences carried the death penalty – breaking machinery (other than threshing machines), destroying buildings, extorting money, being part of a 'crowd whose collective action led to extortion, violence or physical assault, whether he was a direct or willing participant or not' (*ibid.*, 258–9) and penalties imposed were harsh indeed. Pleas for clemency and petitions were sent to the Home Office. Of the 1,976 prisoners tried in 34 counties, 19 were executed, with 505 sentenced to transportation for various terms including life, 644 sentenced to prison, seven were fined and one whipped. Some 800 were acquitted or bound over (*ibid.*, 262). Locally, two men were executed at Winchester, and one at Reading. One young man, Joseph Blatch, aged 20, was convicted for destroying machinery, the property of William Tasker at his Iron Foundry, near Andover, on 20th November, 1830, and following a petition this was later commuted to one year in prison (National Archives HO 17/46/34). Another John Gilmore, of Andover, a labourer aged 25, was sentenced to death although this was commuted to transportation for life (102 inhabitants of Andover having petitioned the sentence, including the prosecutor (HO 17/86/32)).

Select Glossary

abjuror	someone who has renounced their country and taken an oath of perpetual banishment
alod	land owned absolutely
amercement	a fine
appeal	a public accusation
carnifices	executioner
coram rege	court of the King's Bench
Curia Regis	king's court or royal council
deodand	an item that has caused death or personal injury, which is forfeit to the Crown and to be used for a pious purpose
disseisin	the act of wrongfully or unlawfully depriving someone of the freehold possession of property
estray	lost domestic animal
estrepement	needless destruction of land
eyre	circuit court held in each shire from 1176 until the late 13th century
felonies	homicide, theft, arson and rape and certain other trespasses (premeditated assault, extortion and violent disseisin) plus conspiracy from 1305
frankpledge	system of joint suretyship common in England throughout the Early Middle Ages
infangentheof	the right of a lord of a manor to jurisdiction over thieves caught within his liberty
justiciar	chief justice of the realm
outfangantheof	the right of a lord of a manor to jurisdiction over thieves living in his manor but caught outside it
oyer and *terminer*	a commission where justices 'heard and determined' certain defined pleas
sac and *sol, tol* and *theam*	privileges granted by the Crown to landowners under Anglo-Saxon and Anglo-Norman law
shrievalty	the office, term of office, or jurisdiction of a sheriff
suspensores	hangman
tithing	a group of ten men, who were bound to stand pledge in court for their members
tourn	court held by the sheriff twice yearly in each hundred, whose proceedings are generally known as 'view of frankpledge'
wergild	'man payment', a value set in Anglo-Saxon and Germanic law on a human life and paid as compensation to the kin or lord
witenagemot	an assembly of local elders

References

AC Archaeology, 2011 *Excavations at East Anton, Andover, Hampshire Archaeological assessment report* Unpublished report No: ACW209/1/0

Adams, J.B. 1907 'The Descendants of the Curia Regis', *The American Historical Review* **13**, 11–15 https://archive.org/details/jstor-1834884/page/n5 (accessed January 2019)

Afton, B. 1987 'A Want of Good Feeling. A Reassessment of the Economic and Political Causes of the Rural Unrest in Hampshire, 1830', *Proc. Hampshire Fld Club Archaeol. Soc.* **43**, 237–54

AlQahtani, S.J., Hector, M.P. and Liversidge, H.M. 2010 'Brief communication: The London Atlas of Human Tooth Development and Eruption', *Amer. J. Phys. Anthropol.* **142**, 481–90

Ambers, J. 2005 'Assessment of radiocarbon dates', in Carver, M. *Sutton Hoo. A Seventh Century Princely Burial Ground and its Context* London, British Museum Press, 54–5

Ambrose, S.H. 1990 'Preparation and characterization of bone and tooth collagen for isotopic analysis', *J. Archaeol. Sci.* **17**, 431–51

Anderson, L.D. and D'Alonzo, R.T. 1974 'Fractures of the odontoid process of the axis', *J. Bone Joint Surg. (Am)* **56**(8), 1663–74

Arcini, C. 2009 'Losing Face. The Worldwide Phenomenon of Ancient Prone Burial', in Back Danielsson, I.-M., Gustin, I., Larsson, A., Myrberg, N. and Thedeén, S. (eds) *Döda personers sällskap. Gravmaterialens identiteter och kulturella uttryck / On the Threshold. Burial Archaeology in the Twenty-First Century* Stockholm, Stockholm University, 187–202

Armitage, P.L. 1977 *The Mammalian Remains from the Tudor Site of Baynard's Castle, London: A Biometrical and Historical Analysis* Unpublished PhD thesis, Royal Holloway College and British Museum (Natural History)

Aufderheide, A.C. and Rodríguez-Martin, C. 1998 *The Cambridge Encyclopaedia of Human Palaeopathology* Cambridge, Cambridge University Press

Baker, J. 2019 'Meeting in the Shadow of Heroes? Personal Names and Assembly Places', in Carroll, J. Reynolds, A. and Yorke, B. (eds) *Power and Place in Europe in the Early Middle Ages* Oxford, Proceedings of the British Academy **224**, 37–63

Barclay, A., Knight, D., Booth, P., Evans, J., Brown, D.H. and Wood, I. 2016 *A Standard for Pottery Studies in Archaeology* Prehistoric Ceramics Research Group, Study Group for Roman Pottery, Medieval Pottery Research Group

Baring, F.H. 1915 'William the Conqueror's March Through Hampshire in 1066', *Proc. Hampshire Fld Club Archaeol. Soc.* **7**(ii), 33–9

Bartlett, R. (ed.) (2002) *Life and Miracles of St. Modwenna* Oxford, Clarendon Press

Bass, W.M. 1995 *Human osteology: A laboratory and field manual* (4th edn) Columbia, Missouri Archaeological Society

Baxter, S. and Hudson, J. (eds) 2014 *Patrick Wormald Papers Preparatory to the Making of English Law: King Alfred to the Twelfth Century, Vol. II: From God's Law to Common Law* University of London: Early English Laws http://www.earlyenglishlaws.ac.uk/reference/wormald/ (accessed 26 December 2018)

Bayliss, A. 2009 'Rolling out revolution: using radiocarbon dating in archaeology', *Radiocarbon* **51**, 123–47

Bayliss, A., Shepherd Popescu, E., Beavan-Athfield, N., Bronk Ramsey, C., Cook, G.T. and Locker, A. 2004 'The potential significance of dietary offsets for the interpretation of radiocarbon dates: an archaeologically significant example from medieval Norwich', *J. Archaeol. Sci.* **431**, 563–75

Bayliss, A., Beavan, N., Hamilton, D., Köhler, K., Nyerges, É.Á., Bronk Ramsey, C., Dunbar, E., Fecher, M., Goslar, T., Kromer, B., Reimer, P., Bánffy, E., Marton, T., Oross, K., Osztás, A., Zalai-Gaál, I. and Whittle, A. 2013 'Peopling the past: creating a site biography in the Hungarian Neolithic', *Bericht der Römisch-Germanischen Kommission* **94**, 23–91

Beard, F. 2005 'The Arrival of The Hospitallers in Hampshire', *Proc. Hampshire Fld Club Archaeol. Soc.* **60**, 175–86

Beaumont, J. and Montgomery, J. 2016 'The Great Irish Famine: identifying starvation in the tissues of victims using stable isotope analysis of bone and incremental dentine collagen', *PloS ONE* **1**(8), e0160065. doi: 10.1371/journal.pone.0160065

Bennett, A.C. 1931 *The Story of St Mary's Church, Andover* (various publishers and editions)

Bentley, R.A. 2006 'Strontium isotopes from the earth to the archaeological skeleton: a review', *J. Archaeol. Method and Theory* **13**(3), 135–87

Beresford, G. 1975 *The Medieval Clay-Land Village: Excavations at Goltho and Barton Blount* Soc. Med. Arch. Monog. **6**, London

Beresford, M. 2012 *The Dangerous Dead: The Early Medieval deviant burial at Southwell, Nottinghamshire in a wider context* MBArchaeology Local Heritage Series, Number **3** http://www.mbarchaeology.co.uk/wp-content/uploads/2012/02/LHS3%20-%20The%20Dangerous%20Dead.pdf (accessed February 2019)

Berry, R. and Berry, A. 1967 'Epigenetic variation in human cranium', *J. Anatomy* **101**, 361–79

Bird, D. 2018a 'Guildown reconsidered 4: the execution cemetery', *Surrey Archaeol. Soc. Bulletin* **467**, 2–6

Bird, D. 2018b 'Guildown reconsidered 5: the so-called 'Guildown Massacre', *Surrey Archaeol. Soc. Bulletin* **468**, 14–16

Blair, J. 1994 *Anglo-Saxon Oxfordshire* Stroud, Alan Sutton

Blair, J. 1995 'Anglo-Saxon pagan shines and their prototypes', *Anglo-Saxon Stud. Archaeol. Hist.* **8**, 1–28

Blair, J. 2005 *The Church in Anglo-Saxon Society* Oxford, Oxford University Press

Blair, J. 2009 'The dangerous dead in Early Medieval England', in Baxter, S., Karkov, C.E. and Pelteret, I. (eds) *Early Medieval Studies in Memory of Patrick Wormald* Farnham, Ashgate, 539–55

Bocherens, H., Drucker, D.G. and Taubald, H. 2011 'Preservation of bone collagen sulphur isotopic compositions in an early Holocene river-bank archaeological site', *Palaeogeography, Palaeoclimatology, Palaeoecology* **310**, 32–8

Boessneck, J., Müller, H.H. and Teichert, M. 1964 'Osteologische Unterscheidungmerkmale zwischen Schaf (*Ovis aries* Linné) und Ziege (*Capra hircus* Linné)', *Kühn-Archiv, Bd.* **78**, H.1–2

Bonney, D. 1976 'Early Boundaries and Estates in Southern England', in P.H. Sawyer (ed.) *Medieval Settlement* London, Edward Arnold, 72–82

Brettell, R., Evans, J., Marzinzik, S., Lamb, A. and Montgomery, J. 2012 ' 'Impious Easterners': can oxygen and strontium isotopes serve as indicators of provenance in early medieval European cemetery populations?', *European Journal of Archaeology* **15**, 117–45

Brickley, M. and McKinley, J. 2004 'Guidelines to the standards for recording of human remains', *IFA Paper* No. 7

British Geological Survey, 2015 *Geology of Britain viewer* http://mapapps.bgs.ac.uk/geologyofbritain/home.html (accessed 9 December 2015)

British Library, 2018 *Catalogue of Illuminated Manuscripts* https://www.bl.uk/catalogues/illuminatedmanuscripts/ILLUMIN.ASP?Size=mid&IllID=32143 (accessed December 2018)

Brodie, A., Croom, J. and Davies J.O. 2002 *English Prisons. An Architectural History* Swindon, English Heritage

Bronk Ramsey, C. 1995 'Radiocarbon calibration and analysis of stratigraphy', *Radiocarbon* **36**, 425–30

Bronk Ramsey, C. 1998 'Probability and dating', *Radiocarbon* **40**, 461–74

Bronk Ramsey, C. 2001 'Development of the radiocarbon calibration program OxCal', *Radiocarbon* **43**, 355–63

Bronk Ramsey, C. 2009 'Bayesian analysis of radiocarbon dates', *Radiocarbon* **51**, 337–60

Bronk Ramsey, C. and Lee, S. 2013 'Recent and planned developments of the program OxCal', *Radiocarbon* **55**(2–3), 720–30

Bronk Ramsey, C., Dee, M., Lee, S., Nakagawa, T. and Staff, R.A. 2010 'Developments in the calibration and modelling of radiocarbon dates', *Radiocarbon* **52**(3), 953–61

Brooks, S. and Suchey, J.M. 1990 'Skeletal age determination based on the os pubis: a comparison of the Acsádi-Nemeskéri and Suchey–Brooks method', *Human Evolution* **5**, 227–38

Brothwell, D.R. 1981 *Digging up Bones* Oxford, Oxford University Press

Brothwell, D.R. and Møller-Christensen, V. 1963 'Mediohistorical aspects of a very early case of mutilation', *Danish Medical Bulletin* **10**, 21–5

Buck, C.E. and Juarez, M. 2017 'Bayesian radiocarbon modelling for beginners' https://arxiv.org/abs/1704.07141 (accessed 9 May 2017)

Buckberry, J. 2008 'Off with their heads: The Anglo-Saxon execution cemetery at Walkington Wold, East Yorkshire', in Murphy, E.M. (ed.) *Deviant burial in the archaeological record* Oxford: Oxbow Books, 148–68

Buckberry, J.L. 2014 'Osteological evidence of corporal and capital punishment in later Anglo-Saxon England', in Marafioti, N. and Gates, J. (eds) *Capital and corporal punishment in Anglo-Saxon England* Woodbridge, Boydell and Brewer, 131–48

Buckberry, J. 2015 'The (mis)use of adult age estimates in osteology', *Annals of Human Biology* **42**(4), 321–9

Buckberry, J.L and Chamberlain, A.T. 2002 'Age estimation from the auricular surface of the ilium: a revised method', *Amer. J. Phys. Anthropol.* **119**, 231–9

Buckberry, J. and Hadley, D.M. 2007 'An Anglo-Saxon execution cemetery at Walkington Wold, Yorkshire', *Oxford J. Archaeol.* **26**(3), 309–29

Bucknill, R.P. 2003 *Wherwell Abbey and its Cartulary* PhD thesis, King's College London Research Portal https://kclpure.kcl.ac.uk/portal/files/2932847/408128.pdf (accessed January 2019)

Buikstra, J.E. and Ubelaker, D.H. (eds) 1994 *Standards for data collection from human skeletal remains* Arkansas Archeological Survey Research Series **44**, Fayetteville Arkansas

Caley, J., Ellis, H. and Bandinel, B. 1846 *Monasticon Anglicanum: A History of the Abbies and other Monasteries, Hospitals, Frieries and cathedral and collegiate churches with their dependencies in England and Wales* Originally published by Sir William Dugdale Vol. 6 part II, Charing Cross, James Bohn

Cam, H.M. 1930 *The Hundred and the Hundredal Rolls: An outline of local government in medieval England* London, Methuen & Co

Campling, N. 1989 '2 Newbury Street, Andover', in M.F. Hughes (ed.) *Archaeology in Hampshire. Annual Report for 1988* Winchester, Hampshire County Council, 12

Carpenter, D.A. 1996 'England in the Twelfth and Thirteenth Centuries', in Haverkamp, A. and Vollrath, H. (eds) *England and Germany in the High Middle Ages* London, The German Historical Institute / Oxford, Oxford University Press, 105–26

Carrabine, E., Iganski, P., Lee, M., Plummer, K. and South, N. 2004 *Criminology: a sociological introduction* London, Routledge

Carson, E.A. 2006 'Maximum-Likelihood Variance Components Analysis of Heritabilities of Cranial Nonmetric Traits', *Human Biology* **78**(4), 383–402

Carty, N. 2015 ' "The Halved Heads": Osteological Evidence for Decapitation in Medieval Ireland', *Papers from the Institute of Archaeology* **25**(1), 1–20 http://dx.doi.org/10.5334/pia.477 (accessed August 2018)

Carver, M. 2005 *Sutton Hoo. A Seventh Century Princely Burial Ground and its Context* London, British Museum Press

Cayton, H. 1980 'Some contributions from the written sources', in Wade Martins, P. and Yaxley, D. (eds) *Excavations in North Elmham 1967–1972* E. Anglian Archaeol. Rep. **9**, Norfolk Archaeological Unit, Dereham, 303–13

Cessford, C. 2015 'The St. John's Hospital Cemetery and Environs, Cambridge: Contextualizing the Medieval Urban Dead', *Archaeol. J.* **172**(1), 52–120. doi: 10.1080/00665983.2014.984960

Cessford, C., Dickens, A., Dodwell, N. and Reynolds A. 2007 'Middle Anglo-Saxon Justice: the Chesterton Lane Corner execution cemetery and related sequence, Cambridge', *Archaeol. J.* **164**, 197–226

Chapman, A. 2010 *West Cotton, Raunds: a study of medieval settlement dynamics AD 450–1450* Oxford, Oxbow Books (cited in Mays *et al.* 2017)

Chapman, J. and Seeliger, S. 1997 *A Guide to Enclosure in Hampshire 1700–1900* Hampshire Record Series Vol. **XV**, Winchester, Hampshire County Council

Chedzey, J. 2003 'Manuscript production in Medieval Winchester', *Reading Medieval Studies* **XXIX** https://www.reading.ac.uk/web/files/GCMS/RMS-2003-01_J._Chedzey,_Manuscript_Production_in_Medieval_Winchester.pdf (accessed June 2019)

Chenery, C.A., Pashley, V., Lamb, A.L., Sloane, H.J. and Evans, J.A. 2012 'The oxygen isotope relationship between the phosphate and structural carbonate fractions of human bioapatite', *Rapid Communications in Mass Spectrometry* **26**, 309–19

Chenery, C.A., Evans, J.A., Score, D., Boyle, A. and Chenery, S.R. 2014 'A boat load of Vikings?', *Journal of the North Atlantic* **S7**, 43–53

Cherryson, A.K. 2005 *In the Shadow of the Church Burial, practices in the Wessex heartlands c. 600–1100AD* PhD thesis, University of Sheffield http://etheses.whiterose.ac.uk/10321/ (accessed 12 March 2019)

Cherryson, A.K. 2008 'Normal, deviant and atypical: burial variation in late Saxon Wessex c. AD 700–1100', in Murphy, E.M. (ed.) *Deviant burial in the archaeological record* Oxford, Oxbow Books, 115–30

CMS (Church Monument Society), 2018 'Symbolism on monuments' https://churchmonumentssociety.org/resources/symbolism-on-monuments (accessed 24 August 2018)

Clanchy, M.T. 1978 'Highway robbery and trial by battle in the Hampshire eyre of 1249', in Hunnisett, R.F. and Post, J.B. (eds) *Medieval Legal Records edited in memory of C.A.F. Meekings* London, HMSO, 26–61

Clifford, N. 2018 'Ann Baker, hanged for stealing sheep (1801)' https://www.naomiclifford.com/ann-baker/ (accessed 24 August 2018)

Clutterbuck, J. 2018a 'Exploring an Anglo-Norman execution cemetery', *Current Archaeology* May 2018, 22–8

Clutterbuck, J. 2018b 'The excluded dead: An execution cemetery on Weyhill Road, Andover', *British Archaeology* May/June 2018, 36–41

Clutterbuck, R.H. (revised and ed. E.D. Webb) 1898 *Notes on the Parishes of Fyfield, Kimpton, Penton Mewsey, Weyhill and Wherwell in the County of Hampshire* Salisbury, Bennett Bros.

Clutton-Brock, J., Dennis-Bryan, K., Armitage, P.L. and Jewell, P.A. 1990 'Osteology of the Soay sheep', *Bulletin British Museum (Natural History) Zoology Series* **56**(1), 1–56

Coates, R. 1989 *The place-names of Hampshire* London, B.T. Batsford

Cockburn, J.S., King, H.P.F. and McDonnell, K.G.T (eds) 1969 'Religious Houses: House of Knights hospitallers', *A History of the County of Middlesex: Volume 1, Physique, Archaeology, Domesday, Ecclesiastical Organization, the Jews, Religious Houses, Education of Working Classes To 1870, Private Education From Sixteenth Century* London, Victoria County History, 193–204. British History Online http://www.british-history.ac.uk/vch/middx/vol1/pp193-204 (accessed 28 January 2019)

Codrington, T. 1919 *Roman Roads in Britain* (Reprint of 3rd edn) London, Society for Promoting Christian Knowledge https://archive.org/details/romanroadsinbrit00codrrich/page/n5 (accessed 28 October 2018)

Coldicott, D.K. 1998 *Monxton A Hampshire Village History* Andover, D.K. Coldicott

Cole, G., Ditchfield, P.W., Dulias, K., Edwards, C., Reynolds, A. and Waldron, T. (under review), forthcoming 'Summary justice or the King's will? The first case of formal facial mutilation from Anglo-Saxon England', *Antiquity*

Cook, A.M. 1985 'Dress Fasteners and Ornaments', in Cook and Dacre 1985, 73–88

Cook, A.M. and Dacre M.W. 1985 *Excavations at Portway, Andover 1973–1975* Oxford Univ. Comm. Archaeol. Monog. **4**, Oxford, Oxford University Committee for Archaeology

Coppen, M. 2015 *Andover's Norman Church 1080–1840, The Architecture and Development of Old St Mary, Andover, Hampshire* Andover, Andover History and Archaeology Society

Cotswold Archaeology, 2017 *Aldi site, Weyhill Road, Andover, Hampshire. Archaeological Watching Brief and Excavation Interim Report* Unpublished Report No. 17171

Cotter, J. 2011 'Medieval Pottery', in Ford, B. *et al.* 2011, Digital contents, Part 3: Specialist reports, Section 1.3, 1–136

Coulton, G.G. 1927 *Five Centuries of Religion Vol. II The Friars and the Dead Weights of Tradition. 1200–1400 A.D.* Cambridge, Cambridge University Press

Cox, G. and Sealy, J. 1997 'Investigating identity and life histories: isotopic analysis and historical documentation of slave skeletons found on the Cape Town foreshore, South Africa', *Int. J. Hist. Archaeol.* **1**(3), 207–24

Craig, O.E., Biazzo, M., Colonese, A.C., Di Giuseppe, Z., Martinez-Labarga, C., Lo Vetro, D., Lelli, R., Martini, F. and Rickards, O. 2010 'Stable isotope analysis of Late Upper Palaeolithic human and faunal remains from Grotta del Romito (Cosenza), Italy', *J. Archaeol. Sci.* **37**, 2504–12

Craig-Atkins, E. 2017 'Seeking "Norman Burials": evidence for continuity and change in funerary practice following the Norman Conquest', in Hadley, D.M. and Dyer C. (eds) *The Archaeology of the 11th Century. Continuities and Transformations.* Soc. Medieval Archaeol. Monogr. Ser. **38**, Abingdon, Routledge, 139–58

Craig-Atkins, E. and Buckberry, J. (2010) 'Investigating social status using evidence of biological status: a case study from Raunds Furnells', in Buckberry, J. and Cherryson, A. (eds) *Burial in Later Anglo-Saxon England, c.650–1100 AD* Studies in Funerary Archaeology **4**, Oxford, Oxbow http://eprints.whiterose.ac.uk/89892/2/Jo%2520book%2520paper%2520final%2520v.pdf (accessed December 2018)

Crangle, J.N. 2015 *A study of post-depositional funerary practices in Medieval England Volume 1* PhD thesis, University of Sheffield http://etheses.whiterose.ac.uk/13315/1/JNC%20Thesis.pdf (accessed June 2019)

Crittall, E. (ed.) 1959a 'Royal forests', in *History of the County of Wiltshire: Volume 4* London, Victoria County History, 391–433. British History Online http://www.british-history.ac.uk/vch/wilts/vol4/pp391-433 (accessed 21 July 2018)

Crittall, E. (ed.) 1959b 'Roads', in *A History of the County of Wiltshire: Volume 4* London, Victoria County History, 254–71. British History Online http://www.british-history.ac.uk/vch/wilts/vol4/pp254-271 (accessed 2 September 2018)

Crowley, D.A. 1975 'All Cannings', in E. Crittall (ed.) *Victoria County History: A History of the County of Wiltshire: Volume 10* London, Oxford University Press, 20–33

Crummy, N. 1988 *The post-Roman small finds from excavations in Colchester* Colchester Archaeological Report **5**, Colchester, Colchester Archaeological Trust

Cunliffe, B. and Poole, C. 2000 *The Danebury Environs Programme: The Prehistory of a Wessex Landscape Vol. 2, part 2. Bury Hill, Upper Clatford, Hants, 1990* English Heritage and Oxford Univ. Comm. Archaeol. Monogr. **49**

Dacre, M. and Warmington, R. 1977 'Saxon site at Charlton, Andover', *Hampshire Fld Club Newsletter* **7**, 22

Daniell, C. 2002 'Conquest, Crime and Theology in the Burial Record: 1066–1200' in Lucy, S. and Reynolds, A. (eds) *Burial in Early Medieval England and Wales* Soc. Med. Archaeol. Monogr. Ser. **17**, Leeds, Maney, 241–54

Daux, V., Lécuyer, C., Héran, M.-A., Amiot, R., Simon, L., Fourel, F., Martineau, F., Lynnerup, N., Reychler, H. and Escarguel, G. 2008 'Oxygen isotope fractionation between human phosphate and water revisited', *J. Hum. Evol.* **55**(6), 1138–47

Davies, S.M. 1980 'Excavations at Old Down Farm, Andover, part I: Saxon', *Proc. Hampshire. Field Club Archaeol. Soc.* **36**, 161–80

Davies, S.M. 1981 'Excavations at Old Down Farm, Andover, part II: prehistoric and Roman', *Proc. Hampshire Fld Club Archaeol. Soc.* **37**, 81–163

Davies, W. 2006 'Introduction: Community Definition and Community Formation in the Early Middle Ages—Some Questions', in Davies, W., Halsall, G. and Reynolds, A. (eds) *People and Space in the Middle Ages 300–1300* Turnhout, Brepols, 1–12

Denton, J. *et al.* 2014 *Taxatio* HRI Online, Sheffield https://www.dhi.ac.uk/taxatio/forms (accessed 28 August 2018) Data entered from Astle T, Ayscough S. and Caley J. (eds) 1802 *Taxatio ecclesiastica Angliae et Walliae auctoritate P. Nicholai IV*, circa AD1291 Record Commission, London

De Vere Stacpoole, H. (trans.) 1914 *The poems of François Villon* John Lane, New York, 17–19. Internet Archive https://archive.org/details/poemsoffranoisrs00villuoft/page/16 (accessed 30 November 2018)

Dias, G. and Tayles, N. 1997 'Abscess cavity'—a misnomer', *Int. J. Osteoarchaeol.* **7**, 548–54

DNB (Dictionary of National Biography), 1885–1900 Vol. 63 Tout, T.F. 'Zouche, William la', citing '(*Cal. Pat. Rolls*, 1327–30, p. 275)' https://en.wikisource.org/wiki/Zouche,_William_la_(DNB00) (accessed June 2019)

Downer, L.J. 1996, *Leges Henrici Primi repr.* Oxford (92, 8 cited in Daniell 2002, 254)

Driesch, A. von den 1976 *A Guide to the Measurement of Animal Bones from Archaeological Sites* Cambridge, Mass., Peabody Museum Bulletin **1**

Driesch, A. von den and Boessneck, J. 1974 'Kritische Anmerkungen zue Widerristhöhenberechnung aus Langenmassen vor-und frühgeschichlicher Tierknochen', *Saugetierkundliche Mitteilungen* **22**, 325–48

Driscoll, D.J., Rigamonti, D. and Gailloud, P. 2003 *Klippel-Feil Syndrome. NORD Guide to Rare Disorders* Philadelphia, PA Lippincott Williams & Wilkins.

Duggan, K.F. 2018 'The ritualistic importance of gallows in thirteenth-century England', in Butler, S. M. and Kesselring, K.J. (eds) *Crossing borders: boundaries and margins in medieval and early modern Britain. Essays in Honour of Cynthia J. Neville* Leiden, Brill 195–215

Dunbar, E., Cook, G.T., Naysmith, P., Tripney, B.G. and Xu, S. 2016 'AMS ^{14}C dating at the Scottish Universities Environmental Research Centre (SUERC) Radiocarbon Dating Laboratory', *Radiocarbon* **58**(01), 9–23. doi:10.1017/RDC.2015.2

Duxbury, S. 2011 'Bonds of Trade The Port of Southampton and the Merchants of Winchester and Salisbury', in Mitchell, L.E., French, K.L. and Briggs, D.L. (eds) *The Ties that Bind: Essays in Medieval British History in Honor of Barbara Hanawalt* Ashgate, Farnham, 21–37

Eagles, B. 2015 ' "Small Shires" and Regiones in Hampshire and the Formation of the Shires of Eastern Wessex', *Anglo-Saxon Stud. Archaeol. Hist.* **19**, 122–52

Edwards, J.F. 1987 *The Transport System Of Medieval England And Wales - A Geographical Synthesis* PhD thesis, University of Salford https://usir.salford.ac.uk/14831/1/D083029.pdf (accessed August 2018)

EEL (Early English Laws), 2018 http://www.earlyenglishlaws.ac.uk/ (accessed 01 September 2018)

Egan, G. 1991 'Buckles', in Egan, G. and Pritchard, F. *Dress Accessories: Medieval Finds From Excavations in London* London, HMSO, 50–123

Ekwall, E. 1970 *The Oxford Dictionary of English Place-Names* Oxford, Oxford University Press

Elamin, F. and Liversidge H.M. 2013 'Malnutrition Has No Effect on the Timing of Human Tooth Formation', *PLoS ONE* **8**(8), e72274. doi:10.1371/journal.pone.0072274

Ellis, C.J. and Rawlings, M. 2001 'Excavations at Balksbury Camp, Andover 1995–97', *Proc. Hampshire Fld Club Archaeol. Soc.* **56**, 21–94

Evans, J.A., Montgomery, J., Wildman, G. and Boulton, N. 2010 'Spatial variations in biosphere ^{87}Sr/^{86}Sr in Britain', *J. Geological Soc.* **167**, 1–4

Evans, J.A., Chenery, C.A. and Montgomery, J. 2012 'A summary of strontium and oxygen isotope variation in archaeological tooth enamel excavated from Britain', *J. Analytical Atomic Spectrometry* **27**, 754–64

Ex-Classics, 2018 'THOMAS DUN Head of a Gang of Outlaws, on Account of whom King Henry I. is credibly supposed to have built Dunstable. Executed Piecemeal', in *The Newgate Calendar The Malefactors' Bloody Register*, various editions available online as http://www.exclassics.com/newgate/ng2.htm (accessed February 2019)

Falys, C. 2014 'The human bone', in Wallis, S. *The Oxford Henge and Late Saxon Massacre with Medieval and Later Occupation at St John's College, Oxford* Thames Valley Archaeological Services Ltd Monogr. **17**, Reading, Thames Valley Archaeological Services Ltd, 37–158

Falys, C. 2017 'The land at 12 Guildown Avenue, Guildford', *Surrey Archaeol. Soc. Bull.* **465**, 2–4

Falys, C.G. and Lewis, M.E. 2010 'Proposing a way forward: A review of standardisation in the use of age categories and ageing techniques in osteological analysis (2004–2009)', *Int. J. Osteoarchaeol.* **21**, 704–16

Fasham, P.J. and Keevil, G. 1995 'The church' to 'the Burials', and 'Brighton Hill South Site A', in Fasham and Keevil with Coe 1995, 77–83 and 77–146

Fasham, P.J. and Keevil, G. with Coe, D. 1995 *Brighton Hill South (Hatch Warren): an Iron Age Farmstead and Deserted Medieval Village* Hampshire Wessex Archaeology Report **7**, Salisbury, Trust for Wessex Archaeology

Ferembach, D., Schwidetzky, I. and Stloukal, M. 1980 'Recommendations for age and sex diagnoses of skeletons', *J. Hum. Evol.* **9**, 517–49

Fiorato, V., Boylston, A. and Knüsel, C. 2000 *Blood Red Roses: The Archaeology of a Mass grave from the Battle of Towton AD 1461* (1st edn) Oxford, Oxbow Books

Fitzpatrick-Matthews, K.J. 2013 *Britannia in the Ravenna Cosmography: A Reassessment* https://www.academia.edu/4175080/BRITANNIA_IN_THE_RAVENNA_COSMOGRAPHY_A_REASSESSMENT (accessed January 2019)

Flower, C. and Brand, P. 1922–1972 *Curia regis rolls* London, H.M. Stationery Office

Flight, T. 2016 'Aristocratic deer hunting in late Anglo-Saxon England: A reconsideration, based upon the Vita S. Dvnstani', *Anglo-Saxon England* **45**, 311–31

Ford, B., Teague, S., Biddulph, A., Hardy, A. and Brown, L. 2011 *Winchester. A City in The Making: Archaeological excavations between 2001 and 2007 on the sites of the Northgate House, Staple Gardens and the former Winchester Library, Jewry St.* Oxford, Oxford Archaeol. Monogr. **12**

Foxhall Forbes, H. 2013 *Heaven and Earth in Anglo-Saxon England: theology and society in an age of faith* Studies in Early Medieval Britain, Farnham, Ashgate http://dro.dur.ac.uk/11240/1/11240.pdf (accessed 15th February 2019)

Frei, K.M. and Price, T.D. 2012. 'Strontium isotopes and human mobility in prehistoric Denmark', *Archaeol. Anthropol. Sci.* **4**, 103–14

Gardeła, L. 2015 'Face Down: The Phenomenon of Prone Burial in Early Medieval Poland', *Analecta Archaeologica Ressoviensia* **10**, 99–122 http://cejsh.icm.edu.pl/cejsh/element/bwmeta1.element.desklight-c8f3e4d0-3695-4e27-a3bb-f224bf73622b (accessed January 2019)

Garmonsway, G.N. (trans.) 1972 *The Anglo-Saxon Chronicle* London, J.M. Dent

Geake, H. 1997 *The Use of Grave-Goods in Conversion-Period England, c. 600–850* BAR Brit. Ser. **261**, Oxford

Gee, H. and Hardy, W.J. 1914 *Documents illustrative of English church history* London, Macmillan and Co. https://archive.org/details/documentsillustrx00geeh/page/54 (accessed June 2019)

Geltner, G. 2006 'Medieval Prisons: Between Myth and Reality, Hell and Purgatory', *History Compass* 4(2), Blackwell Publishing, 261–74 https://doi.org/10.1111/j.1478-0542.2006.00319.x (accessed October 2019)

Gilchrist, R. 2008 'Magic for the Dead? The Archaeology of Magic in Later Medieval Burials', *J. Med. Arch.* 52(1), 119–59

Gilchrist, R. 2012 *Medieval Life Archaeology and the Life Course* Woodbridge, The Boydell Press

Gilchrist, R. and Sloane B. 2005 *Requiem. The Medieval Monastic Cemetery in Britain* London, Museum of London Archaeology Service

Giles, E. 1970 'Discriminant function sexing of the human skeleton', in Stewart, T.D. (ed.) *Personal Identification in Mass Disaster* Washington DC, National Museum of Natural History, 99–107

Giles, J.A. 1849 (trans.) *Roger of Wendover's Flowers of History* Vol. 2 London, Henry G. Bohn https://archive.org/details/rogerofwendovers02rogeiala/page/n7 (accessed June 2019)

Giles, J.A. (trans) 1852 *Matthew Paris's English History* Vol. I London, H.G. Bohn https://archive.org/details/matthewparissen01rishgoog/page/n6 (accessed June 2019)

Giles, J.A. (trans) 1854 *Matthew Paris's English History* Vol. 3 London, H.G. Bohn https://archive.org/details/matthewparissen01parigoog/page/n127 (accessed September 2019)

Given, J.B. 1977 *Society and Homicide in Thirteenth-Century England* Stanford CA, Stanford University Press

Gomersall, M. and Whinney, R. 2007 'The Hospital of St John The Baptist, Winchester', *Proc. Hampshire Fld Club Archaeol. Soc.* 62, 83–108

Goodall, I.H. 2011 *Ironwork in Medieval Britain: An Archaeological Study* Soc. Med. Archaeol. Monog. Ser. 31, London

Gordon, S. 2014 'Disease, sin and the walking dead in Medieval England, c. 1100–1350: a note on the documentary and archaeological evidence', in Gemi-Iordanou, E., Gordon, S., Matthew, R., McInnes, E. and Pettitt, R. (eds) *Medicine. Healing and Performance* Oxford, Oxbow Books, 55–70

Grant, A. 1982 'The use of tooth wear as a guide to the age of domestic ungulates', in Wilson, B., Grigson, C. and Payne, S. (eds) *Ageing and Sexing Animal Bones from Archaeological Sites* BAR Brit. Ser. 109, Oxford, 91–108

Grant, M. 2009 'The small towns of North Hampshire 1660 – c. 1800. Part 2: Population Growth and Urban Development', *Proc. Hampshire Fld Club Archaeol. Soc.* 64, 182–99

Green, J.A. 2013 'Forest laws in England and Normandy in the twelfth century', *Hist. Res.* 86, 416–31

Green, N.S. 2002 'Folic Acid Supplementation and Prevention of Birth Defects', *J. Nutrition* 132(8), 1 August 2002, 2356S–2360S

Gron, K.J. and Rowley-Conwy, P. 2017 'Herbivore diets and the anthropogenic environment of early farming in southern Scandinavia', *The Holocene* 27, 98–109

Gross C. 1890 *The gild merchant; a contribution to British municipal history* Vol. 2 Oxford, Clarendon Press https://archive.org/details/gildmerchantcont02gros/page/n5 (accessed August 2018)

Gross, C. (ed.) 1896 *Select Cases from the Coroners' Rolls AD 1265–1413* Publications of the Selden Society Vol. 9 Bernard Quaritch, London https://archive.org/details/selectcasesfromc00seldrich/page/n10 (accessed December 2018)

Grundy, G.B. 1921 'The Saxon land charters of Hampshire with notes on place and field names. (1st series)', *Archaeol. J.* 78, 55–173

Grundy, G.B. 1927 'The Saxon Land Charters of Hampshire with Notes on Place and Field Names (4th series)', *Archaeol. J.* 84,160–340

Gurven M. and Kaplan H. 2007 'Longevity among hunter-gatherers: A cross-cultural examination', *Population and Development Review* 33, 321–65

Hadley, D.M. 2010 'Burying the Socially and Physically Distinctive in Later Anglo-Saxon England', in Buckberry J. and Cherryson A. (eds) *Burial in Later Anglo-Saxon England c. 650–1100 AD* Oxford, Oxbow Books, 103–15

Hadley, D and Buckberry, J. 2005 'Caring for the dead in Late Anglo-Saxon England', in Tinti, F. (ed.) *Pastoral Care in Late Anglo-Saxon England* Woodbridge, Boydell, 121–47

Hadley, D.M. and Dyer, C. 2017 'Introduction', in Hadley, D.M. and Dyer, C. (eds) *The Archaeology of the 11th Century: Continuities and Transformations* Soc. Medieval Archaeol. Monogr. Ser. 38 Abingdon, Routledge, 1–13

Haggard, D. 1965 'The Hundred Courts of Hampshire', *Hampshire Magazine April 1965*, 26–8

Halstead, P., Collins, P. and Isaakidou, V. 2002 'Sorting the sheep from the goats: morphological distinctions between the mandibles and mandibular teeth of adult *Ovis* and *Capra*', *J. Archaeol. Sci.* 29, 545–53

Hampshire Archaeology, 1997 *Gymnasium and Car Park, North of Churchill Way, Charlton, Andover. Report on the Watching Brief* Unpublished report

Harding, C., Hines, B., Ireland, R. and Rawlings, P. 1985 *Imprisonment on England and Wales A Concise History* Beckenham, Croom Helm

Harmer, F.L. 1952 *Anglo-Saxon Writs* Manchester, Manchester University Press

Hart, C.R. 1966 *The Early Charters of Eastern England* Leicester, Leicester University Press

Hase, P.H. 1975 *The Development of the Parish in Hampshire, Particularly in the Eleventh and Twelfth Centuries* Unpublished PhD thesis, University of Cambridge

Hase, P.H. 1994 'The Church in the Wessex Heartlands', in M. Aston and C. Lewis (eds), *The Medieval Landscape of Wessex* Oxford, Oxbow Books, 47–82

Hassall, T.G., Halpin, C.E. and Mellor, M. 1989 'Excavations in St. Ebbs, Oxford, 1967–1976: Part 1: Late Saxon and Medieval Domestic Occupation and Tenements, and the Medieval Greyfriars', *Oxoniensia* **54**, 71–277

Hatting, T. 1983 'Osteological investigations on *Ovies aries* L.', *Videnskabelige Meddeleiser dansk naturhistorisk Forening* **144**, 115–35

Hayman, G. and Reynolds, A. 2005 'A Saxon and Saxo-Norman execution cemetery at 42–54 London Road, Staines', *Antiq. J.* **162**, 215–55

Hedges, R.E.M., Clement, J.G., Thomas, C.D.L. and O'Connell, T.C. 2007 'Collagen turnover in the adult femoral mid-shaft: modeled from anthropogenic radiocarbon tracer measurements', *Amer. J. Phys. Anthropol.* **133**, 808–16

Henderson, C.Y., Mariotti, V., Pany-Kucera, D., Villotte, S. and Wilczak, C. 2016 'The New 'Coimbra Method': A Biologically Appropriate Method for Recording Specific Features of Fibrocartilaginous Entheseal Changes', *Int. J. Osteoarchaeol.* **26**(5), 925–32

Hill, N.G. 1937 'Excavations on Stockbridge Down, 1935–36', *Proc. Hampshire Fld Club Archaeol. Soc.* **13**(3), 247–59

Hillson, S. 1996 *Dental Anthropology* Cambridge, Cambridge University Press

Historic England, 2017 'Church of St Michael and All Angels' (record in The National Heritage List for England (NHLE)) https://historicengland.org.uk/listing/the-list/list-entry/1229819 (accessed June 2017)

Historic England, 2018 *PastScape* (records held in the National Record of the Historic Environment (NRHE)) https://www.pastscape.org.uk/ (accessed May 2018)

Hobsbawm, E. and Rudé, G. 2014 *Captain Swing* London, Verso

Hope-Taylor, B. 1977 *Yeavering: An Anglo-British Centre of Early Northumbria* London, HMSO

Hopkins, D. 2004 *Andover Archaeological Assessment Extensive Urban Survey Hampshire and the Isle of Wight* Winchester, Hampshire County Council

Hoppa, R.D. 1992 'Evaluating human skeletal growth: an Anglo-Saxon example', *Int. J. Osteoarchaeol.* **2**, 275–88

Hostettler, J. 2009 *A history of criminal justice in England and Wales* Hook, UK, Waterside Press

House of Commons, 1831 Population Comparative account of the Population of Great Britain in the years 1801, 1811, 1821 and 1831 with the annual value of real property in the year 1815, London, House of Commons

Hughes, S.S., Millard, A.R., Lucy, S.J., Chenery, C.A., Evans, J.A., Nowell, G. and Pearson, D.G. 2014 'Anglo-Saxon origins investigated by isotopic analysis of burials from Berinsfield, Oxfordshire, UK', *J. Archaeol. Sci.* **42**, 81–92

Hunnisett, R.F. 1961 (2008 reprint) *The Medieval Coroner* Cambridge, Cambridge University Press

Hunt, D.R. and Bullen, L. 2007 'The frequency of os acromiale in the Robert J. Terry Collection', *Int. J. Osteoarchaeol.* **17**(3), 309–17

Işcan, M.Y. and Loth, S.R. 1984 'Determination of age from the sternal rib in white males', *J. Forensic Sci.* **31**, 122–32

Işcan, M.Y, Loth, S.R. and Scheuerman, E.H. 1985 'Determination of age from the sternal rib in white females', *J. Forensic Sci.* **31**, 990–9

James, R. and Nasmyth-Jones, R. 1992 'The occurrence of cervical fractures in victims of judicial hanging', *Forensic Sci. Int.* **54**(1), 81–91

Jay, M. and Richards, M.P. 2007 'British Iron Age diet: stable isotopes and other evidence', *Proc. Prehist. Soc.* **73**, 169–90

Jay, M., Montgomery, J., Nehlich, O., Towers, J. and Evans, J. 2013 'British Iron Age chariot burials of the Arras culture: a multi-isotope approach to investigating mobility levels and subsistence practices', *World Archaeol.* **45**(3), 473–91

Jones, L.B. 2014 *A Craniometric Analysis of English Skeletal Samples: Change and Continuity between the Iron Age and Post-Medieval time periods (400 BCE–1850 CE)* Unpublished MA thesis, North Carolina State University

Judd, M.A. and Roberts C.A. 1999 'Fracture Trauma in a medieval British farming village', *Amer. J. Phys. Anthropol.* **109**(2), 229–43

Jurmain, R. 1999 *Stories from the skeleton. Behavioural reconstruction in human osteology* Amsterdam, Gordon & Breach

Kirby, T.F. (ed.) 1896–9 *Wykeham's Register,* 2 vols London and Winchester, Hampshire Record Society

Klinken, G.J. van 1999. 'Bone collagen quality indicators for palaeodietary and radiocarbon measurements', *J. Archaeol. Sci.* **26**, 687–95

Kosiba, S.B., Tykot, R.H. and Carlsson, D. 2007 'Stable isotopes as indicators of change in the food procurement and food preference of Viking Age and Early Christian populations on Gotland (Sweden)', *J. Anthropol. Archaeol.* **26**, 394–411

Lambert, T.B. 2009 *Protection, Feud and Royal Power: Violence and its Regulation in English Law, c. 850 c. 1250* PhD thesis, Durham University http://etheses.dur.ac.uk/2/ (accessed December 2018)

Lanting, J.N. and van der Plicht, J. 1998 'Reservoir effects and apparent ages', *J. Irish Archaeol.* **9**, 151–65

Lavelle, R. 2005 'Why Grateley? Reflections on Anglo-Saxon kingship in a Hampshire landscape', *Proc. Hampshire Fld Club Archaeol. Soc.* **60**, 154–69

Lawes-Long, H. 1836 *Observations upon certain Roman Roads and Towns in the South of Britain* Farnham Nichols and Sons https://books.google.dm/books?id=iGUGAAAAQAAJandprintsec=frontcover#v=onepage andqandf=false (accessed 28 October 2018)

Lawrence, M.J. and Brown, R.W. 1973 *Mammals of Britain Their Tracks, Trails and Signs* (rev. edn) London, Blandford Press

Lee-Thorp, J.A. 2008. 'On isotopes and old bones', *Archaeometry* **50**(6), 925–50

Letters, S. (ed.) 2005a 'The valuation of the town in the Lay Subsidy of 1334 in 'Hampshire', in *Gazetteer of Markets and Fairs in England and Wales To 1516* Kew, British History Online http://www.british-history.ac.uk/list-index-soc/markets-fairs-gazetteer-to-1516/hampshire (accessed 26 August 2018)

Letters, S. 2005b *Gazetteer of Markets and Fairs in England and Wales To 1516* Kew, List and Index Society

Liddell, D.M. 1933 'Excavations at Meon Hill', *Proc. Hampshire Fld Club Archaeol. Soc.* **12**(2), 127–62

Lightfoot, E. and O'Connell, T. 2016 'On the use of biomineral oxygen isotope data to identify human migrants in the archaeological record: intra-sample variation, statistical methods and geographical considerations', *PloS ONE* **11**(4), e0153850. doi:10.1371/journal.pone.0153850

Lloyd, T.H. 1977 *The English Wool Trade in the Middle Ages* Cambridge, Cambridge University Press

Loe, L. and Robson-Brown, K. 2005 'Summary report on the human skeletons', in Holbrook, N. and Thomas, A. 2005 'An early medieval monastic cemetery at Llandough, Glamorgan: excavations in 1994', *Medieval Archaeol.* **XLIX**, 1–92

Loe, L., Boyle, A., Webb, H. and Score, D. 2014 *'Given to the ground': A Viking mass grave on Ridgeway Hill, Weymouth* Oxford, Oxford Archaeology

Lovejoy, C.O., Meindl, R.S., Pryzbeck, T.R. and Mensforth, R.P. 1985 'Chronological metamorphosis of the auricular surface of the illium: a new method for determination of adult skeletal age-at-death', *Amer. J. Phys. Anthropol.* **68**, 15–28

Lowther, A.W.G. 1931. The Saxon cemetery at Guildown, Guildford, Surrey', *Surrey Archaeol. Collect.* **39**, 1–50

MacGregor, A., Mainman, A.J. and Rogers, N.S.H. 1999 *Bone, Antler, Ivory and Horn from Anglo-Scandinavian and Medieval York* Wakefield, York Archaeological Trust

Maitland F.W. 1889 *Select Pleas in Manorial and other Seignorial Courts* Publications of the Selden Society **2** https://archive.org/details/selectpleasinma01maitgoog/page/n6 (accessed 22 December 2018)

Maitland F.W. and Baildon, W.P. (eds) 1890 *The Court Baron* Publications of the Selden Society **4** https://archive.org/details/courtbaronbeingp00bail/page/n6 (accessed 16 December 2018)

Makarewicz, C.A. and Sealy, J. 2015 'Dietary reconstruction, mobility, and the analysis of ancient skeletal tissues: expanding the prospects of stable isotope research in archaeology', *J. Archaeol. Sci.* **56**, 146–58

Manby, G.T. 1985 *Thwing: Excavation and Field Archaeology in East Yorkshire* Yorkshire Archaeology Society, Prehistoric Research Section

Maresh, M.M. 1970 'Measurements from roentgenograms, heart size, long bone lengths, bone, muscles and fat widths, skeletal maturation', in McCammon, R.W. (ed.) *Human growth and development* Springfield IL, Charles C. Thomas, 155–200

Margary, I.D. 1973 '4b Port Way, Silchester–Old Sarum (36 1/4 miles) 96–98' in *Roman Roads in Britain* (3rd edn) London, John Baker

Mariotti, V., Facchini, F. and Belcastro, M.G. 2007. 'The study of entheses: proposal of a standardised scoring method for twenty-three entheses of the postcranial skeleton', *Coll. Antropol.* **31**(1), 291–313

Marzinzik, S. 2003 *Early Anglo-Saxon Belt Buckles (late 5th to early 8th centuries A.D.): Their classification and context* BAR Brit. Ser. **357**, Oxford

Mattison, A. 2016 *The Execution and Burial of Criminals in Early Medieval England, c. 850–1150 An Examination of the changes in judicial punishment across the Norman Conquest* Unpublished PhD thesis, University of Sheffield

Mays, S.A. 1996 'Healed limb amputations in human osteoarchaeology and their causes: a case study from Ipswich, UK', *Int. J. Osteoarchaeol.* **6**, 101–13

Mays, S. 1998 *The Archaeology of Human Bones* Abingdon, Routledge

Mays, S. 2016 'Estimation of stature in archaeological human skeletal remains from Britain', *Amer. J. Phys. Anthropol.* **161**(4), 646–55

Mays, S., Harding, C. and Heighway, C. 2007 *Wharram XI: The Churchyard* WHARRAM Settlement Series Vol. **11**, York, York Archaeological Publications

Mays, S., Fryer, R., Pike, A.W.G., Cooper, M.J. and Marshall P. 2017 'A multidisciplinary study of a burnt and mutilated assemblage of human remains from a deserted Mediaeval village in England', *J. Archaeol. Science Reports* **16**, 441–55

Mays, S. Brickley, M., Dodwell, N. and Sidell, J. 2018 *The Role of the Human Osteologist in an Archaeological Fieldwork Project* Swindon, Historic England

McKern, T.W. and Stewart, T.D. 1957 *Skeletal Age Changes in Young American Males, Analysed from the Standpoint of Identification* Massachusetts Quartermaster Research and Development Command Technical Report EP-45

McKinley, J. 2004 'Compiling a skeletal inventory: disarticulated and co-mingled remains', in Brickley, M. and McKinley, J. (eds) *Guidelines to the standards for recording human remains* IFA paper No. **7**, 7–9

McKisack, M. 1959 *The Fourteenth Century 1307–1399* Oxford, Oxford University Press

McManus, E., Montgomery, J., Evans, J., Lamb, A., Brettell, R. and Jelsma, J. 2013 ' "To the land or to the sea": diet and mobility in early medieval Frisia', *J. Island and Coastal Archaeol.* **8**, 255–77

McNaught, J. 2006 *A clinical and archaeological study of Schmorl's Nodes: using clinical data to understand the past* Unpublished PhD thesis, Durham University

Meaney, A. 1995 'Pagan English Sanctuaries, Place-Names and Hundred Meeting Places', *Anglo-Saxon Stud. Archaeol. Hist.* **8**, 29–42

Meekings, C.A.F. (ed.) 1961 *Crown Pleas of the Wiltshire Eyre, 1249* Wiltshire Archaeological and Natural History Society Records Branch Vol. **XVI** for the year 1960, Devizes

Meindl, R.S. and Lovejoy, C.O. 1985 'Ectocranial suture closure: A revised method for the determination of skeletal age at death based on the lateral-anterior sutures', *Amer. J. Phys. Anthropol.* **68**, 29–45

Merbs, C.F. 1996 'Spondylolysis and Spondylolisthesis: A cost of being an erect biped or a clever adaptation?' *Amer. Jour. Phys. Anthropol.* **101** *(S23) Yearbook of Physical Anthropology* **39**, 201–28

Metzler, I. 2013 *A social history of disability in the Middle Ages: Cultural Considerations of Physical Impairment* London, Routledge

Michopoulou, E., Nikita, E. and Henderson, C.Y. 2017 'A Test of the Effectiveness of the Coimbra Method in Capturing Activity-induced Entheseal Changes', *Int. J. Osteoarchaeol.* **27**(3), 409–17

Midgley, S. 1789 *The History of the Town and Parish of Halifax…* J. Milner, Halifax https://babel.hathitrust.org/cgi/pt?id=nyp.33433071366268;view=1up;seq=9 (accessed 26 January 2019)

Milella, M., Belcastro, M.G., Zollikofer, C.P.E. and Mariotti, V. 2012 'The effect of age, sex, and physical activity on entheseal morphology in a contemporary Italian skeletal collection', *Amer. J. Phys. Anthropol.* **148**(3), 379–88

Miles, A. 1962 'Assessment of age of a population of Anglo-Saxons from their dentition', *Proc. Royal Society of Medicine* **55**, 881–6

Millett, M. with James, S. 1983 'Excavations at Cowdery's Down, Basingstoke, Hampshire 1978–81', *Archaeol. J.* **140**, 151–279

Milner, G.R. and Larsen, C.S. 1991 'Teeth as artifacts of human behaviour: intentional mutilation and accidental modification', in Kelley, M.A. and Larsen, C.S. (eds) *Advances in Dental Anthropology* New York, Wiley-Liss, 357–78

Miquel-Feucht, M.J., Polo-Cerdá, M. and Villalaín-Blanco, J.D. 1999 'El síndrome criboso: cribra femoral vs cribra orbitaria', in *Sistematización Metodológica en Paleopatología, Actas V Congreso Nacional de Paleopatología (Alcalá la Real)*, 221–37

Montgomery, J. 2010 'Passports from the past: investigating human dispersals using strontium isotope analysis of tooth enamel', *Annals of Human Biology* **37**(3), 325–46

Montgomery, J., Evans, J.A. and Cooper, R.E. 2007 'Resolving archaeological populations with Sr-isotope mixing models', *Applied Geochemistry* **22**, 1502–14

Montgomery, J., Müldner, G. and Cook, G. 2009 'Isotope analysis of bone collagen and tooth enamel', in Lowe, C. (ed.), *Clothing for the Soul Divine: Burials at the tomb of St Ninian. Excavations at Whithorn Priory,*

1957–67 Edinburgh, Historic Scotland, Archaeology Report No. **3**, 65–82

Montgomery, J., Grimes, V., Buckberry, J., Evans, J.A., Richards, M.P. and Barrett, J.H. 2014 'Finding Vikings with isotope analysis: the view from wet and windy islands', *Journal of the North Atlantic* **S7**, 54–70

Mook, W.G. 1986 'Business Meeting: recommendations/resolutions adopted by the twelfth international radiocarbon conference', *Radiocarbon* **28**, 799

Moorees, C.F.A., Fanning E.A. and Hunt, E.E. 1963 'Age variation of formation stages for ten permanent teeth', *Journal of Dental Research* **42**, 1490–502

Morgan, M. 1946 *The English Lands of The Abbey of Bec* Oxford, Oxford University Press

Morris, W.A. 1927 *The Medieval English Sheriff to 1300* Manchester, The University of Manchester Press

Mundill, R.R. 2003 'Edward I and the Final Phase of Anglo-Jewry', in Skinner, P. (ed.) *Jews in Medieval Britain Historical, Literary and Archaeological Perspectives* Woodbridge, Boydell Press, 55–70

Musson, A. 2001 *Medieval Law in Context: The Growth of Legal Consciousness from Magna Carta* Manchester, Manchester University Press

Musson, A. 2009, *Crime, Law and Society in the Later Middle Ages* Manchester, Manchester University Press

Needham S. 2014 'Thanet: Fulcrum of the North-Western Seaways' in McKinley, J.I., Leivers, M., Schuster, J., Marshall P., Barclay A.J. and Stoodley, N. 2014 *Cliffs End Farm Isle of Thanet, Kent: A mortuary and ritual site of the Bronze Age, Iron Age and Anglo-Saxon period* Wessex Archaeology Monogr. **31**, Salisbury, Wessex Archaeology, 219–36

Nehlich, O. 2015 'The application of sulphur isotope analyses in archaeological research: a review', *Earth Science Reviews* **142**, 1–17

Nehlich, O. and Richards, M.P. 2009 'Establishing collagen quality criteria for sulphur isotope analysis of archaeological bone collagen', *Archaeol. Anthropol. Sci.* **1**(1), 59–75

Nehlich, O., Fuller, B.T. and Richards, M.P. 2008 'Sulphur isotope measurements reveal additional dietary and breastfeeding information from the late/sub-Roman site of Queenford Farm.' Poster presented at International Symposium on Biomolecular Archaeology 2008

Nehlich, O., Borić, D., Stefanović, S. and Richards, M.P. 2010 'Sulphur isotope evidence for freshwater fish consumption: a case study from the Danube Gorges, SE Europe', *J. Archaeol. Sci.* **37**, 1131–9

Nehlich, O., Fuller, B.T., Jay, M., Smith, C.I., Mora, A., Nicholson, R.A. and Richards, M.P. 2011 'Application of sulphur isotope ratios to examine weaning patterns and freshwater fish consumption in Roman Oxfordshire, UK', *Geochimica et Cosmochimica Acta* **75**, 4963–77

Norden, J. 1607 'Norden's Hampshire 1607', John Norden's map of Hampshire in the version engraved by W. Hole and published in Camden's Britannia,

1607 http://www.geog.port.ac.uk/webmap/hantsmap/hantsmap/norden1/norden1.htm#intro (accessed December 2018)

North, J.J. 1994 *English Hammered Coinage Vol. 1: Early Anglo-Saxon to Henry III, c. 600–1272. Vol. 1* USA, Spink and Son Ltd

Nottingham University 2018 *Key to English Place Names* http://kepn.nottingham.ac.uk/map/place/Hampshire (accessed 26 August 2018)

O'Connell, T.C., Kneale, C.J., Tasevska, N. and Kuhnle, G.G.C. 2012 'The diet-body offset in human nitrogen isotopic values: a controlled dietary study', *Amer. Jour. Phys. Anthropol.* **149**, 426–34

Ogden, A. 2008 'Advances in the palaeopathology of teeth and jaws', in R. Pinhasi and S. Mays (eds), *Advances in Human Palaeopathology* Chichester, Wiley, 283–307

Ortner, D.J. and Putschar, W.G.J. 1981 *Identification of pathological conditions in human skeletal remains* Washington, Smithsonian Institute Press

Page, W. (ed.) 1908 'Houses of Cistercian monks: Abbey of Stoneleigh', in *A History of the County of Warwick: Volume 2* London, Victoria County History, 78–81, British History Online http://www.british-history.ac.uk/vch/warks/vol2/pp78-81 (accessed 7 October 2019)

Page, W. (ed.) 1911a Parishes: Andover with Foxcott', in Page, W. (ed.) '*A History of the County of Hampshire: Volume 4* London, Victoria County History, 345–58, British History Online http://www.british-history.ac.uk/vch/hants/vol4/pp345-358 (accessed 31 August 2018)

Page W., (ed.) 1911b 'Parishes: Penton Mewsey', in Page, W. (ed.) *A History of the County of Hampshire: Volume 4* London, Victoria County History, 381–4, British History Online http://www.british-history.ac.uk/vch/hants/vol4/pp381-384 (accessed 19 January 2018)

Page, W. (ed.) 1911c 'Parishes: Monxton', in Page, W. (ed.) *A History of the County of Hampshire: Volume 4* London, Victoria County History, 379–81. British History Online http://www.british-history.ac.uk/vch/hants/vol4/pp379-381 (accessed 19 December 2018)

Page, W. (ed.) 1911d 'Parishes: Quarley', in Page, W. (ed.) *A History of the County of Hampshire: Volume 4* London, Victoria County History, 385–7. British History Online http://www.british-history.ac.uk/vch/hants/vol4/pp385-387 (accessed 19 December 2018)

Page, W. (ed.) 1911e 'Parishes: Wherwell' 'The hundred of Wherwell', in Page, W. (ed.) *A History of the County of Hampshire: Volume 4* London, Victoria County History, 400–1. British History Online http://www.british-history.ac.uk/vch/hants/vol4/pp400-401 (accessed 20 January 2019)

Page, W. (ed.) 1911f Parishes: Nether Wallop', in Page, W. (ed.) *A History of the County of Hampshire: Volume 4* London, Victoria County History, 525–30. *British History Online* http://www.british-history.ac.uk/vch/hants/vol4/pp525-530 (accessed 19 December 2018)

Page, W. (ed.) 1911g 'Parishes: Basingstoke', in Page, W. (ed.) *A History of the County of Hampshire: Volume 4* London, Victoria County History, 127–40. British History Online http://www.british-history.ac.uk/vch/hants/vol4/pp127-140 (accessed 19 December 2018)

Page, W. 1911h 'Parishes: Fyfield', in Page, W. (ed.) *A History of the County of Hampshire: Volume 4* London, Victoria County History, 366–69. British History Online http://www.british-history.ac.uk/vch/hants/vol4/pp366-369 (accessed 5 February 2019)

Page, W. 1911i 'The hundred of Andover', in Page, W. (ed.) *A History of the County of Hampshire: Volume 4* London, Victoria County History, 333. British History Online http://www.british-history.ac.uk/vch/hants/vol4/p333 (accessed 6 February 2019)

Page, W. 1911j 'Parishes: Weyhill with Penton Grafton', in Page, W. (ed.), *A History of the County of Hampshire: Volume 4* London, Oxford University Press, 394–9. British History Online https://www.british-history.ac.uk/vch/hants/vol4/pp394-399 (accessed October 2019)

Pálsson, H. and Edwards, P. 1976 *Egil's Saga* Harmondsworth, Penguin Books

Pantos, A. 2003 ' "On the Edge of Things": the Boundary Location of Anglo-Saxon Assembly Sites', *Anglo-Saxon Stud. Archaeol. Hist.* **12**, 38–49

Parsons, E. 1945 'The Andover Woollen Industry', *Proc. Hampshire Fld Club Archaeol. Soc.* **16**(2), 178–83 http://www.hantsfieldclub.org.uk/publications/hampshirestudies/digital/1940s/vol16/Parsons.pdf (accessed October 2018)

Payne, S. 1973 'Kill-off patterns in sheep and goats: the mandibles from Aşvan Kale', *Anatolian Studies* **XXIII**, 281–303

Pellegrini, M., Pouncett, J., Jay, M., Parker Pearson, M. and Richards, M.P. 2016 'Tooth enamel oxygen "isoscapes" show a high degree of human mobility in prehistoric Britain', *Scientific Reports* **6**, article no. 34986. doi:10.1038/srep34986

Pokines, J. and Symes, S.A. (eds) 2013 *Manual of Forensic Taphonomy* Boka Raton, CRC Press

Pollard, A.M., Pellegrini, M. and Lee-Thorp, J.A. 2011 'Technical note: some observations on the conversion of dental enamel $\delta^{18}O_p$ values to $\delta^{18}O_w$ to determine human mobility', *Amer. J. Phys. Anthropol.* **145**(3), 499–504

Pollard, A.M., Ditchfield, P., Piva, E., Wallis, S., Falys, C. and Ford, S. 2012 ' "Sprouting like cockle amongst the wheat": the St Brice's Day massacre and the isotopic analysis of human bones from St John's College, Oxford', *Oxford J. Archaeol.* **31**(1), 83–102

Pollard, J. and Reynolds, A. 2002 *Avebury: The Biography of a Landscape* Stroud and Charleston SC, Tempus Publishing

Pollock, F. 1899 'The King's Peace in the Middle Ages', *Harvard Law Review* **13**(3), 177–89 https://www.jstor.org/stable/1322581 (accessed: 07 November 2018)

Pollock, F. and Maitland, F.W. 1898 *The History of English Law Before the Time of Edward I: Volume II* (2nd edn) Cambridge at the University Press https://archive.org/details/historyofenglish00polluoft/page/n4 (accessed December 2018)

Poole, A.L. 1951 *From Domesday Book to Magna Carta 1087–1216* Oxford, Oxford University Press

Poole S. 2008 ' "A lasting and salutary warning": incendiarism, rural order and England's last scene of crime execution', *Rural Hist.* **19**, 163–77

Poore, D., Norton, A. and Dodd, A. 2009 'Excavations at Oxford Castle: Oxford's Western Quarter from Mid-Saxon period to the Late Eighteenth century (Based on Daniel Poore's Tom Hassall lecture for 2008)', *Oxoniensia* **74**, 1–18

Porter, J.A.F. 1977 *A re-assessment of pagan Anglo-Saxon burials and burial rites in Wiltshire* MPhil thesis, Durham University http://etheses.dur.ac.uk/9741/ (accessed December 2018)

Potter, K.R. 1976 (ed. and trans.) *Gesta Stephani* Oxford, Clarendon Press

Power, E. 1922 *Medieval English Nunneries c. 1275 to 1535* Cambridge, Cambridge University Press

Price, T.D., Frei, K.M. and Naumann, E. 2014 'Isotopic baselines in the North Atlantic region', *Journal of the North Atlantic* **S7**, 103–36

Privat, K.L., O'Connell, T.C. and Richards, M.P. 2002 'Stable isotope analysis of human and faunal remains from the Anglo-Saxon cemetery at Berinsfield, Oxfordshire: dietary and social implications', *J. Archaeol. Sci.* **29**, 779–90

Pugh, R. 1968 *Imprisonment in Medieval England* Cambridge, Cambridge University Press (cited in Geltner 2006)

Pugh, R.B. (ed.) 1978 *Wiltshire Gaol Delivery and Trailbaston Trials 1275–1306* Wiltshire Record Society (formerly the Records Branch of the Wiltshire Archaeological and Natural History Society) **33** (for the year 1977) http://www.wiltshirerecordsociety.org.uk/pdfs/wrs_v33.pdf (accessed December 2018)

Pugh, R.B. 1981 'The Knights Hospitallers of England as Undertakers', *Speculum* **56**(3), 566–74

Quensel-von-Kalben, L. 2000 'Putting late burial practice (from Britain) in context', in Pearce, J., Millett, M. and Struck, M. (eds) *Burial, Society and Context in the Roman World* Oxford, Oxbow Books, 217–30

Rabin, A. 2014 'Capital punishment and the Anglo-Saxon judicial apparatus: a maximum view?', in Gates, J.P. and Marafioti, N. (eds) *Capital and Corporal punishment in Anglo-Saxon England* Anglo-Saxon Studies **23**, Woodbridge, The Boydell Press, 181–200

Rackham, O. 1986 *The History of the Countryside* London, J.M. Dent

Rackham, O. 2006 *Woodlands* London, Harper Collins

Rahtz, P.A. 1969 'Upton, Gloucestershire, 1964–1968', *Trans. Bristol Gloucestershire Archaeol. Soc.* **88**, 74–126 (cited in Mays *et al.* 2017)

Ray, J. 1737 *A Collection of English Proverbs* (3rd edn) London, printed by J. Hughs ... for J. Torbuck, O. Payne and T. Woodman, 1737 https://babel.hathitrust.org/cgi/pt?id=nyp.33433082291794&view=1up&seq=328 (accessed September 2019)

Reimer, P.J., Bard, E., Bayliss, A., Beck, J.W., Blackwell, P.G., Bronk Ramsey, C., Buck, C.E., Cheng, H., Edwards, R.L., Friedrich, M., Grootes, P.M., Guilderson, T.P., Haflidason, H., Hajdas, I., Hatté, C., Heaton, T.J., Hoffmann, D.L., Hogg, A.G., Hughen, K.A., Kaiser, K.F., Kromer, B., Manning, S.W., Niu, M., Reimer, R.W., Richards, D. A., Scott, E.M., Southon, J.R., Staff, R.A., Turney, C. S.M. and van der Plicht, J. 2013 'IntCal13 and marine13 radiocarbon age calibration curves 0–50,000 years cal BP', *Radiocarbon* **55**, 1869–87

Reitsema, L.J. and Kozłowski, T. 2013 'Diet and society in Poland before the state: stable isotope evidence from a Wielbark population (2nd C. AD)', *Anthropological Review* **76**, 1–22

Reitsema, L.J., Crews, D.E. and Polcyn, M. 2010. 'Preliminary evidence for medieval Polish diet from carbon and nitrogen stable isotopes', *J. Archaeol. Sci.* **37**, 1413–23

Resnick, D. 1995 *Diagnosis of Bone and Joint Disorders* 6 vols (3rd edn) London, W.B. Saunders Company

Reynard, F.H. 1904 *The Ninth (Queen's Royal) Lancers 1715–1903* London, Blackwood (facsimile Uckfield, Naval & Military Press Ltd)

Reynolds, A. 2005 'From Pagus to Parish: Territory and Settlement in the Avebury Region from the Late Roman Period to the Domesday Survey', in Brown, G., Field, D. and McOmish, D. (eds) *The Avebury Landscape: Aspects of the field archaeology of the Marlborough Downs* Oxford: Oxbow Books, 164–80

Reynolds, A. 2009a *Anglo-Saxon Deviant Burial Customs* Oxford, Oxford University Press

Reynolds, A. 2009b 'The landscape archaeology of secular power in 8th–11th century England', in Conde, F. and Castro-Valdés, C. (eds) *Territorio, Sociedad y Poder*, Anejo **2**, University of Oviedo, 67–88

Reynolds, 2009c *The emergence of Anglo-Saxon judicial practice: the message of the gallows* The Agnes Jane Robertson Memorial Lectures on Anglo-Saxon Studies **1**, Aberdeen, The Centre for Anglo-Saxon Studies, University of Aberdeen

Reynolds, A. 2013 'Judicial culture and social complexity: a general model from Anglo-Saxon England', *World Archaeol.* **45**(5), 699–713

Reynolds, A. 2018 'Lineage, genealogy and landscape: a high-resolution archaeological model for the emergence of supra-local society from early medieval England', *World Archaeology* **50**(1), 121–36

Reynolds, A. and Langlands, A. 2011 'Travel as communication: a consideration of overland journeys in Anglo-Saxon England', *World Archaeol.* **43**(3), 410–27

Ricaut, F-X., Auriol, V., Cramon-Taubadel, N., Keyser, C., Murail, P., Ludes, B. and Crubezy, E. 2010 'Comparison between morphological and genetic data to estimate biological relationship: the case of the Egyin Gol necropolis (Mongolia)', *Amer. J. Phys. Anthropol.* **143**, 355–64

Richards, M.P., Fuller, B.T. and Hedges, R.E.M. 2001 'Sulphur isotopic variation in ancient bone collagen from Europe: implications for human palaeodiet, residence mobility, and modern pollutant studies', *Earth and Planetary Science Letters* **191**(3–4), 185–90

Richards, M.P., Fuller, B.T., Sponheimer, M., Robinson, T. and Ayliffe, L. 2003 'Sulphur isotopes in palaeodietary studies: a review and results from a controlled feeding experiment', *Int. J. Osteoarchaeol.* **13**(1–2), 37–45

Richmond, I.A. and Crawford, O.G.S. 1949 'The British section of the Ravenna Cosmography', *Archaeologia* **93**, 1–50

Riisøy, I.A. 2015 'Deviant Burials: Societal Exclusion of Dead Outlaws in Medieval Norway', in Korpiola, M. and Lahtinen, A. (eds) *Cultures of Death and Dying in Medieval and Early Modern Europe* COLLeGIUM: Studies across Disciplines in the Humanities and Social Sciences **18**, Helsinki, Helsinki Collegium for Advanced Studies, 49–81

Rivet, A.L.F. and Smith, C. 1979 *The Place-names of Roman Britain* London, B.T. Batsford Ltd

Riviello, C. 2017 'A joyless dwelling: exiles and traitors, pilgrims and sinners in Old English poetry', *Medioevo Europeo* **1**(1), 131–60 http://www.medioevoeuropeo-uniupo.com/index.php/mee/article/view/30 (accessed June 2019)

Roberts, C. 2007 'A bioarchaeological study of maxillary sinusitis', *Amer. J. Phys. Anthropol.* **133**(2), 792–807

Roberts, C. and Cox, M. 2003 *Health and disease in Britain* Stroud, Sutton Publishing

Roberts, C. and Manchester, K. 1995 *The Archaeology of Disease* (2nd edn) New York, Cornell University Press

Robinson, D.E. 2003 'Neolithic and Bronze Age agriculture in southern Scandinavia - recent archaeobotanical evidence from Denmark', *Environmental Archaeol.* **8**, 145–65

Rockwood, C.A., Green, D.P. and Bucholz, R.W. 2010 *Rockwood and Green's fractures in adults* (7th edn) Philadelphia PA, Wolters Kluwer Health/Lippincott Williams and Wilkins

Rocque, M., Posick, C. and Hoyle, J. 2015 'Age and Crime', in Jennings, W.G. (ed.) *The Encyclopedia of Crime and Punishment* New York, Wiley, 1–8 https://doi.org/10.1002/9781118519639.wbecpx275 (accessed June 2018)

Rogers, J. and Waldron, T. 1995 *A Field Guide to Joint Disease in Archaeology* Chichester and New York, Wiley

Routledge, B. 2015 *Archaeology and State Theory: Subjects and Objects of Power* London and New York, Bloomsbury

Russel, A.D. 1985 'Foxcotte: the archaeology and history of a Hampshire hamlet', *Proc. Hampshire Fld Club Archaeol. Soc.* **41**, 149–224

Russel, A.D. 2016 'Hung in Chains: A Late Saxon Execution Cemetery at Oliver's Battery, Winchester', *Proc. Hampshire Fld Club Archaeol. Soc.* **71**, 89–109

Salmon, P. and Spencer H., 2009 'Pollen, Sir John Walter, 2nd bt. (1784–1863), of Redenham nr. Andover, Hants', in Fisher, D.R. (ed.) *The History of Parliament: the House of Commons 1820–1832* Cam-bridge, Cambridge University Press https://www.history-ofparliamentonline.org/volume/1820-1832/member/pollen-sir-john-1784-1863 (accessed October 2018)

Salter, H.E. 1912 *Records of Mediaeval Oxford Coroners' Inquests, the Walls of Oxford, Etc.* Oxford, The Oxford Chronicle Company (2018 reprint: London, Forgotten Books)

Salzman, L.F. (ed.) 1951 'Parishes: Stoneleigh', in Salzman, L.F. (ed.) *A History of the County of Warwick: Volume 6, Knightlow Hundred* London, Victoria County History, 229–40. British History Online http://www.british-history.ac.uk/vch/warks/vol6/pp229-240 (accessed 2 February 2019)

Sargent, H.C. and Kitteredge, G.L. *c.* 1904 *English and Scottish popular ballads edited from the collection of Francis James Child* Boston, Houghton Mifflin Co.

Sawyer, P.H. 1968 *Anglo-Saxon Charters: An Annotated List and Bibliography* London, Royal Historical Society

Saxton, 1575 'Southamtoniae', Map engraved by Leonard Terwoort, Antwerp, Netherlands, published by Christopher Saxton, map maker, London? about 1575 http://www.geog.port.ac.uk/webmap/hantsmap/hantsmap/saxton1/sax1smaf.htm (accessed June 2018)

Sayle, K.L., Cook, G.T., Ascough, P.L., Hastie, H.R., Einarsson, Á., McGovern, T.H., Hicks, M.T., Edwald, Á. and Friðriksson, A. 2013 'Application of ^{34}S analysis for elucidating terrestrial, marine and freshwater ecosystems: evidence of animal movement/husbandry practices in an early Viking community around Lake Mývatn, Iceland', *Geochimica et Cosmochimica Acta* **120**, 531–44

Schatzker, J., Rarabeck, C.H. and Waddell, J.P. 1971 'Fractures of the Dens (odontoid process): an analysis of thirty-seven cases', *The Journal of Bone and Joint Surgery* **53**(3), 392–405

Schell, S. 2011 *The Office of the Dead in England: Image and Music in the Book of Hours and Related Texts, c. 1250-c. 1500* PhD thesis, University of St Andrews, St Andrews Research Repository http://hdl.handle.net/10023/2107 (accessed May 2019)

Scheuer, L, and Black, S. 2000 *Developmental Juvenile Osteology* San Diego, CA, Academic Press

Schwartz, J.H. 1995 *Skeleton Keys: An introduction to human skeletal morphology, development, and analysis* USA, Oxford University Press

Scott, E.M. 2003 'The third international radiocarbon intercomparison (TIRI) and the fourth international radiocarbon intercomparison (FIRI) 1990–2002: results, analyses, and conclusions', *Radiocarbon* **45**, 135–50

Scott, E.M., Cook, G.T., Naysmith, P., Bryant, C. and O'Donnell, D. 2007 'A report on phase 1 of the 5th international radiocarbon intercomparison (VIRI)' *Radiocarbon* **49**, 409–26

Scott, E.M., Cook, G.T. and Naysmith, P. 2010 'A report on phase 2 of the fifth international radiocarbon intercomparison (VIRI)', *Radiocarbon* **52**, 846–58

Scott, I.R. 1988 'Penton Mewsey – Harroway Farm (SU 3312 4665)', in *Archaeology in Hampshire. Annual Report for 1987* Winchester, Hampshire County Council, 21

Sealy, J. 2001 'Body tissue chemistry and palaeodiet', in Brothwell, D.R. and Pollard, A.M. (eds) *Handbook of Archaeological Sciences* Chichester, John Wiley and Sons, 269–79

Semple, S. 2007 'Defining the OE Hearg: A Preliminary Archaeological and Topographic Examination of Hearg Place Names and their Hinterlands', *Early Medieval Europe* **15**(4): 364–85

Semple, S. 2013 *Perceptions of the Prehistoric in Anglo-Saxon England: Religion, Ritual, and Rulership in the Landscape* Oxford, Oxford University Press

Shepherd, S.L. 2010, *Anglo-Saxon Labours of the Months: Representing May – a case study* MPhil thesis, University of Birmingham https://etheses.bham.ac.uk/id/eprint/2920/1/Shepherd11MPhil.pdf. (accessed February 2019)

Shore, T.W. 1888 'Ancient Hampshire Forests and Geological Conditions of their Growth', *Hampshire Field Club Papers* **1**, 40–60

Shrewsbury, J.F.D. 1970 *A History of Bubonic Plague in the British Isles* Cambridge, Cambridge University Press

Simpson, J. 2003 'Repentant soul or walking corpse? Debatable apparitions in Medieval England', *Folklore* **114**, 389–402

Sjøvold, T. 1984 'A Report on the Heritability of Some Cranial Measurements and Non-Metric Traits', in van Vark, G.N. and Howells, W.W. (eds) *Multivariate Statistical Methods in Physical Anthropology: A Review of Recent Advances and Current Developments* Netherlands, Springer, 223–46

Sluis, L.G. van der, Hollund, H.I., Kars, H., Sandvik, P.U. and Denham, S.D. 2016 'A palaeodietary investigation of a multi-period churchyard in Stavanger, Norway, using stable isotope analysis (C, N, H, S) on bone collagen', *J. Archaeol. Sci. Reports* **9**, 120–33

Smith, R.F. 1987 *Roadside Settlements in Lowland Roman Britain* BAR Brit. Ser. **157**, Oxford

Smits, E., Millard, A.R., Nowell, G. and Pearson, D.G. 2010 'Isotopic investigation of diet and residential mobility in the Neolithic of the Lower Rhine Basin', *European J. Archaeol.* **13**, 5–31

Sofield, C.M. 2015 'Living with the Dead: Human Burials in Anglo-Saxon Settlement Contexts', *Archaeol. J.* **172**, 351–88 https://doi.org/10.1080/00665983.2015.1038688 (accessed 26 August 2018)

Spaul, J. 1999 'Where is *Laucomagus*?', *Newsletter of the Hampshire Field Club* **31**, 6–7

Spence, M.W., Shkrum, M.J., Ariss, A. and Regan, J. 1999 'Craniocervical injuries in judicial hangings: an anthropological analysis of six cases', *The American Journal of Forensic medicine and pathology* **20**(4), 309–22

Spradley, M.K. and Jantz, R.L. 2011 'Sex Estimation in Forensic Anthropology: Skull Versus Postcranial Elements', *J. Forensic Sci.* **56**, 289–96

Stephen, J.F. 1883 *A history of the criminal law of England in three volumes,* Vol. 1 London, McMillan and Co https://archive.org/details/historyofcrimina01stepuoft/page/n3 (accessed January 2019)

Stenton, F.M. 1971 *Anglo-Saxon England* (3d edn, reissued 2001) Oxford, Oxford University Press

Stevenson, J. 1856 (trans.) 'The Chronicle of Melrose', in *The church historians of England* Vol. 4, part 1 London, Seeleys, 77–242 https://archive.org/details/thechurchhistor104fiskuoft/page/n173 (accessed June 2019)

Stewart, N.A., Gerlach, R.F., Gowland, R.L., Gron, K.J. and Montgomery, J. 'Sex determination of human remains from peptides in tooth enamel', *Proc. Nat. Acad. Sci. USA* **114**(52), 13649–54,

Stirland, A. 1996 'Patterns of Trauma in a unique medieval parish cemetery', *Int. J. Osteoarchaeol.* **6**, 92–100

Stoodley, N. 2006 'Changing Burial Practice in Seventh-Century Hampshire: The Anglo-Saxon Cemetery at Portway West, Andover', *Proc. Hampshire Fld Club Archaeol. Soc.* **61**, 63–80

Stoodley, N. 2013 *The Archaeology of Andover: the Excavations of Andover Archaeological Society 1964–1989* Newbury, Threshold Press

Stuart-Macadam, P.L. 1991 'Anaemia in Roman Britain: Poundbury Camp', in Bush, H. and Zvelebil, M. (eds) *Health in Past Societies: Biocultural Interpretations of Human skeletal remains in archaeological contexts* BAR Int. Ser. **567**, Oxford, Tempus Repartum, 101–13

Stubbs, W. (ed.) 1870 (edn of 1960) *Select Charters and Other Illustrations of English Constitutional History* London, Oxford University Press https://archive.org/details/cu31924014323202/page/n489 (accessed 04 November 2018)

Stuiver, M. and Reimer, P.J. 1986 'A computer program for radiocarbon age calculation', *Radiocarbon* **28**, 1022–30

Stuiver, M. and Reimer, P.J. 1993 'Extended ^{14}C data base and revised CALIB 3.0 ^{14}C age calibration program', *Radiocarbon* **35**, 215–30

Summerson, H. 1996 *Maitland and the Criminal law in the Age of Bracton* Proceedings of the British Academy **89**, 115–43 https://www.thebritishacademy.ac.uk/sites/default/files/89p115.pdf (accessed February 2019)

Summerson, H. 2001 'Attitudes to Capital Punishment in England, 1200–1350', in Prestwich, M., Britnell, R. and Frame, R. (eds) *Thirteenth Century England* **VIII**, *Proceedings of the Durham Conference 1999* Woodbridge, The Boydell Press, 123–33

Swanton, M. 1996 (trans. and ed.) *The Anglo-Saxon Chronicle* London, J.M. Dent

Tanner, T. 1744 *Notia Monastica or an Account of all of the Abbies, Priories and Houses of Friers Heretofore in England and Wales* London, John Tanner https://archive.org/details/notitiamonastica00tann/page/168 (accessed December 2018)

Tarlow, S. and Dyndor, Z. 2015 'The Landscape of the Gibbet', *Landscape History*, Jan 2 2015, **36**(1), 71–88. Published online 2015 Apr 30. doi: 10.1080/01433768.2015.1044284 (accessed December 2018)

Tildesley, M.L. 1933 'Report on human remains from Meon Hill', 137–9 in Liddell, D.M. 'Excavations at Meon Hill', *Proc. Hampshire Fld Club Archaeol. Soc.* **12**(2), 127–62

Tile, M., Helfet, D.L. and Kellan, J.F. 2003 *Fractures of pelvis and acetabulum* (3rd edn) Baltimore MD, Lippincott Williams and Wilkins

Thompson, V. 2002 *Death and Dying in later Anglo-Saxon England* Woodbridge, The Boydell Press

Towers, J., Jay, M., Mainland, I., Nehlich, O. and Montgomery, J. 2011 'A calf for all seasons? The potential of stable isotope analysis to investigate prehistoric husbandry practices', *J. Archaeol. Sci.* **38**, 1858–68

Trotter, M. 1970 'Estimation of stature from intact limb bones', in Stewart T.D. (ed.) *Personal identification in mass disasters* Washington, Smithsonian Institute, 71–83

Trotter, M. and Gleser, G.C. 1958 'A re-evaluation of estimation of stature based on measurements of stature taken during life and of long bones after death', *Amer. J. Phys. Anthropol.* **16**(1), 79–123

Trousdale, A.A. 2013 'Being Everywhere at Once: Delegation and a Royal Authority in Late Anglo-Saxon England', in Owen-Crocker G.R. and Schneider B.W. (eds) *Kingship, Legislation and Power in Anglo-Saxon England* Woodbridge, The Boydell Press, 275–96

Tucker, K. 2014 'The osteology of decapitation burials from Roman Britain: a post-mortem burial rite?' in Knüsel, C. and Smith, M.J. (eds) *The Routledge Handbook of the Bioarchaeology of Human Conflict* London, Routledge, 213–36

Ubelaker, D.H. 1992 'Hyoid fracture and strangulation', *Journal of Forensic Sciences* **37**(5), 1216–22

Uçar D., Uçar B.Y. and Coşar, Y. 2013 'Retrospective cohort study of the prevalence of lumbosacral transitional vertebra in a wide and well-represented population', *Arthritis* **2013**, Article ID 461425

Vince, A.G., Lobb, S.J., Richards, J.C. and Mepham, L. 1997 *Excavations in Newbury, Berkshire 1979–1990* Wessex Archaeology Report No. **13** Salisbury, Trust for Wessex Archaeology Ltd

Vinogradoff, P. 1892 *Villainage in England: essays in English mediaeval history* Oxford, The Clarendon Press https://archive.org/details/villainageinengl00vinouoft/page/n3 (accessed June 2019)

Vinogradoff, P. 1908 *English society in the eleventh century; essays in English mediaeval history* Oxford, The Clarendon Press https://archive.org/details/englishsocietyin00vinoiala/page/328 (accessed June 2019)

Wadmore, J.F. 1897 'The Knight Hospitallers in Kent', *Arch. Cantiana* **22**, 232–74

Wahl, J. and Berszin, C. 2013 'Indirect evidence of Hanging: Lesions of traumatic violence in eighteenth-century execution victims from southwest Germany', in Knüsel, C. and Smith, M.J. (eds) *Routledge Handbook of the Bioarchaeology of Human Conflict* London, Routledge, 473–89

Wainwright, G.J. 1969 'Balksbury Camp, Andover, Hants', *Proc. Hampshire Fld Club Archaeol. Soc.* **26**, 21–55

Wainwright, G.J. and Davies, S.M. 1995 *Balksbury Camp Hampshire: Excavations 1973 and 1981* London, English Heritage

Waldron, A. 1995 'Human bone' 142–5 in Fasham, P.J. and Keevil, G. with Coe D. 1995

Waldron, T. 1996 'Legalized Trauma', *Int. J. Osteoarchaeol.* **6**, 114–18

Waldron, T. 2009 *Palaeopathology* Cambridge, Cambridge University Press

Walker, P.L., Bathurst, R.R., Richman, R., Gjerdrum, T. and Andrushko, V.A. 2009 'The causes of porotic hyperostosis and cribra orbitalia: A reappraisal of the iron-deficiency-anemia hypothesis', *Amer. J. Phys. Anthropol.* **139**, 109–25

Wallis, S. *et al.* 2014 'Chapter 3: A Late Saxon Mass Grave', in Wallis, S. *The Oxford Henge and Late Saxon Massacre with Medieval and Later Occupation at St John's College, Oxford* Thames Valley Archaeological Services Ltd Monogr. **17**, Reading, Thames Valley Archaeological Services Ltd, 37–158

Ward, G.K. and Wilson, S.R. 1978 'Procedures for comparing and combining radiocarbon age determinations: a critique', *Archaeometry* **20**, 19–31

Warham, J. 2011 *Mapping Biosphere Strontium Isotope Ratios Across Major Lithological Boundaries: A systematic investigation of the major influences on geographic variation in the $^{87}Sr/^{86}Sr$ composition of bioavailable strontium above the Cretaceous and Jurassic rocks of England* Unpublished PhD thesis, University of Bradford

Webb, E.C., Newton, J., Lewis, J., Stewart, A., Miller, B., Tarlton, J.F. and Evershed, R.P. 2017 'Sulphur-isotope compositions of pig tissues from a controlled feeding study', *Science and Technology of Archaeological Research* **3**(1), 87–95

Webb, P.A.O and Suchey, J.M. 1985 'Epiphyseal union of the anterior iliac crest and medial clavicle in a modern multiracial sample of American males and females', *Amer. J. Phys. Anthropol.* **68**(4), 457–66

Weiss, K.M. 1972 'On the systematic bias in skeletal sexing', *Amer. J. Phys. Anthropol.* **37**, 239–49

Wessex Archaeology 2007 *Archaeological Excavations at Berwick Field and Old Dairy Cottage, West of Andover Road, Winchester, Hampshire, 1989–1994* Unpublished Client Report Ref: 63020.1

Williams, A. 1995 *The English and the Norman Conquest* Woodbridge, Boydell Press,

Williams, H.M.R. 2002 'Cemeteries as Central Places: Place and Identity in Migration Period Eastern England', in Hårdh, B. and Larsson, L. (eds) *Central Places in the Migration and Merovingian Periods. Papers from the 52nd Sachsensymposium Lund, August 2001* Uppåkrastudier **6**, Lund, 341–62

Williams, H. 2006 *Death and Memory in Early Medieval Britain* Cambridge, Cambridge University Press

Williamson, T. 2013 *Environment, Society and Landscape in Early Medieval England: Time and Topography* Woodbridge, The Boydell Press

Winters, J. 2018 'Forest Law', *Early English Laws* http://www.earlyenglishlaws.ac.uk/reference/essays/forest-law/ (accessed December 2018)

Wood, J., Holman, D., O'Connor, K.A. and Ferrell, R. 2002 'Mortality models for palaeodemography', in Hoppa, R.D. and Vaupel, J.W. (eds) *Paleodemography: Age Distributions from Skeletal Samples* Cambridge, Cambridge University Press (Cambridge Studies in Biological and Evolutionary Anthropology), 129–68

Wormald, P. 1999 T*he Making of English Law, King Alfred to the 12th Century. Vol. I: legislation and its limits* Oxford, Blackwell

Wright, J. 2004 'Excavation of Early Saxon Settlement and Mesolithic activity at Goch Way, near Charlton, Andover', *Proc. Hampshire. Fld Club Archaeol. Soc.* **59**, 116–38

Wright, R.P. 1936 'The Portway at Newton Tony', *Wiltshire Archaeol. Natur. Hist. Mag.* **47**, 513–16, and Plates I–III https://archive.org/details/wiltshirearchaeo471935193/page/n507 (accessed 28 October 2018)

Wright, R.V. 2012 *Guide to using the CRANID6 programs CR6aIND: For linear and nearest neighbours discriminant analysis. 2010* Formerly available at http://www.box.net/shared/static/n9q0zgtr1y. EXE (accessed April 2018)

Wymer, J.J. 1996 'The excavation of a ring-ditch at South Acre', in Wymer, J.J. (ed.) *Barrow Excavations in Norfolk 1984–88* East Anglian Archaeology 77, Gressenhall, Field Archaeology Division, Norfolk Museums Service, 59–89

Yekeler, E., Tunaci, M., Tunaci, A., Dursun, M. and Acunas, G. 2006 'Frequency of Sternal Variations and Anomalies Evaluated by MDCT', *American Journal of Roentgenology* **186**, 956–60

Yorke, B.A.E. 1989 'The Jutes of Hampshire and Wight and the origins of Wessex', in Bassett, S. (ed.) *The Origins of Anglo-Saxon Kingdoms* London, Leicester University Press, 84–96 (cited in Stoodley 2006)

Yorke, B. 1994 'Andover and the late Saxon Kings of England', in *Andover History and Archaeology Society* **1**(5), 90–1

Zeder, M.A. 2002 'Reconciling rates of long bone fusion and tooth eruption and wear in sheep (*Ovis*) and goat (*Capra*)', in Ruscillo, D. (ed.) *Recent Advances in Ageing and Sexing Animal Bones. Proceedings of the 9th ICAZ Conference, Durham 2002* Oxford, Oxbow Books, 87–118

Index

Illustrations are denoted by page numbers in *italics* or by *illus* where figures are scattered throughout the text. Places are in Hampshire unless indicated otherwise. Gr – Grave; SK – skeleton.